The Complete Film Production Handbook

The Complete Film Production Handbook

Eve Light Honthaner

Focal Press

Boston   Oxford   Johannesburg   Melbourne   New Delhi   Singapore

Focal Press is an imprint of Butterworth–Heinemann
⟵ A member of the Reed Elsevier group

∞ Recognizing the importance of preserving what has been written, Butterworth–Heinemann prints its books on acid-free paper whenever possible.

Library of Congress Cataloging-in-Publication Data

Honthaner, Eve Light
    The complete film production handbook / by Eve Light Honthaner.
        p.   cm.
    "Revised version"—Introd.
    Includes indexes.
    ISBN 0-240-80236-5 (pbk.)
    1. Motion pictures—Production and direction—Handbooks, manuals, etc.   I. Title.
PN1995.9.P7H66   1996
791.43'0232—dc20   95-51148
                                                        CIP

British Library Cataloguing-in-Publication Data

A catalogue record for this book is available from the British Library.

The publisher offers discounts on bulk orders of this book.
For information, please write:
        Manager of Special Sales
        Butterworth–Heinemann
        313 Washington Street
        Newton, MA 02158–1626
        Tel: 617-928-2500
        Fax: 617-928-2620

For information on all Focal Press publications available, contact our World Wide Web home page at: http://www.bh.com/fp

10 9 8 7 6 5 4 3 2

Printed in the United States of America

Table of Contents

Introduction

The first version of this book came out in 1993, and I have been more than pleased with the response. For those who found the first book useful, you will appreciate the revised version with its companion computer disk. The information contained within this book has not only been updated, but it is also more comprehensive and reflects current industry trends and concerns.

While recent technological advances have simplified numerous aspects of filmmaking; in general it has become increasingly more complicated. There are a variety of new options to consider when choosing such things as locations, equipment, and post production systems. Unions and guilds are offering a larger selection of low-budget and affirmative action agreements, insurance companies are providing a wider range of coverages, *interactive* and *multimedia* are becoming commonplace terms, and there seems to be no limit to the ever-increasing creation of extraordinary stunts and effects. There are new digital systems to learn about, computer software to master, and new terminology to integrate into our daily routines.

While we are faced with more choices at every turn, the industry has also made tremendous strides in recognizing the need for a greater sense of responsibility. In the past few years, there has been an increase in self-regulation, highlighted by the formation of strict safety guidelines and the *Filmmaker's Code of Conduct*. We must be accountable for the safety of our employees and for our policies, work habits, and behavior. The responsible actions of our industry cannot be stressed enough. I hope this book, in some small way, will help to encourage and promote these policies.

To reiterate how this book came into being, I assembled my first production manual while working as a production executive for an independent production company several years ago. I felt it was important to standardize forms, releases, and procedures on all of the company's shows; to provide important information needed to set up and run a production; and for everyone to know, up front, what the company's policies were. It contained material I had either saved or put together at one time or another to help me on a particular show, or something created to simplify my job or to avoid specific problems I had previously encountered. I designed some of the forms, and some are a compilation of the best of other forms I had accumulated over the years. When it was important to include information I did not have, I found someone who could provide it, thereby customizing the manual to address a wide variety of procedures and situations.

I took the manual with me to the next company I worked for, and the next show, and the show after that, continually using it, adding to it, and sharing the information with the people I worked with. My co-workers were the first to encourage me to have the manual published so I could pass this collection of information on to other companies and individuals who would be able to use it on a daily basis.

This industry-related reference book is different than most others, as it will not teach you how to budget or breakdown a script. It does not include information on videotape production or live television, and just barely scratches the surface of post production. It does not provide union and guild rates, or information on how to locate equipment, locations, services, crews, etc., all of which can be found in other books and directories. What it does contain, however, is a detailed guide to *film* production for production personnel, based solely on the scope of my experience, on the shared experiences of friends and associates, and on what I feel is important to know—information you will not find in other publications.

Use this book as a *guideline.* The information furnished under Establishing Company Policies and Standard Production Forms and Formats are suggestions; and although the chapters pertaining to music and clip clearances, and visa and immigration information, as well as all the enclosed forms, releases, and deal memos, have been approved by an attorney, have your own attorney look everything over before using any of them. Your attorney may want to make changes or add riders that relate to the specifics of your production.

A number of the forms contained in the book, such as the Day-Out-of-Days and Shooting Schedule, are functions automatically prepared by a variety of computer software programs (a list of scheduling programs can be found in Chapter 8). I have kept them in for those who are still learning, for those who wish to breakdown and schedule their show manually, and for those who do not yet own the software.

One last thing . . . for all you new and prospective line producers, production managers, and production coordinators, if it's something you have not yet discovered for yourself, let me be the first to tell you that being in production is *extremely* difficult work. You are the first to arrive in the morning and the last to leave at night. You have the most responsibility and are the first ones to get blamed if anything goes wrong. Your work can never be called *artistic,* the fruits of your labor can rarely be seen on the screen, and you will work just as hard on a bad movie as you do on a good one—sometimes harder. I can honestly say, however, that production can be a lot of fun. There is something extremely satisfying (and even exciting at times, when you're not too tired or too crazed to get excited) about putting all the pieces together and watching a movie come together. It's great to work with and meet new people all the time and wonderful to travel to diverse locations.

Be a team player, and do what has to be done to get the camera rolling and the show finished. Be generous with your knowledge, and don't feel too imposed upon to help or teach others.

Work as hard as you can, learn as much as you can, and never be afraid to ask questions. Be conscientious and organized, but also flexible. Don't lose your sense of humor, and try to find the lighter side of difficult situations. The work is too demanding not to be able to have fun while you're doing it. Your job can be a drudge, or it can be a series of challenging experiences and memorable adventures. It's up to you!

I have been able to add to and update the information in this book, in large part, with the help of my friends and associates, each possessing expertise in different areas of the business. Their collective efforts have helped to make this new and improved version possible.

I would like to sincerely thank my husband Ron for all of his emotional support and endless help. I also extend thanks to Nick Abdo, Patricia O'Brien, Marc Federman, Suzy Vaughan, Cindy Quan, Don Gold, Sheri Galloway, Gig Rackauskas, Martha Cronin, Lisa Matsukawa, Harriet Cheng, Cleve Landsberg, Adam Streltzer, John Poer, Kelly Oxford, Al Marrewa, Leigh von der Esch, Eleanore Robinson, Phil Wylly, Richard Wells, Bill Harrold, and Mike Papadaki. I greatly appreciate all of your suggestions, input, guidance, and encouragement.

I would like to offer a very special thank you to Focal Press, and especially to Marie Lee and Christine Swanson, without whom this terrific new edition and companion computer disk would not have been published. Their professionalism and joint contributions have made working with Focal Press an absolute pleasure.

How to Use this Book

The Complete Film Production Handbook contains many forms, including standard production forms, contracts, deal memos, release forms, and an assortment of miscellaneous forms to help you stay more organized. To illustrate how each form is to be completed, they have all been fully, or partially, filled out.

We have used an assortment of names and situations, all of which are fictitious. The name of our production company is *XYZ Productions*, and the name of the show is *Herby's Summer Vacation*. Note, however, that from situation to situation, *Herby's Summer Vacation* is either a feature film, a movie for cable, a movie for television, or a television series, with the current episode being *Boys Night Out*.

A complete set of blank forms, which are perforated and can be torn out and filled in, are at the back of the book. You can also access the entire collection of forms, releases, contracts, and checklists from the computer disk. Type in the information pertinent to your show, and print out completed forms, releases, and contracts. The checklists can be printed out, tacked up on a bulletin board, or put on a clipboard to help you keep track of everything that needs to be done.

Abbreviations

The following abbreviations are used throughout the book

UPM	Unit Production Manager
DP	Director of Photography
AD	Assistant Director
SAG	Screen Actors Guild
DGA	Directors Guild of America
WGA	Writers Guild of America
AMPTP	Association of Motion Picture and Television Producers

CHAPTER ONE

Pre-production

Pre-production is the period of time used to plan and prepare for the filming and completion of your film. It is the time in which to

Set up production offices

Hire a crew

Evaluate locations, visual effects, special effects, and stunt requirements as per your script

Determine time and cost factors involved and adjust script, budget, and schedule accordingly

Finalize your script and budget

Arrange for insurance and completion bond

Schedule your shoot

Become signatory to the unions and guilds you wish to sign with and post any necessary bonds

Cast your show

Contact film commissions for distant location options

Choose your locations

Build and decorate your sets

Wardrobe actors

Order film, equipment, vehicles, and catering

Book travel and hotel accommodations

Prepare all agreements, releases, contracts, and paperwork

Plan stunt work and special effects

Line up special requirements, such as picture vehicles, animals, mock-ups, miniatures, etc.

Set up accounts with labs; set up editing rooms; schedule routing of dailies; plan your post production schedule, hire post production crew, and prebook scoring, looping, and dubbing facilities

Clear copyrighted music you wish to use in your picture

PLAN AHEAD TO AVOID PROBLEMS

Arrange for *cover sets* should the weather turn bad while filming exteriors.

Know where you can exchange or get additional equipment if needed at *any time*.

Keep names, phone numbers, and resumes of additional crew members should you suddenly need an extra person or two.

Line up alternative locations should your first choice not be available.

The lower the budget, the more prep time you should have. Lower budgeted films do not have the luxury of extra time or money, so it is imperative to be completely prepared. Ironically, the films needing the most prep time are the ones that can least afford it. Many independent producers prepare as much as they can while waiting for their funding, although they are somewhat limited until they can officially hire key department heads.

Many variables, such as budget and script requirements, determine your pre-production schedule. The following is an *example* of what a reasonable schedule (barring any extraordinary circumstances) might look like based on a six-week shoot with a *modest* budget of $4 to $6 million.

An ideal pre-production schedule would allow one and one-half weeks of prep for each week of shooting. Accordingly, a six-week shoot should have a nine-week prep period. The following eight-week schedule, however, should be more than sufficient, as well as cost effective.

Pre-production Schedule

Week 1 (8 weeks of prep)

Starting Crew
Producers
Director
Line Producer and/or Production Manager
Production Accountant
Location Manager
Casting Director
Secretary/Receptionist
Production Assistant #1

To Do
Establish your company, if not done earlier
Set up production offices
Finalize script and budget
Start filling out union/guild signatory papers
Firm up insurance coverage
Begin casting
Start lining up your crew
Start scouting locations
Open accounts with vendors

Week 2 (7 weeks of prep)

Starting Crew
Production Designer

To Do
Start music clearance procedures using either your attorney or a music clearance service to determine if the rights are available and how much the sync license fees are for each piece of music

Week 3 (6 weeks of prep)

Starting Crew
Art Director
Set Designer
Production Coordinator
Assistant Location Manager

Week 4 (5 weeks of prep)

Starting Crew
First Assistant Director
Wardrobe Supervisor
Transportation Coordinator
Property Master
Set Decorator
Production Assistant #2

Week 5 (4 weeks of prep)

Starting Crew
Production Secretary
Assistant Accountant
Costumer #1
Assistant Property Master
Lead Person

To Do
At the end of this week, you should be ready for your first production meeting

Note: Depending on script requirements, the production designer will determine the start dates of the construction coordinator and construction crew. The production manager will determine the start dates of the stunt coordinator and special effects crew. The producer will determine the start date of a visual effects coordinator.

Week 6 (3 weeks of prep)

Starting Crew
Second Assistant Director
Transportation Captain
Swing Crew

Week 7 (2 weeks of prep)

Starting Crew
Director of Photography
Key Grip
Gaffer
Costumer #2
Extra casting, if needed

Week 8 (final week of prep)

Monday

Starting Crew
Script Supervisor
Production Assistant #3
Set Production Assistant
Additional drivers (as needed)

To Do
Post SAG bond by this date (if needed), or you will not be able to issue work calls or clear actors through Station 12
Complete casting and send out actors' contracts
Finalize selection of locations
Order all equipment, vehicles, raw stock, expendables, and catering

Thursday

Starting Crew
Best Boy, electric
Best Boy, grip
Hair Stylist
Makeup Artist
First Assistant Cameraman

To Do
Final location scout for camera, grip, electric

Friday

Starting Crew
Sound Mixer
Production Van Driver

To Do
Hold final production meeting

Pre-production Checklist

Starting from Scratch

- ❏ Find a good attorney who specializes in entertainment law
- ❏ Establish company structure (i.e., corporation or partnership)
- ❏ Obtain business licenses from city, county, and/or state
- ❏ Apply to the IRS for a Federal I.D. number
- ❏ If you have established a corporation, get a corporate seal and a minutes book
- ❏ Obtain workers' compensation and general liability insurance
- ❏ Open a bank account
- ❏ Secure a completion bond (if applicable)
- ❏ Start lining up staff and crew

Legal

Note: Your company's legal or business affairs department or an outside entertainment attorney should do this work.

- ❏ Secure the rights to the screenplay
- ❏ Negotiate (or review) and prepare the contract for the writer of the screenplay
- ❏ Review all financing and distribution agreements
- ❏ Order all copyright and title reports
- ❏ Prepare contracts for principal cast
- ❏ Prepare contracts for the producer, director, director of photography, production designer, costumer designer, and editor
- ❏ Prepare minors' contracts
- ❏ Complete errors and omissions insurance application
- ❏ Review contracts regarding literary material to make sure all required payments are made
- ❏ Review permits and other documents having potential legal significance
- ❏ Prepare (or approve) all necessary release forms
- ❏ Start music clearance procedures

Set Up Production Office

- ❏ Furniture
- ❏ Phone system
- ❏ Copier machine
- ❏ Typewriters
- ❏ Computers and printers
- ❏ Production and accounting software programs
- ❏ Fax machine(s)
- ❏ Office supplies
- ❏ Bottled water
- ❏ Coffee maker
- ❏ Refrigerator
- ❏ Extra keys to the office (keep a list of who has keys)
- ❏ Beepers for key personnel
- ❏ Department head envelopes for messages and approving bills

Paperwork

- ❏ Sign union and/or guild contracts (if applicable)
- ❏ Open accounts with vendors
- ❏ Set up production files
- ❏ Assemble supply of production forms
- ❏ Prepare contact list
- ❏ Prepare chart of accounts for coding bills
- ❏ Start purchase order log
- ❏ Prepare and distribute inventory logs
- ❏ Start raw stock inventory
- ❏ If a television series, prepare a list of episodes, production dates, director, writer, and editor for each show
- ❏ Prepare DGA deal memos
- ❏ Prepare crew deal memos
- ❏ Post and distribute safety and code of conduct guidelines as required
- ❏ Distribute *Acknowledgment of Safety Guidelines* forms for crew to sign
- ❏ Give crew start slips and tax information to payroll
- ❏ Prepare crew list
- ❏ Prepare Crew Startup and Data Sheet
- ❏ Prepare a distribution list

Visual Effects

- ❏ Hire a visual effects supervisor
- ❏ Prepare a breakdown of visual effects shots
- ❏ Have conceptual designs and storyboards prepared, clearly defining each effect
- ❏ Determine methodology and exact elements required to accomplish desired effects Send breakdown, designs, and storyboarded scenarios out to visual effects houses for bids
- ❏ Determine time and expense necessary to accomplish each effect
- ❏ Adjust script to accommodate budgetary and scheduling limitations if necessary
- ❏ Select visual effects houses to create needed effects (i.e., creatures, animation, computer-generated characters)

□ Have effects supervisor prepare a schedule integrating pre-production, production, and post production activities and all work to be done at effects houses

□ Determine which portion of each visual effects shot will need to be shot during production (i.e., process plates) and coordinate with the UPM and first assistant director, so requirements can be integrated into the shooting schedule

□ Determine what special equipment you will need to order to be used during production (i.e., motion control camera, blue screen)

□ Line up additional, specially trained crew to work on the portions of effects that are scheduled to shoot during production

□ Have effects supervisor prepare a contact list, including which effects houses are doing which effects, phone numbers, and names of who is supervising the work at each of the houses

Note: Complicated stunts and special effects to be shot during production should be assessed and planned during the early stages of pre-production, as well as visual effects. Preparation involves many of the same steps as those listed above.

Cast Related

□ Secure SAG bond (if applicable)
□ Finalize casting
□ Prepare cast list
□ Station 12 cast members
□ Prepare cast deal memos
□ Prepare SAG contracts
□ Schedule designated cast for medical exams
□ Complete actors' checklist items: doctor exam, wardrobe notified, contract received, contract signed, script received, etc.
□ Fit wardrobe
□ Hire a stunt coordinator
□ Have stunt coordinator line up stunt doubles
□ Line up photo doubles
□ Hire a dialogue coach
□ Schedule rehearsal(s)
□ Schedule hair and makeup tests
□ Get work permits for minors
□ Hire welfare worker(s), teacher(s)
□ Line up an extras casting agency
□ Interview stand-ins and extras
□ Obtain a good supply of extra vouchers

Script and Schedules

□ Finalize script
□ Type script
□ Duplicate script
□ Distribute script to cast and crew
□ Send script to research company
□ If for television, send scripts to network executives and Standards & Practices
□ Breakdown script, prepare a production board
□ Prepare a One-Line Schedule
□ Prepare a Day-Out-of-Days
□ Prepare a Shooting Schedule
□ Have the script timed

Prepare Breakdowns

□ Atmosphere
□ Production vehicles
□ Picture vehicles
□ Stunts
□ Locations
□ Special effects
□ Visual effects
□ Travel

Budgetary

□ Finalize budget
□ Prepare cash flow chart
□ Send script, budget, and schedule to the completion bond company

Insurance

□ Send script and budget to the insurance companies for bids
□ Secure insurance coverage
□ Make sure errors and omissions insurance application is submitted
□ Provide information for risk management survey
□ Decide on specific endorsements to meet the needs of your picture
□ Secure special coverage for aircraft, boats, railroad, etc.
□ Prepare certificates of insurance for vehicles, equipment, and locations
□ Send travel breakdown to the insurance company
□ Send stunt and effects breakdown to the insurance company, along with resumes of the stunt coordinator and effects supervisors
□ Have a supply of workers' compensation accident forms and insurance information

for office, second assistant director, and company nurse
- ❏ Select doctor approved by insurance company for necessary physicals

Prepare Pre-production Schedule, including:
- ❏ Casting sessions
- ❏ Production meetings (schedule at least two, more if time allows)
- ❏ Location scouts
- ❏ Rehearsals
- ❏ Prerigging

Post Production Related
- ❏ Hire a post production supervisor
- ❏ Determine method of editing
- ❏ Select lab and sound house
- ❏ Set up accounts for lab, sound transfers, video transfers, supplies, etc.
- ❏ Order editing equipment
- ❏ Set up editing room(s)
- ❏ Schedule digital editing training for editor and assistant editor, if necessary
- ❏ Get bids from sound effects houses
- ❏ Book dates and facility for predubbing and final mix
- ❏ Route dailies
- ❏ Schedule screening of dailies
- ❏ Prepare a tentative post production schedule
- ❏ Have script supervisor meet with editor regarding routing of daily notes and any special requests editor may have

Locations
- ❏ Hire a location manager
- ❏ Select a location service to work with, if necessary
- ❏ Complete location agreements
- ❏ Secure certificates of insurance
- ❏ Obtain permits
- ❏ Hire fire and police officers
- ❏ Set up security
- ❏ Arrange for intermittent traffic control
- ❏ Post for parking
- ❏ Obtain signed releases from neighbors
- ❏ Prepare maps to locations
- ❏ Get heaters, fans, air conditioners
- ❏ Get layout board and drop cloths
- ❏ Locate closest medical emergency facilities
- ❏ Set up phones, power, and utilities
- ❏ Locate parking lot(s) if shuttling is necessary

- ❏ Arrange for extra tables, chairs, tent
- ❏ Allocate areas for extras, dressing rooms, eating, hair, makeup, school room, rest area for minors and parents, special equipment, and animals
- ❏ Allocate parking areas for equipment and vehicles
- ❏ Order honeywagons or motor homes with showers for *messy* shooting days when cast will be subjected to rain, mud, etc.
- ❏ Line up nurse or medic for location construction and shoot days

Distant Locations
See Distant Location Checklist in Chapter 13.

Order
- ❏ Raw stock

Note: Discuss raw stock options with director of photography prior to ordering
- ❏ Still film and Polaroid film
- ❏ Camera equipment*
- ❏ Empty cans, camera reports, black bags, and cores (from lab)
- ❏ Steadicam
- ❏ Video assist*
- ❏ Grip and electric equipment*
- ❏ Grip, electric, and camera expendables
- ❏ Dolly(s), crane(s), and condor(s)
- ❏ Generator(s)*
- ❏ Sound equipment*
- ❏ 1/4 inch mag stock
- ❏ Walkie-talkies, bullhorns, and headsets*
- ❏ Cellular phone(s)
- ❏ Portable VCR and monitor (if dailies are shown on set)*
- ❏ Catering

* Note: Most equipment is rented on a weekly basis. If you are using the same equipment for the run of your show, you should be able to negotiate two- or three-day weekly rental rates with each of the equipment houses you are dealing with.

Transportation
- ❏ Motor home(s) and star wagon(s)
- ❏ Honeywagon(s)
- ❏ Camera car(s) and process trailer(s)
- ❏ Water truck
- ❏ Production trailer
- ❏ Hair and makeup trailer
- ❏ Wardrobe trailer

- ❏ Crew cabs and vans
- ❏ Grip and electric truck
- ❏ Camera truck
- ❏ Prop truck
- ❏ Set dressing truck
- ❏ Fuel truck
- ❏ Picture cars

Animals

- ❏ Locate the necessary animals/livestock
- ❏ Contact the American Humane Association for guidelines in the proper care, use, handling, and safety of animals

Locate and hire competent:

- ❏ Animal handlers
- ❏ Trainers
- ❏ Wranglers

Specialty Items

- ❏ Technical advisor(s)
- ❏ Rear screen/process photography
- ❏ Blue or green screen for visual effects shots
- ❏ Motion control camera
- ❏ Stock footage
- ❏ Cycs
- ❏ Mockups
- ❏ Models
- ❏ Special makeup and hair pieces

Preparing for Stage Work

- ❏ Telephones
- ❏ Security
- ❏ Power
- ❏ Remote and bell
- ❏ Heaters, fans, air conditioners
- ❏ Generator (if necessary)
- ❏ Dressing rooms
- ❏ School room
- ❏ Shower facilities for *messy* shooting days when cast members are subjected to such things as rain, mud, whipped cream, etc.
- ❏ Rest area for minors and parents
- ❏ Tables and chairs
- ❏ Area for extras
- ❏ Makeup and hair
- ❏ Darkroom
- ❏ Access to lot medical department or nurse/medic on set

Prepare a *portable file box* (or a legal-size accordion file) with the following paperwork to stay on the set at all times. This box should contain the following:

Copies of:

- ❏ All signed location agreements
- ❏ All permits

Blanks of:

- ❏ Location agreements
- ❏ Call sheets
- ❏ Production reports
- ❏ Workers' compensation accident report forms
- ❏ Automobile accident report forms
- ❏ SAG contracts (a few of each kind)
- ❏ SAG Taft/Hartley report forms
- ❏ Crew deal memo forms
- ❏ Certificates of insurance
- ❏ Check request forms
- ❏ Purchase orders
- ❏ Petty cash envelopes
- ❏ Release forms (an assortment)

Extra copies of:

- ❏ Staff and crew lists
- ❏ Scripts and script changes
- ❏ Cast lists
- ❏ Contact lists
- ❏ Shooting schedules
- ❏ Day-out-of-days
- ❏ Maps to the locations
- ❏ Start slips, W-4s, and I-9s
- ❏ Extra vouchers

Keep on the set at all times:

- ❏ A complete first aid kit
- ❏ Aspirin/Tylenol
- ❏ Several flashlights
- ❏ An assortment of office supplies
- ❏ A typewriter (or laptop computer) and small copier machine (if you have the room and the additional cost is within your budget)

CHAPTER TWO

Establishing Company Policies

Whether you are producing one show or ten a year, your company should have an established set of policy guidelines and basic operating procedures for all employees to follow. These directives will not only help you avoid unnecessary delays in disseminating information, paperwork, and checks, but you will stay better organized and maintain tighter controls over your costs. It is important for staff and crew members to know, coming in, what the company's policies are and what they are specifically responsible for.

Some production companies distribute memos to all new crew members listing their policies. Others attach a list of policies to each *crew deal memo*, integrating the acceptance of these *rules* as a condition of employment. The following are standard industry policies.

STARTUP

All crew members must sign a *deal memo* prior to their first day of work. A start card, W-4, and I-9 must be completed for purposes of payroll, and I-9s must be substantiated with a valid driver's license and social security card, birth certificate, U.S. passport, or alien registration card. Once department heads have confirmed their department's budget with the unit production manager (UPM), they should inform the accounting department of vendors they wish to open accounts with and complete a check request for the amount of petty cash they will need. This is also the time to request

a block of purchase orders, start an inventory log, and inform the production coordinator of any certificates of insurance they might need.

INVENTORIES

Each department should keep an ongoing inventory of all company assets—materials purchased, rented, or built for your production, including prices, rental dates, and serial numbers (wherever applicable). The production office will supply the *Inventory Log forms*. At the completion of principal photography, each department should turn in all remaining inventory along with completed inventory logs to the production office.

Keep inventories on the following:

Equipment and tools

Props and set dressing

Wardrobe

Research books

Raw stock and videocassettes

Office supplies and equipment (including the serial numbers of typewriters, computers, editing equipment, VCRs, etc.)

Keys

Walkie-talkies, chargers, bullhorns (including the serial numbers of each)

Beepers

Supplies and expendables

PRODUCTION ASSISTANTS AND RUNNERS

Production assistants (PAs) and runners should be responsible to the production coordinator or *one* other designated person only. They should not take directions from everyone in the office. The production coordinator (or other designated person) will help to coordinate each PA's duties and schedule runs based on production priorities. If an emergency should arise and a PA is not available, the production coordinator will make alternate arrangements (another PA, messenger service, transportation driver, etc.).

Anyone requesting a pickup or delivery should fill out a *Request for Pickup* or *Request for Delivery* form provided by the production coordinator. Place the completed form, along with any item to be delivered, in the PA's designated box. Each form will contain the following: (1) the name of the person requesting the pickup (delivery), (2) when the item(s) need to be picked up (delivered), (3) street directions, (4) whom to contact (pickup from or deliver to), (5) date and time of each pickup (delivery), and (6) signature of recipient. Keep all completed pickup (delivery) forms on file through the end of production.

Production assistants should call the production office after each run, unless they are on a pager, to see if there is a need for a pickup on their way back.

EMPLOYEES DRIVING THEIR OWN VEHICLES FOR BUSINESS PURPOSES

If an employee is driving a personal vehicle during the business day for business purposes and has an accident, insurance regulations specify that a person's own insurance is primary. The company's *non-owned auto liability policy* covers the production company, not the individual. All employees using personal vehicles for business purposes (especially PAs and runners) need to be informed of this policy and must show proof of auto insurance.

MILEAGE REIMBURSEMENT

Inform your employees of the mileage reimbursement rate. To qualify for mileage reimbursement, they must fill out *Mileage Logs* showing the beginning mileage, destination, purpose, and ending mileage for each run. Estimated mileage is not acceptable. Mileage to and from home is not reimbursable. Employees who receive mileage reimbursement are not reimbursed for gas receipts.

In order to be reimbursed for mileage expenses, submit the Mileage Log, attached to the back of a completed check request, to the UPM or production coordinator for approval. Once approved, the production office will pass it on to accounting for payment. Requests for mileage reimbursement should be submitted on a weekly basis.

ADDITIONAL TAXABLE INCOME

The federal government has set an *allowable limit* for mileage reimbursement, drive-to, and per diems. Any amount over such limit (see your accountant for limit guidelines) is considered taxable income and will be taxed along with the weekly payroll checks.

Box rental monies are also considered taxable income but are generally not taxed on a weekly basis. Those receiving box rentals will receive a 1099 at the end of the year and will be responsible for the taxes on this additional income.

INVOICING

Crew members should turn in their invoices for salary, services, equipment and box rental, vehicle rental, car allowance, or mileage reimbursement at the end of each week for payment the following week. Each invoice must include the employee's name, his or her corporation name, address, and social security number (or federal ID number). A complete description of what the invoice is for (i.e., services rendered or equipment rental) and a week-ending date must also be indicated on the invoice. All invoices are approved by the UPM before payment can be made.

PURCHASE ORDERS

Purchase orders are to be used whenever possible for purchases and/or rentals with vendors the company has, or will have, an account with. Purchase orders are obtained from the production coordinator or production accountant, and must be completely filled out and approved *before* a purchase or rental can be made. If the purchase order is for $500 or less, it should be approved by the production manager. If the purchase order is for more than $500, it should be approved by the producer. Some companies require purchase orders for over $1,000 to be accompanied by bids from three different vendors prior to approval and processing.

If the exact dollar amount of the purchase or rental is not known at the time the purchase order is issued, it should reflect an estimated amount that will not be exceeded. Distribute copies of each purchase order to the following:

1. Vendor (the original)
2. Production manager
3. Accounting department
4. Department head

The production coordinator should keep a running purchase order (P.O.) log, indicating the date, vendor, item(s) being purchased or rented, amount of purchase or rental, date of rental return, and the department to which each P.O. is assigned. Also noted on the P.O. log are purchases that at the end of the show become part of the company's inventory.

CHECK REQUESTS

For payments that require a check, obtain a check request from the production coordinator or the accounting department. Fill it out completely. The UPM must approve it before payment can be made. Each check request should contain as much information as possible, such as

Is this for a purchase, rental, location fee, petty cash, advance, or deposit?

If it is for a deposit, is it *refundable* or to be applied to the final bill?

Is this a partial payment or the first of many?

What are the terms of the purchase, rental, or service?

Is the check to be mailed or held for pickup?

What is the total amount to be?

Specify how quickly you need the check—within normal processing time, within a day or two, or immediately. If needed immediately and the UPM is not present to approve the request, an effort should be made to locate him or her and to obtain verbal approval over the phone or via walkie-talkie. If the UPM cannot be found, approval should be obtained from the producer. If the check request is for the purchase of tools, props, wardrobe, etc. (anything that can be considered inventory), note it on the check request so that these items can be added to the inventory log.

PETTY CASH

Petty cash should be used for small purchases that are not covered by a purchase order or check request, generally for items under $100, such as gas or oil for company vehicles, parking fees, expendable supplies, small props, and miscellaneous office supplies. Requests for petty cash are made by check request and are approved by the UPM. Those receiving petty cash will receive a check in their name and a petty cash envelope to keep track of all petty cash expenditures.

Anyone receiving a petty cash advance from the production manager or accountant will need to sign a *Received of Petty Cash* slip acknowledging receipt of the cash. The person advancing the funds will also sign the slip. When petty cash receipts are turned in, it is the responsibility of the person who had been given the cash to retrieve and discard the Received of Petty Cash slip, so he or she will no longer be responsible for the money.

Petty cash receipts should be numbered and taped to 8½ × 11 sheets of paper, in sequence, each clearly labeled as to exactly what it is for. List the corresponding numbers on the front of the envelope, along with a description of each item. Petty cash should not be used for salaries or box rentals. Meals purchased with petty cash should be pre-approved by the UPM.

Petty cash receipts should all be originals. Approximate costs are not generally accepted, except for such things as phone calls and parking meters. Note any petty cash purchases for inventory items, and add these items to the inventory log.

Submit petty cash envelopes once a week or in advance of running out of money. Date, list, and total all expenditures. Do not seal the envelope. Once approved, the accounting department will issue you a check for the amount of your expenditures, keeping your initial draw at the same balance. At the completion of principal photography or wrap, the balance of receipts and remaining cash must be accounted for as quickly as possible.

DISTRIBUTION

A *Distribution List* is essential to ensure that the immense volume of paperwork and information that must be dispersed to cast, crew, staff, bond company, network, studio, etc. from the production office gets to all those who need it. A Distribution List form can be found in Chapter 14.

RECYCLING

A cardboard box or trash can should be allocated for the collection of empty soda cans and bottles. Place another empty box or can near the copier machine for paper that can be recycled (old scripts, outdated schedules, etc.). Make sure there are no paper clips or staples attached to the paper.

If your city, studio lot, or building does not provide for the pickup of recyclables, locate the nearest recycling center to your office. Have a production assistant or driver drop off your recyclable items as often as it is convenient.

PRODUCT PLACEMENT

Before making a deal with a product placement firm or with an individual company for obtaining wardrobe, props, set dressing, vehicles, locations, or services in exchange for on-air exposure and/or screen credit, please discuss this with your production executive or attorney. If approved, a representative of the company supplying the item(s), service(s), or location(s) will be required to sign an appropriate release form. A Product Placement Release form can be found in Chapter 9.

BETTER SAFE THAN SORRY

Even with the existence of industry safety guidelines and a location code of conduct, efforts must continually be made to be aware, cautious, and thorough. Although this behavior will most certainly prevent many potential problems, be assured that no production company, regardless of size or stature, is totally immune to accidents, grievances, lawsuits, and insurance claims. *Be careful!* It's easy to get so busy on a shoot, that from time to time, a few small details fall between the cracks. And small details can quickly turn into big problems that come back to haunt you later on.

To best protect your own backside, and that of the company, you should:

Keep careful inventories and note when something is lost or damaged.

Put as much information on the back of the production report as possible, including the slightest scratch anyone might receive. When a day passes and there are no injuries, indicate by noting, "No injuries reported today" on the back of the production report.

When someone is injured, complete a workers' compensation (Employer's Report of Injury) report as soon as possible and get it to the insurance agency. Also attach a copy to the daily production report.

Have an ambulance on the set on standby when you are doing stunts that are in the least bit complicated or dangerous. Always know where the closest medical emergency facility near your shooting site is located. If you do not have an ambulance on the set, have a *designated* car and driver ready to take someone to the hospital if necessary.

Confirm all major decisions and commitments in writing; and if an official agreement or contract is not drawn up, write a confirming memo detailing the arrangement.

If you are having trouble with a crew member, keep a log of dates and incidents.

Do not sign a rental agreement for the use of equipment, motor homes, facilities, etc. until you or someone you trust can check out the quality and you know exactly what you are getting.

Favors involving any type of exchange are nice (i.e., the company uses a crew member's car in a chase sequence in exchange for repairs to the car) but can also backfire on you. All such agreements should be backed up with a letter in writing stating the exact terms of the exchange and releasing the company from any further obligations.

CREATE YOUR OWN PRODUCTION MANUAL

The best way to establish your company's policies is to have your own production manual. Having a company manual provides a substantial degree of professionalism to the smallest of production units. Assemble your manuals in large three-ring binders, and make sure all staff and freelance production personnel receive one.

The manual should contain the following:

1. A complete listing of company operating procedures, including crew startup and payroll reporting procedures
2. A contact list containing the names, addresses, and phone numbers of the company's insurance representative, outside legal advisor, travel agent, vendors, storage facilities, labs and post production facilities, applicable union and guild representatives, payroll service, permit service, script research service, music clearance service, messenger service, equipment rental houses, repair contacts, etc.
3. A company staff list, including department designations and phone number extensions
4. Samples of the forms and releases you wish to be used on all company shows
5. Pertinent union and guild rates and regulations, including rules governing the employment of minors
6. Insurance guidelines, contacts, forms, and claim reporting procedures
7. Safety guidelines
8. Code of conduct

. . . and anything else relevant to your company operations.

CHAPTER THREE

Insurance Requirements

Securing insurance should be the first order of business at the start of any new production. Coverage should be obtained from an insurance agency that specializes in insurance for the entertainment industry. You may want to get bids from two or three different companies, or from one insurance broker you have developed a good working relationship with.

As films continually become more complicated in terms of action, stunts, effects, technology, and the reliance on highly paid actors and directors to carry entire pictures on their names alone, levels of financial exposures increase as well. Insurance companies and the agencies who represent them are taking a much closer look than ever before at each picture, vigorously investigating potential exposure, and carefully assessing the risks.

In addition to budgets and schedules, insurance companies examine the track record of the production company, the producer and director; where the show is to be shot; its financing source; distribution and bond company agreements; cast; storyline; all potential hazards; safety guidelines and protection methods to be utilized; proposed travel; crew specifications and anticipated payroll; rare and expensive set dressing, props or wardrobe to be used; the use of animals, motorcycles, special vehicles and equipment, watercraft, aircraft, or railroad cars; and all proposed action, stunts, and effects.

Information necessary to complete a *risk management survey* is now required when applying for production insurance. Risk manage-

ment personnel (i.e., in-house risk managers, brokers, and underwriters) review all scripts, contracts, and budgets, in addition to detailed breakdowns of proposed stunts and effects. The backgrounds and experience levels of stunt coordinators and effects supervisors are scrutinized, and proof of pyrotechnic licenses is required as well.

On films containing action, *loss control representatives* might contact stunt coordinators and effects supervisors to discuss the concerns of the underwriter, how each stunt and effect is to be accomplished, the anticipated use of personnel, and the safety procedures to be implemented. These reps. are extremely knowledgeable in the areas of stunts and effects, and will offer advice and spend time on the set when action sequences are shot. Their sole purpose is to minimize risks and to curb the escalating losses suffered by insurance companies on action pictures. This chapter will touch on the basics of motion picture and television insurance, including both standard and supplemental coverages.

ERRORS AND OMISSIONS

Errors and omissions liability insurance provides coverage for claims made for libel, slander, invasion of privacy, infringement of copyright, defamation of character, plagiarism, piracy, or unfair competition resulting from the alleged unauthorized use of titles, formats, ideas, characters, plots, performances of artists or performers, or other materials. It includes coverage for any legal expenses incurred in the defense of any covered claim as well as indemnity.

Delivery requirements might dictate whether this is to be a one-year or a three-year policy. A three-year policy is cost effective, and renewals should continue at least throughout the distribution period.

Obtain an errors and omissions liability insurance application from your insurance broker immediately upon starting pre-production. This is the only insurance application that is completed by the production company and must be signed by an authorized member of the production company. Submit the application and secure this coverage as soon as possible.

COMPREHENSIVE GENERAL LIABILITY

This coverage typically provides a combined single limit of $1,000,000 per occurrence and $2,000,000 in the aggregate for bodily injury and property damage liability. The liability coverage includes: blanket contractual liability, products and completed operations, non-ownership watercraft legal liability (up to twenty-six feet), personal injury endorsement, fire damage legal liability, and an additional assured employee rider.

Evidence of this coverage is given in the form of a *Certificate of Insurance*. Certificates of Insurance are issued by the production office (or in some cases, the insurance agency) to a third party (i.e., a location owner) as evidence of coverage.

Frequently, you will be requested to name a certificate holder as *additional insured* and/or *loss payee*. If a certificate holder is named as an additional insured, the insurance coverage will protect the certificate holder for claims arising out of the activities of the production company. A certificate holder who is named loss payee is the owner of a vehicle or equipment being used on your film. If there is a claim resulting from the loss or damage to their vehicle or equipment, reimbursement for the loss or damage would be paid to the loss payee.

Your insurance agency may require that you call their office to request additional insured or loss payee certificates when a certificate holder requests this additional coverage. There are times, however, when these certificates may be issued directly from the production office.

You can order certificates of insurance that specify *Additional Insured—Managers or Lessors of Premises*, which are issued to the owner(s) of each filming location, and *Additional Insured/Loss Payee—Equipment*, which are issued to the owners of rented equipment and vehicles. Special coverages that involve the company's use of watercraft, aircraft, or a railroad are always handled through your insurance representative. Certificates involving these activities are never issued by the production office.

When filling out a Certificate of Insurance on a rental vehicle or a picture vehicle, it is a good idea to include the make, model, and I.D. number of the vehicle. If the value of the vehicle exceeds the limits of the policy, additional coverage will be necessary. If you are doing a series, the episode and production number should be indicated on the certificate.

The top copy of the certificate (the original) goes to the owner of the vehicle, property, or equipment. Two copies are to be sent to your insurance representative. One copy should be given to your production executive, and one is to remain in the production files. If the certificate is for a vehicle, a copy should also be kept in the vehicle's glove compartment.

HIRED, LOANED, DONATED, OR NON-OWNED AUTO LIABILITY

This covers all hired or leased vehicles used in connection with the production. Vehicles owned by or leased to the company must be scheduled separately, and a charge is incurred for each vehicle. If an employee should have an accident while driving his or her personal car for company business, his or her own insurance is primary. The company's policy only insures the production company if the employee's coverage is insufficient.

Have your transportation coordinator keep a supply of auto accident forms (Automobile

Loss Notice) on the set at all times. One should be filled out and submitted to the insurance agency immediately after an accident occurs.

HIRED, LOANED, DONATED, OR NON-OWNED AUTO PHYSICAL DAMAGE

This coverage insures hired or leased vehicles against the risks of loss, theft, or damage, including collision for certain vehicles for which the production company is contractually responsible. It covers vehicles rented from crew and staff members if a contractual agreement for the use of a vehicle is entered into between the company and the employee *prior* to any incident that might trigger a claim. As with the auto liability coverage, vehicles owned by or leased to the company must be scheduled separately.

If a vehicle is damaged as a result of more than one incident, notation must be made as to the specific damage caused during each incident, the date and time of each, what the vehicle was being used for (was it a picture vehicle or a production vehicle?), and how the accident occurred. The insurance company *will not* accept miscellaneous vehicle damage accumulated during the length of a production. It treats each occurrence as a separate accident, and a separate deductible applies to each occurrence. If you plan to use a picture vehicle for stunt work, include this information in your breakdown. Be aware that physical damage to vehicles used in stunts is generally not covered.

WORKERS' COMPENSATION AND EMPLOYER'S LIABILITY

All employees are entitled to workers' compensation benefits if they are injured or acquire an illness directly resulting from or during the course of their employment. The benefits are established by state laws.

Workers' compensation coverage should be supplied by the *employer of record*, that is, the paying entity, which is either the payroll service or the production company. Although payroll services generally supply workers' compensation, it is a prudent practice to obtain a certificate of workers' compensation coverage from them prior to any commitment of services. Even if all employees are being paid through the payroll service, prudence further dictates that the production company still carry a minimum premium, insuring *independent contractors*, volunteers, or interns who might work on your picture. A contingent workers' compensation policy would also provide employer liability coverage should the need arise.

If the employer of record is other than the production company or payroll service (for example, a stunt coordinator hiring other stunt personnel or a special effects supervisor hiring his or her own effects crew), you should obtain a Certificate of Insurance from the employer (department head) to show evidence of workers' compensation coverage for his or her employees.

If your workers' compensation coverage is coming from more than one source, generate a memo indicating which staff, crew, and cast members are covered under which policy. The memo should also include information on each of the insurance companies (name, address, and phone number), the name of an insurance agency or payroll company representative to report claims to, the policy numbers of each, and a copy of the accident report form (Employer's Report of Injury) that each insurance company uses. Make sure your company medic and second assistant director have copies of this memo and a supply of both accident forms on the set at all times.

When a staff, cast, or crew member is injured on the set, fill out an Employer's Report of Injury form and note the incident on the back of the daily production report for that particular day. Send the report directly to the insurance agency or payroll company, keep a copy for the production files, and send a copy to your production executive. Also attach an additional copy to the back of the production report. Forward all medical bills, doctor's reports, etc. to the respective insurance agency or payroll company.

When applying for workers' compensation during pre-production, declare the need for coverage for employees hired in your state of operations as well as coverage for any other state where your employees are living at the time of hire. Include an *All States' Endorsement* with your workers' compensation policy to protect the company if employees are hired from a state or states you had not initially declared. Injured employees will receive benefits in accordance with the compensation laws of the state in which they were living at the time of hire. Six states—Nevada, Ohio, West Virginia, Wyoming, North Dakota, and Washington State—are *monopolistic*, meaning that you must purchase workers' compensation coverage directly from their state insurance program if you choose to hire employees from their state.

Your insurance agency representative and/or the state's workers' compensation fund will supply you with appropriate injury report forms. Reporting procedures are the same in every state. Should a SAG-covered performer be injured in the course of employment with your company, the Screen Actors Guild requires that you send a copy of the accident report to them.

GUILD/UNION ACCIDENT COVERAGE

Employees traveling on company business are covered under a *Travel Accident Policy*, which provides coverage as specified in their governing guild or union bargaining agreements. If an employee is not a member of any union or guild, coverage is provided for a minimum amount. No employee, while on the company payroll, is allowed to fly as a pilot or as a member of a flight crew unless specifically hired for that duty and scheduled on the insurance policy.

Under Guild/Union Travel Accident coverage, each production is required to keep track of (1) the number of plane and/or helicopter flights taken by any guild/union member on each show, (2) the number of hours each person may spend in a helicopter, (3) the number of days each guild/union member may be exposed to hazardous conditions, and (4) the number of days any DGA member may be exposed while filming underwater. This specific information may be requested from the insurance company at the completion of principal photography.

PRODUCTION PACKAGE (PORTFOLIO POLICY)

The Production Package provides coverage for cast insurance; negative film and videotape/direct physical loss; faulty stock, camera, and processing; props, sets and scenery, costumes, and wardrobe; miscellaneous rented equipment and office contents; extra expense; and third party property damage.

The premium for the Production Package is usually based upon what is referred to as *net insurable* costs. To determine the cost of a production package, the practice has been to take the final budget and to deduct the costs of post production, story, music, and finance costs. This is starting to change because some productions now include the additional coverage on story, music, and finance costs. Your selection of optional coverages on any one show will be based on script and budgetary considerations, as well as requirements imposed by distributors and bond companies. Your insurance representative will discuss all variables and policy options with you and help you decide which coverages will provide the best protection for your picture.

CAST INSURANCE

This coverage is placed on a designated number of cast members, the director, and possibly the producer or director of photography—any key person whose disability or death would cause a shutdown of the production. If an accident or illness of a covered actress, actor, director, etc. creates a postponement, interruption, or cancellation of production, the production company, subject to a predetermined deductible, would be reimbursed for extra expenses incurred in the completion of principal photography. This policy might also include coverage for kidnapping occurring during pre-production or filming, and can include coverage for the payment of ransom demands. A thorough and complete substantiation of the company's extra costs incurred due to such occurrences must be presented to the insurance company before a claim can be properly adjusted.

Physical exams are required for those who are to be covered under cast insurance, and the insurance agency will furnish you with the name of a physician (or a choice of physicians) with whom you can set up appointments. The insurance company will pay closer attention to a cast member's medical history when that person is either overaged or underaged. When employing minors, your insurance broker needs to be aware of the childhood diseases they have had, because the diseases (e.g., chicken pox, measles, mumps) they have not yet had may be excluded from the cast insurance policy. There may also be specific exclusions imposed upon principals who have had a history of alcohol or substance abuse. If any of these circumstances do exist, they should be brought to the attention of the producer as soon as possible. At times, certain exclusions can be "bought back" or modified (i.e., by using higher deductibles, etc.).

Cast insurance usually starts three to four weeks prior to the commencement of principal photography, although additional prep coverage is often required. An example of this is a key actor who is involved with the project from the very early stages of pre-production.

If at any point during pre-production or production, the director, producer, or one of the designated actors becomes ill, is injured, or is incapacitated in any way, call your insurance representative immediately. If one of them feels ill yet continues working, but you are not sure how he or she will be on the following day, or how the schedule may be affected later in the week, alert the insurance agency as to the possibility of an interruption in filming. *If there is ever a question as to whether you should call or not, DO IT!*

If a cast claim is submitted, the director or performer who is ill or injured should be seen by a doctor as soon as possible. The doctor's report is a necessary factor in substantiating the claim.

ESSENTIAL ELEMENTS

This coverage is an optional endorsement that is becoming more and more popular, especially with large budgeted productions. An *essential element* would be an actor, actress,

producer, or director who carries an entire show on their name alone, someone without whom, if this person were to die or become ill or injured, the picture could not be completed and delivered. At times, more than one key person may be designated as an essential element. If there is essential element coverage, the inability of an essential element to continue working now gives the producer the option of abandoning the project and recouping all expenses. If it is determined, however, that the essential element, after suffering an illness or injury, is likely to recover and resume his or her assigned role or position, the insurance company has the option to delay the abandonment of the insured production for up to sixty days after the occurrence of the injury or onset of the illness.

The additional insurance would begin at the start of pre-production and should be carried until at least two weeks after the completion of principal photography. In the case of an essential director, coverage might have to stay in effect through the director's cut.

Before someone is granted the status of essential element, their name must be on an "A" list of artists, or they must be approved by the underwriter. It is mandatory that he or she have an extensive medical exam and also sign a warranty agreeing to refrain from hazardous activities on and off the set during the entire span of their contract. The payment schedule of the artist being insured is examined, as are any previous disabling illnesses or injuries.

FAMILY DEATH ENDORSEMENT (BEREAVEMENT COVERAGE)

This is another optional endorsement that would reimburse the production for expenses incurred when a key member of the cast or the director must interrupt his or her working schedule due to the death of an immediate family member.

NEGATIVE FILM AND VIDEOTAPE/ DIRECT PHYSICAL LOSS

Subject to specific exclusions, most of which are covered under Faulty Stock, Camera, and Processing (described later), this coverage protects against direct physical loss, damage, or destruction to all negative and videotape elements, including: work prints, cutting copies, fine-grain prints, sound tracks, audiotapes, videotapes, cassettes, and CDs. In addition, coverage is included for accidental magnetic erasure on videotape production and has been adapted to cover the most up-to-date technological developments of videotape production. It also includes coverage on all negative and videotape elements while in transit.

FAULTY STOCK, CAMERA, AND PROCESSING

Subject to certain exclusions, this coverage insures against the loss, damage, or destruction of raw film stock or tape stock, exposed film, recorded videotape, and sound tracks caused by or resulting from fogging or the use of faulty equipment, faulty developing, or faulty processing. It does not cover losses due to mistakes made by the camera crew.

PROPS, SETS AND SCENERY, COSTUMES AND WARDROBE; MISCELLANEOUS RENTED EQUIPMENT; OFFICE CONTENTS

Subject to specified exclusions, these provide coverage against direct physical loss, damage, or destruction to all property (contents, equipment, cameras, sets, wardrobe, lighting equipment, office furnishings, props, supplies, etc.) used in connection with the covered production. Keep running inventories of all set dressing, props, wardrobe, equipment, etc. that are purchased and/or rented for each show. If anyone on your crew notices that something is missing or damaged, inform the insurance agency, make a note of it on the inventory log and on the back of the daily production report, and file a police report if applicable. At the end of the show, the insurance company *may not* honor claims on lost or damaged equipment, props, set dressing, or wardrobe without sufficient documentation. Advise all department heads to inform the production manager or production coordinator of loss and damages as they occur and to not wait until the completion of principal photography to submit invoices for repairs and replacement costs.

In specific cases of missing equipment, props, set dressing, or wardrobe, there must clearly be a theft for a claim to be honored. As

soon as an item is discovered missing, file a police report to substantiate the theft. If at the end of principal photography, however, you discover you are short a few pieces of equipment, a few props, or some pieces of wardrobe and have no idea when any of these items were taken, this is considered "mysterious disappearance." Without a police report and documentation indicating when each item was discovered missing, who discovered it missing, etc., a claim of mysterious disappearance is not covered.

No insurance reimbursements are issued for the loss of employees' personal belongings, such as purses or clothing. If an employee is using his or her own personal computer or typewriter, it is not covered under the company policy unless it is being rented by the company (even if the rental price is $1 a month); and there must be an invoice or deal memo to substantiate the rental, each of which must include substantiation of the producer's contractual responsibility to insure these items.

EXTRA EXPENSE

Claims of this type typically involve the damage or destruction of sets, props, wardrobe, locations, or facilities that actually interrupt, delay, or cause the cancellation of production. It also covers additional expenses resulting from the short circuiting, electrical injury, or failure of any electrical generator, portable or otherwise, used in production. This added protection covers expenditures over and above the total cost normally incurred to complete principal photography when any real and/or personal property is lost due to damage or the destruction of this property.

THIRD PARTY PROPERTY DAMAGE

This coverage pays all sums that the production company shall become legally obligated to pay as damages because of accidental injury to or destruction of property of others while such property is in the care, custody, or control of the production company.

Your insurance representative will advise you as to the specific limits and deductibles of the above-mentioned coverages and any additional optional coverages you might require based on the needs of your production.

SUPPLEMENTAL (OR OPTIONAL) COVERAGES

UMBRELLA (EXCESS LIABILITY)

There will be times, with locations, for example, when higher limits than those provided under General Liability and/or Third Party Property Damage are mandatory. This coverage carries limits of liability in excess of $1,000,000. An Umbrella Liability Policy will indemnify the insured for the ultimate net loss in excess of the underlying limit or the self-insured retention, whichever is the greater, because of bodily injury, personal injury, or property damage to which the insurance applies.

Umbrella liability policies providing limits from $1 million to $25 million, and higher, are available. If, however, increased limits of liability are required for a short period of time only, excess limits can be obtained to comply with specific location or contract requirements. If your operations are to include filming at any museums, airports, or major office or manufacturing locations, umbrella liability is a must.

USE OF AIRCRAFT

Inform your insurance agency as soon as possible if you plan to use any aircraft in your show so that adequate *Non-Owned Aircraft Liability* and/or hull coverages can be secured. Insurance is also available to c er the use of hot air balloons, gliders, sailplanes, and other types of aircraft.

To add protection for the possible negligence of the owner of the aircraft, it is also strongly advisable that the owner be asked to name your production company as *additional insured* under his owner's Hull and Liability Insurance policies. The production should secure a Hold Harmless and Waiver of Subrogation with respect to loss or damage to the hull of the aircraft, so that the production is not responsible for any damage to it. Request a Certificate of Insurance from the owner of the aircraft evidencing the Waiver of Subrogation and including the production company as an additional insured.

USE OF WATERCRAFT

If you are going to be using a boat (water

craft) for the purpose of filming or carrying a film crew and/or equipment, discuss the details with your insurance representative to determine if and what type of *marine coverages* are necessary.

USE OF RAILROADS OR RAILROAD FACILITIES

For the use of railroads or railroad facilities, the production company is often required to indemnify the railroad for the production's negligence as well as the railroad's negligence. The insurance agency will need to review the contract provided by the railroad before proper coverage can be determined.

USE OF VALUABLES

Inform the insurance agency as to the use of fine arts, jewelry, furs, and expensive antiques, and the values of each, so that limits can be increased as required. How these items are to be used with respect to the production must be discussed so that appropriate coverage can be arranged.

USE OF LIVESTOCK OR ANIMALS

If insurance coverage is necessary for livestock or animals to be used in a production, it is arranged on a case-by-case basis and is based on contractual obligations and the value of the animal(s). *Animal mortality insurance* covers the death or destruction of any animal specifically insured. At no time would the limit of coverage be more than the value of the animal covered; and before coverage is issued, a veterinarian certificate on the animal is necessary. Under certain circumstances, an animal may be insured under *Extra Expense*. This coverage reimburses the production company for extra expenses incurred due to the accident, illness, or death of a covered animal.

SIGNAL INTERRUPTION INSURANCE

Insurance coverage is available to protect against exposures in the transmission of signals by satellite or closed circuit television. This coverage indemnifies the insured for loss of revenues resulting from the necessary interruption of business due to breakdown, failure, or malfunction of any equipment that prevent the telecasting or presentation of the scheduled event.

FOREIGN PACKAGE POLICY

When a production is filming outside of the United States, its territories, or possessions, special coverages are necessary. Under these circumstances, it is important to procure Foreign Liability, Foreign Workers' Compensation, and Foreign Auto coverage. A domestic policy will not protect you against lawsuits filed in foreign countries.

POLITICAL RISK INSURANCE

This coverage is recommended for production companies planning to shoot in certain (potentially dangerous) foreign countries. Under this policy, the insurance company pays for loss due to physical property damage to insured assets caused by war, civil war, and insurrection. It includes *forced project relocation coverage*, which pays the additional costs incurred solely and directly as a result of and following relocation of the production to another country. This coverage also includes any production-related confiscation or expropriation by a foreign government.

WEATHER INSURANCE

Weather insurance is available to protect against additional costs incurred in the event your production is interrupted, postponed, or cancelled as a result of weather-related problems. The policy can include coverage not only for precipitation, but can be extended to include coverage for wind, fog, temperature, and any other measurable weather conditions.

COMPLETION BONDS

Completion guarantees, also referred to as *completion bonds*, insure motion picture financiers against cost overruns in excess of their approved budget. In addition, they insure that the film will be delivered in accordance with all specifications contained in the financing and distribution agreements, and in other related contracts that define the deal.

Major studios with the resources to finance pictures, including overages, do not require bonding, as the functions provided by a bond company are handled in house. Bond companies do service smaller studios and independent production companies, whose financiers and distributors will require that their picture be bonded prior to the start of principal photography.

The formal issuance of a completion guaranty involves two separate documents. The *producer's agreement* is signed by the producer and guarantor, and is an acknowledgment and warranty by the producer to produce the film in accordance with the approved script, schedule, and budget. The producer also agrees to take or cause no action that would void the approved insurance coverages or that would otherwise threaten the timely and efficient production of the film. In the event of default by the producer, this document gives the guarantor the ultimate right to take over the film, and to complete and deliver it in the producer's stead.

The *completion guaranty* is signed by the financier(s) and the guarantor. In this document, the guarantor agrees to deliver the film in accordance with the approved script, schedule, budget, and contractual specifications, and to pay any additional costs in excess of the approved budget required to so deliver the project. In the event that the film cannot be delivered as guaranteed, the guarantor agrees to repay all funds that have been therefore advanced by the financier(s) to cover the costs of the approved budget. If the project has to be abandoned, the financier is not put in the position of having spent money on a project that was not completed. In the event that the picture cannot be completed, the financier is repaid his investment. While not able to collect additional revenues from box office grosses, he has not lost anything either.

As do the insurance underwriters, *completion guarantors* carefully assess each project before committing to a bond. They want to know that you have a script with an adequate schedule and budget, and a reputable and insurable cast and crew. They will review all major contracts relating to cast, locations, special effects, insurance, travel, etc. They will assign members of their staff to oversee projects from the beginning of pre-production through delivery; and at times, they will hire an outside person to oversee a particular picture. Bond reps will receive copies of scripts, budgets, schedules, call sheets, production reports, weekly cost reports, etc. Some will attend a production meeting or two and make occasional visits to the set during production. Other bond reps will be more hands-on and remain with the shooting company on a daily basis, involved in all major decisions pertaining to the production. Much will depend on the bond company and its particular style of involvement, the relationship and track record you have with the bond company, and how each film is progressing; the ones that encounter the most difficulties are the ones more closely watched.

The traditional point where a bond company would take over a film is after the production has gone through their entire budget plus the full 10% contingency prior to the completion of the picture. This rarely happens, as the bond company's job is to anticipate potential problems before they occur. It works diligently with the producer, director, cast, and crew to keep things on schedule and on budget. Unless you have one company that you prefer working with, shop around for a completion guarantor, as rates are competitive and often negotiable.

INSURANCE FORMS

Once you have filled out the appropriate applications and coverage is in place, you will be supplied with a copy of your insurance policy (and/or certificates) and the various accident and claim forms needed for each production. Have a supply of the following in the production office and on the set at all times:

1. Certificate of Insurance
2. Automobile Loss Notice
3. Property Loss Notice
4. General Liability Notice of Occurrence/Claim Notice
5. Workers' Compensation—Employer's Report of Occupational Injury or Illness

Some you will use more frequently than others, but you should be familiar with all of them.

CLAIMS REPORTING PROCEDURES

If an accident, injury, or theft occurs; if the director or a cast member becomes ill and unable to work; if you have a scratched negative or damage to equipment, props, set dressing, or any of your sets, report it to the insurance agency as soon as possible. Back up each reported occurrence in writing by completing an appropriate claim form, noting such on the back of the daily production report for that particular day, and/or by writing a letter to the insurance agency containing as much detail as possible—when the incident occurred (date of loss), where it occurred, how it happened, who was there at the time, etc. Report any major theft or accident to the police, and attach a copy of the police report to your letter to the insurance agency. Even if you are not sure a loss would be covered, advise your insurance representative as to the possibility of a claim.

If a serious accident occurs, promptly record the names and phone numbers of witnesses (including staff, cast, and crew members) so that an accurate description of the incident can be determined at a later date. Statements or reports should only be taken by authorized representatives of the production company, and in turn, should be submitted to your insurance representative.

SUBMITTING CLAIMS

When an incident occurs resulting in an insurance claim, the accounting department should begin to tag each related invoice, indicating specific costs (or portions of costs) that were directly incurred as a result of the claim. When the claim is submitted, all related costs and overages should be presented *budget-style* starting with a budget *top sheet* indicating the exact impact to each account. Copies of invoices should be coded and placed behind the top sheet in the correct order of accounts.

In addition to applicable police and doctor reports and copies of invoices, backup should also include call sheets; production reports; and both original and revised schedules, day-out-of-days, cast lists, etc.—anything to substantiate the changes created by the claim.

Depending on the claim, copies of cast and crew deal memos, time cards, travel movement lists, equipment rental agreements, and/or location agreements may also be required. For complicated or ongoing claims, it is a good idea for the producer or production manager to either maintain a *log* of events pertaining to the claim on a day-to-day basis or to write memos to the file on a regular basis.

Begin each claim with a *cover letter* referencing the production, date of occurrence, claim number (if available), a description of the claim, and a brief summary of the backup you are providing. (I suggest binding the backup with brads or in file folders secured with Acco® fasteners.) Start processing insurance claims as soon as they occur. Submit the full claim to the insurance agency as soon as costs can be assessed and backup provided. Do not wait until the end of principal photography to start processing your claims.

Once a claim is reported to your insurance representative, it is then turned over to an insurance agency claim representative. When all the information is in order, the claim is then submitted to the insurance company, who may or may not (depending on the claim) then assign it to an independent insurance auditor. It is often advantageous for the production manager and production accountant to meet with the insurance auditor shortly after the incident occurs to better define the parameters of the claim and to know exactly what backup will be necessary.

The following pages contain four *insurance claim worksheets* that will be helpful in collecting needed information for the submission of insurance claims. For further information regarding any aspect of insurance, contact your insurance agent.

Note: Assistance for this chapter was provided by Marc J. Federman, Sr. Vice President of Near North Insurance Brokerage in Los Angeles.

INSURANCE CLAIM WORKSHEET

(THEFT)

STOLEN ☐ EQUIPMENT
☐ WARDROBE
☐ PROPS
☑ SET DRESSING
☐ VEHICLE

PRODUCTION HERBY'S SUMMER VACATION

DATE ITEM(S) WERE DISCOVERED MISSING JUNE 29, 19XX

DESCRIPTION OF ITEM(S) STOLEN (Include I.D.#'s If Available)

MACINTOSH II si COMPUTER WITH MONITOR & KEYBOARD
SERIAL # XSF23L2762265

DEPARTMENT USED BY SET DRESSING
PERSON USED BY USED AS SET DRESSING ONLY

WHERE WERE ITEM(S) LAST SEEN "HERBY'S BEDROOM" SET

WHO DISCOVERED ITEM(S) MISSING DARLENE DRESSER

ITEM(S) ☐ PURCHASED FOR SHOW—PURCHASE PRICE $
☑ RENTED FOR SHOW
RENTED FROM CAL'S COMPUTER CENTER
ADDRESS 8976 MAIN STREET
STUDIO VILLAGE, CA 90000
PHONE# (818) 555-1767
CONTACT CAL COLLINS

VALUE $ 1,500
RENTAL PRICE $ 200   PER ☐ DAY
☐ WEEK
☑ MONTH

☑ POLICE REPORT ATTACHED
☑ OTHER ATTACHMENTS RENTAL AGREEMENT FROM CAL'S
COMPUTER CENTER

SUBMITTED TO INSURANCE AGENCY ON JULY 2, 19XX
ATTENTION SUSIE
CLAIM # 005327
INSURANCE COMPANY CLAIMS REP. CURTIS CLAIMS

INSUR. CLAIM WORKSHEET COMPLETED BY CONNIE COORDINATES
DATE JULY 2, 19XX TITLE PRODUCTION COORDINATOR

AMOUNT CREDITED TO AGGREGATE DEDUCTIBLE $ 500   DATE 7·15·XX
REIMBURSEMENT CHECK PAID TO XYZ PRODUCTIONS
AMOUNT $ 1,000   DATE 7·20·XX

© ELH Form #01

INSURANCE CLAIM WORKSHEET

DAMAGE TO   ☑ EQUIPMENT
                   ☐ WARDROBE
                   ☐ PROPS
                   ☐ SET DRESSING
                   ☐ LOCATION/PROPERTY

PRODUCTION   HERBY'S SUMMER VACATION

DATE OF OCCURRENCE   6·24·XX   TIME   11 A.M.

WHAT WAS DAMAGED   MOTOROLA HT1000 WALKIE·TALKIE

LOCATION OF OCCURRENCE   HOLLYWOOD RIVER

HOW DID DAMAGE OCCUR   SECOND ASSISTANT DIRECTOR ACCIDENTALLY DROPPED WALKIE·TALKIE IN RIVER WHILE ARRANGING ATMOSPHERE FOR SCENE 25.

WITNESS   MIKE BOOM   POSITION   SOUND MIXER
PHONE#   (213) 555-9993

DAMAGED ITEM(S)   ☐ PURCHASED FOR SHOW—PURCHASE PRICE $ _____
                  ☑ RENTED FROM/OWNER   XXX AUDIO SERVICES
                       ADDRESS   123 GRAND AVE.
                                    HOLLYWOOD, CA 91234
                     PHONE #   (213) 555-5311
                     CONTACT   MACK

           RENTAL PRICE $ 50   PER   ☐ DAY
                                          ☑ WEEK
                                          ☐ MONTH

    VALUE OF DAMAGED ITEM(S) $ 1,000
         ESTIMATE TO REPAIR $ 600
☑ ATTACHMENTS   COPY OF DAILY PRODUCTION REPORT (INCIDENT NOTED) COPY OF REPAIR INVOICE

SUBMITTED TO INSURANCE AGENCY ON   6·29·93
                     ATTENTION   SUSIE
                       CLAIM #   005328
INSURANCE COMPANY CLAIMS REP.   CURTIS CLAIMS

INSURANCE CLAIM WORKSHEET COMPLETED BY   CONNIE COORDINATES
DATE   6·28·XX   TITLE   PRODUCTION COORDINATOR

AMOUNT CREDITED TO AGGREGATE DEDUCTIBLE $ 0   DATE _____
REIMBURSEMENT CHECK PAID TO XXX AUDIO SERVICES
                     AMOUNT $ 600   DATE 7·29·XX

© ELH Form #02

INSURANCE CLAIM WORKSHEET

☑ CAST
☐ EXTRA EXPENSE
☐ FAULTY STOCK

PRODUCTION _____ HERBY'S SUMMER VACATION _____

DATE OF OCCURRENCE __JULY 2, 19XX__ TIME __5:00 P.M.__

DESCRIPTION OF INCIDENT __DIRECTORS CHAIR COLLAPSED WHILE ACTRESS__ __WAS SITTING ON IT BETWEEN TAKES. SHE INJURED HER RIGHT__ __LEG AND SPRAINED HER BACK.__

IF CAST CLAIM, WHICH ARTIST __SCARLET STARLET__

WAS A DOCTOR CALLED IN ☑ YES ☐ NO

NAME OF DOCTOR __A. PAINE, M.D.__
ADDRESS __3327 S. INJECTION BLVD.__
__LOS ANGELES 90000__
PHONE # __(310) 555-1177__

COULD COMPANY SHOOT AROUND INCIDENT ☐ YES ☑ NO
IF YES, FOR HOW LONG _____

HOW MUCH DOWN TIME WAS INCURRED DUE TO THIS INCIDENT __1 DAY__

AVERAGE DAILY COST $ __50,000__

BACKUP TO CLAIM TO INCLUDE · __COPY OF DAILY PRODUCTION REPORT__
· __COPY OF DOCTOR'S REPORT__
· __BACK-UP TO COSTS INCURRED DUE TO DOWN TIME__

SUBMITTED TO INSURANCE AGENCY ON __JULY 12, 19XX__
ATTENTION __SUSIE__
CLAIM # __005329__
INSURANCE COMPANY CLAIMS REP. __CURTIS CLAIMS__
INSURANCE AUDITOR __LAWRENCE LIABILITY__

INSURANCE CLAIM WORKSHEET COMPLETED BY __CONNIE COORDINATES__
DATE __7·11·XX__ TITLE __PRODUCTION COORDINATOR__

AMOUNT CREDITED TO DEDUCTIBLE $ __0__ DATE _____
REIMBURSEMENT CHECK PAID TO __XYZ PRODUCTIONS, INC.__
AMOUNT $ __65,000__ DATE __8·15·XX__

© ELH Form #03

INSURANCE CLAIM WORKSHEET

AUTOMOBILE ACCIDENT

PRODUCTION ___HERBY'S SUMMER VACATION___

DATE OF OCCURRENCE ___JUNE 25, 19XX___ TIME ___9:23 A.M.___

LOCATION OF OCCURRENCE ___CORNER OF 4TH STREET & MAPLE DRIVE___
___STUDIO VILLAGE___

HOW DID ACCIDENT OCCUR ___DRIVER SHUTTLING CAST & CREW TO SET___
___FROM PARKING AREA RAN INTO A CAR IN FRONT OF HIM___
___WHEN OTHER CAR STOPPED SHORT APPROACHING THE___
___INTERSECTION.___

INSURED VEHICLE (Year, Make, Model) ___1996 FORD AEROSTAR___
VEHICLE I.D. # ___1234567X2L7HNZ___ LIC. PLATE # ___XXX 2321___
OWNER OF VEHICLE ___TINSELTOWN FORD___
ADDRESS ___7503 CLUTCH DRIVE · BURBANK, CA 91503___
PHONE # ___(818) 555-3327___ CONTACT ___BUDDY___

DRIVER ___TERRY TEAMSTER___
POSITION ___TRANSPORTATION CAPTAIN___
DRIVER'S LIC. # ___S0030376___ USED W/PERMISSION ☑ YES ☐ NO
ADDRESS ___523 N. BROADWAY, APT. #137___
___GLENDALE, CA 91204___
PHONE # ___(818) 555-0216___

WHERE CAN CAR BE SEEN ___TINSELTOWN FORD___
WHEN ___BETWEEN 9:00 a.m. & 6:00 p.m.___

DAMAGE TO CAR ___DENTED FRONT FENDER BUMPER, GRILL & HOOD___
___FRONT END OUT OF ALIGNMENT___
___DAMAGED RADIATOR___
ESTIMATE(S) TO REPAIR $ ___2,900—___ $ ___3,300—___

DAMAGE TO OTHER VEHICLE (Year, Make, Model) ___1993 DODGE RAM PICK·UP___
LIC. PLATE # ___2376573___

DRIVER OF OTHER VEHICLE ___DENNIS DRIVER___
ADDRESS ___7326 N. HILLTOP RD.___
___LOS ANGELES, CA 90000___
PHONE(S) # ___(213) 555-7676___   # _____

WHERE CAN CAR BE SEEN ___AT MR. DRIVER'S HOME___
WHEN ___EVENINGS BETWEEN 6 p.m. & 8 p.m.___

DAMAGE TO CAR ___DENTED REAR BUMPER & TAILGATE___
___BROKEN TRAILER HITCH___

ESTIMATE(S) TO REPAIR $ ___1,500—___ $ ___1,750—___

© ELH Form #04 (Pg. 1)

INJURED _NO INJURIES_

ADDRESS _____

PHONE # _____

EXTENT OF INJURY _____

WITNESS(ES) _F. STOPP (DIRECTOR OF PHOTOGRAPHY)_   _PATRICK PEDESTRIAN_

ADDRESS _3276 BEL AIR CIRCLE_   _603 N. LUMBERJACK WAY_

BEL AIR, CA 90002   _PASADENA, CA 91332_

PHONE # _(310) 555-1727_   _(818) 555-1017_

☑ POLICE REPORT ATTACHED

☑ OTHER ATTACHMENTS _ESTIMATES TO REPAIR VEHICLES_

SUBMITTED TO INSURANCE AGENCY ON _6·30·XX_

ATTENTION _SUSIE_

CLAIM # _005330_

INSURANCE COMPANY CLAIMS REP. _CURTIS CLAIMS_

INSURANCE CLAIM WORKSHEET COMPLETED BY _ALEX AUTOS_

DATE _6·28·XX_   TITLE _TRANSPORTATION COORDINATOR_

INSURANCE ADJUSTER TO SEE INSURED VEHICLE ON _7·7·XX_

TO SEE OTHER VEHICLE ON _7·8·XX_

AMOUNT CREDITED TO DEDUCTIBLE $ _4,100_   DATE _7·12·XX_

REIMBURSEMENT CHECK PAID TO _____

AMOUNT $ _____   DATE _____

TO _____

AMOUNT $ _____   DATE _____

NOTES: _____

CHAPTER FOUR

Setting Up Production Files

You cannot run an efficient production office without well-organized files. Use this as a guide—delete or add files to fit the specific requirements of your show. The name of the show should appear in capital letters at the top of each file folder label, with the heading underneath. Secure each file with an Acco® fastener so none of the papers fall out.

MOVIES FOR TELEVISION, MOVIES FOR CABLE, OR FEATURES

Art Dept./Set Construction
Budget
Budget/Cash Flow and Chart of Accounts
Budget/Cost Reports
Call Sheets
Camera
Cast List/SAG Contracts
Casting Submissions
Check Requests
Code of Conduct
Completion Bond Company
Contact List
Correspondence/Memos
Crew Lists/Deal Memos
Crew—Wrap Schedule
Day-Out-of-Days
Director

Distribution Agreement
Equipment (Miscellaneous)
Extras
Grip/Electric
Hotel/Motel Accommodations
Insurance—General Policy Info and
    Correspondence
Insurance—Workers' Compensation
Insurance—Insurance Claims
Insurance—Certificates of Insurance
Inventory Logs
Locations/Loc. Agreements and Permits
Locations (Distant)
Miscellaneous
Music
Network (or Cable) Format
Network Standards & Practices (if applicable)
Office (Equipment, Furniture, Keys, etc.)
Payroll Info
Personal Releases
Post Production—Schedule and Delivery
    Requirements
Post Production—Contact List,
    Correspondence, etc.
Post Production—Screen Credits
Producer(s)
Production Reports
Property/Set Dressing
Publicity

Purchase Orders/P.O. Log

Research Report

Resumes

Safety Guidelines

Script

Shooting Schedule/One-Liner

Special Effects

Stunt Breakdown

Transportation

Travel Arrangements/Movement Lists

Union/Guild Information

Visual Effects

Wardrobe

Writer(s)

SERIES FILES

When setting up files for a television series, organize *general production files* with the name of the series in capital letters at the top of each file folder label and the heading underneath. *Episode files* should have the name of the episode in capital letters at the top of each file folder label and the heading underneath.

GENERAL PRODUCTION FILES

Art Dept./Set Construction

Budget

Budget/Cash Flow and Chart of Accounts

Budget/Cost Reports

Camera

Cast List—Regulars

Check Requests

Code of Conduct

Contact List

Correspondence/Memos

Crew List/Deal Memos

Crew—Wrap Schedule

Director(s)

Episode Schedule (including writer, director, and editor for each episode)

Equipment (Miscellaneous)

Extras

Hotel/Motel/Apartment Accommodations

Grip/Electric

Insurance—General Policy Information and Correspondence

Insurance—Workers' Compensation

Insurance—Insurance Claims

Insurance—Certificates of Insurance/Vehicles & Equipment

Insurance—Certificates of Insurance/Locations

Inventory Logs

Locations—Miscellaneous Correspondence and Permits

Locations—Permanent

Locations—Nonpermanent (one file for each episode)

Miscellaneous

Music

Network Format

Network Standards & Practices

Office (Equipment, Furniture, Keys, etc.)

Payroll Information

Personal Releases

Post Production—Schedules and Delivery Requirements

Post Production—Contact List, Correspondence, etc.

Post Production—Screen Credits

Producer(s)

Property/Set Dressing

Publicity

Purchase Orders/P.O. Logs

Resumes

Safety Guidelines

Transportation

Travel Arrangements/Movement Lists

Union/Guild Information

Wardrobe

Writer(s)

EPISODE FILES (THREE FOR EACH EPISODE)

1. Complete script with all changes
2. Call Sheets and Production Reports
3. Cast List, Shooting Schedule, Day-Out-of-Days, One-Liner, Research Report, etc.

DAY FILES

It has become a common practice for production personnel to maintain *day files*. The files are kept in chronological order and labeled as follows:

DAY #1
(Day)/(Date)

with one file for each day of shooting. Each file contains all pertinent information for that day of shooting: call sheet, production report, camera report, sound report, film inventory, catering receipt, etc.

Individual call sheet and production report files can be kept (as indicated earlier); call sheets and production reports can be kept in day files or they can be cross-referenced and kept in both types of files. Use whichever system works best for you.

CHAPTER FIVE

Deal Memos

Each member of a shooting company should sign a *deal memo* prior to his or her first day of work. Everyone must know, up front, what their salary will be, including overtime rates and payment for sixth and seventh days worked; how they will be traveling to location; how much their per diem will be; if they will be receiving screen credit, etc. Not knowing for sure, from the beginning, what is to be given and what is expected can make for a very disgruntled and unhappy cast or crew member (or members) later on down the line.

With the exception of the Directors Guild of America (DGA) deal memos, the others included in this chapter are intended as basic guidelines. You and your legal advisor will want to incorporate specific provisions and/or conditions to the terms of employment as they relate to your production. Many producers also issue forms attached to deal memos, which employees are requested to sign, acknowledging that they have received, reviewed, and thoroughly understand the guidelines governing general safety regulations, sexual harassment, and location code of conduct.

Give each employee a copy of his or her signed deal memo (including all attached riders and forms of acknowledgment). Copies should also be given to the production manager, production accountant, and/or payroll service. The original should be retained for the company's master files. Copies of signed DGA deal memos must be sent to the DGA's Reports Compliance Department, in care of the National Office of the Directors Guild of America at 7920 Sunset Blvd., Los Angeles, CA 90046. Their phone and fax numbers are as follows: (310) 289-2000 (phone) and (310) 289-2029 (fax).

LOANOUTS

A person who is a *loanout* must have a valid corporation (with a federal ID number). The corporation then "loans out" the employee's services to the production company. The employee's compensation is paid directly to the corporation, and the corporation is responsible for all applicable payroll taxes. The employee must also show proof of incorporation and of the workers' compensation coverage it is required to carry before the employee can be paid as a loanout, and loanout agreements between the corporation and the production entity must be signed.

Most production companies will only allow specific categories of employees to be paid in this manner, generally actors, writers, directors, producers, production managers, casting directors, directors of photography, production designers, costume designers, editors, and music composers.

EXEMPT/NON-EXEMPT STATUS

There is a place on the *crew deal memo* where each person must indicate whether he or she is an exempt or a non-exempt employee. At one time, claiming *exempt* meant that no deductions would be taken from your payroll check. In this newer context, *exempt* means that the employee can be paid a *flat salary* (opposed to an *hourly rate*). In theory, this employee is a department head, generally sets his or her own hours, is not under anyone's direct control, and can negotiate his or her own rate, including premium pay for a sixth or seventh day worked. Exempt status is not afforded to many.

Non-exempt employees (everyone else) can no longer be paid flat salaries. Non-union crews are paid straight time for the first eight hours, time-and-a-half from eight to twelve hours, and double time beyond twelve hours, with no guarantee past the first eight hours. On union shoots, time-and-a-half and double time varies from union to union, and certain guarantees are permissible. Both union and non-union crews must now completely fill out their time cards, indicating exact hours in and out each day (including meal breaks). They can no longer merely write *worked* with a line drawn across the time card. Although the exempt/non-exempt ruling was initially imposed by the California Labor Board, the practice is spreading throughout the industry. Your production accountant and/or payroll service representative should be able to answer any questions you may have regarding this policy.

CAST DEAL MEMO

PRODUCTION COMPANY __XYZ PRODUCTIONS, INC.__   DATE __MAY 11, 19XX__

ADDRESS __1234 FLICK DR.__   PHONE # __(213) 555-3331__

__HOLLYWOOD, CA 90038__   FAX # __(213) 555-3332__

SHOW __HERBY'S SUMMER VACATION__   EPISODE _____

CASTING DIRECTOR __DEE CASTOR__   PROD # __0100__

ARTIST __SCARLET STARLET__   SOC.SEC. # __555-55-5555__

ADDRESS __555 SCHOOL ST.__   PHONE # __(213) 555-6262__

__HOLLYWOOD, CA 90038__   MESSAGES __(213) 555-2673__

ROLE __"LAURA"__   START DATE __6·9·XX__

- [✓] ACTOR
- [ ] SINGER
- [ ] STUNT
- [ ] OTHER _____

- [✓] THEATRICAL
- [ ] TELEVISION
- [ ] OTHER _____

- [ ] DAY PLAYER
- [ ] 3-DAY PLAYER
- [✓] WEEKLY

COMPENSATION $ __75,000__   PER   [ ] DAY [ ] WEEK [✓] SHOW

	# DAY/WEEKS	DATES
TRAVEL	2 DAYS	6/9/XX & 6/16/XX
REHEARSAL/FITTINGS	1 DAY - FITTINGS	5/19/XX
PRINCIPAL PHOTOGRAPHY	5 DAYS	6/10 - 15
ADDITIONAL SHOOT DAYS	ALLOW: 2	AS NECESSARY
POST PRODUCTION DAYS	ALLOW: 1	TBD

PER DIEM/EXPENSES __$100 PER DAY__

TRANSPORTATION/TRAVEL __ROUND-TRIP FIRST-CLASS AIR TRAVEL & TRANSPOR-TATION TO & FROM AIRPORT__

ACCOMMODATIONS __FIRST-CLASS HOTEL ACCOMMODATIONS__

OTHER __FIRST-CLASS DRESSING ROOM WHEN ON STAGE - MOBILE HOME WITH TV, VCR & MICROWAVE OVEN WHEN ON LOCATION__

BILLING __SINGLE CARD - MAIN TITLES - 3RD POSITION__

- [✓] PAID ADVERTISING

AGENT __JOE COOL__   HOME # __(310) 555-5663__

AGENCY __TALENT ARTISTS AGENCY__   OFFICE # __(213) 555-2345__

ADDRESS __1515 SUNSET BLVD.__   FAX # __(213) 555-2344__

__HOLLYWOOD, CA 90000__

- [✓] LOAN OUT

CORPORATION NAME __STARLET NIGHTS, INC.__

Address __C/O TAA · 1515 SUNSET BLVD.__

__HOLLYWOOD, CA 90000__

Federal I.D. # __95-1234567__

CONTRACT PREPARED BY __BARBARA BUSINESS AFFAIRS__ DATE SENT OUT __5·15·XX__

SENT: [✓] To Agent   [ ] To Artist   [ ] To Set

[✓] SENT SCRIPT   [✓] NOTIFIED WARDROBE   [✓] STATION 12   [✓] INSURANCE PHYSICAL

APPROVED BY __Swifty Deals__   TITLE __PRODUCER__

CREW DEAL MEMO

PRODUCTION CO. __XYZ PRODUCTIONS, INC.__
SHOW __HERBY'S SUMMER VACATION__
NAME __MIKE BOOM__
ADDRESS __3133 RECORDING PLACE__
__ENCINO, CA 91322__
START DATE __JUNE 4, 19XX__
JOB TITLE __SOUND MIXER__
UNION/GUILD _____
RATE (In Town) __$2,500—__
(Distant Loc.) __$3,000—__
ADDITIONAL DAY(S) PRO-RATED @ __1/5__ (th)
OVERTIME __X 1/2__ After __8__ hours

DATE __5·31·XX__
PROD # __0100__
SOC.SEC. # __123-45-6789__
PHONE (Home) __(818) 555-4500__
(Beeper) __(818) 555-9372__
(Fax) __(818) 555-4501__
ACCOUNT # __835-01__
☐ Exempt ☑ Non-Exempt *(to be paid on hourly basis only)*
Per [Hour][Day][Week] for a [5][6] __5__-day week
Per [Hour][Day][Week] for a [5][6] __6__-day week
Of a week
__XX__ After __14__ hours

BOX RENTAL _____ Per Day/Week
EQUIPMENT/VEHICLE RENTAL __$1,750—__ Per Day/(Week)
MILEAGE ALLOWANCE _____ Per Day/Week

NOTE: Box & Equipment rental & mileage allowance are subject to 1099 reporting.—Any equipment rented by the Production Co. from the employee must be listed or inventoried before rental can be paid.

TRAVEL/ACCOMMODATIONS __ROUND-TRIP BUSINESS-CLASS AIR FARE__
__& TRANSPORTATION TO AND FROM THE AIRPORT__

EXPENSES/PER DIEM __$65/DAY PER DIEM__

OTHER __USE OF A CAR WHILE ON LOCATION__

☑ LOAN OUT
CORP. NAME __BOOM AUDIO RENTALS__ FED. ID# __95-1234567__
ADDRESS (If Different From Above) _____

AGENT __NONE__
ADDRESS _____

AGENCY _____
PHONE # _____
FAX # _____

EMPLOYER OF RECORD __PAULINE'S PAYROLL SERVICE__
ADDRESS __7325 PAYERS LANE__ PHONE # __(818) 555-4444__
__STUDIO VILLAGE, CA__ FAX # __(818) 555-4443__
IF AWARDED SCREEN CREDIT, HOW WOULD YOU LIKE YOUR NAME TO READ _____
__SOUND MIXER — MICHAEL R. BOOM__
APPROVED BY __Fred Filmer__ TITLE __UPM__
ACCEPTED __Mike Boom__ DATE __6·3·XX__

© ELH Form #14

WRITER'S DEAL MEMO

PRODUCTION COMPANY __XYZ PRODUCTIONS, INC.__   DATE __2.28.XX__

ADDRESS __1234 FLICK DRIVE__   PHONE # __(213) 555-3331__

__HOLLYWOOD, CA 90038__   FAX # __(213) 555-3332__

SHOW __HERBY'S SUMMER VACATION__   PROD # __0100__

EPISODE _____

WRITER __F. SCOTT RYDER__   PHONE # __(213) 555-7662__

SOC. SEC. # __555-00-5500__   MESSAGES _____

ADDRESS __9336 W. STOREY ST.__   FAX # __(213) 555-7660__

__LOS ANGELES, CA 90000__

DATES OF EMPLOYMENT _____
__3.1.XX THROUGH 7.31.XX__

COMPENSATION __$150,000 FOR ORIGINAL SCREENPLAY - PLUS ONE__
__ADDITIONAL REWRITE & ONE POLISH__

ADDITIONAL TERMS OF EMPLOYMENT __ONE FIRST-CLASS, ROUND-TRIP__
__AIR FARE TO LOCATION__

BILLING __SCREENPLAY BY__
__F. SCOTT RYDER__

☑ PAID ADVERTISING

WRITER'S AGENT __JOE COOL__   DIRECT # __(213) 555-5663__

AGENCY __TALENTED ARTISTS AGENCY__   PHONE # __(213) 555-2345__

ADDRESS __1515 SUNSET BLVD.__   FAX # __(213) 555-2344__

__HOLLYWOOD, CA 90000__

☑ LOAN OUT

CORPORATION NAME __GREAT RYDERS, INC.__

ADDRESS __(SAME AS ABOVE)__

FED. I.D. # __95-3367323579__

CONTRACT PREPARED BY __BARBARA BUSINESS AFFAIRS__

DATE SENT OUT __3.1.XX__

APPROVED BY __Swifty Deals__

TITLE __PRODUCER__   DATE __2.28.XX__

© ELH Form #15

WRITING TEAM DEAL MEMO

PRODUCTION COMPANY __XYZ PRODUCTIONS, INC.__   DATE __6·10·XX__

ADDRESS __1234 FLICK DR.__   PHONE # __(213) 555-3331__

__HOLLYWOOD, CA 90038__   FAX # __(213) 555-3332__

SHOW __HERBY'S SUMMER VACATION__   PROD # __0100__

EPISODE __"BOY'S NIGHT OUT"__

WRITERS __JASON PENN__   __SAMUEL INKK__

SOC.SEC. # __555-02-3657__   __555-72-7632__

ADDRESS __1723 LINCOLN BLVD.__   __313 WASHINGTON ST.__

__LOS ANGELES, CA 90000__   __CULVER CITY, CA 90230__

PHONE # __(213) 555-7321__   __(310) 555-9636__

FAX # __(213) 555-7322__   __(310) 555-9637__

DATES OF EMPLOYMENT __6·12·XX THROUGH 8·31·XX__

COMPENSATION __$80,000__

ADDITIONAL TERMS OF EMPLOYMENT _____

BILLING __SCREENPLAY BY__
__JASON PENN and SAMUEL INKK__

☑ PAID ADVERTISING

WRITER'S AGENTS __JOE COOL__   __(SAME)__

AGENCY __TALENTED ARTISTS AGENCY__

ADDRESS __1515 SUNSET BLVD.__

__HOLLYWOOD, CA 90000__

PHONE # __(213) 555-2345__

☑ LOAN OUT

CORP. NAME __PENN AND INK PRODUCTIONS, INC.__

ADDRESS __9o TAA - 1515 SUNSET BLVD.__

__HOLLYWOOD, CA 90000__

FED. I.D. # __95-7291346782__

CONTRACT PREPARED BY __BARBARA BUSINESS AFFAIRS__

DATE SENT OUT __6·15·XX__

APPROVED BY __Swifty Deale__

TITLE __PRODUCER__   DATE __6·12·XX__

© ELH Form #16

DIRECTOR DEAL MEMORANDUM

This confirms our agreement to employ you to direct the project described as follows:

Name: SID CELLULOID   S.S. # 999·88·7777

Loanout (if applicable): _____   Tel. # _____

Address: 3563 DIRECTION CIRCLE

Salary: $ SCALE   ☐ per week   ☐ per day   ☑ per show

Additional Time: $ SCALE   ☑ per week   ☐ per day

Start date: 7·12·XX   Guaranteed Period: 13 WKS.   ☐ pro rata

Project Information:

Picture or Series Title: HERBY'S SUMMER VACATION

Episode/Segment Title: _____   Epsd.# _____

Length of Program: 2 HOUR   Is this a Pilot? ☐ Yes ☑ No

Produced Primarily/Mainly for:

☑ Theatrical   ☐ Network   ☐ Syndication
☐ Basic Cable   ☐ Disc/Cassette   ☐ Pay-TV: _____
                                                        (service)

Theatrical Film Budget (check one)   Free Television/Pay Television
☐ A. Under $500,000   ☐ Network Prime Time (type)
☐ B. Between $500,000 and $1,500,000   ☐ Other than Network Prime Time (type)
☑ C. Over $1,500,000

Check one (if applicable):   ☐ Segment   ☐ Second Unit

The INDIVIDUAL having final cutting authority over the film is: SWIFTY DEALS, PRODUCER

Other conditions (including credit above minimum): $100 PER DIEM; 1ST CLASS, ROUND·TRIP AIR
FARE & HOTEL ACCOMMODATIONS; RENTAL CAR; MOTORHOME WHILE ON LOC.

This employment is subject to the provisions of the Directors Guild of America Basic Agreement of 1993.

Accepted and Agreed: Signatory Co: XYZ PRODUCTIONS, INC.
Employee: Sid Celluloid   By: Swifty Deals, Producer
Date: 7·9·XX   Date: July 9, 19XX

RC300/070193

ADDENDUM TO THE DIRECTOR'S DEAL MEMORANDUM
POST PRODUCTION SCHEDULE
(FOR A THEATRICAL MOTION PICTURE OR TELEVISION MOTION PICTURE 90 MINUTES OR LONGER)

DIRECTOR'S NAME: SID CELLULOID   DATE FOR SPECIAL PHOTOGRAPHY
SOCIAL SECURITY #: 999·88·7777   & PROCESSES (IF ANY): NONE
PROJECT TITLE: HERBY'S SUMMER VACATION   DATE FOR DELIVERY OF ANSWER PRINT: 1·10·XX
COMPANY NAME: XYZ PRODUCTIONS   DATE OF RELEASE (THEATRICAL FILM): 1·14·XX
DIRECTOR'S CUT: START DATE: 10·18·XX   DATE OF NETWORK BROADCAST
            FINISH DATE: 11·28·XX   (IF APPLICABLE): _____

UNIT PRODUCTION MANAGER AND
ASSISTANT DIRECTOR FILM DEAL MEMORANDUM

This confirms our agreement to employ you on the project described below as follows:

Name: __ALICE DEES__   S.S. #: __666·55·4456__

Loanout: _____   Tel. #: __(818) 555-6541__

Address: __12353 AVE. OF THE STARS__
__HOLLYWOOD, CA 90028__

- [ ] Unit Production Manager
- [✓] First Assistant Director
- [ ] Key Second Assistant Director
- [ ] 2nd Second Assistant Director

- [✓] Principal Photography
- [ ] Second Unit
- [ ] Both

- [ ] Additional Second Assistant Director
- [ ] Technical Coordinator

Salary: $ __SCALE__ $ _____   [✓] per week   [ ] per day
            (studio)   (location)

Production Fee: $ _____ $ __SCALE__
                    (studio)   (location)

Start Date: __7·12·XX__   Guaranteed Period: __2 WEEKS__

Film or Series Title: __HERBY'S SUMMER VACATION__

Episode Title: __"BOYS NIGHT OUT"__   Length of Show: __1 HOUR__

Intended Primary Market:

- [ ] Theaters
- [ ] Basic Cable
- [✓] Network
- [ ] Discs/Cassettes
- [ ] Syndication
- [ ] Pay TV: _____
                    (service)

Other Terms (e.g., credit, suspension, per diem, etc.): __1ST CLASS, ROUND·TRIP AIR FARE; $50 PER__
__DIEM AND $15 PER DAY - INCIDENTAL ALLOWANCE WHILE ON DISTANT__
__LOCATION__

- [ ] Studio
- [ ] Distant Location
- [✓] Both

- [ ] Check if New York Area Amendment Applies

This Employment is subject to the Provisions of the Directors Guild of America, Inc. Basic Agreement of 1993.

Accepted and Agreed: Signatory Co.: __XYZ PRODUCTIONS__

Employee: _Alice Dees_   By: _Swifty Deals, Producer_

Date: _July 12, 19XX_   Date: _7·12·XX_

RC301/070193

EXTRA TALENT VOUCHER

DATE WORKED __JUNE 10, 19XX__

PRODUCTION __HERBY'S SUMMER VACATION__   PROD # __0100__

EXTRA CASTING AGENCY __RAZMATAZ EXTRA CASTING__

CONTACT __BAMBI__   PHONE # __(213) 555-7366__

EMPLOYER OF RECORD __PAULINE'S PAYROLL SERVICE__

ADDRESS __7325 PAYERS LANE__
__STUDIO VILLAGE, CA__

PHONE # __(818) 555-4444__

NAME (Please Print) __ADAM ATMOSPHERRE__

ADDRESS __950 BACKGROUND LN.__
__HOLLYWOOD, CA 90028__

PHONE # __(213) 555-9831__

SOC. SEC. # __562-11-3698__

☐ Married   ☑ Single   O Exemptions   ☑ Completed I-9

			BASE RATE		
REPORTING TIME	7A	8 HRS. of S.T.	@ 5.00	per. hr.	$40-
MEAL	1-1:30P	4 HRS. of 1 1/2X	@ 7.50	per. hr.	$30-
2ND MEAL		1 HRS. of 2X	@ 10.00	per. hr.	$10-
DISMISSAL TIME	8:30P	ADJUSTMENT(S)			

TOTAL HRS. WORKED: __13__   GROSS TOTAL: __$80-__

MILEAGE REIMBURSEMENT __$12-__
WARDROBE REIMBURSEMENT __$10-__
OTHER REIMBURSEMENT _____

I acknowledge receipt of the compensation stated herein as payment in full for all services rendered by me on the days indicated. I hereby grant to my employer permission to photograph me and to record my voice, performances, poses, acts, plays and appearances, and use my picture, photograph, silhouette and other reproductions of my physical likeness and sound in the above-named production and in the unlimited distribution, advertising, promotion, exhibition and exploitation of the production by any method or device now known or hereafter devised in which the same may be used. I agree that I will not assert or maintain against you, your successors, assigns and licensees, any claim, action, suit or demand of any kind or nature whatsoever in connection with your authorized use of my physical likeness and sound in the production as herein provided.

SIGNATURE __Adam Atmospherre__
(If minor, parent or guardian must sign)

APPROVED BY __Will Light__

TITLE __2ND ASSISTANT DIRECTOR__

LOANOUT AGREEMENT

This agreement, dated as of _JUNE 25, 19XX_, is between

XYZ PRODUCTIONS, INC., ("Producer") and

GREAT RYDERS, INC., ("Employer")

for the services of _F. SCOTT RYDER_, ("Employee")

in connection with the _MOTION PICTURE_

tentatively entitled _HERBY'S SUMMER VACATION_.

You, the Employer, warrant and represent that you have the exclusive right to lend Employee's services to Producer under all terms and conditions hereof, and that Employee is free to render such services. Employer maintains that if applicable, Employee is a member in good standing of such union or guild as may have jurisdiction, to the extent required by law and applicable collective bargaining agreements. You further warrant and represent to us that you are a duly organized and existing corporation and are currently in good standing under the laws of the state or country of your incorporation.

In consideration of the mutual covenants and agreements herein contained, Producer and Employer agree as follows:

Producer shall pay directly to you all of the compensation that would have been payable to Employee had Employee rendered services directly for us, and we shall not be obligated to make any such payments of any nature whatsoever directly to Employee. In no event shall your failure to pay any amount to Employee be deemed a breach of this agreement.

Producer will not withhold, report or pay payroll taxes from the compensation payable to Employer. Should Producer be subjected to any expenses or other liability by reason of such failure to withhold, report or pay such taxes (including but not limited to penalties, interest and reasonable attorneys' fees), Employer agrees that Employer and Employee will indemnify and hold Producer harmless therefrom.

Employer has, and will maintain at all times while Employee is rendering services hereunder, Workers' Compensation insurance as required by law.

Kindly sign this agreement in the space provided below to confirm your understanding of our agreement.

Very truly yours,

Swifty Deals

AGREED TO AND ACCEPTED

By _F. Scott Ryder_

PRESIDENT
Title

Name of Corporation _GREAT RYDERS, INC._

Federal ID# _95-33226543_

By _SWIFTY DEALS, PRODUCER_

XYZ PRODUCTIONS, INC.
Name of Production Company

Address _1234 FLICK DR._

HOLLYWOOD, CA 90038

Phone Number _(213) 555-3331_

CHAPTER SIX

Unions and Guilds

All major studios and many independent production companies are signatory to certain basic union and guild agreements, the most common being the *Screen Actors Guild* (SAG), representing actors, stunt coordinators, stunt performers, professional singers, puppeteers, airplane pilots, and extras; the *Directors Guild of America* (DGA), representing directors, unit production managers, and assistant directors; the *Writers Guild of America* (WGA), representing writers; the *International Alliance of Theatrical Stage Employees* (*IATSE* or IA), covering various crew classifications (each represented by their own *local*); and the *Teamsters*, with jurisdiction over drivers and location managers. There are a few others (such as National Association of Broadcast Employees and Technicians [NABET] and American Federation of Television and Radio Artists [AFTRA]), but when it comes to shooting a feature film or movie for television or cable, these are the primary unions and guilds you will be dealing with.

Many of the unions and guilds, in addition to having offices in both Los Angeles and New York, have additional branch offices in various other locations around the country. The IA does not have branch offices, but does maintain individual locals in different cities throughout the country. To locate the specific union or guild branch office, or IA local, closest to you, contact one of their main offices or your film commission for assistance.

THE ALLIANCE OF MOTION PICTURE AND TELEVISION PRODUCERS (AMPTP)

On the West Coast, what stands between the unions and guilds, the producers who employ union and guild members, and those applying for union membership is the AMPTP, the *Alliance of Motion Picture and Television Producers*. The AMPTP provides services to studios and independent production companies covering all aspects of employment within the television and theatrical motion picture industry and other issues that affect the industry as a whole. They represent their member companies in industrywide bargaining with the unions and guilds, including grievance and arbitration decisions, and interpreting and administering agreements with the WGA, DGA, SAG, IATSE, West Coast studio local unions, and basic crafts unions.

The AMPTP assists member companies in complying with the myriad of laws that impact the employment process, responds to equal employment opportunity inquiries from SAG based upon reports that are required under the existing collective bargaining agreement, and oversees the Human Resources Coordinating Committee meetings for the purpose of implementing the script submission and trainee programs under the Writers Guild of America agreements. They also initiated and continue to participate in an industrywide safety committee composed of *producer* representatives and unions and guilds representing persons involved in the production process. The AMPTP has drafted and disseminated joint safety bulletins over the past several years in conjunction with the unions and guilds.

Under the auspices of the AMPTP, the *Contract Services Administration Trust Fund* is the entity that specifically maintains work rosters and coordinates qualifications committees, develops and administers training and apprenticeship programs, administers controlled substance abuse testing, collects and maintains *I-9* files, schedules expedited arbitrations, handles step two conciliation grievances, handles *material breach* claims, and provides labor relations advice.

The two major considerations relating to unions and guilds are as follows: (1) As an individual—should you join, what are the advantages of union membership and are you eligible to join? (2) As a producer—which unions and guilds, if any, should you sign with?

BECOMING A UNION MEMBER

The requirements for membership differ with each union and guild, because each has its own set of variables, depending upon the classification you are seeking. It is definitely advantageous to become a member of a union or guild with benefits such as overtime, meal penalties, health insurance, pension, vacation and holiday pay, etc. Although preferable to the longer hours and lower wages generally associated with non-union shows, union and guild membership is not open to just anyone who wants in. It is quite difficult to join most of the unions and guilds, because a primary function of their existence is to protect the employment of their current membership by limiting the number of new members they accept.

Contact the union or guild you are interested in joining to inquire as to their membership requirements. Although you need only to sell a script to a signatory company to become a member of the Writers Guild and can get into SAG by way of employment on a SAG production (requiring a Taft/Hartley), many others require that you work a specified number of

hours or days at a particular (non-union) job and prove a certain level of expertise in a given field. If that is the case, you will need to keep careful records documenting your work history. Even if you are far from reaching your goal, gather the substantiating data as you go along, because it is very difficult to go back and collect pieces of information long after a production has been completed. Keep copies of things such as deal memos, paycheck stubs, call sheets, production reports, and crew lists. Some unions will require letters from producers or department heads you worked under confirming work dates and job responsibilities. Occasionally, you will be asked for proof of screen credits. Find out what the requirements are, and set up a file box to start accumulating all the necessary paperwork.

BECOMING A UNION SIGNATORY

As a producer, it will be your responsibility to determine which unions and guilds to sign with. Consider the following points:

Will your budget accommodate union wages and benefits? Will the film be shot in a right-to-work state or in a metropolitan area where you are likely to be visited by picketers should you not sign a particular union agreement?

Are there certain people you want on your show who are union members and cannot work for you unless you become signatory to their contract?

Will you be working on a studio lot that only allows for the employment of union members?

Many unions and guilds now have low-budget and affirmative action agreements, offering less expensive pay scales and more flexible working conditions to those who qualify. These special contracts are granted to companies who would not otherwise be able to sign union agreements, and allows the production entity to pay union benefits to cast and crew members who might not otherwise receive them. They also encourage keeping certain productions *in town*, as opposed to shooting else where, where labor rates are less costly. Each union and guild offering a low-budget and/or affirmative action agreement has its own qualification guidelines and requirements. Check to see if you qualify before assuming that you cannot afford to become a signatory.

DIRECTORS GUILD OF AMERICA (DGA)

The DGA has a low-budget agreement and a low-low budget agreement. Each is negotiated on a case-by-case basis and is not only between the producer and the guild, but must be approved by the DGA members as well—the *director, unit production manager,* and *assistant directors*—who will be working on the picture. If a *producer* or the production company he represents is not known to the DGA, they may ask for a bond to be put up during preproduction to insure the payment of their members. This is also negotiated on a case-by-case basis.

For those interested, be aware that the DGA does have an *assistant director's training program,* which is administered jointly by the DGA and the AMPTP. The guild also has a special agreement with the AMPTP, referred to as the *Third Area Qualifications List.* Production companies may hire non-union UPMs and assistant directors when shooting outside of the southern California and New York areas. Although non-union at the time of hire, these employees must become guild members once the company signs a DGA agreement. They can continue to work outside of the southern California and New York areas under the Third Area Qualifications List while accumulating days. Once they have accumulated a required number of days, they become eligible to work on any DGA show without restrictions. Contact the DGA and/or the AMPTP for further information concerning these programs.

SCREEN ACTORS GUILD (SAG)

The Screen Actors Guild currently offers a low-budget agreement for productions with budgets of $2 million or under and an affirmative action agreement for productions with budgets of $2.75 million and under. These agreements provide for pay scales that are two contract terms behind the current wage structure. Films produced under this contract must be filmed entirely in the United States and have an initial theatrical release. A modified low-budget agreement is now being offered on a trial basis for productions with budgets under $300,000. With limited availability, these contracts are granted to encourage local production and to determine their effectiveness in generating work for guild members. The biggest obstacle to the modified low-budget agreement is that the film must have an initial theatrical release—it cannot be released directly to video without first appearing in at least one theater. If a film made under a modified low-budget agreement is not released theatrically, the production entity is obligated to retroactively compensate all SAG performers who appeared in the film at the rate of the basic agreement at the time of principal photography.

SAG does not offer low-budget agreements for television productions, and there are separate video agreements for films made exclusively for video release. All SAG agreements require that the *producer* show proof of copyright ownership to the screenplay prior to the start of principal photography. This requirement impacts the guild's security interest in maintaining its rights, especially with regard to residual obligations.

PRODUCTION COORDINATORS

Because this book is written for the benefit of production personnel, and even though this chapter does not include specific information on most of the other unions, guilds and locals, *Locals 717 and 161* deserve special mention. A significant member of any production team is that of the *production coordinator.* In Los Angeles, *production coordinators* and *assistant production coordinators* (in addition to *production accountants* and *assistant production accountants*) are represented by Local 717 of the IATSE. This local is different from the others in that, although a part of the IA, it is not part of the basic collective bargaining agreement administered by the AMPTP; therefore, Local 717 members do not automatically receive union benefits just by virtue of the fact that they belong to an IA local. Producers who wish to pay their *production coordinators* and *production accountants* union scale wages and benefits are asked to sign an agreement with Local 717 that is independent of the one they sign with the IA. Local 717's counterpart in New York is Local 161. Producers who wish to employ 161 members are required to sign separate agreements with this local as well.

SAG, DGA, AND WGA—FORMS AND REPORTS

Many films are shot using non-union crews, but few production units are not signatory to the Screen Actors Guild, the Directors Guild, and the Writers Guild. Each of these three guilds have their own very distinct forms, reports, and guidelines that signatory companies are asked to adhere to. As a signatory to SAG, DGA, and WGA, you will have copies of each of the guild contracts and should know the rules and rates associated with each.

The following is a sampling of the most often used guild contracts and report forms. Note that (1) DGA *deal memos* are not included in this section but can be found in the chapter on deal memos, and (2) there are no samples of pension, health, and welfare reports or gross earning reports in the following pages. The reporting of such are functions of either your *production accountant* or the payroll company handling your show, and are not generally prepared by production personnel.

WRITERS GUILD—NOTICE OF TENTATIVE WRITING CREDITS

TELEVISION

Before writing credits are finally determined, you are required to send a copy of the *Notice of Tentative Writing Credits—Television* to the Writers Guild and all participating writers concurrently. At the completion of principal photography, you are required to send two copies of the revised final shooting script to each participating writer. The notice should state the company's choice of credit on a tentative basis.

THEATRICAL MOTION PICTURES

Before the writing credits are finally determined, you are required to file a copy of the *Notice of Tentative Writing Credits—Theatrical Motion Pictures* with the Writers Guild Credits Department (within three days after completion of principal photography). The notice should state the company's choice of credit on a tentative basis. Copies must be sent concurrently to all participating writers and to the Writers Guild, along with a copy of the final shooting script to each participant. The Notice of Tentative Writing Credits should be submitted to the Writers Guild office you signed with, either:

The Writers Guild of America, West
8955 Beverly Blvd.
Los Angeles, CA 90048

(213) 550-1000

or

The Writers Guild of America, East
555 W. 57th Street
New York, NY 10019

(212) 245-6180

Note: Samples of both the television and theatrical motion picture Notice of Tentative Writing Credits forms are found at the end of this chapter.

SCREEN ACTORS GUILD

DAILY CONTRACT
(DAY PERFORMER)
FOR TELEVISION MOTION PICTURES OR VIDEOTAPES

Company __XYZ PRODUCTIONS__   Date __JUNE 1, 19XX__

Production Title __HERBY'S SUMMER VACATION__   Performer Name __JOHN DOE__

Production Number __0100__   Address __123 ACTORS ALLEY RD. HOLLYWOOD, CA 90028__

Date Employment Starts __JUNE 2, 19XX__   Telephone No.: (213) __555-1962__

Role __HERBY'S NEIGHBOR__   Social Security No. __124-23-9637__

Daily Rate $ __SCALE & 10% AGENCY COMMISSION__ Date of Performer's next engagement _____

Weekly Conversion Rate $_____

Wardrobe supplied by performer   Yes ☐   No ☑

If so, number of outfits _____ @ $_____

(formal) _____ @ $_____

COMPLETE FOR "DROP-AND-PICK-UP" DEALS **ONLY**:
Firm recall date on _____
or on or after * __JULY 13, 19XX__
("On or after" recall only applies to pick-up as Weekly Performer)
As ☐ Day Performer ☑ Weekly Performer
*Means date specified or within 24 hours thereafter.

THIS AGREEMENT covers the employment of the above-named Performer by __XYZ PRODUCTIONS__ in the production and at the rate of compensation set forth above and is subject to and shall include, for the benefit of the Performer and the Producer, all of the applicable provisions and conditions contained or provided for in the applicable Screen Actors Guild Television Agreement (herein called the "Television Agreement"). Performer's employment shall include performance in non-commercial openings, bridges, etc., and no added compensation shall be payable to Performer so long as such are used in the role and episode covered hereunder in which Performer appears; for other use, Performer shall be paid the added minimum compensation, if any, required under the provisions of the Screen Actors Guild agreements with Producer.

Producer shall have all the rights in and to the results and proceeds of the Performer's services rendered hereunder, as are provided with respect to "photoplays" in Schedule A of the applicable Screen Actors Guild Codified Basic Agreement and the right to supplemental market use as defined in the Television Agreement.

Producer shall have the unlimited right throughout the world to telecast the film and exhibit the film theatrically and in supplemental markets in accordance with the terms and conditions of the Television Agreement.

If the motion picture is rerun on television in the United States or Canada and contains any of the results and proceeds of the Performer's services, the Performer will be paid for each day of employment hereunder the additional compensation prescribed therefor by the Television Agreement, unless there is an agreement to pay an amount in excess thereof as follows:

SAG MINIMUM

If there is foreign telecasting of the motion picture as defined in the Television Agreement, and such motion picture contains any of the results and proceeds of the Performer's services, the Performer will be paid the amount in the blank space below for each day of employment hereunder, or if such blank space is not filled in, then the Performer will be paid the minimum additional compensation prescribed therefor by the Television Agreement. $_____

If the motion picture is exhibited theatrically anywhere in the world and contains any of the results and proceeds of the Performer's services, the Performer will be paid $ __SAG MIN__ , or if this blank is not filled in, then the Performer will be paid the minimum additional compensation prescribed therefor by the Television Agreement.

If the motion picture is exhibited in supplemental markets anywhere in the world and contains any of the results and proceeds of the Performer's services, then Performer will be paid the supplemental market fees prescribed by the applicable provisions of the Television Agreement.

If the Performer places his or her initials in the box below, he or she thereby authorizes Producer to use portions of said television motion picture as a trailer to promote another episode or the series as a whole, upon payment to the Performer of the additional compensation prescribed by the applicable provisions of the Television Agreement.

** BILLING : END CREDITS, SHARED CARD, PLACEMENT AT PRODUCER'S DISCRETION.

Initial

By _Swifty Deals_
Producer

John Doe
Performer

Production time reports are available on the set at the end of each day, which reports shall be signed or initialed by the Performer.

NOTICE TO PERFORMER: IT IS IMPORTANT THAT YOU RETAIN A COPY OF THIS CONTRACT FOR YOUR PERMANENT RECORDS.

* AS AGENTS DO NOT COLLECT COMMISSION ON "SCALE", 10% IS ADDED TO THE COMPENSATION RATE FOR THOSE ACTORS WHO HAVE AGENTS & ARE RECEIVING "SCALE" FOR THEIR PERFORMANCE.

** INCLUDING THE "BILLING" (SCREEN CREDIT) IS NOT REQUIRED, BUT IT IS AN IMPORTANT PART OF THE PERFORMER'S DEAL WORTH ADDING TO THE SIGNED CONTRACT.

THE PERFORMER MAY NOT WAIVE ANY PROVISION OF THIS CONTRACT WITHOUT THE WRITTEN CONSENT OF SCREEN ACTORS GUILD, INC.

MINIMUM THREE-DAY CONTRACT
FOR TELEVISION MOTION PICTURES OR VIDEOTAPES
THREE-DAY MINIMUM EMPLOYMENT

THIS AGREEMENT is made this ___15TH___ day of __MAY__, 19_XX_, between ___XYZ PRODUCTIONS, INC.___, a corporation, hereinafter called "Producer," and ___RAYMOND BURRMAN___, hereinafter called "Performer."

WITNESSETH:

1. **Photoplay: Role and Guarantee.** Producer hereby engages Performer to render service as such in the role of ___ELLIOT___, in a photoplay produced primarily for exhibition over free television, the working title of which is now __HERBY'S SUMMER VACATION__. Performer accepts such engagement upon the terms herein specified. Producer guarantees that it will furnish Performer not less than __THREE__ days' employment. (If this blank is not filled in, the guarantee shall be three (3) days.)

2. **Salary.** The Producer will pay to the Performer, and the Performer agrees to accept for three (3) days (and pro rata for each additional day beyond three (3) days) the following salary rate: $ __SCALE__ .

3. Producer shall have the unlimited right throughout the world to telecast the film and exhibit the film theatrically and in Supplemental Markets in accordance with the terms and conditions of the applicable Screen Actors Guild Television Agreement (herein referred to as the "Television Agreement").

4. If the motion picture is rerun on television in the United States or Canada and contains any of the results and proceeds of the Performer's services, the Performer will be paid the additional compensation prescribed therefor by the Television Agreement, unless there is an agreement to pay an amount in excess thereof as follows:

___SAG MINIMUM___

5. If there is foreign telecasting of the motion picture as defined in the Television Agreement, and such motion picture contains any of the results and proceeds of the Performer's services, the Performer will be paid the amount in the blank space below plus an amount equal to one-third (1/3) thereof for each day of employment in excess of three (3) days, or, if such blank space is not filled in, then the Performer will be paid the minimum additional compensation prescribed therefor by the Television Agreement. $ __SAG MIN__ .

6. If the motion picture is exhibited theatrically anywhere in the world and contains any of the results and proceeds of the Performer's services, the Performer will be paid $ __SAG MIN__ , plus an amount equal to one-third (1/3) thereof for each day of employment in excess of three (3) days. If this blank is not filled in, the Performer will be paid the applicable minimum additional compensation prescribed therefor by the Television Agreement.

7. If the motion picture is exhibited in Supplemental Markets anywhere in the world and contains any of the results and proceeds of the Performer's services, the Performer will be paid the supplemental market fees prescribed by the applicable provisions of the Television Agreement.

8. **Term.** The term of employment hereunder shall begin on __JUNE 20, 19XX__ , on or about* _____ and shall continue thereafter until the completion of the photography and recordation of said role.

* The "on or about clause" may only be used when the contract is delivered to the Performer at least three (3) days before the starting date.

9. **Incorporation of Television Agreement.** The applicable provisions of the Television Agreement are incorporated herein by reference. Performer's employment shall include performance in non-commercial openings, closings, bridges, etc., and no added compensation shall be payable to Performer so long as such are used in the role and episode covered hereunder and in which Performer appears; for other use, Performer shall be paid the added minimum compensation, if any, required under the provisions of the Screen Actors Guild agreements with Producer. Performer's employment shall be upon the terms, conditions and exceptions of the provisions applicable to the rate of salary and guarantee specified in Paragraphs 1. and 2. hereof.

10. **Arbitration of Disputes.** Should any dispute or controversy arise between the parties hereto with reference to this contract, or the employment herein provided for, such dispute or controversy shall be settled and determined by conciliation and arbitration in accordance with and to the extent provided in the conciliation and arbitration provisions of the Television Agreement, and such provisions are hereby referred to and by such reference incorporated herein and made a part of this agreement with the same effect as though the same were set forth herein in detail.

11. **Performer's Address.** All notices which the Producer is required or may desire to give to the Performer may be given either by mailing the same addressed to the Performer at 123 ELM ST. – HOLLYWOOD, CA 90028 or such notice may be given to the Performer personally, either orally or in writing.

12. **Performer's Telephone.** The Performer must keep the Producer's casting office or the assistant director of said photoplay advised as to where the Performer may be reached by telephone without unreasonable delay. The current telephone number of the Performer is (213) 555-3621 .

13. If Performer places his initials in the box, he thereby authorizes Producer to use portions of said television motion picture as a trailer to promote another episode or the series as a whole, upon payment to the Performer of the additional compensation prescribed by the Television Agreement.

RB

14. **Furnishing of Wardrobe.** The Performer agrees to furnish all modern wardrobe and wearing apparel reasonably necessary for the portrayal of said role; it being agreed, however, that should so-called "character" or "period" costumes be required, the Producer shall supply the same. When Performer supplies any wardrobe, Performer shall receive the cleaning allowance and reimbursement specified in the Television Agreement.

15. **Next Starting Date.** The starting date of Performer's next engagement is _____.

IN WITNESS WHEREOF, the parties have executed this agreement on the day and year first above written.

BILLING: END CREDITS, SHARED CARD, POSITION AT PRODUCER'S DISCRETION.

By _Swifty Deals_
_____
Producer

Raymond Burrman
_____
Performer

173-21-6342
_____
Social Security No.

Production time reports are available on the set at the end of each day. Such reports shall be signed or initialed by the performer.

Attached hereto for your use is a Declaration Regarding Income Tax Withholding ("Part Year Employment Method of Withholding"). You may utilize such form by delivering same to Producer.

NOTICE TO PERFORMER: IT IS IMPORTANT THAT YOU RETAIN A COPY OF THIS CONTRACT FOR YOUR PERMANENT RECORDS.

**THE PERFORMER MAY NOT WAIVE ANY PROVISION OF THIS CONTRACT
WITHOUT THE WRITTEN CONSENT OF SCREEN ACTORS GUILD, INC.**

SCREEN ACTORS GUILD

**MINIMUM FREE LANCE WEEKLY CONTRACT
FOR TELEVISION MOTION PICTURES OR VIDEOTAPES**
Continuous Employment – Weekly Basis – Weekly Salary
One Week Minimum Employment

THIS AGREEMENT is made this _____28 TH_____ day of __MAY__ , 19 XX , between
___XYZ PRODUCTIONS, INC.___ , a corporation, hereinafter called "Producer," and
___NANCY NICELY___ , hereinafter called "Performer."

WITNESSETH:

1. **Photoplay: Role and Guarantee.** Producer hereby engages Performer to render services as such, in the role of ___MOM___ , in a photoplay produced primarily for exhibition over free television, the working title of which is now __HERBY'S SUMMER VACATION__ . Performer accepts such engagement upon the terms herein specified. Producer guarantees that it will furnish Performer not less than __TWO (2)__ weeks employment. (If this blank is not filled in, the guarantee shall be one week.)

2. **Salary.** The Producer will pay to the Performer, and the Performer agrees to accept weekly (and pro rata for each additional day beyond guarantee) the following salary rate: $ __SCALE__ per "studio week." (Schedule B Performers must receive an additional overtime payment of four (4) hours at straight time rate for each overnight location sixth day).

3. Producer shall have the unlimited right throughout the world to telecast the film and exhibit the film theatrically and in Supplemental Markets, in accordance with the terms and conditions of the applicable Screen Actors Guild Television Agreement (herein referred to as the "Television Agreement").

4. If the motion picture is rerun on television in the United States or Canada and contains any of the results and proceeds of the Performer's services, the Performer will be paid the additional compensation prescribed therefor by the Television Agreement, unless there is an agreement to pay an amount in excess thereof as follows:

___SAG MINIMUM___

5. If there is foreign telecasting of the motion picture, as defined in the Television Agreement, and such motion picture contains any of the results and proceeds of the Performer's services, the Performer will be paid $_____ plus pro rata thereof for each additional day of employment in excess of one week, or, if this blank is not filled in, the Performer will be paid the minimum additional compensation prescribed therefor by the Television Agreement.

6. If the motion picture is exhibited theatrically anywhere in the world and contains any of the results and proceeds of the Performer's services, the Performer will be paid $ __SAG MIN__ plus pro rata thereof for each additional day of employment in excess of one week, or, if this blank is not filled in, the Performer will be paid the minimum additional compensation prescribed therefor by the Television Agreement.

7. If the motion picture is exhibited in Supplemental Markets anywhere in the world and contains any of the results and proceeds of the Performer's services, the Performer will be paid the supplemental market fees prescribed by the applicable provisions of the Television Agreement.

8. **Term.** The term of employment hereunder shall begin on __JUNE 21, 19XX__ , on or about*_____ and shall continue thereafter until the completion of the photography and recordation of said role.

*The "on or about clause" may only be used when the contract is delivered to the Performer at least three (3) days before the starting date.

9. **Incorporation of Television Agreement.** The applicable provisions of the Television Agreement are incorporated herein by reference. Performer's employment shall include performance in non-commercial openings, closings, bridges, etc., and no added compensation shall be payable to Performer so long as such are used in the role and episode covered hereunder and in which Performer appears; for other use, Performer shall be paid the added minimum compensation, if any, required under the provisions of the Screen Actors Guild agreements with Producer. Performer's employment shall be upon the terms, conditions and exceptions of said provisions applicable to the rate of salary and guarantee specified in Paragraphs 1. and 2. hereof.

10. **Arbitration of Disputes.** Should any dispute or controversy arise between the parties hereto with reference to this contract, or the employment herein provided for, such dispute or controversy shall be settled and determined by conciliation and arbitration in accordance with and to the extent provided in the conciliation and arbitration provisions of the Television Agreement, and such provisions are hereby referred to and by such reference incorporated herein and made a part of this agreement with the same effect as though the same were set forth herein in detail.

11. **Performer's Address.** All notices which the Producer is required or may desire to give to the Performer may be given either by mailing the same addressed to the Performer at 4321 ORANGE RD. - LOS ANGELES CA 90000 or such notice may be given to the Performer personally, either orally or in writing.

12. **Performer's Telephone.** The Performer must keep the Producer's casting office or the assistant director of said photoplay advised as to where the Performer may be reached by telephone without unreasonable delay. The current telephone number of the Performer is (310) 555-7997 .

13. If Performer places his initials in the box, he thereby authorizes Producer to use portions of said television motion picture as a trailer to promote another episode or the series as a whole, upon payment to the Performer of the additional compensation prescribed by the Television Agreement.

14. **Furnishing of Wardrobe.** The Performer agrees to furnish all modern wardrobe and wearing apparel reasonably necessary for the portrayal of said role; it being agreed, however, that should so-called "character" or "period" costumes be required, the Producer shall supply the same. When Performer supplies any wardrobe, Performer shall receive the cleaning allowance and reimbursement specified in the Television Agreement.

15. **Next Starting Date.** The starting date of Performer's next engagement is _____ .

IN WITNESS WHEREOF, the parties have executed this agreement on the day and year first above written.

BILLING: MAIN TITLES, SINGLE CARD, 3RD POSITION

By _Swifty Deals_
_____ Producer
Nancy Nicely
_____ Performer
372·46·2232
_____ Social Security No.

Production time reports are available on the set at the end of each day. Such reports shall be signed or initialed by the performer.

NOTICE TO PERFORMER: IT IS IMPORTANT THAT YOU RETAIN A COPY OF THIS CONTRACT FOR YOUR PERMANENT RECORDS.

THE PERFORMER MAY NOT WAIVE ANY PROVISION OF THIS CONTRACT WITHOUT THE WRITTEN CONSENT OF SCREEN ACTORS GUILD, INC.

SCREEN ACTORS GUILD

DAILY STUNT PERFORMER CONTRACT
FOR TELEVISION MOTION PICTURES OR VIDEOTAPES

Company _XYZ PRODUCTIONS, INC._ Date _JUNE 24, 19XX_

Date Employment Starts _JUNE 25, 19XX_ Stunt Performer Name _JOHNNY ROCKETT_

Role _STUNT DOUBLE_ Address _9326 HOLLYWOOD HILLS RD. HOLLYWOOD, CA 90028_

 Stunt Double for* _____ Telephone No.: (213) _555-1007_

 Other (description) _____ Social Security No. _552-11-7627_

Production Title _HERBY'S SUMMER VACATION_ Daily Rate $ _SCALE_

Weekly Conversion Rate $ _____

Stunt Adjustment(s):

$ _1,000_ for _HIGH FALL_ No. of takes _3_

$ _____ for _____ No. of takes _____

Wardrobe supplied by performer Yes ☐ No ☑

If so, number of outfits _____ @ $ _____

(formal) _____ @ $ _____

Date of Stunt Performer's next engagement: _____

COMPLETE FOR "DROP-AND-PICK-UP" DEALS ONLY:

Firm recall date on _____

or on or after * _____

("On or after" recall only applies to pick-up as Weekly Performer)

As ☐ Day Performer ☐ Weekly Performer

*Means date specified or within 24 hours thereafter.

WITNESSETH:

1. THIS AGREEMENT covers the employment of the above-named Performer by _XYZ PRODUCTIONS_ in the production and at the rate of compensation set forth above and is subject to and shall include, for the benefit of the Performer and the Producer, all of the applicable provisions and conditions contained or provided for in the Screen Actors Guild Television Agreement (herein called the "Television Agreement"). Performer's employment shall include performance in non-commercial openings, bridges, etc., and no added compensation shall be payable to Performer so long as such are used in the role and episode covered hereunder in which Performer appears.

2. Producer shall have the unlimited right throughout the world to telecast the film and exhibit the film theatrically and in supplemental markets in accordance with the terms and conditions of the Television Agreement.

3. If the motion picture is rerun on television in the United States or Canada and contains any of the results and proceeds of the Performer's services, the Performer will be paid for each day of employment hereunder the additional compensation prescribed therefor by the Television Agreement, unless there is an agreement to pay an amount in excess thereof as follows: _SAG MINIMUM_ _____

_____

_____

* NOTE: STUNT DAY PERFORMERS MUST RECEIVE A SEPARATE DAY'S PAY AND CONTRACT FOR EACH PERSON DOUBLED

4. If there is foreign telecasting of the motion picture as defined in the Television Agreement, and such motion picture contains any of the results and proceeds of the Performer's services, the Performer will be paid in the amount in the blank space below for each day of employment hereunder, or if such blank space is not filled in, then the Performer will be paid the minimum additional compensation prescribed therefor by the Television Agreement. $SAG MIN.

5. If the motion picture is exhibited theatrically anywhere in the world and contains any of the results and proceeds of the Performer's services, the Performer will be paid $ SAG MIN. , or if this blank is not filled in, then the Performer will be paid the minimum additional compensation prescribed therefor by the Television Agreement.

6. If the motion picture is exhibited in supplemental markets anywhere in the world and contains any of the results and proceeds of the Performer's services, then Performer will be paid the supplemental market fees prescribed by the applicable provisions of the Television Agreement.

By _Swifty Deals_____
                              Producer

_Johnny Rockett_____
                              Stunt Performer

Production time reports are available on the set at the end of each day, which reports shall be signed or initialed by the Performer.

Attached hereto for your use are the following: (1) Declaration Regarding Income Tax Withholding ("Part Year Employment Method of Withholding") and (2) Declaration Regarding Income Tax Withholding. You may utilize the applicable form by delivering same to Producer. Only one of such forms may be used.

NOTICE TO PERFORMER: IT IS IMPORTANT THAT YOU RETAIN A COPY OF THIS CONTRACT FOR YOUR PERMANENT RECORDS.

SCREEN ACTORS GUILD
STUNT PERFORMER'S
MINIMUM FREELANCE THREE-DAY CONTRACT
FOR TELEVISION MOTION PICTURES

STUNT PERFORMER **ARNOLD WEISMULLER** DATE OF AGREEMENT **JULY 19, 19XX**

ADDRESS **1300 TARZANA GARDENS**

TARZANA, CA 91333

TELEPHONE **(213) 555-7134** SOCIAL SECURITY NO. **331-32-4476**

COMPANY/PRODUCER **XYZ PRODUCTIONS, INC.**

PRODUCTION TITLE **HERBY'S SUMMER VACATION** PRODUCTION NO. **0100**

AGENT/AGENCY

ADDRESS

1. **DESCRIPTION OF SERVICES:** Producer hereby engages Stunt Performer to render services as **UTILITY STUNT PERFORMER**. Stunt Performer accepts such engagement upon the terms herein specified.

2. **COMPENSATION/TERM/GUARANTEE:** Producer will pay Stunt Performer and Stunt Performer agrees to accept the following three-day compensation (excluding location premiums) of $_____ (and pro rata services). The total guaranteed compensation shall be $ **2,500** for the total guaranteed period of **THREE (3) DAYS**. If this space is not filled in, the guarantee shall be three (3) days. Stunt Performer shall receive sixth day location premium where applicable.

3. **START DATE:** The term of engagement shall begin on _____. or "on or about" * **JULY 21, 19XX**.

4. **NEXT START DATE:** The start date of Stunt Performer's next engagement is _____.

5. **STUNT ADJUSTMENTS:** It is understood that the rate of compensation specified may be adjusted depending upon the nature of the stunt activities Producer may require. If so, a stunt adjustment will be agreed upon between the parties through good faith bargaining and said adjustment shall be noted on Stunt Performer's daily time report or time card.

The parties shall agree upon the compensation to be paid before the stunt is performed if they may readily do so; however, it is expressly agreed that production shall not be delayed for the purpose of first determining the compensation for a stunt. Such adjustment shall increase Stunt Performer's compensation for the three-days in the manner prescribed in Schedule H-II or H-III of the Screen Actors Guild Codified Basic Agreement.

6. **INCORPORATION OF PRODUCER-SCREEN ACTORS GUILD COLLECTIVE BARGAINING AGREEMENT:** All provisions of the Screen Actors Guild Codified Basic Agreement as the same may be supplemented and/or amended to date shall be deemed incorporated herein. Stunt Performer's engagement shall include performance in non-commercial openings, closings, bridges, etc., and no added compensation shall be payable to Stunt Performer so long as such are used in the Motion Picture covered hereunder and in which Stunt Performer appears or with respect to which Stunt Performer is paid compensation hereunder. Stunt Performer's engagement shall be upon the terms, conditions and exceptions of said provisions applicable to the rate of compensation specified.

The "on or about" clause may only be used when this Agreement is delivered to Stunt Performer at least three (3) days before the Start Date.

7. **RIGHTS:** Producer shall have the unlimited right throughout the universe and in perpetuity to exhibit the Motion Picture in all media, now or hereafter known, and Producer, as employer-for-hire of Stunt Performer, shall own all rights in the results and proceeds of Stunt Performer's services hereunder.

8. **ADDITIONAL COMPENSATION:** If the Motion Picture covered hereby is exhibited, containing any of the results and proceeds of Stunt Performer's services hereunder, in any of the following media:

   (i) "Free" television reruns in the United States or Canada, or both;
   (ii) Television exhibition anywhere in the universe outside the United States and Canada;
   (iii) Theatrical exhibition anywhere in the universe;
   (iv) Supplemental Market exhibition anywhere in the universe;
   (v) Basic Cable exhibition anywhere in the universe,

   as to each such medium in which the motion picture is so exhibited, Producer will pay, and Stunt Performer will accept as payment in full, the minimum additional compensation provided therefor in the Screen Actors Guild Codified Basic Agreement or Television Agreement, as the case may be, except as compensation in excess of such minimum, if any, has been provided in this Agreement.

9. **CONTINUOUS EMPLOYMENT AND RIGHT TO ROLE (when applicable):** If Stunt Performer portrays a role or has dialogue, Stunt Performer shall be entitled to "continuous employment" and "Right to Role," if any, only to the extent prescribed by the Screen Actors Guild Codified Basic Agreement. Stunt Performer shall receive a separate contract for such services.

10. **MOTION PICTURE AND TELEVISION FUND:** Stunt Performer [does] [does not] hereby authorize Producer to deduct from the compensation hereinabove specified an amount equal to _____ percent of each installment of compensation due Stunt Performer hereunder, and to pay the amount so deducted to the Motion Picture and Television Fund of America, Inc.

11. **WAIVER:** Stunt Performer may not waive any provision of the Screen Actors Guild Codified Basic Agreement or Television Agreement, whichever is applicable, without the written consent of the Screen Actors Guild, Inc.

12. **SIGNATORY:** Producer makes the material representation that either it is presently a signatory to the Screen Actors Guild collective bargaining agreement covering the engagement contracted for herein, or that the Motion Picture is covered by such collective bargaining agreement under the "Independent Production" provisions (Section 24) of the General Provisions of the Screen Actors Guild Codified Basic Agreement.

Signing of this Agreement in the spaces below signifies acceptance by Producer and Stunt Performer of all of the above terms and conditions and those on the reverse hereof and attached hereto, if any, as of the date specified above.

PRODUCER _Swifty Deals_   STUNT PERFORMER _Arnold Weiss_

BY _SWIFTY DEALS_

Production time reports and/or time cards are available on the set at the beginning and end of each day, which reports and/or time cards shall be signed or initialed by Stunt Performer and must indicate any agreed stunt adjustments.

NOTICE TO STUNT PERFORMER: IT IS IMPORTANT THAT YOU RETAIN A COPY OF THIS AGREEMENT FOR YOUR PERMANENT RECORDS.

SCREEN ACTORS GUILD

**STUNT PERFORMER
MINIMUM FREE LANCE WEEKLY CONTRACT
FOR TELEVISION MOTION PICTURES OR VIDEOTAPES**

Weekly Basis—Weekly Salary
One Week Minimum Employment

THIS AGREEMENT, made this _____19TH_____ day of _____AUGUST_____, 19XX, between

_____XYZ PRODUCTIONS, INC._____, a corporation, hereinafter called "Producer."

and _____CLIFF HANGER_____, hereinafter called "Performer."

WITNESSETH:

1. PHOTOPLAY, ROLE AND GUARANTEE. Producer hereby engages Performer to render services as such,

   Check One:

   ☐ in the Role of _____ , or

   ☑ as Stunt Double for _____RAYMOND BURRMAN_____ , or

   ☐ as Utility Stunt Performer, or

   ☐ other (describe work) _____

   in a photoplay produced primarily for exhibition over free television, the working title of which is now
   _____HERBY'S SUMMER VACATION_____ . Performer accepts such engagement upon the terms
   herein specified. Producer guarantees that it will furnish Performer not less than _____ONE (1)_____ weeks employment.
   (If this blank is not filled in, the guarantee shall be one week.)

2. SALARY. The Producer will pay to the Performer, and the Performer agrees to accept weekly (and pro rata for
   each additional day beyond guarantee) the following salary rate: $_____SCALE_____ per "studio week." (Schedule H-II
   Performers must receive an additional overtime payment for four (4) hours at straight time rate for each overnight
   location Saturday.)

3. STUNT ADJUSTMENTS. It is understood between the parties that the salary rate specifed above may require
   adjustment depending upon the nature of the stunt activities Producer requires. If so, a Stunt Adjustment will be
   agreed upon between the parties through good faith bargaining and said adjustment shall be noted on the
   Performer's daily time sheet or time card. Such adjustment shall increase the Performer's compensation for the
   week in the manner prescribed in Schedule H of the Screen Actors Guild Codified Basic Agreement.

4. Producer shall have the unlimited right throughout the world to telecast the film and exhibit the film theatrically
   and in supplemental markets, in accordance with the terms and conditions of the Screen Actors Guild Television Agreement (herein referred to as the "Television Agreement").

5. If the motion picture is rerun on television in the United States or Canada and contains any of the results and
   proceeds of the Performer's services, the Performer wili be paid the additional compensation prescribed therefor
   by the Television Agreement unless there is an agreement to pay an amount in excess thereof as follows:
   _____SAG MINIMUM_____

6. If there is foreign telecasting of the motion picture as defined in the Television Agreement, and such motion picture contains any of the results and proceeds of the Performer's services, the Performer will be paid $_SAG MIN._
   plus pro rata thereof for each day of employment in excess of one week, or, if this blank is not filled in, then the
   Performer will be paid the minimum additional compensation prescribed therefor by the Television Agreement.

7. If the motion picture is exhibited theatrically anywhere in the world and contains any of the results and proceeds of the Performer's services, the Performer will be paid $SAG MIN. plus pro rata thereof for each day of employment in excess of one week, or, if this blank is not filled in, the Performer will be paid the minimum additional compensation prescribed therefor by the Television Agreement.

8. If the motion picture is exhibited in supplemental markets anywhere in the world and contains any of the results and proceeds of the Performer's services, then Performer will be paid the supplemental market fees prescribed by the applicable provisions of the Television Agreement.

9. TERM. The term of employment hereunder shall begin

   on ___AUGUST 20, 19XX___ , OR on or about* _____

10. CONTINUOUS EMPLOYMENT AND RIGHT TO ROLE. If the Stunt Performer portrays a role or has dialogue, such Performer shall be entitled to continuous employment and "right to role" and shall receive payment for the entire period from the Performer's first call to work on the picture until completion of the photography and recordation of said role.

11. INCORPORATION OF TELEVISION AGREEMENT. The applicable provisions of the Television Agreement are incorporated herein by reference. Performer's employment shall include performance in non-commercial openings, closings, bridges, etc., and no added compensation shall be payable to Performer so long as such are used in the role(s) and episode(s) covered hereunder and in which Performer appears. Performer's employment shall be upon the terms, conditions and exceptions of said provisions applicable to the rate of salary and guarantee specified in Paragraphs 1 and 2 hereof.

12. PERFORMER'S ADDRESS. All notices which the Producer is required or may desire to give to the Performer may be given either by mailing the same addressed to the Performer at 333 ROSE AVE.-LOS ANGELES, CA or such notice may be given to the Performer personally, either orally or in writing.   90000

13. PERFORMER'S TELEPHONE. The Performer must keep the Producer's casting office or the assistant director of said photoplay advised as to where the Performer may be reached by telephone without unreasonable delay. The current telephone number of the Performer is (213) 555-2323.

14. NEXT STARTING DATE. The starting date of the Performer's next engagement is _____.

IN WITNESS WHEREOF, the parties have executed this agreement on the day and year first above written.

PRODUCER _Swifty Deals_____ STUNT PERFORMER _Cliff Hanger_____

BY _SWIFTY DEALS_____ SOCIAL SECURITY # 134-76-1328

*The "on or about" clause may only be used when the contract is delivered to the Performer at least three (3) days before the starting date.

The Production time reports are available on the set at the end of each day, which reports shall be signed or initialed by the Performer and must indicate any agreed stunt adjustments.

Attached hereto for your use is a Declaration Regarding Income Tax Withholding.

NOTICE TO STUNT PERFORMER: IT IS IMPORTANT THAT YOU RETAIN A COPY OF THIS CONTRACT FOR YOUR PERMANENT RECORDS.

SCREEN ACTORS GUILD

DAILY CONTRACT
(DAY PERFORMER)
FOR THEATRICAL MOTION PICTURES

Company __XYZ PRODUCTIONS, INC.__   Date __JUNE 10, 19XX__

Date Employment Starts __JUNE 23, 19XX__   Performer Name __HOLLYWOOD MANN__

Production Title __HERBY'S SUMMER VACATION__   Address __3465 HORTENSE ST WONDERLAND, CA 90000__

Production Number __0100__   Telephone No.: __(818) 555-7737__

Role __GEORGE__   Social Security No. __231-56-6789__

Daily Rate $ __1,000__   Legal Resident of (State) __CALIFORNIA__

Weekly Conversion Rate $ _____   Citizen of U.S. ☑ Yes ☐ No

COMPLETE FOR "DROP-AND-PICK-UP" DEALS ONLY:

Firm recall date on _____

or on or after * _____

("On or after" recall only applies to pick-up as Weekly Performer)

As ☐ Day Performer ☐ Weekly Performer

*Means date specified or within 24 hours thereafter.

Wardrobe supplied by Performer   Yes ☐   No ☑

If so, number of outfits _____ @ $_____

(formal) _____ @ $_____

Date of Stunt Performer's next engagement: _____

BILLING: END CREDITS · CO-STARRING FIRST POSITION

The employment is subject to all of the provisions and conditions applicable to the employment of DAY PERFORMER contained or provided for in the Producer-Screen Actors Guild Codified Basic Agreement as the same may be supplemented and/or amended.

The performer (does)[does not] hereby authorize the Producer to deduct from the compensation hereinabove specified an amount equal to _____ .5 _____ per cent of each installment of compensation due the Performer hereunder, and to pay the amount so deducted to the Motion Picture and Television Relief Fund of America, Inc.

Special Provisions: _____

PRODUCER _Swifty Deals_   PERFORMER _Hollywood Mann_

BY __SWIFTY DEALS__

Production time reports are available on the set at the end of each day. Such reports shall be signed or initialed by the Performer.

Attached hereto for your use is Declaration Regarding Income Tax Withholding.

NOTICE TO PERFORMER: IT IS IMPORTANT THAT YOU RETAIN A COPY OF THIS CONTRACT FOR YOUR PERMANENT RECORDS.

SCREEN ACTORS GUILD

**SCREEN ACTORS GUILD
MINIMUM FREE LANCE CONTRACT
FOR THEATRICAL MOTION PICTURES**

Continuous Employment—Weekly Basis—Weekly Salary
One Week Minimum Employment

THIS AGREEMENT, made this ___2ND___ day of ___MAY___ , 19____ , between _____
_____XYZ PRODUCTIONS, INC._____ , hereafter called "Producer," and
_____CLARK GRABLE_____ , hereafter called "Performer."

1. PHOTOPLAY, ROLE, SALARY AND GUARANTEE. Producer hereby engages Performer to render services as
   such in the role of ____HERBY_____ , in a photoplay, the working title of which is now
   HERBY'S SUMMER VACATION , at the salary of $ _2,500_ per "studio week" (Schedule B Performers must
   receive an additional overtime payment of four (4) hours at straight time rate for each overnight location
   Saturday). Performer accepts such engagement upon the terms herein specified. Producer guarantees that it
   will furnish Performer not less than __SIX (6)_____ week's employment (if this blank is not filled in, the
   guarantee shall be one week). Performer shall be paid pro rata for each additional day beyond guarantee until
   dismissal.

2. TERM: The term of employment hereunder shall begin on
                    on _JUNE 1, 19XX_

          on or about* _____

   and shall continue thereafter until the completion of the photography and recordation of said role.

3. BASIC CONTRACT. All provisions of the collective bargaining agreement between Screen Actors Guild, Inc.
   and Producer, relating to theatrical motion pictures, which are applicable to the employment of the Performer
   hereunder, shall be deemed incorporated herein.

4. PERFORMER'S ADDRESS. All notices which the Producer is required or may desire to give to the Performer
   may be given either by mailing the same addressed to the Performer at _1234 FIRST ST. -MALIBU, CA 90272_
   or such notice may be given to the Performer personally, either orally or in writing.

5. PERFORMER'S TELEPHONE. The Performer must keep the Producer's casting office or the assistant director
   of said photoplay advised as to where the Performer may be reached by telephone without unreasonable delay.
   The current telephone number of the Performer is _(310) 555 - 7332_ .

6. MOTION PICTURE AND TELEVISION RELIEF FUND. The Performer (does) [does not] hereby authorize the
   Producer to deduct from the compensation hereinabove specified an amount equal to _1 (ONE)_ per cent
   of each installment of compensation due the Performer hereunder, and to pay the amount so deducted to the
   Motion Picture and Television Relief Fund of America, Inc.

7. FURNISHING OF WARDROBE. The (Producer) (Performer) agrees to furnish all modern wardrobe and wearing
   apparel reasonably necessary for the portrayal of said role; it being agreed, however, that should so-called
   "character" or "period" costumes be required, the Producer shall supply the same. When Performer furnishes
   any wardrobe, Performer shall receive the cleaning allowance and reimbursement, if any, specified in the basic
   contract.

                    Number of outfits furnished by Performer _____ @ $_____
                                            (formal) _____ @ $_____

*The "on or about" clause may only be used when the contract is delivered to the Performer at least seven days before the
starting date. See Codified Basic Agreement, Schedule B, Schedule C, otherwise a specific starting date must be stated.

8. ARBITRATION OF DISPUTES. Should any dispute or controversy arise between the parties hereto with reference to this contract, or the employment herein provided for, such dispute or controversy shall be settled and determined by conciliation and arbitration in accordance with the conciliation and arbitration provisions of the collective bargaining agreement between the Producer and Screen Actors Guild relating to theatrical motion pictures, and such provisions are hereby referred to and by such reference incorporated herein and made a part of this Agreement with the same effect as though the same were set forth herein in detail.

9. NEXT STARTING DATE. The starting date of Performer's next engagement is _____.

10. The Performer may not waive any provision of this contract without the written consent of Screen Actors Guild, Inc.

11. Producer makes the material representation that either it is presently a signatory to the Screen Actors Guild collective bargaining agreement covering the employment contracted for herein, or that the above-referred-to photoplay is covered by such collective bargaining agreement under the Independent Production provisions of the General Provisions of the Screen Actors Guild Codified Basic Agreement as the same may be supplemented and/or amended.

IN WITNESS WHEREOF, the parties have executed this agreement on the day and year first above written.

PRODUCER _Swifty Deals_ PERFORMER _Clark Gable_

BY ___SWIFTY DEALS___ Social Security No. _637-17-6992_

BILLING: MAIN TITLES, SINGLE CARD, FIRST POSITION

Production time reports are available on the set at the end of each day, which reports shall be signed or initialed by the Performer.

Attached hereto for your use are the following: (1) Declaration Regarding Income Tax Withholding ("Part Year Employment Method of Withholding") and (2) Declaration Regarding Income Tax Withholding. You may utilize the applicable form by delivering same to Producer. Only one of such forms may be used.

NOTICE TO PERFORMER: IT IS IMPORTANT THAT YOU RETAIN A COPY OF THIS CONTRACT FOR YOUR PERMANENT RECORDS.

SCREEN ACTORS GUILD

STUNT PERFORMER'S
DAILY CONTRACT
FOR THEATRICAL MOTION PICTURES

STUNT PERFORMER _DARREN DEVIL_   DATE OF AGREEMENT _SEPT. 5, 19XX_

ADDRESS   _17602 VINE ST., APT. 306_

HOLLYWOOD, CA 90038

TELEPHONE _(213)555-1902_   SOCIAL SECURITY NO. _195-02-7274_

COMPANY/PRODUCER _XYZ PRODUCTIONS, INC._

PRODUCTION TITLE _HERBY'S SUMMER VACATION_ PRODUCTION NO. _0100_

AGENT/AGENCY _____

ADDRESS _____

DAILY RATE _SCALE_   SERIES _____

WEEKLY CONV. RATE $ _____   START DATE _SEPT. 6, 19XX_

---

1. **DESCRIPTION OF SERVICES:** Producer hereby engages Stunt Performer to render services as _STUNT DOUBLE_. Stunt Performer accepts such engagement upon the terms herein specified.

2. **TERM/GUARANTEE:** Producer guarantees to furnish Stunt Performer not less than _2 (TWO)_ days engagement. If this space is not filled in, the guarantee shall be one (1) day.

3. **STUNT ADJUSTMENTS:** It is understood that the rate of compensation specified may be adjusted depending upon the nature of the stunt activities Producer may require. If so, a stunt adjustment will be agreed upon between the parties through good faith bargaining and said adjustment shall be noted on Stunt Performer's daily time report or time card. The parties shall agree upon the compensation to be paid before the stunt is performed if they may readily do so; however, it is expressly agreed that production shall not be delayed for the purpose of first determining the compensation for a stunt. Such adjustment shall increase Stunt Performer's compensation for the day in the manner prescribed in Schedule H of the Screen Actors Guild Codified Basic Agreement.

4. **INCORPORATION OF PRODUCER-SCREEN ACTORS GUILD COLLECTIVE BARGAINING AGREEMENT:** All provisions of the Screen Actors Guild Codified Basic Agreement and Television Agreement as the same may be supplemented and/or amended to date shall be deemed incorporated herein. Stunt Performer's engagement shall be upon the terms, conditions and exceptions of said provisions applicable to the rate of compensation and guarantee specified.

5. **RIGHTS:** Producer shall have the unlimited right throughout the universe and in perpetuity to exhibit the Motion Picture in all media, now or hereafter known, and Producer, as employer-for-hire of Stunt Performer, shall own all rights in the results and proceeds of Stunt Performer's services hereunder.

6. **ADDITIONAL COMPENSATION:** If the Motion Picture covered hereby is exhibited, containing any of the results and proceeds of Stunt Performer's services hereunder, in any of the following media:
   (i) "Free" television exhibition anywhere in the universe;
   (ii) Supplemental market exhibition anywhere in the universe;
   (iii) Basic Cable exhibition anywhere in the universe,

as to each such medium in which the motion picture is so exhibited, Producer will pay, and Stunt Performer will accept as payment in full, the minimum additional compensation provided therefor in the Screen Actors Guild Codified Basic Agreement or Television Agreement, as the case may be, except as compensation in excess of such minimum, if any, has been provided in this Agreement.

7. **CONTINUOUS EMPLOYMENT AND RIGHT TO ROLE (when applicable):** If Stunt Performer portrays a role or has dialogue, Stunt Performer shall be entitled to "continuous employment" and "Right to Role," if any, only to the extent prescribed by the Screen Actors Guild Codified Basic Agreement. Stunt Performer shall receive a separate contract for such services.

8. **MOTION PICTURE AND TELEVISION FUND:** Stunt Performer [does] [does not] hereby authorize Producer to deduct from the compensation hereinabove specified an amount equal to _____ percent of each installment of compensation due Stunt Performer hereunder, and to pay the amount so deducted to the Motion Picture and Television Fund of America, Inc.

9. **WAIVER:** Stunt Performer may not waive any provision of the Screen Actors Guild Codified Basic Agreement without the written consent of the Screen Actors Guild, Inc.

10. **SIGNATORY:** Producer makes the material representation that either it is presently a signatory to the Screen Actors Guild collective bargaining agreement covering the engagement contracted for herein, or that the Motion Picture is covered by such collective bargaining agreement under the "Independent Production" provisions (Section 24) of the General Provisions of the Screen Actors Guild Codified Basic Agreement.

Signing of this Agreement in the spaces below signifies acceptance by Producer and Stunt Performer of all of the above terms and conditions and those on the reverse hereof and attached hereto, if any, as of the date specified above.

PRODUCER _Swifty Deals_ STUNT PERFORMER _Darrin Devil_

BY _SWIFTY DEALS_

Production time reports and/or time cards are available on the set at the beginning and end of each day, which reports and/or time cards shall be signed or initialed by Stunt Performer and must indicate any agreed stunt adjustments.

NOTICE TO STUNT PERFORMER: IT IS IMPORTANT THAT YOU RETAIN A COPY OF THIS AGREEMENT FOR YOUR PERMANENT RECORDS.

S-3 (7-92)

**THE ARTIST MAY NOT WAIVE ANY PROVISION OF THIS CONTRACT
WITHOUT THE WRITTEN CONSENT OF SCREEN ACTORS GUILD, INC.**

 SCREEN ACTORS GUILD
STUNT PERFORMER'S
MINIMUM FREELANCE WEEKLY CONTRACT
FOR THEATRICAL MOTION PICTURES

STUNT PERFORMER _DANGEROUS DANN_   DATE OF AGREEMENT _JULY 5, 19XX_

ADDRESS _P.O. BOX 9876_

TINSELTOWN, CA 90000

TELEPHONE _(213)555-1136_   SOCIAL SECURITY NO. _961-83-2765_

COMPANY/PRODUCER _XYZ PRODUCTIONS, INC._

PRODUCTION TITLE _HERBY'S SUMMER VACATION_ PRODUCTION NO. _0100_

AGENT/AGENCY _____

ADDRESS _____

1. **DESCRIPTION OF SERVICES:** Producer hereby engages Stunt Performer to render services as _UTILITY STUNT PERFORMER_. Stunt Performer accepts such engagement upon the terms herein specified.

2. **COMPENSATION/TERM/GUARANTEE:** Producer will pay Stunt Performer and Stunt Performer agrees to accept the following weekly compensation (excluding location premiums) of $ _SCALE_ (and pro rata for each additional day beyond the guarantee until completion of services). The total guaranteed compensation shall be $_____ for the total guaranteed period of _____. If this space is not filled in, the guarantee shall be one (1) week. Stunt Performer shall receive sixth day location premium where applicable.

3. **START DATE:** The term of engagement shall begin on _JULY 6, 19XX_.
   or "on or about" * _____.

4. **NEXT START DATE:** The start date of Stunt Performer's next engagement is _____.

5. **STUNT ADJUSTMENTS:** It is understood that the rate of compensation specified may be adjusted depending upon the nature of the stunt activities Producer may require. If so, a stunt adjustment will be agreed upon between the parties through good faith bargaining and said adjustment shall be noted on Stunt Performer's daily time report or time card.

   The parties shall agree upon the compensation to be paid before the stunt is performed if they may readily do so; however, it is expressly agreed that production shall not be delayed for the purpose of first determining the compensation for a stunt. Such adjustment shall increase Stunt Performer's compensation for the week in the manner prescribed in Schedule H-II or H-III of the Screen Actors Guild Codified Basic Agreement.

6. **INCORPORATION OF PRODUCER-SCREEN ACTORS GUILD COLLECTIVE BARGAINING AGREEMENT:** All provisions of the Screen Actors Guild Codified Basic Agreement as the same may be supplemented and/or amended to date shall be deemed incorporated herein. Stunt Performer's engagement shall be upon the terms, conditions and exceptions of said provisions applicable to the rate of compensation and guarantee specified.

7. **RIGHTS:** Producer shall have the unlimited right throughout the universe and in perpetuity to exhibit the Motion Picture in all media, now or hereafter known, and Producer, as employer-for-hire of Stunt Performer, shall own all rights in the results and proceeds of Stunt Performer's services hereunder.

*The "on or about" clause may only be used when this Agreement is delivered to Stunt Performer at least three (3) days before the Start Date.

8. **ADDITIONAL COMPENSATION:** If the Motion Picture covered hereby is exhibited, containing any of the results and proceeds of Stunt Performer's services hereunder, in any of the following media:

(i) "Free" television reruns in the United States or Canada, or both;
(ii) Television exhibition anywhere in the universe outside the United States and Canada;
(iii) Theatrical exhibition anywhere in the universe;
(iv) Supplemental Market exhibition anywhere in the universe;
(v) Basic Cable exhibition anywhere in the universe,

as to each such medium in which the motion picture is so exhibited, Producer will pay, and Stunt Performer will accept as payment in full, the minimum additional compensation provided therefor in the Screen Actors Guild Codified Basic Agreement or Television Agreement, as the case may be, except as compensation in excess of such minimum, if any, has been provided in this Agreement.

9. **CONTINUOUS EMPLOYMENT AND RIGHT TO ROLE (when applicable):** If Stunt Performer portrays a role or has dialogue, Stunt Performer shall be entitled to "continuous employment" and "Right to Role," if any, only to the extent prescribed by the Screen Actors Guild Codified Basic Agreement. Stunt Performer shall receive a separate contract for such services.

10. **MOTION PICTURE AND TELEVISION FUND:** Stunt Performer [does] (does not) hereby authorize Producer to deduct from the compensation hereinabove specified an amount equal to _____ percent of each installment of compensation due Stunt Performer hereunder, and to pay the amount so deducted to the Motion Picture and Television Fund of America, Inc.

11. **WAIVER:** Stunt Performer may not waive any provision of the Screen Actors Guild Codified Basic Agreement or Television Agreement, whichever is applicable, without the written consent of the Screen Actors Guild, Inc.

12. **SIGNATORY:** Producer makes the material representation that either it is presently a signatory to the Screen Actors Guild collective bargaining agreement covering the engagement contracted for herein, or that the Motion Picture is covered by such collective bargaining agreement under the "Independent Production" provisions (Section 24) of the General Provisions of the Screen Actors Guild Codified Basic Agreement.

Signing of this Agreement in the spaces below signifies acceptance by Producer and Stunt Performer of all of the above terms and conditions and those on the reverse hereof and attached hereto, if any, as of the date specified above.

PRODUCER *Swifty Deals*   STUNT PERFORMER *Dangerous Dan*

BY ___SWIFTY DEALS___

Production time reports and/or time cards are available on the set at the beginning and end of each day, which reports and/or time cards shall be signed or initialed by Stunt Performer and must indicate any agreed stunt adjustments.

NOTICE TO STUNT PERFORMER: IT IS IMPORTANT THAT YOU RETAIN A COPY OF THIS AGREEMENT FOR YOUR PERMANENT RECORDS.

S-2 (7-92)

THE PERFORMER MAY NOT WAIVE ANY PROVISION OF THIS CONTRACT WITHOUT THE WRITTEN CONSENT OF SCREEN ACTORS GUILD, INC.

SCREEN ACTORS GUILD

PERFORMER CONTRACT FOR INTERACTIVE PROGRAMMING

Company _XYZ PRODUCTIONS, INC._   Date _AUGUST 23, 19XX_

Production Title _HERBY'S SUMMER VACATION_   Performer Name _FLASH GORDON_

Production Number _0100_   Address _P.O. BOX 1237 · HOLLYWOOD, CA_

Date Employment Starts _AUGUST 24, 19XX_   Telephone No.: _(213) 555-6126_

Role _POLICE SGT._   Social Security No.: _243-76-4432_

Daily Rate $_____   Date of Performer's next engagement _____

3 Day Rate $_____

Weekly Rate $ _SCALE_

Special Provisions $_____

_____

Wardrobe supplied by Performer ☐ Yes ☑ No

If so, number of outfits _____ @ $_____

(formal) _____ @ $_____

Complete for "Drop-And-Pick-Up" Deals ONLY:

Firm recall date on _____

or on or after* _____

("On or after" recall only applies to pick-up as Weekly Performer)

As ☐ Day Performer ☐ Weekly Performer

*Means date specified or within 24 hours thereafter.

THIS AGREEMENT covers the employment of the above-named Performer by _XYZ PRODUCTIONS_ in the production and at the rate of compensation set forth above and is subject to and shall include, for the benefit of the Performer and the Producer, all of the applicable provisions and conditions contained or provided for in the applicable Screen Actors Guild Interactive Agreement, and/or the Screen Actors Guild Television Agreement. Performer's employment shall include performance in non-commercial openings, bridges, etc., and no added compensation shall be payable to Performer so long as such are used in the role and project(s) covered hereunder in which Performer appears; for other use, Performer shall be paid the added minimum compensation, if any, required under the provisions of the Screen Actors Guild agreements with Producer.

Producer shall have all the rights in and to the results and proceeds of the Performer's services rendered hereunder, as are provided with respect to "photoplays" in Schedule A of the applicable Screen Actors Guild Codified Basic Agreement and the right to supplemental market use as defined in the Television Agreement.

Producer shall have the unlimited right throughout the world to telecast the film and exhibit the film theatrically and in supplemental markets in accordance with the terms and conditions of the Television Agreement.

By _Swifty Deals_   _Flash Gordon_

Producer   Performer

_243.76.4432_

Performer's Social Security No.

Production time reports are available on the set at the end of each day, which reports shall be signed or initialed by the Performer.

NOTICE TO PERFORMER: IT IS IMPORTANT THAT YOU RETAIN A COPY OF THIS CONTRACT FOR YOUR PERMANENT RECORDS.

#37A

SCREEN ACTORS GUILD
TAFT/HARTLEY REPORT

#15

ATTENTION: (CURRENT ADMINISTRATOR OF UNION SECURITY DEPT.)   ATTACHED?: ☑ RESUME*   ☑ PHOTO

EMPLOYEE INFORMATION

NAME __GOLDIE LOCKS__   SS# __111-22-1111__

ADDRESS __433 BEARHOUSE LANE__   AGE (IF MINOR) _____

CITY/STATE __WOODLAND HILLS, CA__ ZIP __91364__   PHONE __(818) 555-6226__

EMPLOYER INFORMATION

NAME __XYZ PRODUCTIONS, INC.__   Check one: ☐ AD AGENCY
☐ STUDIO
☑ PRODUCTION COMPANY

ADDRESS __1234 FLICK DR.__

CITY/STATE __HOLLYWOOD, CA__   ZIP __90038__   PHONE ( )

EMPLOYMENT INFORMATION

Check one: CONTRACT: ☑ DAILY   CATEGORY: ☑ ACTOR
☐ 3-DAY   ☐ SINGER   ☐ OTHER
☐ WEEKLY   ☐ STUNT

WORK DATE(S) __JULY 26, 19XX__   SALARY __SCALE__

PRODUCTION TITLE __HERBY'S SUMMER VACATION__   PROD'N/COM'L # __0100__

SHOOTING LOCATION (City & State) __VENICE BEACH, CALIFORNIA__

REASON FOR HIRE (be specific) __WHILE SHOOTING A SCENE ON THE STRAND AT VENICE BEACH, DIRECTOR DECIDED THAT MORE "LOCAL COLOR" WAS NEEDED TO MAKE THE SCENE MORE COMPLETE. MS. LOCKS, A ROLLER-SKATING STREET PERFORMER OF EXCEPTIONAL ABILITY WHO WAS PERFORMING ON THE STRAND AT THE TIME, WAS ASKED TO PARTICIPATE IN THE SCENE AND TO INTERACT WITH THE FILM'S ACTORS.__

Employer is aware of General Provision, Section 14 of the Basic Agreement that applies to Theatrical and Television production, and Schedule B of the Commercials Contract, wherein Preference of Employment shall be given to qualified professional actors (except as otherwise stated). Employer will pay to the Guild as liquidated damages, the sums indicated for each breach by the Employer of any provision of those sections.

SIGNATURE __Swifty Deals__   DATE __JULY 26, 19XX__
Producer or Casting Director – Indicate which

PRINT NAME __SWIFTY DEALS, PRODUCER__   PHONE __(213) 555-3331__

*PLEASE BE CERTAIN RESUME LISTS ALL TRAINING AND/OR EXPERIENCE IN THE ENTERTAINMENT INDUSTRY.

SAG EXTRA

15A.
rev. 6/25/92

TAFT/HARTLEY REPORT

ATTENTION: (CURRENT ADMINISTRATOR, ATTACHED?: ☑ RESUME ☑ PHOTO
OF UNION SECURITY DEPT.)

EMPLOYEE INFORMATION

NAME CARY GOOPER   SS# 433-27-6327

ADDRESS 103 YORK BLVD.   AGE (IF MINOR) _____

CITY/STATE LOS ANGELES, CA   ZIP 90000   PHONE (213) 555-6126

EMPLOYER INFORMATION

NAME XYZ PRODUCTIONS, INC.   Check one: ☐ CASTING OFFICE
                                           ☐ STUDIO
ADDRESS 1234 FLICK DR.   ☑ PRODUCTION COMPANY

CITY/STATE HOLLYWOOD, CA   ZIP 90038   PHONE (213) 555-3331

EMPLOYMENT INFORMATION

CHECK ONE: General Extra ☐   Special Ability Extra ☑   Dancer ☐

WORK DATE(S) JULY 22, 19XX   SALARY SCALE

PRODUCTION TITLE HERBY'S SUMMER VACATION

SHOOTING LOCATION (City & State) DOWNTOWN (5TH & BROADWAY) LOS ANGELES

REASON FOR HIRE (be specific) MR. GOOPER WAS HIRED TO PLAY A
CARD SHARK STREET HUSTLER BECAUSE OF HIS
SPECIAL ABILITY IN "TRICK" CARD DEALING.

Employer is aware of General Provision, Section 14.G of the Screen Actors Guild Codified Basic Agreement of 1989 for Independent Producers as amended that applies to Theatrical and Television production, wherein Preference of Employment shall be given to qualified professional extras (except as otherwise stated). Employer will pay to the Guild as liquidated damages, a sum which shall be determined by binding arbitration for each breach by the Employer of any provision of those sections.

SIGNATURE Swifty Deals   DATE 7.22.XX
Producer or Casting Director (indicate which)

PRINT NAME SWIFTY DEALS, PRODUCER   PHONE (213) 555-3331

SAG EXTRA VOUCHER

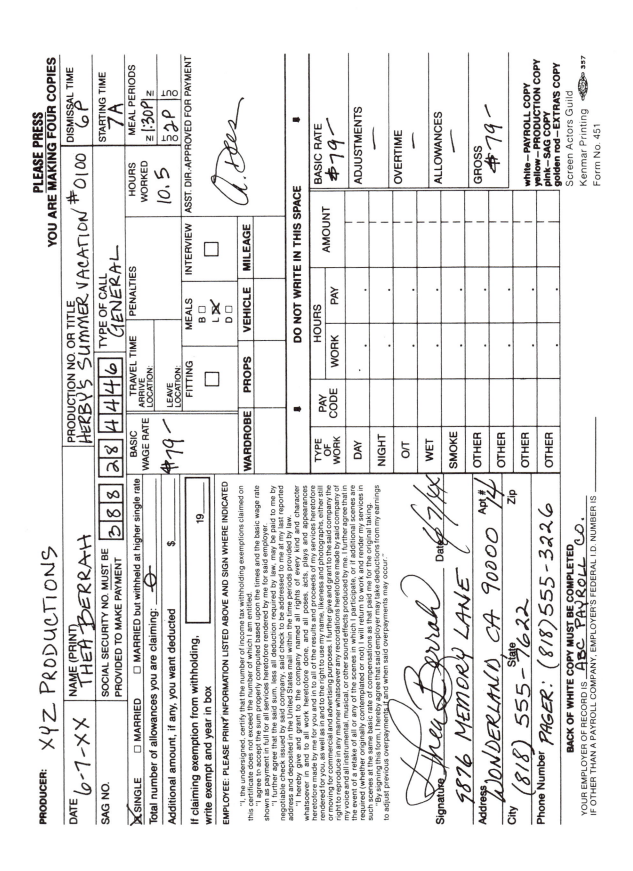

PLEASE PRESS
YOU ARE MAKING FOUR COPIES

PRODUCER: XYZ PRODUCTIONS

DATE 6-7-XX

NAME (PRINT) THEA BERRAH

PRODUCTION NO. OR TITLE
HERBY'S SUMMER VACATION #0100

SAG NO.

SOCIAL SECURITY NO. MUST BE PROVIDED TO MAKE PAYMENT   3 8 8   2 8 4 4 4 6

X SINGLE   □ MARRIED   □ MARRIED but withheld at higher single rate

Total number of allowances you are claiming: — 0 —

Additional amount, if any, you want deducted $ _____

If claiming exemption from withholding, write exempt and year in box   19___

TYPE OF CALL
GENERAL

STARTING TIME
7A

DISMISSAL TIME
6P

MEAL PERIODS
1:30P IN 2
3:2P OUT 1:00

HOURS WORKED
10.5

BASIC WAGE RATE
$79—

ASST. DIR. APPROVED FOR PAYMENT

EMPLOYEE: PLEASE PRINT INFORMATION LISTED ABOVE AND SIGN WHERE INDICATED

"I, the undersigned, certify that the number of income tax withholding exemptions claimed on this certificate does not exceed the number of which I am entitled.

"I agree to accept the sum properly computed based upon the times and the basic wage rate shown as payment in full for all services heretofore rendered by me for said employer.

"I further agree that the said sum, less all deduction required by law, may be paid to me by negotiable check issued by said company, said check to be addressed to me at my last reported address and deposited in the United States mail within the time periods provided by law.

"I hereby give and grant to the company named all rights of every kind and character whatsoever in and to all work heretofore done, and all poses, acts, plays and appearances heretofore made by me for you and in to all of the results and proceeds of my services heretofore rendered for you, as well as in and to the right to use my name, likeness and photographs, either still or moving for commercial and advertising purposes. I further give and grant to the said company the right to reproduce in any manner whatsoever any recordations heretofore made by said company of my voice and all instrumental, musical, or other sound effects produced by me. I further agree that in the event of a retake of all or any of the scenes in which I participate, or if additional scenes are required (whether originally contemplated or not) I will return to work and render my services in such scenes at the same basic rate of compensations as that paid me for the original taking.

"By signing this form, I hereby agree that said employer may take deductions from my earnings to adjust previous overpayments if and when said overpayments may occur."

Signature (Thea Berrah)   Date 6/7/XX

Address 9876 MEMORY LANE   Apt # 4

City WONDERLAND   State CA   Zip 90000

Phone Number (818) 555-7622   PAGER: (818) 555-3226

	TRAVEL TIME		PENALTIES	INTERVIEW
ARRIVE LOCATION:				□
LEAVE LOCATION:				
FITTING □		MEALS B □ / L ☒ / D □		
WARDROBE	PROPS	VEHICLE	MILEAGE	

DO NOT WRITE IN THIS SPACE

		HOURS		AMOUNT
TYPE OF WORK	PAY CODE	WORK	PAY	
DAY		·	·	·
NIGHT			·	·
O/T			·	·
WET			·	·
SMOKE				
OTHER				
OTHER				
OTHER				
OTHER				

BASIC RATE
$79—

ADJUSTMENTS
—

OVERTIME

ALLOWANCES
—

GROSS
$79—

white—PAYROLL COPY
yellow—PRODUCTION COPY
pink—SAG COPY
golden rod—EXTRAS COPY

Screen Actors Guild
Kenmar Printing   357
Form No. 451

BACK OF WHITE COPY MUST BE COMPLETED

YOUR EMPLOYER OF RECORD IS ABC PAYROLL CO.
IF OTHER THAN A PAYROLL COMPANY, EMPLOYER'S FEDERAL I.D. NUMBER IS

SCREEN ACTORS GUILD THEATRICAL & TELEVISION SIGN-IN SHEET

PRODUCER: SWIFTY DEALS
PROD'N CO: XYZ PRODUCTIONS
PROD'N OFFICE
PHONE # (213) 555-3331

AUDITION DATE: 5-10-XX

CASTING REP: DEE CASTOR
CASTING REP. PHONE: (213) 555-7632
PRODUCTION TITLE: HERBY'S SUMMER VACATION
EPISODE: "BOYS NIGHT OUT"

Dee Castor
Casting Director's Signature

(1) NAME	(2) SOCIAL SECURITY	(3) ROLE	(4) AGENT	(5) PROVIDED? PARK	(5) PROVIDED? SCRIPT	(6) ARRIVAL TIME	(7) APPT. TIME	(8) TIME SEEN (Cast. rep.)	(9) TIME OUT	(10) TAPED?	(11) ACT. INI.
CLARK GRABLE	332·62·7749	HERBY	JOE COOL	✓	✓	8:55A	9A	9A	9:25A	✓	
CARY GOOPER	523·76·5351	HERBY	HOLLY WOODS	✓	✓	9:30A	9:30A	9:25A	10A		
JAMES BONDY	237·12·3678	HERBY	RON REPPS	✓	✓	10:05A	10A	10:05A	10:25A		
MARTY MELROSE	176·42·6104	HERBY	JOE COOL	✓	✓	10:25A	10:30A	10:35A	11:05A		
SCARLET STARLET	234·36·3721	LAURA	JOE COOL	✓	✓	11:10A	11A	11:15A	11:40A	✓	
MARY MARVELOUS	542·71·1134	LAURA	RON REPPS	✓	✓	11:30A	11:30A	11:45A	12:10P		
GOLDIE LOCKS	176·43·7662	LAURA	HOLLY WOODS	✓	✓	11:55A	12 P	12:15A	12:35P		
BEVERLY FAIRFAX	332·27·1341	LAURA	JOE COOL	✓	✓	12:15P	12:30P	12:45A	1:15P		

ACTORS PRODUCTION TIME REPORT

PICTURE TITLE: HERBY'S SUMMER VACATION   PROD. # 0100   DATE MON. 6/7/XX   IS TODAY A DESIGNATED DAY OFF?* YES ☐ NO ☑

CAST Worked - W / Rehearsal - R / Started - S / Hold - H / Travel - TR ; Finished - F / Test - T	CHARACTER	W H S F R T / TR	MAKEUP WDBE.	WORKTIME REPORT ON SET	WORKTIME DISMISS ON SET	B K F S T	MEALS 1ST MEAL	MEALS 2ND MEAL	TRAVEL TIME LEAVE FOR LOCATION	TRAVEL TIME ARRIVE ON LOCATION	TRAVEL TIME LEAVE LOCATION	TRAVEL TIME ARRIVE AT STUDIO	STUNT ADJUST.	WARDROBE NO. OF OUTFITS PROVIDED	ACTORS SIGNATURE
CLARK GRABLE	HERBY	W	8A	8:30A	6P		1:30P	2P	7A	8A	6:15P	7:15P			Clark Grable
SCARLET STARLET	LAURA	W	7:30A	10A	8P	Ñ	1:30P	2P	6:45A	7:30A	8:15P	9P			Scarlett Starlett
HOLLYWOOD MANN	GEORGE	SW	9A	10A	8P		1:30P	2P							Hollywood Mann
KENNY SMILES	MARC	W	8A	8:30A	6P		1:30P	2P							Kenny Smiles
WILL PERFORMER	JED	W	8A	8:30A	6P		1:30P	2P							Will Performer
DARREN DEVIL	ND STUNTS	SW/F	9A	10A	7P		1:30P	2P					$500		Darren Devil

* This refers to the 2 days (1 day on overnight location) which producer can designate as day(s) off for the production.

SCREEN ACTORS GUILD

CASTING DATA REPORT

See Reverse For Instructions

THIS FORM MUST BE COMPLETED FOR EACH MOTION PICTURE AND EACH EPISODE OF EACH SERIES PRODUCED FOR THE QUARTER IN WHICH PRINCIPAL PHOTOGRAPHY WAS COMPLETED.

1) PRODUCTION COMPANY **XYZ PRODUCTIONS**
2) QUARTER and YEAR **3RD QUARTER - 19XX**
3) PROJECT (Title, Prod. No., etc.) **HERBY'S SUMMER VACATION - #0100**
4) DESCRIPTION (Feature, M.O.W., TV Series, etc.) **FEATURE**
5) TOTAL NO. OF DAYS OF PRODUCTION (Principal Photography Only) **58**

6) DATA SUBMITTED BY **CONNIE COORDINATES** (NAME)
   TELEPHONE NUMBER **(713) 555-3331**
7) CHECK IF APPROPRIATE [✓] NO STUNTS

PART I

CATEGORY		FORM OF HIRING DAILY	WEEKLY	SERIES	CAST TOTALS	NO. OF DAYS WORKED	AGE: UNDER 40	40 and over	UNKNOWN
MALE	LEAD		3		3	170	2	1	
	SUPPORT	21			21	84	11	9	1
FEMALE	LEAD		2		2	100	2		
	SUPPORT	16			16	48	11	5	

PART II

CATEGORY		DAILY M	DAILY F	WEEKLY M	WEEKLY F	SERIES M	SERIES F	DAYS M	DAYS F	UNDER 40 M	UNDER 40 F	40 & OVER M	40 & OVER F	UNKNOWN M	UNKNOWN F
ASIAN/PACIFIC	LEAD			1				58				1			
	SUPPORT	2	3					10	15	2	3				
BLACK	LEAD			1	1			58	50	1	1				
	SUPPORT	3	3					17	18		3	3			
CAUCASIAN	LEAD			1	1			54	50		1	1			
	SUPPORT	9	10					50	15	9	5		5		
LATINO / HISPANIC	LEAD														
	SUPPORT	5						5		1		4			
N. AMERICAN INDIAN	LEAD														
	SUPPORT														
UNKNOWN / OTHER	LEAD														
	SUPPORT	2						2						1	

INSTRUCTIONS

(After reading the following, if you have any further questions, please call 213/549-6644.) (For your convenience, our fax number is 213/549-6647.)

1. Indicate the name of the signatory Production Company (e.g., "THE ABC COMPANY").

2. Indicate the quarter/year when **principal photography** was completed (e.g., "1st quarter 1981"). Make one report only for full project even though it might span more than one quarter.

   The quarters consist of:

January	-	March	(1st)
April	-	June	(2nd)
July	-	September	(3rd)
October	-	December	(4th)

3. Indicate the <u>name</u> of the film for which you are reporting.

4. Indicate the <u>type</u> of project (feature, television movie, television pilot, television series, animation.

5. Use a number to respond to this question.

6. Indicate the name of person completing this form and the telephone number for same.

7. Two separate reports are required, one for <u>Performers</u> only and one for <u>Stunt Performers</u> only. If there were no Stunt Performers employed on the film, check the "No Stunt" box. If Stunt Performers were employed, complete the casting data report form for Stunt Performers.

8. **Part I.** Indicate the total number of lead and supporting Performers in each of the applicable categories. Series performers column is provided for episodic TV shows only. Daily column is for daily contract & 3-day contract performers only. Weekly column is for weekly contract and run-of-the-picture performers. A day contract performer upgraded to a weekly contract performer in a drop/pick-up situation should be listed in the weekly column (**do <u>not</u> count** the performer twice).

9. Use numbers only to indicate the total number of Performers in the category.

10. Use numbers only to indicate the total number of days worked by <u>ALL</u> Performers in the category. (Include all days paid for including hold, rehearsal days, etc.)

11. Use numbers only to indicate how many Performers were in each age group.

12. **Part II.** Indicate the total number of males and females in each category.

13. Use number only to indicate the total number of days worked by <u>ALL</u> the Performers in male and female category.

14. Use numbers only to indicate how many Performers were in each age group.

<u>NOTE</u>: PLEASE MAKE EVERY EFFORT TO INSURE THAT YOUR NUMBERS CORRESPOND ACROSS AND AMONG <u>PART I AND PART II</u>.

![logo] SCREEN ACTORS GUILD

CASTING DATA REPORT FOR STUNT PERFORMERS ONLY

THIS FORM MUST BE COMPLETED FOR EACH MOTION PICTURE AND EACH EPISODE OF EACH SERIES PRODUCED FOR THE QUARTER IN WHICH PRINCIPAL PHOTOGRAPHY WAS COMPLETED.

| | **See Reverse For Instructions** |

1) PRODUCTION COMPANY XYZ PRODUCTIONS, INC.
2) QUARTER and YEAR 3RD QUARTER, 19XX
3) PROJECT (Title, Prod. No., etc.) HERBY'S SUMMER VACATION
4) DESCRIPTION (Feature, M.O.W., TV Series, etc.) MOW
5) TOTAL NO. OF DAYS OF PRODUCTION (Principal Photography Only) 30

6) DATA SUBMITTED BY CONNIE COORDINATES (NAME)
   TELEPHONE NUMBER (213) 555-3331
7) NAME OF STUNT COORDINATOR CLIFF HANGER

PART I

8) CATEGORY	DAILY	WEEKLY	SERIES	9) PERFORMER TOTALS	10) NUMBER DAYS WORKED	11) AGE — UNDER 40	40 AND OVER	UNKNOWN	12) STUNT SUMMARY — DESCRIPT	NON-DESCRIPT
MALE	6	2		8	31	3	4	1	4	4
FEMALE	2	1		3	13	2	1		2	1

PART II

13) CATEGORY	8) FORM OF HIRING — DAILY M	DAILY F	WEEKLY M	WEEKLY F	SERIES M	SERIES F	14) NUMBER DAYS WORKED M	F	15) AGE — UNDER 40 M	F	40 AND OVER M	F	UNKNOWN M	F	16) STUNT SUMMARY — DESCRIPT M	F	NON-DESCRIPT M	F
ASIAN/PACIFIC	1						1		1						1			
BLACK	1	1					17	2	1	1			1		1	1	1	
CAUCASIAN	3	1		1			11	1	3	1					2	1	2	
LATINO / HISPANIC								10				1						1
N. AMERICAN INDIAN	1						2		1									1
OTHER / UNKNOWN																		

STUNT INSTRUCTIONS

**There are two separate report forms required.
Complete one report for Performers and one report for Stunt Performers.

(After reading the following, if you have any further questions, please call 213/549-6644.) (For your convenience, our fax number is 213/549-6647.)

1. Indicate the Production Company (e.g., "THE ABC COMPANY").

2. Indicate the quarter/year (e.g., "1st quarter 1981").

   The quarters consist of:

January	-	March	(1st)
April	-	June	(2nd)
July	-	September	(3rd)
October	-	December	(4th)

3. Indicate the <u>name</u> of the film for which you are reporting.

4. Indicate the <u>type</u> of project (feature, television movie, television pilot, television series, animation.

5. Use a number to respond to this question.

6. Indicate the name of person completing this form and the telephone number for same.

7. Provide the name of the stunt coordinator for the film.

Part I
8. Indicate the total number of males and females in each category.

9. Use numbers only to indicate the total number of stunt performers in the category.

10. Use numbers only to indicate the total amount of days worked by all stunt performers in the category.

11. Use numbers only to indicate how many stunt performers are in a certain age group.

12. Use numbers only to indicate the stunts as **descript*** or **non-descript***.

   *Descript = **A stunt performer who doubles for an actor.**

   *Non-descript = **A stunt performer doing a utility or faceless stunt.**

Part II
13. Indicate the total number of males and females in each category.

14. Use numbers only to indicate the total number of days worked by <u>all</u> the Performers in each category.

15. Use numbers only to indicate how many performers were in each age group.

16. Indicate the stunts as descript or non-descript.

NOTE: **Please make every effort to insure that your numbers correspond across categories and among <u>Part I and Part II</u>.**

SCREEN ACTORS GUILD

See Reverse For Instructions

THIS FORM MUST BE COMPLETED FOR EACH MOTION PICTURE AND EACH EPISODE OF EACH SERIES PRODUCED FOR THE QUARTER IN WHICH PRINCIPAL PHOTOGRAPHY WAS COMPLETED.

1) PRODUCTION COMPANY XYZ PRODUCTIONS, INC.
2) QUARTER and YEAR 4TH QUARTER - 19XX
3) PROJECT (Title, Prod. No., etc.) HERBY'S SUMMER VACATION
4) DESCRIPTION (Feature, M.O.W., TV Series, etc.) FEATURE
5) TOTAL NO. OF DAYS OF PRODUCTION (Principal Photography Only) 36

6) DATA SUBMITTED BY CONNIE COORDINATES   NAME
   TELEPHONE NUMBER (213) 555-3331
7) CHECK IF APPROPRIATE [✓] NO STUNTS

PART I

CATEGORY		FORM OF HIRING DAILY	WEEKLY	SERIES	CAST TOTALS	NO. OF DAYS WORKED	AGE: UNDER 40	40 TO 60	60 & OVER
MALE	LEAD		1		1	36		1	
	SUPPORT	6	1		7	37	4	1	2
FEMALE	LEAD		2		2	68	2		
	SUPPORT	4	1		5	18	2	2	1

PART II

CATEGORY		FORM OF HIRING DAILY M	DAILY F	WEEKLY M	WEEKLY F	SERIES M	SERIES F	NO. OF DAYS WORKED M	F	AGE UNDER 40 M	F	40 TO 60 M	F	60 & OVER M	F
ASIAN/PACIFIC	LEAD														
	SUPPORT	1	1					3	2	1			1		
BLACK	LEAD								32		1				
	SUPPORT	2	1					3	2	1	1		1		
CAUCASIAN	LEAD	1	1					36	36	1		1			
	SUPPORT	3	2					6	11	2	1		1		
LATINO / HISPANIC	LEAD														
	SUPPORT	1						25	3	1	1				1
N. AMERICAN INDIAN	LEAD														
	SUPPORT														
UNKNOWN / OTHER	LEAD														
	SUPPORT														

INSTRUCTIONS

1. Indicate the Production Company (e.g., "THE ABC COMPANY").

2. Indicate the quarter/year (e.g., "1st quarter 1981").

   The quarters consist of:

January	–	March	(1st)
April	–	June	(2nd)
July	–	September	(3rd)
October	–	December	(4th)

3. Indicate the <u>name</u> of the film for which you are reporting.

4. Indicate the <u>type</u> of project (feature, television movie, television pilot, television series, animation).

5. Use a number to respond to this question.

6. Indicate the name of person completing this form and the telephone number for same.

7. Two separate reports are required, one for <u>Performers</u> only and one for <u>Stunt Performers</u> only. If there were no Stunt Performers employed on the film, check the "No Stunt" box. If Stunt Performers were employed, complete the casting data report form for Stunt Performers.

8. <u>Part I</u>. Indicate the total number of lead and supporting Performers in each of the applicable categories.

9. Use numbers only to indicate the total number of Performers in the category.

10. Use numbers only to indicate the total number of days worked by <u>ALL</u> Performers in the category.

11. Use numbers only to indicate how many Performers were in each age group.

12. <u>Part II</u>. Indicate the total number of males and females in each category.

13. Use number only to indicate the total number of days worked by <u>ALL</u> the Performers in male and female category.

14. Use numbers only to indicate how many performers were in each age group.

**<u>NOTE</u>: PLEASE MAKE EVERY EFFORT TO INSURE THAT YOUR NUMBERS CORRESPOND ACROSS AND AMONG <u>PART I AND PART II.</u>

FINAL CAST LIST INFORMATION SHEET

DATE
FILED: _8·2·XX_   #10

PICTURE TITLE _HERBY'S SUMMER VACATION_   SHOOTING LOCATION _LOS ANGELES, CALIF._

PRODUCTION COMPANY _XYZ PRODUCTIONS_   START DATE _6·1·XX_   COMPLETION DATE _7·30·XX_

ADDRESS _1234 FLICK DR. - HOLLYWOOD CA 90038_   FEDERAL I.D. # _____   STATE I.D. # _____

PHONE _(213) 555-3331_ CONTACT _CONNIE COORDINATES_   PICTURE # _0100_

DISTRIBUTOR _MIRACLE PICTURES_   Check One: MP ☑ MOW ☐ OTHER TV ☐ INDUSTRIAL ☐ OTHER ☐

To establish Residual payments, see Section 5.2 of the 1980 Basic Agreement.

PLAYER NAME & SOCIAL SECURITY NUMBER	PLAYER ADDRESS INCLUDING ZIP	(1) PERIOD WORKED # WKS	# DYS	(1) START DATE	(1) FINISH DATE	(2) CONTRACT TYPE	(3) PLAYER TYPE	(4) TOTAL GROSS SALARY	(5) BASE SALARY	TIME UNITS	SALARY UNITS	TOTAL UNITS	FOR SAG USE ONLY
CLARK GRABLE 332·62·7749	1234 FIRST STREET MALIBU CA 90272	6		6/1	7/12	W	A	$4,325—	$2,000— PER WK.				
SCARLET STARLET 823·76·7737	555 SCHOOL STREET HOLLYWOOD CA 90038	3		6/1	6/19	W	A	$5,860—	$1876— PER WK.				
GOLDIE LOOKS 111·22·3333	453 BEARHOUSE LANE WOODLAND HILLS CA 91364		1	7/26	7/26	D	A	$540—	$540— PER DAY				
DANGEROUS DANN 332·42·9159	P.O. BOX 456 LOS ANGELES, CA 90000	1		7/6	7/10	W	ST	$2851—	$1876— PER WK.				
JOHNNY ROCKETT 552·11·7627	123 HOLLYWOOD HILLS RD. HOLLYWOOD CA 90028		3	6/25	6/29	D	ST	$2120—	$540— PER DAY				

(1) Include days not worked, but considered worked under continuous employment provisions. Report contractually guaranteed work period or actual time worked, whichever is longer.
(2) Insert D for Daily or W for Weekly type of contract.
(3) Insert: A = Actor; ST = Stunt; P = Pilot; SG = Singer; ADR = Automated Dialogue Replacement.
(4) Include all salary, Overtime, Premium, and Stunt Adjustments. Do not include any Penalties paid (e.g., Meal Penalties, Forced Calls, etc.).
(5) List base contractual salary (e.g., $1,500.00/week or $500.00/day).

To establish Residual payments, see Section 5.2 of the 1980 Basic Agreement.

PLAYER NAME & SOCIAL SECURITY NUMBER	PLAYER ADDRESS INCLUDING ZIP	(1) PERIOD WORKED # WKS	# DYS	(1) START DATE	(1) FINISH DATE	(2) CONTRACT TYPE	(3) PLAYER TYPE	(4) TOTAL GROSS SALARY	(5) BASE SALARY	TIME UNITS	SALARY UNITS	TOTAL UNITS	FOR SAG USE ONLY

(1) Include days not worked, but considered worked under continuous employment provisions. Report contractually guaranteed work period or actual time worked, whichever is longer.
(2) Insert D for Daily or W for Weekly type of contract.
(3) Insert: A = Actor; ST = Stunt; P = Pilot; SG = Singer; ADR = Automated Dialogue Replacement.
(4) Include all salary, Overtime, Premium, and Stunt Adjustments. Do not include any Penalties paid (e.g., Meal Penalties, Forced Calls, etc.).
(5) List base contractual salary (e.g., $1,500.00/week or $500.00/day).

SCREEN ACTORS GUILD
MEMBER REPORT
ADR THEATRICAL/TELEVISION

It is the responsibility of the reporting member to file a copy of this report with the Screen Actors Guild within forty-eight (48) hours of each session and to deliver a copy to the employer or the employer's representative at the conclusion of each session. If there is a contractor, he shall assume these responsibilities with respect to each session.

Work Date __8/20/XX__   Title __HERBY'S SUMMER VACATION__

Episode Title __BOYS NIGHT OUT__   Prod. No. __0100__

Production Co./Employer __XYZ PRODUCTIONS__

Address __1234 FLICK DR.__
__HOLLYWOOD, CA__
__90038__

Phone # __(213) 555-3331__

Studio Facility __ABC SOUND SERVICES__

Address __9123 VINE ST.__
__HOLLYWOOD, CA__
__90028__

Phone # __(213) 555-9000__

Sound Supervisor Editor __DAN DUBBER__

Sound Engineer/Mixer __LARRY LOOPER__

ADR Supervisor __SCOTT SOUNDER__

Employer Rep. __PAULA POST__

Type of Film: Theatrical ☐   TV Series ☑   TV MOW ☐   TV Pilot ☐   Other _____

Performer's Name	Performer's Social Security #	Character of 6+ Lines (sync)	Additional sets of up to 3 characters under 5 sync lines each	Studio Time Report/Dismiss	Meal Period From/To	Performer's Initials
BOB HOPEFULL	332-62-7749	BALL GAME ANNOUNCER	—	7A – 11A	—	BH
ROBERT BLUFORD	432-76-7737	—	BALL GAME SPECTATOR	10A – 4P	1 – 1:30P	RB
LORETTA OLDER	372-44-2232	—	"	10A – 4P	1 – 1:30P	
RICKY MOONEY	173-21-6342	—	"	10A – 4P	1 – 1:30P	RM
BRANDON MARLOW	519-36-2173	PITCHER	—	3P – 6P	—	BM

Reel #s Recorded: __#4__

NOTES: _____

This engagement shall be governed by and be subject to the applicable terms of the Screen Actors Guild Codified Basic or Television Agreement.

Production Co./EMPLOYER __XYZ PRODUCTIONS, INC.__

Signature of Employer or Employer Representative __Paula Post__, __POST PRODUCTION SUPERVISOR__

SAG Reporter _____ (Print name) _____

SAG Reporter's Phone # (____) _____ Date _____

SCHEDULE A – EXHIBIT I

DIRECTORS GUILD OF AMERICA
WEEKLY WORK LIST

From: _XYZ PRODUCTIONS_
(signatory company)
1234 FLICK DR.
(address)
HOLLYWOOD, CA 90038

Return to:
Directors Guild of America, Inc.

Week Ending: _6·12·XX_

Name	Soc. Sec. #	Cat.	Project
SID CELLULOID	123·45·6789	DIRECTOR	HERBY'S SUMMER VACATION
FRED FILMER	234·56·7890	UPM	
ALICE DEES	456·78·9012	1ST ASST. DIR.	
WILL LIGHT	567·89·0123	2ND ASST DIR.	
LAURA LAS PALMAS	678·90·1233	2ND, 2ND A.D.	

CONNIE COORDINATES
Prepared by
_(213) 555-3331_
Phone #

RC314/031489

DGA EMPLOYMENT DATA REPORT

DATE: _8·2·XX_   PREPARED BY: _FRED FILMER_   PHONE #: _(213)555-3331_

SIGNATORY COMPANY: _XYZ PRODUCTIONS_

QUARTER COVERED: _3RD_

PROJECT: _HERBY'S SUMMER VACATION_

DIRECTOR

	C	B	H	A	AI	UNKNOWN
MALE		/				
FEMALE						

UNIT PRODUCTION MANAGER

	C	B	H	A	AI	UNKNOWN
MALE	/					
FEMALE						

FIRST ASSISTANT DIRECTOR

	C	B	H	A	AI	UNKNOWN
MALE						
FEMALE		/				

SECOND ASSISTANT DIRECTOR

	C	B	H	A	AI	UNKNOWN
MALE	/					
FEMALE			/			

FIRST TIME DIRECTOR

	C	B	H	A	AI	UNKNOWN
MALE						
FEMALE						

The minority codes utilized in this report represent the following:

C	-	CAUCASIAN
B	-	BLACK
H	-	HISPANIC
A	-	ASIAN
AI	-	AMERICAN INDIAN

When completing this report the employment statistics must be reported in order that two (2) types of statistics can be obtained; the first statistic will indicate the number of persons employed in the respective category (referenced above) during that quarter. The second statistic will indicate the number of days worked or guaranteed in the respective categories for that quarter. Therefore in each category, there will be two (2) separate sets of statistics, one on top of the other, separated by a horizontal slash (example below). The top statistic will represent the number of employees working, the bottom statistic will be the number of days worked or guaranteed during the same quarter.

Example:

DIRECTOR

	C	B	H	A	AI	UNKNOWN
MALE	1/56					
FEMALE		1/25				

In the above example there was one (1) male Caucasian Director working during the quarter for a total of fifty-six (56) days worked or guaranteed. There was one (1) female Black Director working for a total of twenty-five days worked or guaranteed.

This report is to be submitted on a per-production basis not on a per episode basis. In instances where the same DGA employee is employed for multiple episodes in a continuing series, such employee will only be counted once in the number of employee statistics but such employee's cumulative days worked shall be included in that statistic.

NOTICE OF TENTATIVE WRITING CREDITS—THEATRICAL

Date _5. 29 . XX_

TO: Writers Guild of America

AND

All Participating Writers (or to the current agent if that participant so elects)

NAMES OF PARTICIPATING WRITERS   ADDRESS

F. SCOTT RYDER   _9336 W. STOREY STREET_
                                   LOS ANGELES, CA 90000

Title of Photoplay _HERBY'S SUMMER VACATION_
Executive Producer _HARRY HONCHO_
Producer _SWIFTY DEALS_
Director _SID CELLULOID_

Other Production Executives, including their titles, if
    Participating Writers _____

According to the provisions of Schedule A of the Writers Guild of America Theatrical and Television Basic Agreement of 1985 credits are now being determined on the above entitled production.

ON SCREEN, the tentative writing credits are as follows:
            SCREENPLAY BY F. SCOTT RYDER

SOURCE MATERIAL upon which the photoplay is based, if any:

ON SCREEN, <u>FORM</u> of Source Material credit, if any:

PRESENTATION or PRODUCTION credits, if any, which are intended for use in advertising and/or on-screen:
            XYZ PRODUCTIONS PRESENTS
            A SID CELLULOID FILM
The above tentative writing credits will become final unless a protest is communicated to the undersigned not later than 6:00 P.M. on _6|15| XX_

                        XYZ PRODUCTIONS
                        (Signatory Company)
                    BY _Swifty Deals_
                    NAME _SWIFTY DEALS_
                    ADDRESS _1234 FLICK DR. - HOLLYWOOD CA 90038_
                    PHONE _(213) 555-3331_

Revised
Feb. 1985

NOTICE OF TENTATIVE WRITING CREDITS—TELEVISION

Date 5·14·XX

TO: Writers Guild of America

      AND

      Participating Writers

NAMES OF PARTICIPATING WRITERS

JASON PENN

SAMUEL INKK

ADDRESS

1723 LINCOLN BLVD.—LOS ANGELES, CA

313 WASHINGTON ST.—CULVER CITY, CA

Title of Episode BOYS NIGHT OUT   Prod. No. 0100

(If Pilot or MOW or other special or unit program, indicate Network and length.)

Series Title HERBY'S SUMMER VACATION

Producing Company XYZ PRODUCTIONS

Executive Producer HARRY HONCHO

Producer SWIFTY DEALS   Assoc. Producer ADAM DARK

Director SID CELLULOID   Story Editor J. MILLER
                            (or Consultant)

Other Production Executives, if
   Participating Writers _____

Writing credits on this episode are tentatively determined as follows:

ON SCREEN: SCREENPLAY BY JASON PENN AND SAMUEL INKK

Source Material credit ON THIS EPISODE (on separate card, unless otherwise indicated), if any:

Continuing source material or Created By credit APPEARING ON ALL EPISODES OF SERIES (on separate card):

Revised final script was sent to participating writers on 5·21·XX .

The above tentative writing credits will become final unless a protest is communicated to the undersigned not later than 6:00 P.M. on 5/28/XX .

XYZ PRODUCTIONS
(Company)

BY Swifty Deals

CHAPTER SEVEN

Talent

FOLLOW-THROUGH AFTER AN ACTOR HAS BEEN SET

Once an actor has been set for a particular role, the casting office should send a *booking slip* to the actor's agent verifying the role, a minimum guaranteed number of days or weeks of employment and salary. A booking slip should be issued no later than the day preceding the actor's first day of employment. If engagement occurs after 6:00 p.m. of the day prior to the start of work, the booking slip may be included with the script.

Casting will notify production of the actor's name, address, and phone number and the actor's agent's name and phone number. Production then (1) notifies wardrobe of the actor's name and phone number, (2) sends the actor a script, and (3) arranges a physical examination for insurance purposes (if applicable).

A *deal memo* (which outlines the terms of the actor's employment on a particular film) is issued by the casting office and copies are sent to a predetermined distribution list. When the entire cast has been set, the casting office will issue a final *cast list*. Partial cast lists should be done prior to all roles being set. See Chapter 8 for a sample cast list.

Cast lists should also be sent to a predetermined distribution list. (Make sure cast lists are given to your wardrobe, hair, makeup, and transportation people.) Some cast lists may contain an additional column containing the actors' deals, but those are only to be given to a select few: the producer, production manager, assistant directors, production coordinator, and production accountant. Actors' deals are not for general distribution.

A final cast list, detailed on the designated *SAG Final Cast List Information Sheet*, is to be submitted to the Screen Actors Guild no later than 120 days after the completion of principal photography or 90 days after the completion of post production, whichever is sooner. (If the guild is holding a security deposit, the final cast list is submitted directly after the last performer's payroll following principal photography.)

Contracts for lead talent are often prepared by the production company's legal affairs department or by the company's entertainment attorney. The casting office generally prepares standard *SAG contracts* (although sometimes they are prepared and sent out from the production office) with all company related riders and appropriate tax (W-4 and I-9) forms attached. *Weekly* and *three-day player contracts* are sent directly to the respective agents, with a cover letter instructing them as to where to return the contract once it has been signed by their client. Be sure all lines, spaces, boxes, etc. that need to be signed or initialed by the actor are clearly indicated with red Xs and/or paper clips to mark the spot.

The following is a sample of a *cover letter* that would be sent to agents with a client's contract [also enclosed would be any applicable rider(s); all payroll forms; and a self-addressed, stamped, return envelope]:

Today's Date

Agent's Name
Name of Agency
Address
City, State Zip

Dear (Agent's Name):

Enclosed please find an agreement *for (actor's name)*'s services on *("name of project")*. Please have (*him or her*) sign the contract where indicated and complete the attached payroll start slip, W-4, and I-9 forms. We would appreciate it if you would send I-9 verification at the time you return the signed agreement (a copy of a driver's license and social security card or passport).

Enclosed is a self-addressed, stamped envelope for your convenience. In addition to the contract and payroll forms, please return a check authorization form if you wish (*name of actor*)'s checks to be sent directly to your office.

Once the contract is fully executed, a copy will be returned to you for your files. If you have any questions, please do not hesitate to call me at (*production office phone number*).

Sincerely yours,

If an actor does not have an agent, the contract should be sent directly to the actor and the cover letter should read:

Today's Date

Actor's Name
Address
City, State Zip

Dear (Actor's Name):

Enclosed please find an agreement for your services on *("name of project")*. Please sign the contract where indicated and complete the attached payroll start slip, W-4, and I-9 forms. We would appreciate it if you would send I-9 verification at the time you return the signed agreement (a copy of a drivers license and social security card or passport).

Enclosed is a self-addressed, stamped envelope for your convenience. Once the contract is fully executed, a copy will be returned to you for your files. If you have any questions, please do not hesitate to call me at (*production office phone number*).

Sincerely yours,

Day-player contracts are often prepared with the work date left off and given to the production coordinator. The date may be filled in the evening before an actor works and the contract sent to the set the next day for signature. Standard employment contracts must be available for signature no later than the first day of employment. Be careful when communicating with a day player if there is a chance that the part may be canceled. Sending an actor a script (or *sides*) and having wardrobe contact the actor constitutes an *engagement,* even if a firm work date has not yet been given and a contract has not yet been drawn up.

Stunt performer contracts are generally prepared and sent out from the production office. Specific SAG contracts exist for the employment of stunt players.

The casting office will *Station 12* each actor (a SAG procedure to make sure the actors are in good standing with the guild) prior to reporting for work. The production office should Station 12 all actors (such as stunt performers) whose contracts originate from the production office and have not already been checked through the casting office. The burden is on the production company (and not the actor) to notify the guild of all SAG performers it is employing prior to their start dates. Not only should calls be made to the guild to Station 12 actors, but verification calls from the guild back to the casting or production office clearing each performer should be monitored to make sure that all are okayed to work.

Reasons that performers may not be cleared through Station 12 might be (1) they are delinquent in the payment of guild dues and must pay up before being allowed to work; (2) they must be Taft/Hartleyed or they may fall under the category of *"must join"* status for membership (after being Taft/Hartleyed once before). It is therefore advantageous to clear an actor through Station 12 as soon as possible, so these additional steps (if necessary) can be taken. The fine for not clearing a performer who is not in good standing with the guild is presently $500.

Once a contract has been signed by an actor, it should be returned to the production coordinator. A copy of each contract, all accompanying W-4s and I-9s, and a copy of the *Actors Production Time Report* (containing the actors' signatures) for each day of filming is to be turned in to the production accountant. Note that a payroll check cannot be withheld from an actor who has not yet signed a contract as long as the actor has submitted a W-4 and I-9.

Make sure the actors' work times listed on the time report are the same as the times listed on the Daily Production Report, and that the actors' signatures on the report are in ink. The top (original) copies of the SAG Time Sheets should be sent to SAG approximately once a week (to the attention of their production department). A photocopy of each time sheet should be attached to the corresponding Daily Production Report.

The production coordinator will have the producer sign the SAG contracts after they have been signed by the actors and will then distribute all fully executed copies. The white (original) copy should be sent to your production executive for the company's legal files. Subsequent copies are for the production files, the production accountant, and the actor's agent (or the actor if the actor does not have an agent).

The following is a sample of a short letter that would accompany a copy of a *fully executed contract* that is returned to each respective agent:

Today's Date

Agent's Name
Name of Agency
Address
City, State Zip

Dear (*Agent's Name*):

Enclosed you will find a fully executed copy of (*actor*)'s contract for (*his or her*) services on (*"name of project"*). If you have any questions, please do not hesitate to call me.

Sincerely,

Again, if the performer has no agent, the letter should read as follows:

Today's Date

Actor's Name
Address
City, State Zip

Dear (*Actor's Name*):

Enclosed you will find a fully executed copy of your contract for your services on (*"name of project"*). If you have any questions, please do not hesitate to call me.

Sincerely,

All *script revisions* are to be sent to actors via the production office.

WORK CALLS

The assistant director will give all *"first" work calls* to the casting office. They, in turn, will call all respective agents with detailed information as to time, location, and scenes to be shot the following day. The assistant director will usually follow-through and call the actors that evening to confirm that they have received calls from their agents and have been given the proper information. The assistant director will also handle all work calls other than first calls.

If actors call the production or casting office to find out their calls for the next day, they should be informed as to what the call sheet reads, but it must be made clear that this is not a final call and is *subject to change*. Remind all actors that the assistant director will call them each evening with a definite work call for the next day.

Production should make sure casting gets a call sheet each day and is kept up to date on all schedule changes. Your SAG representative should be informed of schedule changes as well.

PERFORMER CATEGORIES

SAG members are classified by category as follows:

Schedule A: Day performers

Schedules B and C: Freelance weekly performers (determined by the amount of compensation paid to the performer)

Schedule D: Multiple-picture performers

Schedules E and F: Contract performers (determined by the amount of compensation)

Schedule G-I: Professional singers employed by the day

Schedule G-II: Professional singers employed by the week (a professional singer is a person who is employed primarily to sing a set piece of music on a given pitch, either as a solo or in a group requiring unison, melody, and harmony)

Schedule H-I: Stunt performers employed by the day

Schedules H-II and H-III: Stunt performers employed by the week (depending on their salary)

Schedule H-IV: Stunt performers under term contracts

Schedule I: Airline pilots—a pilot who is employed to fly or taxi aircraft (including helicopters) before the camera in the photographing of motion pictures

Schedule J: Extra performers

Note that puppeteers do not have a separate schedule.

All categories are determined by the amount of compensation received by the performer. Compensation rates are determined at the contract year's end and are adjusted yearly.

STUNT PERFORMER CATEGORIES

Stunt double: (Daily Performer Contract) may perform only for the character he or she agreed to double. Any other stunt work performed on any given day requires an additional contract.

Utility stunt: (Weekly Performer Contract) may double more than one character during a single day and may perform any other stunt work that might be required without an additional contract(s) for these additional services. This type of employment is permitted only when hired under a weekly stunt contract.

ND stunt: nondescript stunt or generic stunt work is designated on a daily contract. Such performer may not double a specific character without an additional contract for that day.

INTERVIEWS

Day performers (TV and theatrical) are not paid for interviews if they are dismissed within one hour from the time of their appointment. If detained beyond one hour, the performer is paid at straight time in one-half hour units. Three-day performers (TV) and weekly performers (TV and theatrical) do not receive compensation unless they are required to speak lines given them to learn outside the studio or they are kept waiting for more than one hour. All interviews or auditions for television or theatrical films must have sign-in sheets available.

WORKWEEK

The performer's workweek consists of any five consecutive days out of seven consecutive days—or, on an overnight location, any six consecutive days out of seven consecutive—as designated by the producer on each production unit. Any actor or extra who works on the designated sixth or seventh day of the workweek is not entitled to *premium pay* unless such a day is the performer's sixth or seventh consecutive day worked.

Performers are entitled to an additional day's pay for work on the fifth day of the workweek that spills over, that is, goes past midnight, into a sixth day of work. They are not entitled to premium pay for such work on the sixth day unless they are required to report for an additional call on the sixth day.

Producers are allowed to switch the production workweek (without penalty) once, to get on a Monday through Friday workweek, or once off and then back on, to a Monday through Friday workweek. Performers shall be entitled to payment for any days off beyond four between switched workweeks. Further, performers shall be entitled to premium payment if between switched workweeks they do not receive at least one day off.

REST PERIODS

Actors working in town being given *studio calls* are entitled to a twelve consecutive-hour rest period from the time of dismissal until the first call for the next day, whether for makeup, wardrobe, hairdress, or any other purpose.

For a *nearby location* where exterior photography is required on the day preceding and the day following the rest period, the rest period may be reduced from twelve to ten hours once every fourth consecutive day. There is also a provision that allows for the rest period to be reduced by fifteen minutes at the end of a workday if assistance is required with wardrobe or the removal of makeup after wrap. The rest period may not be reduced from twelve to ten hours on the first day of each performer's employment in a television production.

On *overnight locations*, the twelve-hour rest period may be reduced to eleven hours twice a week, but not on consecutive days. This is permitted on theatrical films only. If a performer reporting to an overnight location arrives at the hotel after 9 p.m. and does not work that night, the performer may be given a ten-hour turnaround. A performer who is required to travel by air for more than four hours to a location may not be called for work without a ten-hour rest period.

All performers are entitled to one *weekly rest period* of fifty-four hours provided they are not called before 6:00 a.m. on the first day of the following week. On a six-day location week, the weekly rest period is thirty-six hours. Violation of either the daily or weekly rest period is known as a *forced call,* and the penalty is one day's pay or $950, whichever is the lesser sum.

CONSECUTIVE EMPLOYMENT

Performers are generally paid on a consecutive day's basis from the first day they are instructed to report for work, or when shooting on any overnight location, beginning with the *travel day*, which constitutes the first day of employment. For example, weekly free-lance players scheduled to work on a Monday and Tuesday, *on hold* Wednesday and Thursday, and scheduled again for Friday, will be paid for the entire week, even if they are not given a work call for Wednesday and Thursday. Additionally, because they are employed by the production company for the entire week, they are subject to being called in for work on Wednesday or Thursday should there be a change in schedule.

Weekly performers who are on hold for several days during the schedule and are then called back to work for another day or two cannot be taken off payroll as weekly performers and converted to a daily contract when called back for those additional days. These actors must be compensated on a weekly basis until their services on the film are completed.

A day performer can be converted to a weekly performer or may be returned on a weekly basis as a *drop/pickup*. For a drop/pickup schedule to exist, the performer must first be on a day performer contract and must be notified of the pickup date before wrapping the original engagement. The intervening time must be for more than ten calendar days for films produced in the United States, and fourteen calendar days for films produced outside the United States. Under these circumstances, compensation need not be given for the intervening time, and the performer is independent of any responsibility to the production. Day performers picked up on a weekly contract may be given an *on or after* pickup date (which refers to a specific date or the following day), thus allowing the producer a twenty-four hour leeway. Day performers picked up on another day performer contract must be given a specific pickup date. One such break in employment is allowed for each performer per production. A weekly performer may never be converted to a day performer contract.

On episodic television only, day performers earning not less than two times minimum scale can be recalled once during each episode without payment for the intervening time. Consecutive employment does not apply to stunt performers, unless the stunt performer has dialogue, which constitutes a role.

Recalls for looping, added scenes, process shots, trailers, retakes, etc. after the close of an actor's work in principal photography shall break consecutive employment. Performers may be recalled at their contractual rate provided such additional services are commenced within four months after termination of their employment. After the four-month period, performers are free to renegotiate their contracts for any additional work requested by the producer.

TRANSPORTATION AND LOCATION EXPENSES

Transportation to distant location supplied by the producer must be first class. If six or more performers travel on the same flight and in the same class on jet flights within the continental United States, then coach class shall be acceptable. For interviews and auditions *only*, a performer may travel other than first class on a regularly scheduled jet aircraft. Bus and train transportation (in the best class available) are acceptable.

In addition to single room accommodations, the producer is to provide per diem meal allowance at not less than the current minimum scheduled rates. If the minimum rates are not sufficient to meet prevailing reasonable costs for meals on a specific location, the producer must make appropriate adjustments. Producers must pay the per diem prior to the day or week of work. If the per diem is paid by check, then facilities must be made available to cash such checks.

LOOPING

Day performers may be recalled to loop for a four-hour session and paid one half of their contractual daily salary. A day player (not being recalled and working on a picture for the first time) must receive a full day's pay for a looping session. Weekly freelance performers recalled to loop after completion of principal photography for four hours or less are paid an additional one-half day's pay. If more than four hours are required, a full day's pay shall be required.

Producers may negotiate for a specified number of loop days to be included in a weekly performer's contract if the actor's compensation for the picture is over scale. The producer may also bargain with a day player guaranteed $5,000 or more per day to include not more than one looping day in the performer's contract.

DUBBING (FOR THEATRICAL MOTION PICTURES ONLY)

Producers are required to employ performers at rates not less than specified in SAG's current Dubbing Agreement when dubbing a SAG theatrical motion picture into a language other than English in the United States.

EMPLOYMENT OF MINORS

When finalizing a deal for the *employment of minors*, make sure their work permits are up to date. Most importantly, you need to be aware of both the *child labor laws* in the state in which minors are being hired and SAG policies regarding the employment of minors, and to know which set of regulations apply to your production. Before you can hire minors, many states will have you apply for a *Permit to Employ Minors*, in addition to requiring you to supply them with a certificate of insurance to show proof of your workers' compensation coverage.

Note that California has some of the most stringent child labor laws in the country, which apply to both minors hired in California and to those hired in other states but brought to California to work. If a minor is hired in California by a California-based company and the production company chooses to shoot the film in another state, California regulations apply. If a company based in another state shoots their film in California, the minors they employ are also subject to California laws.

If, however, minors are being employed by a company based in and shooting in a state other than California, where child labor laws are less stringent, then SAG regulations would take precedence.

Regulations regarding the employment of minors are very precise. Depending on the age of the children, they are allowed a required number of hours in which to work, to attend school, and to rest. They cannot work earlier than a specified time in the morning nor past a specified time at night; if under sixteen years of age, minors must be accompanied by a parent or guardian. These regulations also cover the employment of teacher/welfare workers and the number of children each teacher may teach and/or supervise. Producers must hire teachers with credentials appropriate to the level of education required by the minors to be taught on the set.

In addition, California and New York have procedures whereby a judge will both *confirm* a contract with a minor (to prevent the minor from changing his or her mind later) and, at the same time, require the production company to put a portion of the minor's compensation into a supervised bank account until the minor reaches the age of majority (the amount is generally 25% of the gross). Discuss this with your legal department or attorney to determine if court approval should be sought. Parents should also be informed of this when making the deal and should agree to cooperate in obtaining proper approvals.

It is important to be aware of the time frame necessary to secure a court order and to establish a trust account for the minor, because the production company is still bound by the terms of the agreement for the payment of compensation. Whether you are governed under state or SAG guidelines, make sure you and your assistant directors are fully acquainted with all the policies pertaining to the employment of minors.

TAFT/HARTLEY

The Taft/Hartley is a federal law that allows a nonmember of a union or guild to work on a union show for thirty days. At the end of that time period, he or she *must join* the union to continue working on that particular show or for another signatory company.

A producer will generally choose to hire a performer who is not a member of the Screen Actors Guild for a few different reasons. The first scenario is when a decision to hire a nonmember is made after lengthy interviews to find a specific look or type, or someone with very specific abilities that cannot be met by a SAG member. The second scenario happens on the set during filming, on the spur of the moment, when the *director* decides another performer is needed to make a scene more complete and upgrades an extra or stand-in who happens to be there at the time. This situation may also apply to well-known or famous people brought in to portray themselves. If in doubt as to whether a non-SAG performer can be hired under the Taft/Hartley ruling, always check with the guild first.

Whenever a nonmember is hired to perform on a SAG signatory show, a Taft/Hartley form must be completed and submitted to the Screen Actors Guild. A Taft/Hartley form submitted on a television or theatrical film must be received within fifteen calendar days of the performer's first day of work. Submissions postmarked on the fifteenth day do not count and may be subject to a fine. Submissions from commercials must be received within fifteen business days.

Taft/Hartley forms require the performer's name, address, phone number, social security number, information on your production, and *reason for hire*. If the reason for hire does not satisfactorily explain why this person was hired instead of a guild member, the production may be subject to a fine.

Production companies are more apt to be fined for this type of violation when they Taft/Hartley an excessive number of performers on one show, which automatically raises doubt as to the need for so many people with special abilities or qualities that cannot be found from within the SAG membership. Damages for the employment of a performer in violation of provisions that pertain to the Taft/Hartley law are currently $500.

Also requested along with a completed Taft/Hartley form is a professional resume and photograph of the performer. If the performer does not have a professional photograph, a Polaroid taken on the set can be attached, but an explanation is required if a professional resume and/or photo does not exist. As soon as a performer is Taft/Hartleyed, he or she can join the guild. In all states (other than right-to-work states), a performer can work for thirty days from his or her first date of employment (or any amount of days within that thirty-day period) without having to join the guild. Once the thirty days has lapsed, the performer must join before he or she can be employed on another SAG film.

In a right-to-work state (Alabama, Arizona, Arkansas, Florida, Georgia, Idaho, Iowa, Kansas, Louisiana, Mississippi, Nebraska, Nevada, North Carolina, North Dakota, South Carolina, South Dakota, Tennessee, Texas, Utah, Virginia, and Wyoming), a performer may join but is not required to. The performer may work union or non-union films, and the production cannot be fined for hiring a non-SAG member who has worked on other SAG productions. Performers working on a union show, even if they are not guild members, must be cleared through Station 12 and Taft/Hartley letters must be submitted. In addition, pension and health benefits must be paid by the production company, and performers' employment must be reported to the guild.

NUDITY

The rules pertaining to nudity are as follows:

1. The producer's representative is to notify the performer (or their representative) of any nudity or sex acts expected in the role (if known by management at the time) prior to the first interview or audition. Producers may not require total nudity at an audition or interview, and performers must be permitted to wear pasties and a g-string or its equivalent.
2. During any production involving nudity or sex scenes, the set shall be closed to all persons having no business purpose in connection with the production.
3. No still photography of nudity or sex acts will be authorized by the producer to be made without the consent of the performer.

4. The appearance of a performer in a nude or sex scene, or the doubling of a performer in such a scene, shall be conditioned upon the performer's prior written consent. Such consent may be obtained by letter or other writing prior to a commitment or written contract being made or executed. Such consent must include a general description as to the extent of the nudity and the type of physical contact required in the scene. If a performer has agreed to appear in such scene and then withdraws consent, the producer shall also have the right to double the performer. Consent may not be withdrawn for film already photographed. The producer shall also have the right to double young children or infants in nude scenes (not in sex scenes).

Body doubles employed in scenes requiring nudity or conduct of a sexual nature shall be principal performers; however, the provisions relating to residuals, screen credit, consecutive employment, and preference of employment provisions do not apply to these performers. Notwithstanding the foregoing, body doubles shall be paid for intervening days on an overnight location when required to remain at such location by the producer, and the preference of employment provisions of the applicable extra performer schedule shall apply to the employment of body doubles.

WORK IN SMOKE

Principal performers must be notified in advance when scheduled to work in smoke. If a principal performer is not notified and cannot work in smoke for health reasons, such performer shall receive a half-day's pay or payment for time actually worked, whatever is greater.

WORKING WITH ANIMALS

There is an availability of trained animals that can perform with realism and without danger of injury or death. To ensure the responsible, decent, and humane treatment of animals, producers are encouraged to work with the American Humane Association pertaining to the use of animals in their films.

Producers cannot use any performer in a scene in which an animal is intentionally mistreated or killed, except when the animals being killed are subject to the provisions of a legal hunting season. Producers need to notify the American Humane Association prior to the commencement of any work involving an animal(s) and to advise them as to the nature of the work to be performed. Scripted scenes involving animals should be made available to the American Humane Association, and representatives of the association may be present at any time during the filming of a motion picture in which animals are used.

SAG EXTRAS

The different categories of SAG extras are as follows:

General extras: A performer of atmospheric business that includes the normal actions, gestures, and facial expressions of the extra performer's assignment.

Special ability extras: An extra specifically called and assigned to perform work requiring special skill, such as tennis, golf, choreographed social dancing, swimming, skating, riding animals, driving livestock, nonprofessional singing (in groups of fifteen or fewer), professional or organized athletic sports, amputees, driving that requires a special skill and a special license, motorcycle driving, insert work, and practical card dealing.

Stand-in: An extra used as a substitute for another actor for the purpose of focusing shots, setting lights, etc. but not actually photographed. Stand-ins may also be used as general extras.

Photo double: An extra who is actually photographed as a substitute for another actor.

Omnies: Extras who produce indistinguishable background noise and chatter, typically used in a party or restaurant scene.

An extra who is directed to deliver a line of dialogue or speech may be eligible for an *upgrade* to a principal performer. Certain circumstances allow extras to receive rate adjustments. Examples are rough or dangerous work; work requiring the performer to get wet or work in smoke; having to wear body makeup, a skull cap, hair goods, or a natural full-grown beard; and for supplying wardrobe and personal props.

Contact SAG for a complete set of rules and rates pertaining to the employment of extras, especially the guidelines governing the number of union extras you are required to employ before you may use non-union extras. These regulations are still relatively new and are not yet uniform throughout the country.

There are specific voucher forms supplied by SAG and extra casting agencies to be used by SAG extras. Taft/Hartley rules are the same for SAG extras as they are for other SAG performers, but there are different Taft/Hartley forms to fill out in such cases. Samples of both forms can be found in Chapter 6.

INTERACTIVE AND INDUSTRIAL/EDUCATIONAL CONTRACTS

The Screen Actors Guild now offers a contract for producers hiring actors who perform in interactive/multimedia programs. This agreement is mentioned in more detail in Chapter 18. SAG also offers a contract that specifically addresses the employment of principal and extra performers working on industrial and educational shows. The contract covers two categories of programs.

Category I programs are designed to train, inform, promote a product, or perform a public relations function, and are exhibited in classrooms, museums, libraries, or other places where no admission is charged. Included are closed circuit television transmission and teleconferences. Also included are sales programs that are designed to promote products or services of the sponsor but will be shown on a restricted basis only.

Category II programs are intended for unrestricted exhibition to the general public. Category II programs must be designed primarily to sell specific products or services to the consuming public (1) at locations where the products or services are sold, or (2) at public places such as coliseums, railroad stations, air/bus terminals, or shopping centers. These programs may be supplied free of charge to customers as a premium or inducement to purchase specific goods or services. A five-year use limitation applies to all Category II programs.

Contact SAG for further information or to obtain contract digests outlining these agreements.

Rules pertaining to casting and the employment of actors are varied and many. Additions and revisions are enacted every three years when the Screen Actors Guild negotiates a new contract with the AMPTP. In addition to some of the basic regulations outlined in this chapter, you should have a good working knowledge of pay scales and specific rules pertaining to engagement and cancellation; makeup, hairdressing, wardrobe, and fitting calls; employment contracts; billing and screen credit; overtime; location and travel time; meal penalty violations; night work; time of payment and late payments; reuse of film; and affirmative action. Also be aware of the specifics on the employment of extras, minors, stunt performers, dancers, etc.

Keep a copy of the latest SAG contract (and contract digest pamphlets) close at hand. When in doubt of specific rules, contact your legal department or attorney, or call your local SAG representative.

SCREEN ACTORS GUILD OFFICES

NATIONAL HEADQUARTERS
5757 Wilshire Boulevard
Los Angeles, CA 90036-3600

Main Switchboard	(213) 954-1600
(open 9 a.m. til 5 p.m.)	
Theatrical Contracts	(213) 549-6828
Television Contracts	(213) 549-6835
Production Services	(213) 549-6811

Station 12	(213) 549-6794
(open 9 a.m. til 6:30 p.m.)	
SAG Extras	(213) 549-6811
Residuals	(213) 549-6505
Signatory Status	(213) 549-6869
Affirmative Action	(213) 549-6644
Actors to Locate	(213) 549-6737
Agent Contracts	(213) 549-6745
Legal Affairs	(213) 549-6627
Industrial/Ed-Interactive	(213) 549-6850

ARIZONA
1616 E. Indian School Rd., Suite 330
Phoenix, AZ 85016
Phone: (602) 265-2712;   Fax: (602) 264-7571

BOSTON
11 Beacon Street, Room 512
Boston, MA 02108
Phone: (617) 742-2688;   Fax: (617) 742-4904

CHICAGO
75 E. Wacker Drive, 14th Floor
Chicago, IL 60601
Phone: (312) 372-8081;   Fax: (312) 372-5025

CLEVELAND*
1030 Euclid Ave, 429
Cleveland, OH 44114
Phone: (216) 579-9305;   Fax: (216) 781-2257

COLORADO, NEVADA, NEW MEXICO, UTAH
950 South Cherry Street, Suite 502
Denver, CO 80222
Phone: (303) 757-6226;   Fax: (303) 757-1769
        (800) 527-7517

DALLAS-FORT WORTH
6060 N. Central Expressway, Suite 302, LB 604
Dallas, TX 75206-5293
Phone: (214) 363-8300;   Fax: (214) 363-5386

DETROIT
28690 Southfield Road, #290A&B
Lathrup Village, MI 48076
Phone: (810) 559-9540;   Fax: (810) 559-7163
Hotline: (810) 559-0703

FLORIDA
7300 N. Kendall Drive, #620
Miami, FL 33156-7840
Phone: (305) 670-7677;   Fax: (305) 670-1813

GEORGIA
455 E. Paces Ferry Road, N.E., #334
Atlanta, GA 30305
Phone: (404) 239-0131, ext. 10;
Fax: (404) 239-0137

HAWAII
949 Kapiolani Blvd., Suite 105
Honolulu, HI 96814
Phone: (808) 596-0388;   Fax: (808) 593-2636
Hotline: (808) 956-0389

HOLLYWOOD
5757 Wilshire Blvd.
Los Angeles, CA 90036-3600
Phone: (213) 549-6612;   Fax: (213) 549-6603

HOUSTON
2650 Fountainview Dr., Suite 326
Houston, TX 77057
Phone: (713) 972-1806;   Fax: (713) 780-0261

MINNEAPOLIS*
708 N. First Street, #343A
Minneapolis, MN 55401
Phone: (612) 371-9120;   Fax: (612) 371-9119

NASHVILLE
P.O. Box 121087
Nashville, TN 37212
Phone: (615) 327-2944;   Fax: (615) 329-2803

NEW YORK HEADQUARTERS
1515 Broadway, 44th Floor
New York, NY 10036
Phone: (212) 827-1474;   Fax: (212) 944-6774

PHILADELPHIA
230 South Broad Street, 10th Floor
Philadelphia, PA 19102
Phone: (215) 545-3150;   Fax: (215) 732-0086

SAN DIEGO
7827 Convoy Court, #400
San Diego, CA 92111
Phone: (619) 278-7695;   Fax: (619) 278-2505

SAN FRANCISCO
235 Pine Street, 11th Floor
San Francisco, CA 94104
Phone: (415) 391-7373, ext. 315;
Fax: (415) 391-1108
General Number: (415) 391-7510

SEATTLE*
601 Valley Street, Suite 100
Seattle, WA 98109
Phone: (206) 282-2506;   Fax: (206) 282-7073

ST. LOUIS*
906 Olive Street, Suite 1006
St. Louis, MO 63101
Phone: (314) 231-8410;   Fax: (314) 231-8412

WASHINGTON, D.C./BALTIMORE
4340 East West Highway, #204
Bethesda, MD 20814
Phone: (301) 657-2560;   Fax: (301) 656-3615

* These are AFTRA offices that also administer SAG contracts.

CHAPTER EIGHT

Standard Production Forms and Formats

The following are examples of some of the most frequently used standard production forms and samples of how to do a shooting schedule, one-line schedule, crew list, cast list, and contact list, all of which are used on every show.

COMPUTER SOFTWARE

A few of the computer software programs that will break down your script and automatically produce a day-out-of-days, shooting schedule, and one-liner are *Movie Magic Scheduling/Breakdown* by Screenplay Systems, *Production Scheduler* by MacTool Kit, and *Turbo A.D.* by Quantum Films. *Film Works* by Carlan, Graham & Associates offers both hardware and software that will not only schedule your film but will generate call sheets and production reports as well. (Most of these companies also provide budgeting programs.) For those who wish to go through the process manually, the forms you will need are in this chapter.

Not included in this chapter are certain accounting forms, including *cash flow* and *cost report* formats. These forms can be found in one of five or six excellent production accounting software programs that are available through the major payroll companies, each having developed its own program. You can lease one of the software packages without engaging the services of the respective payroll company; but if you do use the payroll service, the software is made

available to you at no additional charge. Discuss the options with your production accountant, who will probably have a preference for both a particular payroll company and a corresponding software package.

SCRIPT REVISIONS

The term *final draft* almost never means final. It would be ideal if all script changes could be made in the early stages of pre-production, but reality is that changes (even if they are small ones) are often made not only up to, but also throughout, principal photography. Script revisions need to be indicated in a precise manner in order for everyone to know if and how each change will affect them or their department.

It is not necessary to run off entire new scripts every time there are changes. The accepted standard is to distribute colored change pages. For example, the first set of change pages are copied onto blue paper, the second set onto pink, and so forth. The color progression runs *white, blue, pink, yellow, green, goldenrod, buff, salmon, cherry, tan, gray, and ivory.* Once you have gone through each color and eleven sets of script revisions, you could begin again by using white change pages, then blue, then pink, etc. Some studios have made it a practice to come out with an entire blue-paged script once the original script has gone through all eleven sets of multicolored revision pages. Changes to a blue script would start with pink pages, and continue to progress through the same cycle of colors.

Just as important as the various colors are to differentiate between sets of changes, it is also very important to indicate the changes by typing *Revised/(date)* at the top left-hand corner of every change page and by indicating the individual changes with asterisks (*) in the right-hand margin next to the specific line where the change occurs. When a scene is omitted, the scene number remains in the script with the word *omitted* typed next to it and an asterisk in the right margin.

Once a show has been scheduled, do not change the scene numbers. If you wish to add a scene, for example, between scenes 4 and 5, you would number the new scene, *4A*. An addition to that would be scene 4B, and so on. In the same vein, do not change the page numbers. If you want to lengthen a scene that appears on page 20 and now runs a page-and-a-half, do not disturb page 21, but instead type the additional half-page onto a new page that is numbered *21A*. All new pages and scene numbers are also to be noted with asterisks.

Your *script supervisor* will keep track of all *revised* page counts and the revised number of scenes on his or her daily log, which will in turn be transferred to the daily production report. With each set of new pages, members of the cast and crew insert each of the latest pages into their scripts, replacing the original white or outdated colored change pages. By the time most shows have completed filming, the scripts are rainbow-colored.

When change pages are generated, it is imperative that they are distributed to the people who need them immediately. In addition to the producer(s), director, and production manager, the first assistant director will need to know if and how these changes will affect the schedule; the casting director and/or specific cast members will need to know if there are changes in their dialogue; and the location manager will need to know if any location has been deleted or a new one added. The same will be true for each department head. Will new equipment or props have to be ordered? Will more or less extras be needed? Again, changes need to be distributed to those who need them as soon as possible.

Once a show has finished filming and post production is completed, a truly *final* script is generated. It is called a *continuity script* and contains the exact (word-for-word) dialogue and action as it appears in the final cut version of the picture. Continuity scripts are for purposes of distribution and are required as part of your delivery requirements.

BREAKDOWN SHEET

BREAKDOWN PAGE # __3__

SHOW __HERBY'S SUMMER VACATION__ PRODUCTION # __0100__
EPISODE __"BOYS NIGHT OUT"__ DATE __5/17/XX__
LOCATION __SWEETWATER ROAD — HOLLYWOOD LAKE__

SCENE #'S	DESCRIPTION	NO. OF PAGES
	(INT)(EXT) ROAD LEADING TO LAKE (DAY)(NIGHT)	
6	THE BOYS WALK TO THE LAKE	1/8
7	THE BOYS SPOT LAURA SUNBATHING	1/8
8 & 9	THE BOYS HIDE & WATCH LAURA	5/8
	TOTAL	7/8

NO.	CAST	BITS/DOUBLES	ATMOSPHERE
1.	HERBY		6 SUNBATHERS
3.	LAURA		MAN WALKING DOG
6.	MARC		2 KIDS PLAYING BALL
7.	JED	WARDROBE	PROPS/SET DRESSING
		BOYS IN T-SHIRTS & SHORTS LAURA IN WHITE BIKINI	BEACH CHAIRS UMBRELLAS / BALL SUNTAN LOTION SUNGLASSES
		SPEC. EFFECTS	TRANS/PIC VEHICLES
			LAURA'S CAR PARKED ON SIDE OF ROAD

STUNTS	MUSIC/SOUND/CAMERA	WRANGLERS/LIVESTOCK
		N.D. DOG

HAIR/MAKE-UP	SPECIAL REQUIREMENTS
CUT ON HERBY'S HAND	DOG TRAINER

© ELH Form #05

DAY-OUT-OF-DAYS

PRODUCTION COMPANY __XYZ PRODUCTIONS__
PRODUCTION TITLE __HERBY'S SUMMER VACATION__
EPISODE TITLE __"BOY'S NIGHT OUT"__
PRODUCTION # __0100__
SCRIPT DATED __FEB. 16, 19XX__

DATE __JUNE 1, 19XX__
PRODUCER __SWIFTY DEALS__
DIRECTOR __SID CELLULOID__
UNIT PRODUCTION MGR. __FRED FILMER__
FIRST ASST. DIRECTOR __A. DEES__

MONTH →		JUNE													JULY								
DAY OF WEEK →		F	S	S	M	T	W	TH	F	S	S	M	T	W	TH	F	S						
(date)		18	19	20	21	22	23	24	25	26	27	28	29	30	1	2	3	TRAVEL	START	FINISH	WORK	IDLE	TOTAL
SHOOTING DAYS →		1	2	3	4	5	6	7	8	9	10	11	12	13	14								
#	NAME / CHARACTER																						
1	CLARK GRABLE — HERBY	TR/S	W	W	W	W	W	H	W	W		W	W	H	W	W	TR/F	2	6/18	7/3	10	2	14
2	ROCKY RIZZO — JAKE	TR/S	W	W	H	H	H	W	H	H		H	H	W	W	W	TR/F	2	6/18	7/3	7	5	14
3	SCARLET STARLET — LAURA			TR/S	W	W	W	W	W	W		W	TR/F					2	6/21	6/30	6	1	9
4	NANCY NICELY — MOM			TR/S	W	W	H	H	H	W		W	W	H	W	TR/F		2	6/21	7/2	5	4	11
5	HOLLYWOOD MANN — GEORGE							TR/F										2	6/22	6/26	3	—	5
6	KENNY SMILES — MARC			TR/S	W	W	W	H	W	TR/F		W	TR/F					2	6/21	6/29	4	2	8
7	LLOYD NELSON — POLICE SGT.			TR/S	W	W	W	H	H	W		W	TR/F					2	6/21	6/29	4	2	8
8	RAYMOND BURRMAN — ELLIOT							SU/F										1	6/24	6/24	1	—	1

© ELH Form #06

CALL SHEET

PRODUCTION COMPANY _XYZ PRODUCTIONS, INC._
SHOW _HERBY'S SUMMER VACATION_
SERIES EPISODE _____
PROD# _0100_   DAY # _6_   OUT OF _8_
IS TODAY A DESIGNATED DAY OFF? ☐ YES ☑ NO
CREW CALL _7A_
LEAVING CALL _—_
SHOOTING CALL _8:30 A_

DATE _FRIDAY, JULY 2, 19XX_
DIRECTOR _SID CELLULOID_
PRODUCER _SWIFTY DEALS_
LOCATION _SWEETWATER RD - HOLLYWOOD_
SUNRISE _6:20A_ SUNSET _7:40P_
ANTICIPATED WEATHER _85°_

☐ Weather Permitting
☑ Report to Location

☑ See Attached Map
☐ Bus to Location

Set Description	Scene Nos.	Cast	D/N	Pages	Location
					HOLLYWOOD LAKE
EXT. ROAD TO LAKE (BOYS ON WAY TO LAKE)	6	1,6,7	D	1/8	
EXT. BUSHES (BOYS WATCH LAURA)	7,8,9	1,3,6,7	D	6/8	
EXT. LAKE (GEORGE JOINS LAURA)	10,11	3,5	D	3 2/8	↓
			TOTAL:	4 1/8 PGS.	

Cast	Part Of	Leave	Makeup	Set Call	Remarks
CLARK GRABLE	HERBY (1)	7:15A	8A	8:30A	TO BE PICKED UP @ 7A
SCARLET STARLET	LAURA (3)	6:30A	7A	9:30A	TO BE PICKED UP @ 6:15A
HOLLYWOOD MANN (NEW)	GEORGE (5)	—	9A	10A	REPORT TO LOC.
KENNY SMILES	MARC (6)	—	8A	8:30A	REPORT TO LOC.
WILL PERFORMER	JED (7)	—	8A	8:30A	REPORT TO LOC.

Atmosphere & Stand-ins	
3 STANDINS	REPORT TO LOC @ 7:30A
6 SUNBATHERS	
1 MAN WALKING DOG	
2 KIDS PLAYING BALL	

NOTE: No forced calls without previous approval of unit production manager or assistant director.   All calls subject to change.

Advance Schedule Or Changes

MON. 7-5-XX
INT. HERBY'S BEDROOM (N) SCS. 5, 8, 115 THRU 123   STG. 14
INT. HERBY'S KITCHEN (N) SCS. 7, 14, 15, 22
INT. HERBY'S FRONT DOOR (N) SC. 73

Assistant Director _Alice Dees_   Production Manager _Fred Filmer_

PRODUCTION REQUIREMENT

SHOW: HERBY'S SUMMER VACATION   PROD #: 0100   DATE: 7.2.XX

NO.	STAFF & CREW	TIME	NO.	STAFF & CREW	TIME	NO.	EQUIPMENT	
1	Production Mgr. FILMER	7A	1	Gaffer	7A	2	Cameras PANAFLEX	
1	1st Asst. Dir. DEES	7A	1	Best Boy			ARRI	
1	2nd Asst. Dir. DURHAM	6:30A	1	Lamp Oper.		1	Dolly CHAPMAN	
1	2nd 2nd Asst. Dir. T.C.	6:30A	1	Lamp Oper.			Crane	
	DGA Trainee			Lamp Oper.			Condor	
1	Script Supervisor KANDU	8A		Local 40 Man				
1	Dialogue Coach WILKES	8A					Sound Channel	
1	Prod. Coordinator	8A	1	Prod. Designer			Video	
1	Prod. Sect'y	8A	1	Art Director				
1	Prod. Accountant	8A		Asst. Art Dir.				
1	Asst. Accountant	8A	1	Set Designer			Radio Mikes	
1	Location Manager	6:30A		Sketch Artist		8	Walkie/talkies	
1	Asst. Location Mgr.	6:30A						
1	Teacher/Welfare Worker	8A	1	Const. Coord.		5	Dressing Rooms	
3	Production Assts.	6:30A	1	Const. Foreman		1	Schoolrooms	
				Paint Foreman		1	Rm. for Parents	
1	Dir. of Photography			Labor Foremen				
1	Camera Operator			Const. First Aid			Projector	
1	Camera Operator						Moviola	
	SteadyCam Operator		1	Set Decorator				
1	Asst. Cameraman		1	Lead Person			Air Conditioners	
1	Asst. Cameraman			Swing Crew			Heaters	
	Asst. Cameraman			Swing Crew			Wind Machines	
1	Still Photographer			Swing Crew				
	Cameraman-Process			Drapery				
	Projectionist							
1	VIDEO ASSIST	7:30A		Technical Advisor			SUPPORT	
1	Mixer			Publicist			PERSONNEL	TIME
1	Boomman			MEALS			Policemen	
1	Cableman			Caterer			Motorcycles	
	Playback		25	Breakfasts ND READY @	7A		Fireman	
	Video Oper.			Wlkg. Breakfasts rdy @			Guard	
			10	Gals. Coffee			Night Watchman	
1	Key Grip		75	Lunches rdy @ 12N Crew @ 1P				
1	2nd Grip			Box Lunches				
1	Dolly Grip			Second Meal				
1	Grip							
1	Grip							
	Grip			DRIVERS			VEHICLES	
			1	Trans. Coord.	6A	1	Prod. Van	
	Greensman		1	Trans. Capt.	6A	1	Camera	
			1	Driver	6:30A		Grip	
	S/By Painter		1	Driver			Electric	
1	Craftservice		1	Driver			Effects	
1	First Aid		1	Driver		1	Props	
			1	Driver		1	Wardrobe	
	Spec. Efx		1	Driver		1	Makeup	
	Spec. Efx		1	Driver		1	Set Dressing	
			1	Driver			Crew Bus	
1	Propmaster		1	Driver		1	Honeywagon	
1	Asst. Props		1	Driver		2	Motorhomes	
	Asst. Props		1	Driver		1	Station Wagons	
			1	Driver		2	Mini-buses	
1	Costume Designer		1	Driver			Standby Cars	
	Costume Supervisor		1	Driver			Crew Cabs	
1	Costumer		1	Driver			Insert Cars	
1	Costumer		1	Driver		1	Generators	
			1	Driver			Water Wagon	
1	Makeup Artist	6:30A	1	Driver		1	Picture Cars	
	Makeup Artist		1	Driver			LAURA'S CAR	
1	Body Makeup							
1	Hairstylist			Stunt Coord.				
	Hairstylist			Wranglers				
			1	Animal Handlers	8A		Livestock	
1	Editor	D/C				1	Animals ND DOG	
1	Asst. Editor							
	Apprentice Editor							

DEPARTMENT	SPECIAL INSTRUCTIONS
PROPS / SET DRESSING	BEACH CHAIRS, UMBRELLAS, BALL, SUNTAN LOTION, SUNGLASSES
MAKEUP	BODY MAKEUP FOR LAURA

© ELH Form #07A

DAILY PRODUCTION REPORT

	1st Unit	2nd Unit	Reh.	Test	Travel	Holidays	Change Over	Retakes & Add. Scs.	Total	Schedule	
No. Days Sched	30	4			2				36		Ahead
No. Days Actual	6				1				7		Behind

Title: **HERBY'S SUMMER VACATION** Prod. # **0100** Date **MON., JUNE 7, 19XX**
Producer: **SWIFTY DEALS** Director: **SID CELLULOID**
Date Started: **6-1-XX** Scheduled Finish Date: **7-16-XX** Est. Finish Date: **7-16-XX**

Sets: **(EXT.) ROAD & FENCE ALONG LAURA'S HOUSE - (EXT.) LAKE SHORE**
Location: **SWEETWATER RD. - HOLLYWOOD LAKE**
Crew Call: **7A** Shooting Call: **8:30A** First Shot: **9:30A** Lunch: **1:30P** Til: **2P**
1st Shot After Lunch ____ 2nd Meal ____ Til ____ Camera Wrap ____ Last Man Out ____
Company dismissed at ☐ Studio ☑ Location ☐ Headquarters Round Trip Mileage **18 MI.** Is Today A Designated Day Off? ☐ YES ☑ NO

SCRIPT SCENES AND PAGES			MINUTES		SETUPS		ADDED SCENES		RETAKES		
										PAGES	SCENES
	SCENES	PAGES	Prev.	31:37	Prev.	83	Prev.	4	Prev.	4 1/8	3
			Today	2:15	Today	23	Today	0	Today	4/8	1
Script	215	117 6/8	Total	33:52	Total	106	Total	4	Total	45/8	4
Taken Prev.	76	35 5/8	Scene No.	3, 4, 5, 26, 27, 30							
Taken Today	6	5 3/8									
Total to Date	82	40 5/8	Added Scenes								
To be Taken	133	77 1/8	Retakes	Sc. 15			Sound Tracks				

FILM STOCK	FILM USE	GROSS	PRINT	NO GOOD	WASTE	1/4" ROLLS	FILM INVENTORY 5296	
5296	Prev.					10	Starting Inv.	20,000
	Today					2	Additional Rec'd.	0
							Today	0
	To Date					12	Total	20,000

FILM STOCK	FILM USE	GROSS	PRINT	NO GOOD	WASTE		FILM INVENTORY 5293	
5293	Prev.	21,386	12,860	5,536	2,990		Starting Inv.	10,260
	Today	4,730	1,850	1,150	610		Additional Rec'd.	0
							Today	3,610
	To Date	26,116	14,710	6,686	3,600		Total	6,650

FILM STOCK	FILM USE	GROSS	PRINT	NO GOOD	WASTE		FILM INVENTORY 5247	
5247	Prev.						Starting Inv.	18,250
	Today						Additional Rec'd.	0
							Today	0
	To Date						Total	18,250

CAST - WEEKLY & DAY PLAYERS
Worked - W Rehearsal - R Finished - F
Started - S Hold - H Test - T
Travel - TR

CAST	CHARACTER	W H S F R T TR	MAKEUP WDBE.	REPORT ON SET	DISMISS ON SET	OUT	IN	LEAVE FOR LOC.	ARRIVE ON LOC.	LEAVE LOCATION	ARRIVE AT HDQ.	STUNT ADJ.
CLARK GRABLE	HERBY	W	8A	8:30A	6P	1:30P	2P	7A	8A	6:15P	7:15P	
SCARLET STARLET	LAURA (XX)	W	7:30A	10A	8P	1:30P	2P	6:45A	7:30A	8:15P	9P	
HOLLYWOOD MANN	GEORGE	SW	9A	10A	8P	1:30P	2P					
KENNY SMILES	MARC	W	8A	8:30A	6P	1:30P	2P					
WILL PERFORMER	JED	W	8A	8:30A	6P	1:30P	2P					

XX = N.D. BREAKFAST * = DISMISS TIME INCLUDES 15 MIN. MAKEUP / WARD. REMOVAL
X = NOT PHOTOGRAPHED S = SCHOOL ONLY

EXTRA TALENT

No.	Rate	1st Call	Set Dismiss	Final Dismiss	Adj.	MPV	No.	Rate	1st Call	Set Dismiss	Final Dismiss	Adj.	MPV
3	SCALE	7:30A	8P		+ WARD								
2	SCALE	10A	2P										
1	SCALE	10A	2:30P		+ WARD								
1	SCALE	8A	8P										

Assistant Director _(signature)_ Production Manager _(signature)_
© ELH Form #08

Standard Production Forms and Formats **103**

SHOW: HERBY'S SUMMER VACATION PROD #: 0100 DATE: 6·7·XX

NO.	STAFF & CREW	TIME	NO.	STAFF & CREW	TIME	NO.	EQUIPMENT
1	Production Mgr. F. FILMER	7A	1	Gaffer		1	Cameras PANAFLEX
1	1st Asst. Dir. A. DEES	7A	1	Best Boy		1	ARRI
1	2nd Asst. Dir. R. DURHAM	6:30A	1	Lamp Oper.		1	Dolly CHAPMAN
1	2nd 2nd Asst. Dir. T.C.	6:30A	1	Lamp Oper.			Crane
	DGA Trainee		1	Lamp Oper.			Condor
1	Script Supervisor K. KANDU	8A		Local 40 Man			
1	Dialogue Coach A. WILKES	8A					Sound Channel
1	Prod. Coordinator C. COORDINATES	8A	1	Prod. Designer			
1	Prod. Sect'y G. AIDES	7:30A	1	Art Director			Video
1	Prod. Accountant AARON A.	8A	1	Asst. Art Dir.			
1	Asst. Accountant	8A	1	Set Designer			Radio Mikes
1	Location Manager B. SCOUT	6:30A	1	Sketch Artist		8	Walkie/talkies
1	Asst. Location Mgr. BOBS.	6:30A	1				
1	Teacher/Welfare Worker	8A	1	Const. Coord.		5	Dressing Rooms
3	Production Assts. JONES,	6:30A	1	Const. Foreman		1	Schoolrooms
	SMITH, MILLER		1	Paint Foreman		1	Rm. for Parents
1	Dir. of Photography F. STOPP	7:30A	1	Labor Foremen			
1	Camera Operator S. SHUTTER	7:30A	1	Const. First Aid			Projector
	Camera Operator						Moviola
	SteadyCam Operator		1	Set Decorator			
1	Asst. Cameraman		1	Lead Person			Air Conditioners
1	Asst. Cameraman		1	Swing Crew			Heaters
1	Asst. Cameraman		1	Swing Crew			Wind Machines
1	Still Photographer		1	Swing Crew			
	Cameraman-Process			Drapery			
1	Projectionist						
				Technical Advisor			SUPPORT
1	Mixer			Publicist			PERSONNEL / TIME
1	Boomman			MEALS		2	Policemen 6:30A
1	Cableman			Caterer	6:30A	2	Motorcycles 6:30A
	Playback		25	Breakfasts			Fireman
	Video Oper.		120	Wlkg. Breakfasts rdy @		1	Guard
			15	Gals. Coffee		1	Night Watchman
1	Key Grip			Lunches rdy @ Crew @			
1	2nd Grip			Box Lunches			
1	Dolly Grip			Second Meal			
1	Grip						
1	Grip						
1	Grip			DRIVERS			VEHICLES
			1	Trans. Coord.		1	Prod. Van
1	Greensman		1	Trans. Capt.		1	Camera
			1	Driver		1	Grip
1	S/By Painter		1	Driver		1	Electric
1	Craftservice		1	Driver			Effects
1	First Aid		1	Driver		1	Props
			1	Driver		1	Wardrobe
1	Spec. Efx		1	Driver		1	Makeup
1	Spec. Efx		1	Driver		1	Set Dressing
			1	Driver			Crew Bus
1	Propmaster		1	Driver		1	Honeywagon
1	Asst. Props		1	Driver		2	Motorhomes
1	Asst. Props		1	Driver		1	Station Wagons
			1	Driver		2	Mini-buses
1	Costume Designer		1	Driver		2	Standby Cars
	Costume Supervisor		1	Driver			Crew Cabs
1	Costumer		1	Driver			Insert Cars
1	Costumer		1	Driver		2	Generators
			1	Driver		1	Water Wagon
1	Makeup Artist		1	Driver		2	Picture Cars
	Makeup Artist		1	Driver			LAURA'S CAR
	Body Makeup						GEORGE'S CAR
1	Hairstylist			Stunt Coord.			
1	Hairstylist			Wranglers			
				Animal Handlers			Livestock
1	Editor					1	Animals NO DOG
1	Asst. Editor						
1	Apprentice Editor						

COMMENTS-DELAYS (EXPLANATIONS)-CAST, STAFF & CREW ABSENCE

- SCARLET STARLET 30 MIN. LATE TO SET
- MACINTOSH COMPUTER w/ MONITOR & KEYBOARD DISCOVERED MISSING FROM HERBY'S BEDROOM SET. POLICE REPORT FORTHCOMING.

- NO ACCIDENTS REPORTED TODAY

© ELH Form #08A

CHECK REQUEST

SHOW __HERBY'S SUMMER VACATION__   PROD # __0100__

COMPANY __XYZ PRODUCTIONS__

ADDRESS __1234 FLICK DRIVE__   PHONE #__(213) 555-3331__

__HOLLYWOOD, CA 90038__   FAX #__(213) 555-3332__

DATE __6·10·XX__   AMOUNT $ __180—__

CHECK PAYEE __CAL'S COMPUTER CENTER__

ADDRESS __9876 FLORES ST.__

__STUDIO VILLAGE, CA 90000__

PHONE # __(818) 555-1000__   FAX # __(818) 555-1003__

ATTN: __CAL__

PAYEE SS # OR FED. I.D. # __95-3654 21769__

DESCRIPTION	CODING	AMOUNT
2 MONTH RENTAL OF	865-55	$90— PER MO.
HP LASER JET PRINTER		
(STARTS 6·15·XX) FOR		
USE BY ACCNTG. DEPT.		

TAX: _____

TOTAL: $ __180—__

☐ PURCHASE
☑ RENTAL   CHECK NEEDED: ☐ IMMEDIATELY
☐ DEPOSIT   ☑ WITHIN NEXT DAY OR TWO
☐ ADVANCE   ☐ WITHIN NORMAL PROCESSING TIME
☐ 1099
☐ INVENTORY

WHEN READY: ☐ PLEASE MAIL CHECK
          ☑ PLEASE GIVE CHECK TO __CINDY FIGURES__

CHECK REQUESTED BY __AARON ACCOUNTANT__   DEPT. __ACCOUNTING__

APPROVED BY __Fred Filmer__   DATE __6·12·XX__

(INVOICE SUBSTANTIATION MUST FOLLOW THIS REQUEST)

PAID BY CHECK # __1327__   DATE __6·15·XX__

© ELH Form #09

PURCHASE ORDER

DATE JUNE 14, 19XX

P.O. # 0125

SHOW HERBY'S SUMMER VACATION

PROD # 0100

COMPANY XYZ PRODUCTIONS

ADDRESS 1234 FLICK DR.

HOLLYWOOD, CA 90038

PHONE # (213) 555-3331

FAX # (213) 555-3332

VENDOR EASTERN COSTUME CO.

ADDRESS 123 HOLLYWOOD WAY

HOLLYWOOD, CA 90028

PHONE # (818) 555-0900

FAX # (818) 555-0901

CONTACT LULU

VENDOR SS # OR FED. I.D. # 95-76513215

☐ PURCHASE   ☑ RENTAL   ☐ SERVICE

DESCRIPTION	CODING	AMOUNT
ASSORTED T-SHIRTS & SHORTS		
FOR HERBY, MARC & JED	831-56	$75
TATTERED CLOTHES FOR JAKE	831-56	$25

INCL. TAX IF APPLICABLE: _____

SET #(s) _____

TOTAL COST: $ 100

Per Show ☐
Day ☐
Week ☑
Month ☐

IF TOTAL COST CANNOT BE DETERMINED
AT THIS DATE, ESTIMATE OF COSTS WILL
NOT EXCEED $ _____

IF P.O. IS FOR A <u>RENTAL</u>, PLEASE ESTIMATE DATE OF RETURN 7·10·XX

ORDER PLACED BY FRIEDA FITTER

DEPT. WARDROBE

APPROVED BY Fred Filmer

DATE 6·15·XX

cc: Vendor (Orig)   Accounting Dept.
      Production Manager   Department Head

© ELH Form #10

PETTY CASH ACCOUNTING

ENVELOPE # 1

NAME PAULA PROPPS   SHOW HERBY'S SUMMER VACATION   AMOUNT RECEIVED $ 500.— *   DATE 6/9/XX

DEPARTMENT PROPERTY   FROM JUNE 1, 19 XX   TO JUNE 8, 19 XX   CHECK # 0037

DATE	NO.	PAID TO	FOR	ACCOUNT	AMOUNT
6/1	1	ACE SPORTING GOODS	BASKETBALL		$ 23.50
6/2	2	JOE'S MARKET	CANNED FOOD		15.37
6/2	3	SHADES INC.	SUNGLASSES		62.05
6/3	4	FOOD-TO-GO	COOKED DINNER		130.63
6/4	5	AL'S DRUGS	SUNTAN LOTION		6.52
6/4	6	ABC DEPT. STORE	MAKE-UP		53.17
6/5	7	BED & BATH SHOP	BEACH TOWELS		33.64
6/5	8	RALPH'S OPTICAL CO.	LAURA'S GLASSES		150.06
6/6	9	AL'S DRUGS	CIGARETTES		10.36
6/7	10	ELMER'S ELECTRONICS	WALKMAN		25.17
6/8	11	ACE SPORTING GOODS	BAT/BALL		28.39
6/8	12	HARRY'S HARDWARE	SHOVEL		43.21
6/8	13	JOE'S MARKET	SOFT DRINKS		27.09
6/8	14	PICNICS GALORE	COOLERS		
				TOTAL: **	$ 609.16

FOR ACCOUNTING USE ONLY

ACCOUNT	AMOUNT

AMOUNT ADVANCED* $ 500.—

TOTAL ACCOUNTED FOR** $ 609.16

CASH ON HAND   -OR-

AMT. TO BE REIMBURSED $ 109.16

NOTE: EACH RECEIPT SHOULD BE CLEARLY LABELED WITH A DATE AND DESCRIPTION AS TO WHAT THEY ARE FOR AND ATTACHED IN THE SAME ORDER IN WHICH THEY APPEAR ON THE ENVELOPE.

APPROVED _Bill Filmer_

AUDITED _Aaron Accountant_   ENTERED 6/10/XX

SIGNATURE _Paula Propps_

PETTY CASH ADVANCE/REIMBURSEMENT		
RECEIVED IN CASH $ 609.16	ON 6/10 , 19 XX	

© ELH Form #11

```
AMOUNT $ 400—                          NO. 27

              RECEIVED OF PETTY CASH

                                DATE  5·25·XX

NAME _____ FRIEDA FITTER _____

DEPARTMENT ___ WARDROBE _____

DESCRIPTION _____
_____
_____
_____

☑ PETTY CASH TO BE ACCOUNTED FOR

APPROVED BY                    RECEIVED BY
Fred Filmer, UPM               Frieda Fitter
© ELH Form #12
```

"HERBY'S SUMMER VACATION" - PROD # 0100

SHOOTING SCHEDULE

PRODUCER:	SWIFTY DEALS	<u>FILM SHOOTS - 36 DAYS</u>:
DIRECTOR:	SID CELLULOID	TUESDAY, JUNE 1, 19XX
PRODUCTION MANAGER:	FRED FILMER	THROUGH
1ST ASST. DIRECTOR:	A. DEES	FRIDAY, JULY 17, 19XX

DATE	SET/SCENES	CAST	LOCATION
1ST DAY TUESDAY 6/1/9X	<u>EXT. LAUREL ROAD</u> - D D-1 1 1/8 Pg. Scs. 6,7,8 The boys discover a hole in the fence and look through to the other side. <u>NOTES</u>:	1. HERBY 3. JED 4. MARC <u>ATMOS</u> 2 elderly ladies (passers-by) <u>VEHICLES</u> old truck next to fence	SWEETWATER ROAD PACIFIC PALISADES <u>PROPS</u> Marc's ball <u>WARDROBE/MAKEUP</u> Herby's cut hand
	<u>EXT. LAURA'S BACKYARD</u> D-1 1 4/8 Pgs. Scs. 9 & 10 The boys see Laura sunbathing by her pool. <u>NOTES</u>:	1. HERBY 2. LAURA 3. JED 4. MARC <u>VEHICLES</u> Laura's Mercedes (in driveway)	(SAME AS ABOVE) <u>PROPS</u> Towel Makeup bag Laura's sunglasses <u>WARDROBE/MAKEUP</u> Laura's white bikini <u>SPEC. EFX</u> Light steam off pool
	<u>EXT. LAURA'S BACKYARD</u> D-1 2 4/8 Pgs. Sc. 11 Steve joins Laura and chases the boys away from the fence. <u>NOTES</u>:	1. HERBY 2. LAURA 3. JED 4. MARC 7. STEVE <u>VEHICLES</u> Laura's Mercedes Steve's BMW	(SAME AS ABOVE) <u>PROPS</u> Same as above <u>WARDROBE/MAKEUP</u> Steve in sport shirt and jacket

END OF DAY #1	TOTAL PAGES:	5 1/8

"HERBY'S SUMMER VACATION" - PROD# 0100

ONE-LINE SCHEDULE

PRODUCER:	SWIFTY DEALS
DIRECTOR:	SID CELLULOID
PRODUCTION MANAGER:	FRED FILMER
1ST ASST. DIRECTOR:	A. DEES

FILM SHOOTS - 36 DAYS:
TUESDAY, JUNE 1, 19XX
THROUGH
FRIDAY, JULY 16, 19XX

FIRST DAY - TUESDAY, JUNE. 1, 19XX

Sc.   1   EXT. PIER AT SUNRISE - D 1/8 pg.
Sunrise over pier and Venice Beach

Scs.   2-13   EXT. VENICE BEACH - D 1 6/8 pgs.
Steve jogs

Sc.   23   EXT. FRONT OF HOTEL - D 1/8 pg.
Steve jogs up to front of hotel

Scs. 46-52   EXT. STRAND VENICE - D 2 3/8 pgs.
Steve greets friends on way out
to jog. He smiles at Laura

Scs. 87-90   EXT. VENICE STRAND - D 6/8 pg.
Nick and Cory walk together

Sc.   95   EXT. VENICE STRAND - D 4/8 pg.
Steve & Laura talk to Herby

Sc.   101   INT. VENICE RESTAURANT - D 1/8 pg.
Inside - people wave hello to
Steve & Laura

Sc.   91   EXT. STRAND AREA (NEAR PIER) - D 6/8 pg.
Marc skates for them

END OF FIRST DAY	**TOTAL PAGES:**	**6 4/8 pgs.**

SECOND DAY - WEDNESDAY, JUNE, 2, 19XX

Sc.   60   INT. GIFT SHOP - D 3/8 pg.
George spots Steve & Laura outside

Sc.   61   EXT. BEACH - VENICE STRAND - D 4 3/8 pgs.
Steve gets dope on horse from Jake

Scs. 63 & 64   EXT. BIKE PATH - VENICE - D 1 5/8 pgs.
Steve & Laura ride on bicycle-
built-for-two

Sc.   66   EXT. BIKE PATH - VENICE - D 1/8 pg.
George's POV of Steve & Laura on
bicycle - from high window

END OF SECOND DAY	**TOTAL PAGES:**	**6 4/8 pgs.**

CREW LIST

9/15/XX

XYZ Productions
1234 Flick Drive
(213) 555-3331 (phone); (213) 555-3332 (fax)
HERBY'S SUMMER VACATION -- Production No. 0100

EXECUTIVE PRODUCER	MARVIN MOGUL 555 School Street Los Angeles, CA 90001	Office: Home: Pager:	(213) 555-7250 (818) 555-5554 (213) 555-1166
PRODUCER	SWIFTY DEALS 12353 Rhodes Ave. Toluca Lake, CA 91150	Office: Home: Car:	(213) 555-7254 (714) 555-0897 (213) 207-5687
DIRECTOR	SID CELLULOID 2764 Carson Street Valencia, CA 90477	Fax:	(818) 555-6033 (818) 555-6031

(Continue listing information for each crew member as indicated above. The EXECUTIVE PRODUCER, PRODUCER, DIRECTOR, ASSOCIATE PRODUCER, PRODUCTION MANAGER, ASSISTANT DIRECTORS, and the PRODUCTION COORDINATOR are generally positioned first. There are no set rules to prioritize the order of the remaining crew, although departments should be grouped together, with the department head listed first.)

ASSOCIATE PRODUCER
PRODUCTION MANAGER
1ST ASSISTANT DIRECTOR
2ND ASSISTANT DIRECTOR
PRODUCTION COORDINATOR
PRODUCTION ACCOUNTANT
ASSISTANT ACCOUNTANT
SCRIPT SUPERVISOR
CASTING DIRECTOR
EXTRA CASTING
LOCATION MANAGER
ASSISTANT LOCATION MANAGER
TEACHER/WELFARE WORKER
PUBLICIST
PRODUCTION DESIGNER
ART DIRECTOR
SET DESIGNER
SET DECORATOR
LEAD PERSON
SWING PERSON
CONSTRUCTION COORDINATOR
PROPERTY MASTER
ASSISTANT PROPERTY MASTER
VISUAL EFFECTS SUPERVISOR
SPECIAL EFFECTS SUPERVISOR
DIRECTOR OF PHOTOGRAPHY
CAMERA OPERATOR
STEADICAM OPERATOR
ASSISTANT CAMERAMAN
2ND ASSISTANT CAMERAMAN
STILL PHOTOGRAPHER

GAFFER
BEST BOY/ELECTRICIAN
ELECTRICIAN
KEY GRIP
BEST BOY/GRIP
DOLLY GRIP
GRIP
SOUND MIXER
BOOM OPERATOR
CABLE PERSON
COSTUME DESIGNER
WARDROBE SUPERVISOR
COSTUMER
HAIR STYLIST
MAKEUP ARTIST
POST PRODUCTION SUPERVISOR
FILM EDITOR
ASSISTANT EDITOR
APPRENTICE EDITOR
MUSIC EDITOR
STUNT COORDINATOR
SPECIAL EFFECTS
VISUAL EFFECTS
TRANSPORTATION COORDINATOR
TRANSPORTATION CAPTAIN
DRIVER
WRANGLER
CRAFT SERVICE
PRODUCTION ASSISTANT
SET SECURITY
CATERING

CAST LIST

PRODUCTION CO.: XYZ PRODUCTIONS, INC.

ADDRESS: 1234 FLICK DR. - HOLLYWOOD, CA

PHONE/FAX: (213) 555-3331 / (213) 555-3332

SHOW TITLE: HERBY'S SUMMER VACATION

PRODUCER: SWIFTY DEALS

DIRECTOR: SID CELLULOID

CASTING DIRECTOR: DEE CASTOR

PRODUCTION #: 0100

ROLE	ACTOR Address/Phone/SS #	AGENT Address/Phone	START DATE	DEAL/BILLING
GEORGE	HOLLYWOOD MANN 3465 HORTENSE ST. WONDERLAND, CA 90000 (818) 555-1000 SS# 123·45·6892	JOE COOL TALENTED ARTISTS AGENCY 1515 SUNSET BLVD. HOLLYWOOD, CA 90002 (213) 555·2345	6·25·XX	$10,000 PER WEEK 6-WK. GUARANTEE 2 POST PROD. DAYS MAIN TITLES · SINGLE CARD · 4TH POSITION

EXECUTIVE STAFF LIST

It is helpful to add the company's EXECUTIVE STAFF LIST to the back of your crew list.

9/15/XX

XYZ Productions
1234 Flick Drive
Hollywood, CA 90038
(213) 555-3331 (phone); (213) 555-3332 (fax)

PRESIDENT

HARRY HONCHO
5678 Constitution Place
Beverly Hills, CA 90222

Office: Ext. 340
Home: (818) 555-8000
Car: (818) 555-8001

Asst: Alice Abet
Sec'y: Terri Types

VICE PRESIDENT
LEGAL AFFAIRS

VICE PRESIDENT
DEVELOPMENT

VICE PRESIDENT
BUSINESS AFFAIRS

VICE PRESIDENT
PRODUCTION

PRODUCTION
EXECUTIVE

VICE PRESIDENT
POST PRODUCTION

CONTROLLER

OFFICE MANAGER

...and so forth

CONTACT LIST

Supply your production staff with a listing of company contacts and services they will need in setting up and running their production. List companies you have used in the past that have given you good service and good rates. (If you use many of the same suppliers on all your shows, you are more likely to be given discounted rates.) Your contact list should look something like this:

9/15/XX

XYZ Productions
1234 Flick Drive
Hollywood, CA 90038
(213)555-331 (phone); (213)555-3332 (fax)

HERBY'S SUMMER VACATION — Production No. 0100

ATTORNEY	CHARLES CHEATEM DEWEY, CHEATEM & HOWE 100 S. Whiskey Road Los Angeles, CA 90004	(213) 555-7789 Fax#: 555-9000
INSURANCE COMPANY	ABC INSURANCE COMPANY 4579 W. Frederick St. Burbank, CA 91502	(818) 555-2345 Fax#: 555-8090
	CONTACT: Darryl Deductible	Dir#: 555-5555

INSURANCE DOCTOR
COMPLETION BOND CO.
ACCOUNTING FIRM
PAYROLL SERVICE
BANK
PUBLIC RELATIONS FIRM
TRAVEL AGENT
EXTRA CASTING AGENCY
EXTRA PAYROLL SERVICE
LAB
SOUND TRANSFERS
SCRIPT RESEARCH CO.
MUSIC CLEARANCE CO.
FILM PERMIT SERVICE
FIRE/POLICE OFFICERS
VEHICLE RENTALS
HONEYWAGON RENTAL
CATERING CO.
RAW STOCK
CAMERA EQUIPMENT
SOUND EQUIPMENT/WALKIE-TALKIES
BULLHORNS/HEADSETS
BEEPERS
GRIP/ELECTRIC EQUIPMENT
DOLLYS
CRANES/CONDORS
EXPENDABLES

GENERATORS
OFFICE SUPPLIES
STORAGE FACILITIES
COPIER MACHINE
RENTAL/REPAIR
TYPEWRITER
RENTAL/REPAIR
COMPUTER
RENTAL/REPAIR
FAX MACHINE
RENTAL/REPAIR
TELEPHONE EQUIPMENT/SERVICING
PRODUCT PLACEMENT FIRMS
WARDROBE RENTAL HOUSES
PROP/SET DRESSING RENTAL HOUSES
BOTTLED WATER/REFRIGERATORS
COFFEE MACHINES/KITCHEN SUPPLIES
MESSENGER SERVICE
OVERNIGHT COURIER SERVICE
SCRIPT TYPING SERVICE
WEATHER REPORT(S)
EDITING ROOMS
POST PRODUCTION FACILITIES
SCREENING ROOMS
STRIKE/CLEANING SERVICE

... and any other services you may need/use.

CHAPTER NINE

Clearances and Release Forms

Obtaining *clearances* is the process of obtaining permission to use someone's likeness, name, logo, photograph, product, premises, publication, film clip, stock footage, music, or song in your film, and, in most circumstances, is in exchange for a fee. Use of stock footage and music is granted through a *license*. Other clearances are secured with a signed *release form*, each designed to grant permission for the use of that particular element (likeness, name, logo, photo, product, etc.).

Both your insurance agency and attorney will request that you have your script *researched* and then follow through on securing needed clearances. When you send your script to a *research service*, they will send back a report itemizing which elements of the script have to be cleared. You will need to follow through to make sure all such items are cleared or licensed. The distributor of your film will insist on receiving copies of all license agreements and release forms. Releasing a picture without the proper clearances may result in costly lawsuits or insurance claims.

Your attorney or legal affairs department may wish to handle any complicated clearances. Music clearances are generally handled through a *music clearance service*; and clearances necessary for the use of clips, stills and news footage are often cleared through a *clearance service* or are handled by individuals with extensive clearance experience, hired on a freelance basis to work on a particular show. You should be able to secure most routine clearances on your own. Many of the release forms found in this chapter can be used for this purpose. If you need a release form that is not here, your attorney or legal affairs department can prepare one for you. Again, even though they have all been approved by an attorney, have *your own* attorney look them over before you use them. The following are some general rules pertaining to clearances.

LIKENESS

Permission to use a performer's likeness is incorporated into his or her SAG contract, and extras grant permission by signing an extra voucher. Occasionally, people who are not *extras* are filmed as "background" or "atmosphere." This may occur when the director decides that, although there were no extras planned for the day, some atmosphere in the background would make a scene more complete. It may also occur when the director does not have enough extras, and on the spur-of-the-moment people walking down a street are recruited to participate in a scene. In this situation, each person filmed as *background* (whether being paid for their appearance or not) should sign a *Personal Release*; or if there are several people, a *Group Release* would be appropriate.

When a large group of people are recruited for an audience that will be filmed, post signs in easy-to-read locations stating that their presence as a member of this audience constitutes their permission for the production company to use their likeness. The same would apply to shooting a street scene within a confined locale or when filming in a specific *area* such as a shopping center. Signs would be posted indicating that filming is taking place, people entering the area may appear in the picture, and by entering the area they grant permission to the production company to use their likeness. (Exact wording for these signs is included in this chapter.) Clearance would not be required if the passersby being filmed are an incidental part of the background or if they will not be recognizable in the picture.

LOCATIONS

Permission to use a premises or property as a shooting location is obtained when the owner of the property signs a release form called a *Location Agreement*.

NAMES

Although a *fictional* character may share a common name with an actual person, the names of actual persons (printed or spoken) should not be used unless permission is granted by that person. *Public figures* may be referenced, providing such references are not derogatory.

NAMES OF ACTUAL BUSINESSES OR ORGANIZATIONS

The use of the actual name of a business, organization, building, etc. that is a shooting location is permissible, providing the location agreement grants the right to use such name. If the name of a business, organization, or building is featured in your film but is not used as a shooting location, then permission for *Use of Name* or *Use of Trademark or Logo* is necessary.

TELEPHONE NUMBERS

Since it is difficult to clear references to identifiable phone numbers, most films use phone numbers that begin with the prefix *555* (a prefix that does not exist in any area code except for directory information).

LICENSE PLATES

As it is also difficult to clear identifiable license plates, prop houses will manufacture fictitious plates for you.

DEPICTION OF PUBLIC AUTHORITIES

Clearance is required for the portrayal of police officers, firemen, prison guards, and other public authorities of identifiable departments or locations, whether uniforms are used or not. Wardrobe and prop departments will supply *generic* uniforms and related paraphernalia if clearances cannot be obtained.

STREET ADDRESSES

Referencing or identifying an actual street address must be cleared.

DEPICTION OR IDENTIFICATION OF ACTUAL PRODUCTS

A depiction or reference to an actual product does not have to be cleared if the depiction or reference is *incidental* and not derogatory. Featuring a product or service trademark or logo does, however, require a clearance. A *Use of Trademark or Logo* release form would be appropriate in this situation.

Often, goods or services (such as wardrobe, food and soft drink products, plane tickets, or the use of vehicles) are given to the production in exchange for using or referencing a product or service in the picture. In most cases, the provider of the goods or services would also receive screen credit in the end titles of the film. *Product Placement Release Forms* cover the necessary clearances associated with this type of arrangement.

MUSIC

See Chapter 11.

GUIDELINES FOR THE USE OF CLIPS, STILLS, AND NEWS FOOTAGE IN MULTIMEDIA PROGRAMS

The following information was provided by Suzy Vaughan of Suzy Vaughan Associates, Inc. of Los Angeles. Suzy is an attorney with many years of clearance experience. Her firm provides clearance services for producers who are doing programs that require the use of excerpts from other projects.

LITERARY WORKS

Literary works, which include books, films, television programs, art works, and still photos, among other things, must be licensed from their owners. The Copyright Act gives creators of literary works the right to sell or license these works and to make money from them for the period of the copyright, which is 50 years plus the life of the author in the United States and in some foreign countries, and 100 years in other foreign countries. Once the copyright runs out, the creative works falls into the public domain and can be used freely by anyone without payment or licensing. If the work is not public domain, it is considered literary property and permission must be obtained from the owner for use of the material. The Copyright Act provides substantial penalties for copyright infringement, ranging from $10,000 for accidental infringement to $100,000 for willful infringement.

NEWS AND/OR STOCK FOOTAGE

News organizations can license the footage they have shot at press conferences to other entities. However, they can only license the copyright. They cannot give the licensee rights to the appearances of people who appear in the clips, including the anchor people, the news reporters, and ordinary people who are interviewed on the show. Use of these names and likenesses will require additional clearances (discussed further later).

FILM CLIPS

Any excerpt from a feature film must be licensed from the copyright holder, and pay

ment for use of the clips must be negotiated. Most studios charge a fee on the basis of a minute or fraction thereof. Most of them will not license footage on an aggregate basis but will base their fees on a per clip or per cut, per minute basis.

The cost per clip depends on the rights required. It is more expensive to license all rights in perpetuity than it is to license five years of worldwide distribution, assuming that a studio would grant you perpetuity. Many studios are currently putting together their own interactive and multimedia divisions, and therefore refuse to license material for other multimedia projects. Studios rarely grant permission to use clips in advertising and promotion, even when the producer offers substantial fees for the use. Some studios have reciprocal arrangements with other studios and provide clips at a much lower fee on that basis. If your project is affiliated with a studio, it is important to determine up front if that studio has reciprocal deals in place that might apply to your project.

Contrary to popular belief, there is no rule that says you can use five seconds for free. That five seconds will cost the same as one minute. Therefore, it behooves you to use the entire scene you have licensed, rather than using two-second clips from six scenes. Studio contracts also stipulate that you may not edit scenes within a film clip. Although an interview that cuts from the interview to the clip and back again is a form of editing, the studios do not generally consider this a problem. The licensing agreements the studios send you to sign are rarely negotiable and are very stringent, demanding concessions from end credits to a guarantee that you will clear all the talent and music used in the clip as well as an agreement that you will indemnify them against any claim that may arise as a result of the broadcast of the clip.

TELEVISION CLIPS

Television clips are owned by studios, independent production companies, and TV networks, and are handled in the same fashion as described earlier with regard to film clips from feature films. Currently, all licensors are very concerned about usage of their material in *interactive* projects, fearing that the images will be manipulated and altered to the point that they are no longer recognizable. As they will not allow this to happen, the word *interactive* in any letter requesting permission to license clips may elicit an immediate "no," unless you can convincingly explain that the material will not be changed.

STILL PHOTOS

Still photos fall into several categories.

Publicity photos (star headshots) have traditionally not been copyrighted. Since they are disseminated to the public, they are generally considered public domain, and therefore, clearance by the studio that produced them is not necessary (even if you could determine which studio produced them).

Production stills (photos taken on the set of a film or TV show during principal photography) must be cleared with the studio and can cost anywhere between $150 and $500.

Lobby cards (film posters) are generally lumped into the same category as publicity photos and do not require clearance.

Paparazzi photos must be cleared with the photographer. If not cleared, you risk a lawsuit and the possibility of the photographer showing up to demand much more money than he or she would have charged had you gone to him or her in the first place.

Magazine and book covers involve clearances from both the magazine or book publisher and the photographer who took the photo.

Still photo houses will generally license photos they own the rights to for $100 to $500 and up.

Samples of still photo releases are included in this chapter, both for the copyright owner of the photo and for the person(s) appearing in the photo.

PUBLIC DOMAIN FILMS AND STILLS

A film or still is protected by copyright if it is less than 75 years old. A work of art obtains a copyright as an unpublished work as soon as it is "fixed in a tangible medium of expression." If that work of art was not registered for copyright or does not have a notice of copyright on it and it is then *published* (which is accomplished by distribution to the public), it loses its unpublished copyright status and falls into the public domain. Once it is in the public domain, it can be reused by anyone without fear of copyright infringement since the copyright no longer exists. Since 1976, however, the fact that a television program may not have a visible copyright notice on it does not indicate that it is public domain, since it could have been registered with the Library of Congress. The only way to determine whether a film or television show is copyrighted is to do a copyright search at the Library of Congress. This applies to all works prior to 1988.

In 1988, the United States joined the Berne Copyright Convention, which states that no formalities are required to obtain a copyright, so therefore no copyright notice is required, nor is registration with the Library of Congress required. A program is copyrighted whether or not it has a copyright notice or is registered with the Library of Congress. However, most copyright holders still register their works with the Library of Congress and put copyright notices on them, since there are benefits to doing so with regard to lawsuits that arise out of the Copyright Act itself.

TALENT CLEARANCE

News Footage
Public Figures in News Footage

Right of privacy. Under U.S. law, an individual has the right of privacy, and his image cannot be used by another until he either consents to that use and thereby waives this right or until he becomes a public figure. One becomes a public figure by placing himself in the limelight and making himself a person of public interest (such as becoming an actor or politician), or by some act that gives him a news significance. Consent is not required of a public figure whose likeness appears in news footage, and that includes material shot at a news conference covered by more than one news camera or celebrities arriving at an event such as the Academy Awards for which they were not contracted but appeared in public voluntarily. They are aware that by appearing at an event such as a press conference, they give permission for use of their appearances in the footage anywhere it might appear. This situation also applies to newsreels that ran in movie theaters in the forties and fifties and are very obviously news.

Public Figures in News Television Programs (interviewers-interviewees). Public figures who appear in news programs must be cleared because these programs were produced under a union contract. The union contracts require current consent and a negotiated payment for use of the appearance of any artist prior to the use of an excerpt from these programs in another program.

Deceased Persons and the Right of Publicity. A deceased person has no right of privacy. The right is triggered only when a person's image is used to sell or endorse products in print ads and commercials, and does not generally apply to feature films or television programs, since they tell a story or disseminate information and do not sell a product. Music videos are a borderline situation, as they are created as tools to sell records and are occasionally considered to be musical commercials. However, the unions do require consent to be obtained from a deceased person's estate when requesting use of that person's likenesses in film clips for multimedia projects, television programs, etc.

Feature Films

Actors. The Screen Actors Guild agreement specifies that when a producer desires to use an excerpt from a feature film, that producer must obtain current consent from all SAG members appearing in the clip and that payment must be negotiated for no less than current union scale. Stars may waive scale payment if they choose. Extras do not have to be cleared or paid. SAG also provides that if consent from an actor is not obtained prior to broadcast of the clip, the fine for violation of this regulation will be three times what the actor made the day he worked on that scene.

Stuntmen. Obtaining clearances from stuntmen can be a challenging objective. First of all, the identification of specific stunt players may be difficult without the help of the stunt coordinator who hired them to appear in the picture to begin with. Locating the stunt coordinator and hoping he or she is available to help you is another matter. Clearances on stuntmen could also get quite expensive,

because the clip you want may feature one action sequence in which several stunt players worked. In addition, many studios are leery of claims and refuse to license footage in which stuntmen appear. Recently, SAG changed the rules slightly to allow producers to find and pay stuntmen during and after the project is completed, and no negotiations are necessary with regard to fees. Stunt performers must accept SAG scale, and violations are no longer levied for late clearances.

Pre-1960 Theatrical Feature Films. Prior to 1960, there was no provision in the SAG agreement granting actors residuals for their performances in feature films. Therefore, actors appearing in a clip from a film made prior to 1960 did not require clearance or payment. The guild recently revised this to require clearance of and payment for the use of clips, unless the name of the film is *billboarded* (either verbally as a voice-over or visually with a chyron) while the clip is on the screen. It must be readable and must appear every time the clip does, making montages impossible to do without clearing all the talent. This rule also applies to stuntmen.

SAG Waivers. Permission not to have to clear and pay actors is very difficult to obtain from SAG. Waivers may only be granted when there is a special reason, such as profits from the show going to charity. Only stars can be asked to waive. You would still be required to gain consent and pay union scale to nonstars.

Agent's Fees. Agents are not allowed to take commission on scale payments. Therefore, when contacting an agent to obtain permission to use his client's performance in a clip, it is customary to offer a 10% agency commission over and above the scale payment you are offering to the actor.

You cannot buy out an actor for the use of clips. Each additional run requires an additional payment to the actors, with payment for the second run at 100% and then 75% on down. If, however, you have hired the actor to appear live on your program for an overscale fee, this fee will include the use of the actor's clips on a buyout.

Television Programs

AFTRA puts major emphasis on obtaining current consent from talent appearing in television programs, and there is no time frame cutoff. This translates to having to clear actors who appeared in shows going back to approximately 1948. The pre-1960 rule does not apply here.

AFTRA is the union governing tape programs, such as soap operas and variety shows. Many other tape programs, such as situation comedies, are governed by SAG rules, as listed earlier. AFTRA's payment schedules are more complicated than SAG's in that there is a separate scale payment for a half-hour show, an hour show, a ninety-minute show, etc. There are also different rates for specialty acts, under five lines, and special business. Dancers and singers must also be cleared and paid. You do not even have to be able to see a dancer's face, just his or her body. Once again, extras do not require clearance or payment. However, determining who is an extra can be tricky, because it does not depend on whether they speak, but how they were hired on the show. The worst-case cost for AFTRA comes in the supplemental market area, where they generally require that you approach the performers for a waiver, since supplemental markets are not addressed in the AFTRA agreement. The waiver can specify payment to each performer of double scale for television shows and single scale for videocassette. Many times, in practice, producers do not obtain waivers and simply pay single scale to all performers. These are considerations decided on a case-by-case basis.

AFTRA has an advantage over SAG, because there are no triple damage penalties. Each rerun of a show featuring AFTRA performers requires an additional payment, with the second run at 75% on down. A talent release for use of a performer's name and likeness in a film or TV clip is included in this chapter.

DIRECTORS AND WRITERS PAYMENTS

Rates. The Directors Guild and the Writers Guild have schedules of payments required each time clips are used in a multimedia program, film, or television show. There are separate schedules depending on whether the clip came from a feature film or a television show. Fees for use of feature film clips break at a thirty-second rate, while fees for television clips are much more expensive, changing rates at a ten-second cutoff. Payment schedules can be obtained from the guilds.

Waivers. These guilds do not grant waivers, except for such things as the Oscars and the Emmys.

One-Time Only. Payments made to the Directors and Writers Guilds for use of clips are one-time only. There is no second payment when the show reruns or is distributed on home video.

Schedules. A producer is required to keep track of the film or television programs in which the clips appear, the writers and directors involved with each, and the amount of time used for each. This information is then submitted with a check to the appropriate guild. Episode titles are required for television shows by the Writers Guild. The guilds, in turn, issue checks to their members. DGA charges a 12.5% pension and welfare fee on top of the clip fee, while WGA does not charge for pension and welfare.

Compilation Rate. If a producer is producing a program that is an anniversary show or "Best of . . . ," the DGA and WGA will levy a *compilation rate*, which is a penalty for using all clips and not creating new material. All of the unions would rather that a producer hire live talent rather than use clips. The compilation rate is dreaded, as it is much more than the per-clip use rate would be. There are also several versions depending on the union: the daytime rate, the prime-time rate, the variety rate. The rate is arrived at by multiplying the standard writer rate times 250% times the number of half-hours in the program. Even if you pay a compilation rate, you must keep track of all clips used, their length, and the writers and directors, so that the unions can divide up the payment you make among the various writers and directors. The only time you would benefit from the compilation rate is when you are using many short television clips. If your program is comprised of many different elements, then a clip rate is much more economical.

DISTRIBUTION OF RELEASE FORMS

Copies of fully executed release forms should be given to:

1. The person who signs the release
2. The production coordinator
3. The production accountant (when a payment is involved)
4. Assistant directors should receive copies of fully executed Location Agreements to have on the set with them at each location.

The original release should be given to your production executive to be stored in permanent company files.

LOCATION AGREEMENT

June 10, 19XX

XYZ PRODUCTIONS
1234 Flick Drive
Hollywood, CA 90028

Dear **Gentlemen:**

You have advised the undersigned that you are producing a **motion picture** tentatively entitled **"HERBY'S SUMMER VACATION"** (the "Picture"). In consideration of your payment to the undersigned for the sum of **$2,500,** you and the undersigned hereby agree as follows:

1. The undersigned hereby irrevocably grants you and your agents, employees, licensees, successors and assigns:

    (a) The right to enter and remain upon the property, which shall include not only real property but any fixtures, equipment or other personal property thereat or thereon, located at: **THE OFFICES OF DEWEY, CHEATEM AND HOWE at 1000 ATLANTIC BLVD., SUITE 700 - LOS ANGELES, CA 90067** (the "Property"), with personnel and equipment (including without limitations, props, temporary sets, lighting, camera and special effects equipment) for the purpose of photographing scenes and making recordings of said Property in connection with the production of the Picture on the following date(s): Prep: **June 14, 19XX**; Shoot: **June 15, 19XX**; Strike: **June 16, 19XX**. If the weather or other conditions are not favorable for such purpose on such date(s), the date(s) shall be postponed to **July 5, 7 and 8, 19XX.**

    (b) The right to take motion pictures, videotapes, still photographs and/or sound recordings on and of any and all portions of the Property and all names associated there with or which appear in, on or about the Property.

    (c) All rights of every nature whatsoever in and to all films and photographs taken and recordings made hereunder, including without limitation of all copyrights therein and renewals and extensions thereof, and the exclusive right to reproduce, exhibit, distribute, and otherwise exploit in perpetuity throughout the universe (in whole or in part) such films, photographs and recordings in any and all media, whether now known or hereafter devised, including without limitation in and in connection with the Picture and the advertising and other exploitation thereof.

2. You agree to indemnify and to hold the undersigned harmless from and against all liability or loss which the undersigned may suffer or incur by reason of any injury to or death of any person, or damage to any property (ordinary wear and tear excepted), directly caused by any of your agents or employees when present on the Property or by reason of the use by any of your agents or employees or any equipment brought by them on to the property.

3. The undersigned warrants and represents (as a condition to the payment of the compensation referred to above), that the undersigned has the full right and authority to enter into this agreement and grant the rights herein granted, and that the consent or permission of no other person, firm, or entity is necessary in order to enable you to exercise or enjoy the rights herein granted.

4. The undersigned hereby releases you from, and covenants not to sue you for, any claim or cause of action, whether known or unknown, for defamation, invasion of his privacy, right of publicity or any similar matter, or any other claim or cause of action, based upon or relating to the exercise of any of the rights referred to in Paragraph 1 hereof; provided, however, that the foregoing shall not affect your obligations to indemnify the undersigned pursuant to Paragraph 2 hereof.

5. The undersigned further warrants neither he/she or anyone acting for him/her, gave or agreed to give anything of value, except for use of the Property, to anyone at **XYZ PRODUCTIONS** or anyone associated with the production for using the Property as a shooting location.

6. This agreement shall inure to benefit of and shall be binding upon your and our respective successors, licensees, assigns, heirs and personal representatives. You shall not be obligated actually to exercise any of the rights granted to you hereunder; it being understood that your obligations shall be fully satisfied hereunder by payment of the compensation referred to above. The agreement constitutes the entire agreement between the parties with respect to the subject matter hereof and cannot be amended except by a written instrument signed by the parties.

Very truly yours,

ACCEPTED & AGREED TO:

_____
(Signature)

By _____

_____
(Please print name)

_____
(Title)

_____
(Address)

_____

_____
(Phone Number)

_____
(Business Phone)

_____
(Fed. ID # or Soc. Sec. #)

PERSONAL RELEASE

June 23, 19XX

XYZ PRODUCTIONS
1234 Flick Drive
Hollywood, CA 90028

Gentlemen:

I, the undersigned, hereby grant permission to **XYZ PRODUCTIONS** to photograph me and to record my voice, performances, poses, acts, plays and appearances, and use my picture, photograph, silhouette and other reproductions of my physical likeness and sound as part of the **movie for television** tentatively entitled **"HERBY'S SUMMER VACATION"** (the "Picture") and the unlimited distribution, advertising, promotion, exhibition and exploitation of the Picture by any method or device now known or hereafter devised in which the same may be used, and/or incorporated and/or exhibited and/or exploited.

I agree that I will not assert or maintain against you, your successors, assigns and licensees, any claim, action, suit or demand of any kind or nature whatsoever, including but not limited to, those grounded upon invasion of privacy, rights of publicity or other civil rights, or for any other reason in connection with your authorized use of my physical likeness and sound in the Picture as herein provided. I hereby release you, your successors, assigns and licensees, and each of them, from and against any and all claims, liabilities, demands, actions, causes of action(s), costs and expenses whatsoever, at law or in equity, known or unknown, anticipated or unanticipated, which I ever had, now have, or may, shall or hereafter have by reason, matter, cause or thing arising out of your use as herein provided.

I affirm that neither I, nor anyone acting for me, gave or agreed to give anything of value to any of your employees or any representative of any television station, network or production entity for arranging my appearance on the Picture.

I have read the foregoing and fully understand the meaning and effect thereof and, intending to be legally bound, I have signed this release.

Very truly yours,

_____
(Signature)

_____
(Please print name)

_____

_____
(Address)

_____
(Phone number)

Rel #02

PERSONAL RELEASE - PAYMENT

June 25, 19XX

XYZ PRODUCTIONS
1234 Flick Drive
Hollywood, CA 90028

Gentlemen:

In consideration of payment to me of the sum of **$50**, receipt of which is hereby acknowledged, I, the undersigned, hereby grant permission to **XYZ PRODUCTIONS** to photograph me and to record my voice, performances, poses, acts, plays and appearances, and use my picture, photograph, silhouette and other reproductions of my physical likeness and sound as part of the **movie for cable** tentatively entitled **"HERBY'S SUMMER VACATION"** (the "Picture") and the unlimited distribution, advertising, promotion, exhibition and exploitation of the Picture by any method or device now known or hereafter devised in which the same may be used, and/or incorporated and/or exhibited and/or exploited.

I agree that I will not assert or maintain against you, your successors, assigns and licensees, any claim, action, suit or demand of any kind or nature whatsoever, including but not limited to, those grounded upon invasion of privacy, rights of publicity or other civil rights, or for any other reason in connection with your authorized use of my physical likeness and sound in the Picture as herein provided. I hereby release you, your successors, assigns and licensees, and each of them, from and against any and all claims, liabilities, demands, actions, causes of action(s), costs and expenses whatsoever, at law or in equity, known or unknown, anticipated or unanticipated, which I ever had, now have, or may, shall or hereafter have by reason, matter, cause or thing arising out of your use as herein provided.

I affirm that neither I, nor anyone acting for me, gave or agreed to give anything of value to any of your employees or any representative of any television station, network or production entity for arranging my appearance on the Picture.

I have read the foregoing and fully understand the meaning and effect thereof and, intending to be legally bound, I have signed this release.

Very truly yours,

_____
(Signature)

_____
(Please print name)

_____

_____
(Address)

_____
(Phone number)

_____
(Fed. ID # or Soc. Sec. #)

Rel #03

GROUP RELEASE

June 27, 19XX

XYZ PRODUCTIONS
1234 Flick Drive
Hollywood, CA 90028

Gentlemen:

I, the undersigned, hereby grant permission to **XYZ PRODUCTIONS** to photograph me and to record my voice, performances, poses, acts, plays and appearances, and use my picture, photograph, silhouette and other reproductions of my physical likeness and sound as part of the **motion picture** tentatively entitled **"HERBY'S SUMMER VACATION"** (the "Picture") and the unlimited distribution, advertising, promotion, exhibition and exploitation of the Picture by any method or device now known or hereafter devised in which the same may be used, and/or incorporated and/or exhibited and/or exploited.

I agree that I will not assert or maintain against you, your successors, assigns and licensees, any claim, action, suit or demand of any kind or nature whatsoever, including but not limited to, those grounded upon invasion of privacy, rights of publicity or other civil rights, or for any other reason in connection with your authorized use of my physical likeness and sound in the Picture as herein provided. I hereby release you, your successors, assigns and licensees, and each of them, from and against any and all claims, liabilities, demands, actions, causes of action(s), costs and expenses whatsoever, at law or in equity, known or unknown, anticipated or unanticipated, which I ever had, now have, or may, shall or hereafter have by reason, matter, cause or thing arising out of your use as herein provided.

I affirm that neither I, nor anyone acting for me, gave or agreed to give anything of value to any of your employees or any representative of any television station, network or production entity for arranging my appearance on the Picture.

I have read the foregoing and fully understand the meaning and effect thereof and, intending to be legally bound, I have signed this release.

NAME	ADDRESS	SOC. SEC. #
_____	_____	_____
_____	_____	_____
_____	_____	_____
_____	_____	_____
_____	_____	_____
_____	_____	_____
_____	_____	_____
_____	_____	_____
_____	_____	_____
_____	_____	_____
_____	_____	_____
_____	_____	_____

Rel #04

USE OF NAME

June 28, 19XX

XYZ PRODUCTIONS
1234 Flick Drive
Hollywood, CA 90028

Gentlemen:

For good and valuable consideration, receipt of which I hereby acknowledge, I hereby grant to you and to your successors, assigns, distributees and licensees forever, throughout the universe, the sole, exclusive and unconditional right and license to use, simulate and portray my name to such extent and in such manner as you in your sole discretion may elect, in or in connection with your **movie for television** tentatively entitled **"HERBY'S SUMMER VACATION"** (including reissues, remakes of and sequels to any such production) prepared by you or any successor to your interest therein, together with the right to publish synopses thereof, and to advertise, exploit, present, release, distribute, exhibit and/or otherwise utilize said productions and publications throughout the world.

I agree that I will not bring, institute or assert or consent that others bring, institute or assert any claim or action against you or your successors, licensees, distributees, or assigns, on the ground that anything performed in any such production or contained in the advertising or publicity issued in connection therewith is libelous, reflects adversely upon me, violates my right of privacy, or violates any other rights, and I hereby release, discharge, and acquit you and them of and from any and all such claims, actions, causes of action, suits and demands whatsoever that I may now or hereafter have against you or them.

In granting of the foregoing rights and licenses, I acknowledge that I have not been induced so to do by any representation or assurance by you or on your behalf relative to the manner in which any of the rights or licenses granted hereunder may be exercised; and I agree that you are under no obligation to exercise any of the rights or licenses granted hereunder.

Very truly yours,

_____
(Signature)

ACCEPTED & AGREED TO:

By _____

_____
(Please print name)

_____

_____
(Address)

_____
(Phone Number)

Rel #05

USE OF TRADEMARK OR LOGO

June 28, 19XX

XYZ PRODUCTIONS
1234 Flick Drive
Hollywood, CA 90028

Gentlemen:

For good and valuable consideration, receipt of which is hereby acknowledged, the undersigned hereby grants to you, your successors, licensees and assigns, the non-exclusive right, but not the obligation to use and include all or part of our trademark(s), logo(s), and/or animated or identifiable characters (the Mark(s)) listed below in the **motion picture** tentatively entitled **"HERBY'S SUMMER VACATION"** (the "Picture"), and to utilize and reproduce the Mark(s) in connection with the Picture, without limitation as to time or number of runs, for reproduction, exhibition and exploitation, throughout the world, in any and all manner, methods and media, whether now known or hereafter known or devised, and in the advertising, publicizing, promotion, trailers and exploitation thereof.

The undersigned acknowledges, as does the company which he represents, that, under the Federal Communications Act, it is a federal offense to give or agree to give anything of value to promote any product, service or venture in connection with the Picture on the air, and warrants and represents that neither he nor they have done or will do so.

The undersigned and the company he represents, hereby warrant, represent and affirm that he and the company have the right to grant the rights granted herein, free of claims by any person or entity.

Mark(s): **The COUNTRY ROADS COLLECTION logo**

Very truly yours,

_____
(Signature)

_____
(Please print name)

ACCEPTED & AGREED TO:

_____
(Title)

By _____

_____
(Address)

_____
(Phone Number)

Rel #06

USE OF LITERARY MATERIAL

June 29, 19XX

XYZ PRODUCTIONS
1234 Flick Drive
Hollywood, CA 90028

Gentlemen:

I am informed that you are producing a **movie for television** tentatively entitled **"HERBY'S SUMMER VACATION"** (the "Picture") and that you have requested that I grant you the right to use the title and/or portions of the following literary material owned and published by the undersigned for inclusion in the Picture:

THE COMPLETE FILM PRODUCTION HANDBOOK

For good and valuable consideration, receipt of which is hereby acknowledged, I (the undersigned) do hereby confirm the consent hereby given you with respect to your use of the above title and/or literary material (the "Materials") in connection with the Picture, and I do hereby grant to you, your successors, assigns and licensees, the perpetual right to use the Materials in connection with the Picture. I agree that you may record the Materials on tape, film or otherwise and use the Materials and recordings in and in connection with the exhibition, advertising, promotion, exploitation, and any other use of the Picture as you may desire.

I hereby release you, your agents, successors, licensees and assigns, and each of them, from and against any and all claims, liabilities, demands, actions, causes of action, costs and expenses, whatsoever, at law or in equity, known or unknown, anticipated or unanticipated, suspected or unsuspected, which I ever had, now have, or may, shall or hereafter have by any reason, matter, cause or thing whatsoever, arising out of your use of the Materials as provided herein in connection with the Picture. I realize that in using the Materials, you are relying upon the rights granted to you hereunder.

Very truly yours,

ACCEPTED & AGREED TO:

_____
(Signature)

By _____

_____
(Please print name)

_____

_____
(Address)

_____
(Phone Number)

Rel #07

USE OF STILL PHOTOGRAPH(S)
(Person in Photo/Free)

June 25, 19XX

XYZ PRODUCTIONS
1234 Flick Drive
Hollywood, CA 90028

Gentlemen:

For good and valuable consideration, receipt of which is hereby acknowledged, I, the undersigned, hereby grant to you, your successors, licensees and assigns, the non-exclusive right, but not the obligation to use and include my physical likeness in the form of still photograph(s) (the Still(s)) as described below in the **television series** tentatively entitled **"HERBY'S SUMMER VACATION"** (the "Picture"), and to utilize and reproduce the Still(s) in connection with the Picture, without limitation as to time or number of runs, for reproduction, exhibition and exploitation, throughout the world, in any and all manner, methods and media, whether now known or hereafter known or devised, and in the advertising, publicizing, promotion, trailers and exploitation thereof.

I agree that I will not assert or maintain against you, your successors, assigns and licensees, a claim, action, suit or demand of any kind or nature whatsoever, including but not limited to, those grounded upon invasion of privacy, rights of publicity or other civil rights, or for any other reason in connection with your authorized use of the Still(s) in the Picture as herein provided. I hereby release you, your successors, assigns and licensees from any and all such claims, actions, causes of action, suits and demands whatsoever that I may now or hereafter have against you or them.

In the granting of the foregoing rights and licenses, I acknowledge that I have not been induced to do so by any representative or assurance by you or on your behalf relative to the manner in which any of the rights or licenses granted hereunder may be exercised; and I agree that you are under no obligation to exercise any of the rights or licenses granted hereunder.

Description of the Still(s): **1985 HEAD SHOT OF SCARLET STARLET**

Very truly yours,

ACCEPTED & AGREED TO:

_____
(Signature)

By _____

_____
(Please print name)

_____
(Title)

_____
(Address)

_____
(Phone Number)

Rel #08

USE OF STILL PHOTOGRAPH(S)
(Person in Photo/Payment)

June 25, 19XX

XYZ PRODUCTIONS
1234 Flick Drive
Hollywood, CA 90028

Gentlemen:

In consideration of the payment of the sum of **$500** and other good and valuable consideration, receipt of which is hereby acknowledged, I, the undersigned hereby grant to you, your successors, licensees and assigns, the non-exclusive right, but not the obligation to use and include my physical likeness in the form of the still photograph(s) (the Still(s)) as described below in the **movie for cable** tentatively entitled **"HERBY'S SUMMER VACATION"** (the "Picture"), and to utilize and reproduce the Still(s) in connection with the Picture, without limitation as to the number of runs, for reproduction, exhibition and exploitation, throughout the world, in any and all manner, methods and media, whether now known or hereafter known or devised, and in the advertising, publicizing, promotion, trailers and exploitation thereof.

I agree that I will not assert or maintain against you, your successors, assigns and licensees, a claim, action, suit or demand of any kind or nature whatsoever, including but not limited to, those grounded upon invasion of privacy, rights of publicity or other civil rights, or for any other reason in connection with your authorized use of the Still(s) in the Picture as herein provided. I hereby release you, your successors, assigns and licensees from any and all such claims, actions, causes of action, suits and demands whatsoever that I may now or hereafter have against you or them.

In the granting of the foregoing rights and licenses, I acknowledge that I have not been induced to do so by any representative or assurance by you or on your behalf relative to the manner in which any of the rights or licenses granted hereunder may be exercised; and I agree that you are under no obligation to exercise any of the rights or licenses granted hereunder.

Description of the Still(s): **HEADSHOT OF HOLLYWOOD MANN**

Very truly yours,

_____
(Signature)

ACCEPTED & AGREED TO:

_____
(Please print name)

By _____

_____
(Address)

_____
(Phone Number)

_____
(Fed. ID # or Soc. Sec. #)

Rel #09

USE OF STILL PHOTOGRAPH(S)
(Copyrighted Owner
Not Person in Photo/Free)

June 28, 19XX

XYZ PRODUCTIONS
1234 Flick Drive
Hollywood, CA 90028

Gentlemen:

For good and valuable consideration, receipt of which is hereby acknowledged, the undersigned Licensor hereby grants to you, the Licensee, your successors, licensees and assigns, the non-exclusive right, but not the obligation to use and include the still photograph(s) (the Still(s)) as described below in the **motion picture** tentatively entitled **"HERBY'S SUMMER VACATION"** (the "Picture"), and to utilize and reproduce the Still(s) in connection with the Picture, without limitation as to time or number of runs, for reproduction, exhibition and exploitation, throughout the world, in any and all manner, methods and media, whether now known or hereafter known or devised, and in the advertising, publicizing, promotion, trailers and exploitation thereof.

You agree to indemnify and hold harmless the undersigned Licensor and its respective agents, representatives, associates, affiliates, predecessors, successors and assigns, parent and subsidiary corporations, and their officers, directors, and employees and each and all of them, of and from any and all claims, losses, costs, damage, liability and expenses, including reasonable attorneys' fees and costs, arising out of any claim which may arise as the result of the broadcast or release of the Picture.

The undersigned Licensor acknowledges, as does the company which he represents, that, under the Federal Communications Act, it is a federal offense to give or agree to give anything of value to promote any product, service or venture in connection with the Picture on the air, and warrants and represents that neither he nor they have done or will do so.

The undersigned and the company he represents, hereby warrant, represent and affirm that he and the company have the right to grant the rights granted herein, free of claims by any person or entity.

Description of the Still(s): **HEADSHOT OF CLARK GRABLE**

Very truly yours,

ACCEPTED & AGREED TO:

_____
(Signature)

By _____

_____
(Please print name)

_____
(Title)

_____
(Address)

_____
(Phone Number)

Rel #10

USE OF STILL PHOTOGRAPH(S)
(Copyrighted Owner
Not Person in Photo/Payment)

June 29, 19XX

XYZ PRODUCTIONS
1234 Flick Drive
Hollywood, CA 90028

Gentlemen:

In consideration of the payment of the sum of **$350** and other good and valuable consideration, receipt of which is hereby acknowledged, the undersigned Licensor hereby grants to you, the Licensee, your successors, licensees and assigns, the non-exclusive right, but not the obligation to use and include the still photograph(s) (the Still(s)) as described below in the **motion picture** tentatively **entitled "HERBY'S SUMMER VACATION"** (the "Picture"), and to utilize and reproduce the Still(s) in connection with the Picture, without limitation as to time or number of runs, for reproduction, exhibition and exploitation, throughout the world, in any and all manner, methods and media, whether now known or hereafter known or devised, and in the advertising, publicizing, promotion, trailers and exploitation thereof.

You agree to indemnify and hold harmless the undersigned Licensor and its respective agents, representatives, associates, affiliates, predecessors, successors and assigns, parent and subsidiary corporations, and their officers, directors, and employees and each and all of them, of and from any and all claims, losses, costs, damage, liability and expenses, including reasonable attorneys' fees and costs, arising out of any claim which may arise as the result of the broadcast or release of the Picture.

The undersigned Licensor acknowledges, as does the company which he represents, that, under the Federal Communications Act, it is a federal offense to give or agree to give anything of value to promote any product, service or venture in connection with the Picture on the air, and warrants and represents that neither he nor they have done or will do so.

The undersigned and the company he represents, hereby warrant, represent and affirm that he and the company have the right to grant the rights granted herein, free of claims by any person or entity.

Description of the Still(s): **1980 HEADSHOT OF ROCKY RIZZO**

Very truly yours,

ACCEPTED & AGREED TO:

_____
(Signature)

By _____

_____
(Please print name)

_____
(Title)

_____

_____
(Address)

_____
(Phone Number)

_____
(Fed. ID # or Soc. Sec. #)

Rel #11

WORDING FOR MULTIPLE SIGNS

(To be placed in several clearly visible locations)

IN A STUDIO WHEN TAPING OR FILMING BEFORE A LIVE AUDIENCE:

PLEASE BE ADVISED THAT YOUR PRESENCE AS A MEMBER OF THE STUDIO AUDIENCE DURING THE **TAPING** OF THE PROGRAM ENTITLED **"HERBY'S SUMMER VACATION"** CONSTITUTES YOUR PERMISSION TO **XYZ PRODUCTIONS** TO USE YOUR LIKENESS ON THE AIR IN ANY FORM AND AS OFTEN AS THEY DEEM APPROPRIATE AND DESIRABLE FOR PROMOTIONAL OR BROADCAST PURPOSES.

IF FOR ANY REASON YOU OBJECT TO YOUR LIKENESS BEING SO USED, YOU SHOULD LEAVE THE STUDIO AT THIS TIME. IF YOU REMAIN, YOUR PRESENCE AT THIS TAPING/FILMING WILL CONSTITUTE YOUR APPROVAL OF THE FOREGOING.

Rel #12A

WORDING FOR MULTIPLE SIGNS

(To be placed in several clearly visible locations)

IN AN "AREA" DURING THE TAPING OR FILMING OF A SHOW:

PLEASE BE ADVISED THAT **FILMING** IS TAKING PLACE IN CONNECTION WITH THE PRODUCTION OF A **MOTION PICTURE** TENTATIVELY ENTITLED **"HERBY'S SUMMER VACATION"**. PEOPLE ENTERING THIS AREA MAY APPEAR IN THE PICTURE. BY ENTERING THIS AREA, YOU GRANT TO **XYZ PRODUCTIONS** THE RIGHT TO FILM AND PHOTOGRAPH YOU AND RECORD YOUR VOICE AND TO USE YOUR VOICE AND LIKENESS IN CONNECTION WITH THE PICTURE AND THE DISTRIBUTION AND EXPLOITATION THEREOF, AND YOU RELEASE **XYZ PRODUCTIONS** AND ITS LICENSEES FROM ALL LIABILITY IN CONNECTION THEREIN. YOU AGREE AND UNDERSTAND THAT **XYZ PRODUCTIONS** WILL PROCEED IN RELIANCE UPON SUCH GRANT AND RELEASE.

XYZ PRODUCTIONS DOES NOT ASSUME RESPONSIBILITY FOR ANY INJURY TO YOUR PERSON OR DAMAGE OR LOSS TO YOUR PROPERTY.

THE USE OF CAMERAS AND RECORDING EQUIPMENT IS PROHIBITED DUE TO UNION AND COPYRIGHT REGULATIONS.

SMOKING IS PROHIBITED IN THIS AREA . . . THANK YOU!

Rel #12B

SUPPLYING A FILM/TAPE CLIP OF YOUR SHOW
FOR PROMOTIONAL PURPOSES

June 25, 19XX

TALK SHOW PRODUCTIONS
"The Evening Show"
1000 W. Miracle Mile Avenue
Los Angeles, CA 90036

Gentlemen:

The undersigned hereby authorizes you to use a FILM/TAPE CLIP from the **movie for television** tentatively entitled **"HERBY'S SUMMER VACATION"** for promotional purposes only in the program entitled **"THE EVENING SHOW"** currently scheduled for broadcast on **June 30, 19XX**.

The undersigned hereby affirms that neither he nor anyone acting on his behalf or any company which he may represent, gave or agreed to give anything of value (except for the FILM/TAPE CLIP) which was furnished for promotional purposes solely on or in connection with **"THE EVENING SHOW"** to any member of the production staff, anyone associated in any manner with the program or any representative of **TALK SHOW PRODUCTIONS** for mentioning or displaying the name of any company which he may represent or any of its products, trademarks, trade-names or the like.

The undersigned understands that any broadcast identification of the FILM/TAPE CLIP (or the name of any company, product, etc. which he may represent) which **XYZ PRODUCTIONS** may furnish, shall, in no event, be beyond that which is reasonable related to the program content.

The undersigned is aware, as is the company which he may represent, that it is a federal offense unless disclosed to **TALK SHOW PRODUCTIONS** prior to broadcast if the undersigned gives or agrees to give anything of value to promote any product, service or venture on the air.

The undersigned represents that he is fully empowered to execute this letter on behalf of any company which he may represent.

The undersigned warrants that he or the company which he may represent has the right to grant the license herein granted, and agrees to indemnify you for all loss, damage and liability, excluding the payment of any guild related talent fees or performing rights fees in the music included in said clip, if any (which you agree to pay or cause to be paid), arising out of the use of the above material.

Very truly yours,

ACCEPTED & AGREED:

_____
(Signature)

By _____

_____
(Please print name)

_____
(Title)

Rel #13

PRODUCT PLACEMENT RELEASE

June 25, 19XX

XYZ PRODUCTIONS
1234 Flick Drive
Hollywood, CA 90028

Gentlemen:

The undersigned ("Company") agrees to provide the following product(s) and/or service(s) to **XYZ PRODUCTIONS** for use in the motion picture now entitled **"HERBY'S SUMMER VACATION"** (the "Picture"):

2 dozen pair, assorted sunglasses
1 basketball
1 bat
2 softballs
2 beachballs
3 pairs roller skates

The Company grants to you, your successors, licensees and assigns, the non-exclusive right, but not the obligation to use and include all or part of the trademark(s), logo(s) and/or identifiable characters (the "Mark(s)") associated with the above listed product(s) and/or service(s) in the Picture, without limitation as to time or number of runs, for reproduction, exhibition and exploitation, throughout the world, in any and all manner, methods and media, whether now known or hereafter known or devised, and in the advertising, publicizing, promotion, trailers and exploitation thereof.

The Company warrants and represents that it is the owner of the product(s) or direct provider of the service(s) as listed above or a representative of such and has the right to enter this agreement and grant the rights granted to **XYZ PRODUCTIONS** hereunder.

In full consideration of the Company providing the product(s) and/or service(s) to **XYZ PRODUCTIONS**, **XYZ PRODUCTIONS** agrees to accord the Company screen credit in the end titles of the positive prints of the Picture in the following form: **"SPORTING GOODS AND SUNGLASSES** furnished by **HOLLYWOOD PROMOTIONS, INC."**.

The Company understands that any broadcast identification of its products, trademarks, trade names or the like which **XYZ PRODUCTIONS** may furnish, shall in no event, be beyond that which is reasonably related to the program content.

As it applies to any and all television broadcasts of the Picture, the Company is aware that it is a federal offense to give or agree to give anything of value to promote any product, service or venture on the air. The Company affirms that it did not give or agree to give anything of value, except for the product(s) and/or service(s) to any member of the production staff, anyone associated in any manner with the Picture or any representative of **XYZ PRODUCTIONS** for mentioning or displaying the name of the Company or any of its products, trademarks, trade names, or the like.

I represent that I am an officer of the Company and am empowered to execute this form on behalf of the Company.

I further represent that neither I nor the Company which I represent will directly or indirectly publicize or otherwise exploit the use, exhibition or demonstration of the above product(s) and/or service(s) in the Picture for advertising, merchandising or promotional purposes without the express written consent of **XYZ PRODUCTIONS**.

Sincerely yours,

_____
(Authorized Signatory)

ACCEPTED & AGREED TO:

By _____

_____
(Please print name)

_____
(Title)

_____
(Name of Company)

_____

_____
(Address)

_____
(Phone Number)

Rel #14

FILM/TAPE FOOTAGE RELEASE

LICENSOR: **STOCK SHOTS, INC.**

LICENSEE: **XYZ PRODUCTIONS**

DESCRIPTION OF THE FILM/TAPE FOOTAGE: **ESTABLISHING SHOT OF DOWNTOWN MILWAUKEE, WISCONSIN**

LENGTH OF FOOTAGE: **40'**

PRODUCTION: **"HERBY'S SUMMER VACATION"**   (The "Picture")

LICENSE FEE, if any   **$1,000**

Licensor hereby grants to Licensee, Licensor's permission to edit and include all or portion of the above-mentioned Footage in the Picture as follows:

1. Licensor grants to Licensee a non-exclusive license to edit and incorporate the Footage in the Picture. Licensee may broadcast and otherwise exploit the Footage in the Picture, and in customary advertising and publicity thereof, throughout the world in perpetuity in any media now known or hereafter devised.

2. Licensee shall not make any reproductions whatsoever of or from the Footage except as described hereunder.

3. Licensee agrees to obtain, at Licensee's expense, all required consents of any person whose appearances are contained in the Footage pursuant to this agreement, and to make any payments to such persons, guilds or unions having jurisdiction thereof and music publishers, when necessary. Licensor agrees to supply the identity of such persons, if known.

4. Licensor represents and warrants that: (1) Licensor has the right and power to grant the rights herein granted, and (2) neither Licensee's use of the Footage pursuant to this license nor anything contained therein infringes upon the rights of any third parties.

5. Licensor and Licensee each agree to indemnify and hold the other harmless from and against any and all claims, losses liabilities, damages and expenses, including reasonable attorneys' fees, which may result from any breach of their respective representations and warranties hereunder.

6. As between Licensor and Licensee, the Picture shall be Licensee's sole and exclusive property. Licensee shall not be obligated to use the Footage or the rights herein granted or to produce or broadcast the Picture.

7. Licensor acknowledges that, under the Federal Communications Act, it is a Federal offense to give or agree to give anything of value to promote any product, service or venture in the Picture, and Licensor warrants and represents that Licensor has not and will not do so.

8. This agreement constitutes the entire understanding between the parties, supersedes any prior understanding relating thereto and shall not be modified except by a writing signed by the parties. This agreement shall be irrevocable and shall be binding upon and inure to the benefit of Licensor's and Licensee's respective successors, assigns and licensees.

Kindly sign below to indicate your acceptance of the foregoing.

Licensor:

CONFIRMED:

_____
(Signature)

_____
(Please print name)

By _____

_____
(Title)

_____
(Company)

_____

_____
(Address)

_____
(Phone Number)

_____
(Fed. ID # or Soc. Sec. #)

Rel #15

TALENT
USE OF NAME & LIKENESS
IN A FILM OR TV CLIP

June 25, 19XX

Mr. Joe Cool
TALENTED ARTISTS AGENCY
1515 Sunset Blvd.
Hollywood, CA 91111

Dear **Mr. Cool:**

I am writing to you with regard to a **motion picture** being produced by **XYZ PRODUCTIONS** and tentatively entitled **"HERBY'S SUMMER VACATION"** (the "Picture"). The Picture is scheduled for **release** on **December 7, 19XX.**

A brief description of the Picture is as follows:

This poignant, coming-of-age story is set in Milwaukee, Wisconsin in 1968. While visiting his grandmother one summer, Herby, an 11-year-old boy, witnesses a murder, discovers his sexuality and learns what it means to be a friend.

In conjunction with this Picture, we are requesting permission to use the appearance of **SCARLET STARLET** in a clip from **her 1968 appearance in the television series, "MARSHAL DILLON OF DODGE," the episode entitled, "The Saloon Girl," Scene #45.**

In consideration for **Ms. Starlet**'s permission and in conjunction with the current SAG Agreement, **XYZ PRODUCTIONS** hereby offers to pay **Ms. Starlet** a fee of **$(SAG minimum) plus 10% agency commission.** This sum represents the total payment for **XYZ PRODUCTION's** use of **Scarlet Starlet's** name and likeness in the above described clip in and in connection with the Picture and in promotion for the Picture. Compensation to **Ms. Starlet** for any further use of the Picture in any media shall be governed by the then applicable collective bargaining agreements pertaining to such use.

I would appreciate it if you would have **Ms. Starlet** complete the information requested below and acknowledge **her** assent to the Agreement by signing below. Once executed, please return a copy of this letter to us for our records.

Please do not hesitate to call should you have any questions.

Sincerely yours,

ACCEPTED & AGREED TO:

By: _____   Date _____

_____   SS# _____

_____   Fed. Tax ID# _____

_____

Loan-Out Corporation Name and Address

Rel #16

REQUEST FOR VIDEOCASSETTE

November 15, 19XX

Mr. F. Stopp
8365 Iris Boulevard
Beverly Hills, CA 90212

Dear **Mr. Stopp:**

You accept delivery of the **1/2"** videocassette ("Recording") of **"HERBY'S SUMMER VACATION"** (the "Picture"), and in consideration of our delivery of it, agree as follows:

1. You warrant, represent and agree that the Recording shall be used solely for your private, personal library purpose or for screenings in connection with an in-house demo reel; and the Recording will never be publicly exhibited in any manner or medium whatsoever. You will not charge or authorize the charge of a fee for exhibiting the Recording. You will not duplicate or permit the duplication of the Recording. You will retain possession of the Recording at all times.

2. All other rights in and to the Picture, under copyright or otherwise, including but not limited to title to, are retained by **XYZ PRODUCTIONS.**

3. The permission which we have granted to you for the use of the Recording itself will be non-assignable and non-transferable.

4. You agree to indemnify us against and hold us harmless from claims, liabilities and actions arising out of your breach of this agreement.

5. You agree to reimburse us for the cost of making the Recording available to you.

This will become a contract between you and us upon your acceptance of delivery of the Recording.

Sincerely yours,

ACCEPTED & AGREED:

By _____

_____
(Signature)

_____
(Please print name)

_____

_____
(Address)

_____
(Phone Number)

Rel #17

CHAPTER TEN

A Guide to Music Clearance

If you are planning to use anything other than originally scored music throughout your entire film, you should contact a music clearance service during the early stages of pre-production. You will want to know if the rights to the copyrighted musical material are available, how much each would cost to license, and if your music budget will cover the cost of the music you wish to use. Early music planning could save you a lot of time and money by knowing exactly which pieces of music you can and cannot incorporate into your film.

The following guide prepared by *The Clearing House, Ltd.* answers the most frequently asked questions about the field of music clearance. Any additional questions you may have about music rights clearances should be directed to your attorney or music clearance service.

A GUIDE TO MUSIC CLEARANCE
Provided By *The Clearing House, Ltd.*

The music we hear every day on radio and television, or see performed in nightclubs and concerts, is subject to federal copyright protection. The U.S. Copyright Act, and other copyright laws around the world, give the owners of copyrighted music certain rights and controls over the use of their music and the fees that will be paid for that use. This system of law, which makes it possible for artists to earn a living from their creations, also requires that producers desiring to use protected musical material secure proper permission to do so.

EXACTLY WHAT IS MUSIC CLEARANCE?

Simply, it is the process of securing permission to use songs or recordings owned by someone else. More specifically, however, it involves (1) determining who owns the copyright to any given musical material, (2) negotiating permission for use of that material for the territories and media in which exhibition or distribution is planned, and (3) paying the license fees to the copyright owners. These steps should be taken before you are committed to using specific songs and recordings in order to eliminate musical material that may be too expensive or that the copyright owners do not want used.

The term *musical material* includes songs, and particular recordings of songs as well, since recordings may be protected by copyright law, state antipiracy statutes, and other legal theories. The song "Thriller" (written by Rod Temperton and controlled by Almo/Irving Music) and the recorded performance of "Thriller" (by Michael Jackson and owned by Sony Music Entertainment, Inc.) are two separate copyrights, each of which may require prior clearance, depending upon the circumstances.

You should start the music clearance process early in the planning stages of your project to assure the availability of the material for its intended use and subsequent exploitation. An early phone call to an attorney or music clearance service is highly recommended.

WHAT ARE MY RESPONSIBILITIES FOR CLEARING THE MUSIC USED IN MY TELEVISION, MOTION PICTURE, OR VIDEO PROJECT?

Both as a matter of copyright law and the producer's own distribution or exhibition agreements, it is generally the producer's responsibility to secure the clearance of musical material used in his or her television, motion picture, or video production. This is required to avoid liability for copyright infringement, to meet broadcaster or distributor delivery requirements, and to comply with errors and omissions insurance procedures.

WHO OWNS THE MUSIC I WISH TO USE?

This is a very complex question since several people can collaborate to create a single composition. Further, a copyright can be divided into separate parts, with each part owned either individually or by several parties.

Generally, a writer sells or assigns the copyright in his or her song to a music publisher, who pays the writer a share of the royalties derived from its exploitation. It is most often the publisher, not the writer, who has the authority to grant permission for its use. However, a publisher that either owns or administers the copyright may be contractually required to ask for the writer's approval before allowing its use.

It is now common for ownership of a copyright to be divided by percentages and territories, so that several publishers could own rights in the United States, while several others could own rights for the rest of the world. The people who own music copyrights frequently transfer the right to grant permission and the right to collect royalties for specific types of rights to outside agencies who do the collecting and paperwork (administration) for them. All of this may result in situations in which several parties must agree to the license, thereby increasing the difficulty in obtaining clearance.

Recordings are usually owned by the record company that paid for the recording session, or that had the recording artist under contract. However, the terms of recording contracts can require certain artist approvals before the record company can grant a license.

WHAT WAS THE U.S. SUPREME COURT'S "REAR WINDOW" DECISION, AND HOW DOES IT AFFECT MUSIC LICENSING?

A full discussion of the so-called "Rear Window" decision is far beyond the scope of this material. However, in broad and general terms, songs copyrighted before January 1, 1978 are entitled to two terms of copyright protection—a first copyright term of 28 years and a renewal term of 47 years, for a total of 75 years. If you use certain songs that are still in the first term of copyright, your licenses may become unenforceable if the songwriter dies in the first term of copyright.

No producer wants to be in a position of losing the rights to a song after he has recorded it into his production or after he has paid for the rights. Your attorney or music clearance service should advise you as to which songs are affected by the decision and the legal and business ramifications of using such songs.

WHAT RIGHTS DO I NEED TO OBTAIN IN ORDER TO MAKE SURE THAT THE MUSICAL MATERIAL USED IN MY PRODUCTION IS PROPERLY CLEARED?

In general, the rights commonly required in order to use musical material (songs and recordings) in television and film productions may be divided into the following categories.

Public Performing Rights
These refer to the rights to do such things as recite, play, sing, dance, act out, or broadcast a composition in public. However, there is a vast difference between the rights required to merely sing a song on a bare stage and the rights required to dramatize or tell the story of a song using sets, costumes, props, etc. While a detailed explanation of dramatic and nondramatic rights is beyond the scope of this guide, remember that the rights required and the complexity of their clearance will depend upon the way the song is to be performed.

Reproduction Rights
A music publisher has the right to control the reproduction (recording) of a composition. Reproduction rights are referred to in television and film production as *synchronization rights*

because the protected material is recorded as part of a soundtrack in synchronization with visual images. *Sync rights*, as they are called, should not be confused with *mechanical rights*, which have historically referred to the reproduction of songs on audio records, CDs, or tapes for distribution to the general public.

Record companies also have the right to control the reproduction of their recordings. A license to reproduce a record in an audio/visual work is generally referred to as a *master use* license.

Adaptation Rights

A copyright owner has the right to control the alteration or adaptation of musical compositions, including arrangements, parodies, comedic uses, lyric changes, translations, etc. If a song or recording is to be used in adapted form, specific permission directly from the copyright owner may be required before exhibition or distribution. Some copyright owners, while open to the use of their material as it was originally written or recorded, will not grant permission for any adaptations.

The way in which a song or recording is performed or used will determine the applicability of these various rights. The media in which distribution is planned (broadcast television, home video, feature film, etc.) will significantly affect how these rights are negotiated, with whom they are negotiated, and how much will have to be paid for the rights.

FROM WHOM MAY I OBTAIN THESE MUSIC RIGHTS?

The previously mentioned rights are generally not handled at one source but instead are often licensed individually by separate parties. For certain rights, you may have to deal directly with the songwriter, the songwriter's heirs, attorneys, publishers, agents, performing artists, record companies, and unions. If several parties own a composition, each may have to be contacted.

Public performing rights are customarily obtained by broadcasters from the music performing rights organizations that represent composers and publishers. They are the American Society of Composers, Authors, and Publishers (ASCAP), Broadcast Music, Inc. (BMI), and the Society of European Stage Authors and

Composers (SESAC). Performing rights licensing for media other than broadcast television, such as feature films, nontheatrical, and nonbroadcast uses, may be handled in a completely different manner.

Synchronization rights and the right to adapt the composition are generally obtained by approaching the owner directly. Some music publishers, while retaining the function of quoting the fees and approving the uses, prefer to do so through an intermediary organization that they retain to license those rights on their behalf. Record companies generally control and license their recordings themselves; however, in some instances the prior approval of the performing artist may be required.

As a producer working in television, film, or music video, you have no reason to personally keep track of the ownership and representation of the thousands of protected compositions and recordings that may be available. However, if you did, your basic problems would be where to start, with whom to talk, what paperwork to do, and how to negotiate the license fees in accordance with current industry standards. All of this takes a great deal of time, even if you have the basic information readily at hand.

CAN THE COPYRIGHT OWNER KEEP ME FROM USING A COMPOSITION, EVEN IF I AM WILLING TO PAY FOR IT?

Yes. The owner of the composition can, except in very rare cases, restrict or deny permission for its reproduction or adaptation. In certain circumstances, the performing rights organizations also allow the owner to restrict the public performance of music that is normally subject to blanket performance clearance. Some popular music, freely broadcast on radio or used in nightclub performances, may be blocked from use on commercial television or in motion pictures. The Copyright Law leaves the final decision up to the owner or owners of the work.

WHAT IS A MUSIC CUE SHEET AND WHY IS IT SO IMPORTANT?

A music cue sheet is a document that lists all of the music contained in a production, including the title, composer(s), publisher(s), performing rights affiliation, and use and timing of each musical cue. The cue sheet tells the performing rights societies which composers and publishers are to receive royalty distributions. Additionally, the information contained in the music cue sheet determines how much certain broadcasters will pay to the societies.

The timely delivery of an accurate music cue sheet has always been a requirement in most production/distribution/station license agreements. Practically speaking, the music cue sheet is also a delivery requirement for music publishers and record companies whose music has been used in the production.

WHAT HAPPENS IF I USE A SONG WITHOUT CLEARING IT?

If no one ever catches you, nothing. However, if the matter is discovered by the copyright owner, you, as the producer of the project and any broadcaster or distributor, may be held liable for copyright infringement as well as other actionable claims. Under the Copyright Act, an infringer may be liable for both the damages sustained by the copyright owner and the profits resulting from the unauthorized use of the protected material. Even if the copyright owner cannot show what the damages or profits are, he can still be awarded substantial statutory damages as provided in the Copyright Act.

You may find yourself facing an injunction, paying an out-of-court settlement to the copyright owner, or going back to your finished program and making extensive changes to remove the uncleared material. A producer with a completed project from which release prints or dubs have already been made may find himself or herself incurring costs that are many times what the original clearance and license fees might have been.

WHAT ABOUT OLD SONGS? AREN'T THESE SONGS IN THE PUBLIC DOMAIN AND FREE TO BE USED WITHOUT RESTRICTION?

There is a certain amount of music for which all copyright protection on a worldwide basis has lapsed. Some musical material that may be in the public domain in the United States may still be protected in other countries. Failure to obtain proper international copyright clearance may severely limit exploitation of the project.

If you plan to use public domain material, you must be sure that *any* arrangement created for your use is based on the original public domain version and not on a subsequent copyrighted or protected version, which would require additional clearance. Actual clearance of material should still be carefully undertaken to ensure its public domain status and to comply with errors and omissions insurance procedures. It can take as much time and expense to determine whether a composition is in the public domain as to clear one that is not.

MAY I USE EIGHT BARS OF A SONG WITHOUT PAYING FOR IT?

No! This is one of the most common misconceptions regarding music and its protection under U.S. Copyright Law. Any unauthorized use of material that is recognizable as having come from a copyrighted source is a potential infringement of copyright.

WHAT IS "FAIR USE"?

There is an exception to the exclusive rights of copyright owners called *fair use*, which permits the limited use of copyrighted material in special circumstances without requiring the owner's consent. In theory, the public interest in the dissemination of ideas and information is served when uses for such purposes as criticism, comment, news reporting, scholarship, teaching, parody, social commentary, etc. are freely permitted. *However*, caution is strongly recommended. Since the factors that courts look to in these cases are neither clear nor definitive, it is difficult to determine in advance what may or may not be a permissible "fair use." If you are faced with a question of this nature, it would be prudent to contact your attorney or music clearance service.

MAY I USE THE TITLE OF A SONG AS MY PROGRAM TITLE?

While titles are not protected under copyright law, they may be protected under other legal doctrines. Use of the title and story line of a song may involve the clearance of dramatic rights or require negotiations similar to those required for the acquisition of rights in a literary property. For protection, your attorney should advise you as to whether the title may be freely used, or if specific permission should be obtained from the owner of the song.

MUST A LICENSE BE SECURED IF SONG LYRICS ARE SPOKEN IN DIALOGUE?

The copyright of a song protects the lyrics as well as the music. Therefore, if an identifiable part of a song lyric is used in dialogue, a license may have to be secured in order to avoid potential liability.

MAY I CHANGE THE LYRICS TO AN EXISTING SONG?

Changes made to the copyrighted lyrics of the song, including what may appear to be only minor changes, usually have to be cleared by obtaining specific permission from the copyright owner. This may even apply to the translation of the original lyrics into a foreign language.

IF I CLEAR A SONG FOR ONE EPISODE OF A TELEVISION SERIES, MAY IT BE USED IN OTHER EPISODES WITHOUT ADDITIONAL PERMISSION?

No. Licenses are normally granted on a show-by-show basis, and unless the song was cleared for use in multiple episodes of the series, it can only be used in a single episode without violating the rights of the owner. In addition, a new episode containing clips from previous episodes will usually require additional licenses for the music contained in the clips.

DO I HAVE TO CLEAR MUSIC THAT IS TO BE USED IN COMMERCIALS?

Yes. In order for copyrighted music to be used in the advertising of products and services, the entire procedure for clearing music must be followed. Popular songs are frequently changed or adapted to fit the product or service being promoted. Accordingly, specific permission for use must be obtained from the copyright owner, based upon the markets and media to be exploited.

MAY I USE RECORDS OR COMPACT DISCS ON MY TELEVISION SHOW?

Be careful. This is a complex and gray area of both law and practice. Some use of records on television teen dance shows, for instance, has been permitted by record companies because this use is considered promotional. Other uses of records in television, home video, and motion picture productions may require permission in advance from any number of involved parties, including the music publisher, record company, artist, performer's unions, etc.

Commercial phonograph recordings made and released after February 15, 1972 are eligible for federal copyright protection. Recordings made prior to that date, though not copyrightable, may still be protected under state antipiracy statutes and other legal theories.

IF I OBTAIN A LICENSE TO USE A FILM CLIP FROM A TELEVISION PROGRAM OR FEATURE FILM IN MY PROJECT, WILL THAT LICENSE INCLUDE THE RIGHT TO USE THE MUSIC CONTAINED ON THE SOUND TRACK?

Generally, no. Film clip licenses are usually granted with the producer acknowledging that he or she will be responsible for obtaining all third party rights and clearances. The film clip owner may not own the music, or may have acquired rights for its use in his or her production only. Therefore, if the music on the soundtrack is not specifically covered in the film clip license agreement, it will be your responsibility to obtain additional clearances for its use in your project. The music publishing division of a motion picture company and the production or publicity division of the same company can have completely different outlooks on what you may or may not use.

IF A RECORD COMPANY GIVES ME A MUSIC VIDEO CLIP FOR USE IN MY PROJECT, WILL I NEED FURTHER MUSIC CLEARANCES?

As with other programs, the proper licensing of the music contained in a "promotional" music video requires public performance rights, synchronization rights, and also may require "dramatic" performing rights if the video is telling the story of the song. A producer wishing to use a music video clip in his or her program must first determine which of the above-mentioned music rights, if any, have been granted to him or her by the licensor of the music video (usually a record company). Music videos are typically licensed with the user being responsible for all third-party licensing obligations, including the payments required to be made pursuant to the collective bargaining agreements of any performer's unions. Record companies are not often willing to assume the responsibility of securing or granting synchronization licenses for your purposes.

IS IT TRUE THAT A SYNCHRONIZATION LICENSE IS NOT NECESSARY FOR THE FIRST U.S. NETWORK RUN OF AN ORIGINAL LIVE OR TAPED TELEVISION PROGRAM?

That is correct. In current practice, this is a very limited exception to traditional licensing procedure. However, U.S. network broadcasts occurring more than six months after the first network run and syndicated broadcasts usually require full music rights clearances. Even if no synchronization license is required, all other rights, such as performance and adaptation rights, must be cleared for the first network run. Foreign runs may require synchronization licenses from the first broadcast.

WILL THE NETWORKS' MUSIC CLEARANCE DEPARTMENTS ASSIST ME?

The television networks maintain music clearance personnel to carry out the reporting and clearance requirements of their licenses with the performing rights organizations. Each network may have a different policy. However, they generally do not negotiate synchronization or adaptation rights on behalf of independent producers, but primarily maintain the licenses that provide for blanket clearance of performing rights. In most production contracts, it is the producer's responsibility to inform the broadcaster of the music to be used, to deliver the program with rights secured, and to indemnify the broadcaster or distributor for any resulting liability, no matter who clears the music.

WHAT RIGHTS ARE REQUIRED TO RELEASE A PROGRAM FOR SALE IN THE HOME VIDEO/MULTIMEDIA MARKETPLACE?

Home video distribution, as that term is generally defined in the entertainment industry, requires that the producer obtain the right to reproduce the musical work on the sound track of the program (much like synchronization rights), and the right to manufacture and distribute copies of the program containing the musical work throughout the territories in which distribution is planned. There are currently no public performance rights involved in home video distribution, as long as the program is not displayed at a place open to the public or any place where a substantial number of people outside of a normal family and its social acquaintances is gathered.

HOW ARE MUSIC RIGHTS LICENSED FOR FEATURE FILMS?

In feature films, music rights, whether for a song or a recording, are usually licensed worldwide for the duration of the copyright. This is partly because of the tremendous investment required to make a feature film and the complicated contractual arrangements involved in feature film distribution. Unlike other types of production for which rights may be licensed on a medium-by-medium basis, the producer of a feature film will usually secure a very broad grant of rights so that the film can be exploited in all possible media existing now or in the future.

For antitrust reasons, the performing rights societies are not allowed to collect performing fees from motion picture theaters in the United States. Therefore, a producer must secure a U.S. theatrical performance license directly from the publisher or its agent when securing a synchronization license. Outside of the United States, local performing rights societies collect a percentage of the net box office receipts from theaters exhibiting feature films.

WHAT RIGHTS ARE REQUIRED TO DISTRIBUTE A PROGRAM TO PUBLIC BROADCASTING STATIONS?

The U.S. copyright law provides that a copyright owner must grant a license (a "compulsory" license) for the public (noncommercial) broadcasting of nondramatic musical works and popular recordings. Compulsory license rates are established by the copyright royalty tribunal and are published in the *Federal Register*.

The law also allows public broadcasters and copyright owners or their representatives to enter into voluntary agreements that prevail over compulsory license rates. Such agreements with the Harry Fox Agency, SESAC, and others for the licensing of synchronization rights, and with ASCAP and BMI for the licensing of performance rights, allow covered music to be incorporated into a production at the negotiated rates without the necessity of preclearing the music with the publisher.

Popular music not covered by voluntary agreements may be used pursuant to the compulsory license; however, this only applies to "nonprofit" producers. "For-profit" producers must negotiate synchronization licenses directly with any publisher who is not signatory to a negotiated agreement.

Regardless of the above, dramatic uses and other adaptations will still require permission in advance from the copyright owners. Remember that the license covers only public broadcasting use. Non-PBS exhibition of the program will likely require licenses from all of the parties involved.

HOW MUCH WILL IT COST TO CLEAR A SONG FOR USE IN MY TELEVISION OR FILM PROJECT?

This depends on a number of factors, including the nature of the clearance you are attempting to obtain. Many television producers can get by with a one-, three-, or five-year synchronization license for just the United States; others need worldwide rights and/or possibly longer terms. Feature film producers must make sure they obtain perpetual worldwide motion picture rights, as well as television rights, for eventual domestic and foreign syndication, home video, and other "new" media.

The new technologies have complicated the matter even further, and the rights for these areas are frequently obtained on a medium-by-medium basis. There is no established pattern for these fees, because they vary from composition to composition and must be computed separately for each project's specific rights and releasing requirements.

WHAT IF I HIRE A COMPOSER TO WRITE ORIGINAL MUSIC FOR MY TELEVISION OR FILM PROJECT?

Depending on your agreement with the composer, the musical material created for your project on an "employee for hire" basis may belong to you as the employer. You should discuss the ramifications of "employee for hire" agreements with your attorney before hiring a composer. If the composer has incorporated existing compositions into the score, care must be taken to make sure that those existing compositions have been cleared. Also, the actual status of any public domain material that may have been used should be thoroughly reviewed.

WHAT IS A NEEDLE DROP?

This refers to the use of a single portion, or *cue*, of an existing recording (placing the needle down on the recording and then lifting it) in synchronization with filmed or taped images. If you use a needle drop or cue from a commercially produced popular recording, you may have to deal with all of the normal clearance requirements previously discussed with respect to the song, the recording of the song, the recording artist, and the performer's unions.

There are organizations known as *production music* libraries that provide commercially produced recordings specifically for background broadcast and film use at a variety of reasonable license rates. The libraries will usually issue one license that includes rights for the music and the recording of the music. Some production music companies include so-called sound-alike recordings of popular artists in their libraries. Remember that if such recordings are used, the producer must still secure a license from the publisher of the song. If you are a union signatory, or are producing for a union signatory company, be sure to use caution, because some production music may not comply with union requirements.

WHAT HAPPENS WHEN LICENSES EXPIRE?

If the right to use music contained in a program has been granted for a limited period of time or for limited media (e.g., free television only), those licenses will have to be renewed or expanded if continued or additional exploitation of the program is contemplated. Broadcasts of the program without licenses that contemplate additional time or media may constitute an infringement of the music copyrights. Be careful, because there are well-known cases in which composers and publishers of popular songs have refused to renew expired licenses or have charged exorbitant fees for license renewals.

MAY I, OR SOMEONE ON MY PRODUCTION STAFF, OBTAIN THE REQUIRED MUSIC RIGHTS CLEARANCES FOR MY PROJECT?

Yes, if you or one of the people on your staff has a day-to-day working knowledge of music clearance procedures, and the research and computer information at hand necessary to resolve questions of ownership, licensing practice, and availability. This is a rapidly evolving and specialized area. Most producers have neither the available full-time staff nor the business affairs support required to carry out the task. While an attorney's direct input is not necessarily required in the process, there are continuing questions that must be addressed in order to comply with both the legal and contractual requirements of production. In common practice, many producers use a music clearance service.

The Clearing House, Ltd. (TCH), based in Los Angeles, maintains a staff of industry professionals who specialize in all aspects of music for television and film production and broadcast. Combining highly customized business affairs practices with constantly updated industry source data, TCH provides producers with complete music research, clearance, licensing, and publishing administration services.

The Clearing House, Ltd. clears and licenses all types of musical material for major motion pictures, network series and specials, music videos, video cassettes, and all other media. The company works with producers, artists, publishers, record companies, and business affairs executives worldwide.

CHAPTER ELEVEN

Safety

In an effort to promote a safer work environment, numerous states have enacted legislation implementing injury prevention programs, the training of employees in general safe and healthy work practices, and the adoption of occupational safety and health standards.

In addition to state safety guidelines, the AMPTP, various unions and guilds, major television networks and studios, and many independent production companies have adopted their own safety programs, many in conjunction with an *Industry-Wide Labor-Management Safety Board*. The AMPTP has drafted and disseminated joint safety bulletins over the past several years in conjunction with the unions and guilds. Numbered in succession, each details safety precautions relating to specific potentially hazardous situations and activities. Most of the unions, guilds, studios, etc. use these bulletins as the basis for their own safety program, the most recognized being the producer's *On Production Injury and Illness Prevention Program* (IIPP). Much of the emphasis of the industry-based safety programs is placed on the holding of *safety meetings* and on the *education and training* of employees.

SAFETY MEETINGS

It is strongly recommended that a brief safety meeting be held with the cast and crew at the beginning of each shooting day, as necessary, to discuss the day's activities, especially if the company has moved to a new location

or if there are scenes involving stunts, special effects, aircraft, wild animals, or other potentially hazardous conditions. In addition, safety meetings and/or training are required whenever new potential hazards are introduced and whenever new equipment and/or procedures are implemented. All safety meetings should be documented on the daily production report. Potentially hazardous situations must be clearly identified on the call sheet and marked at the spot, if possible. If appropriate, an AMPTP safety bulletin or other special notification addressing the particular hazard should be attached to the call sheet or posted at the location. In all cases, every attempt should be made to eliminate any hazardous situation, if possible, before it becomes a danger to cast and crew.

SAFETY TRAINING

Basic safety training should begin by emphasizing the company's intent and attitude toward safety and by familiarizing new employees with all company safety policies, rules, and procedures. New employees should be provided with written job descriptions and safety procedures pertaining to their specific areas of responsibility, reinforcing actual on-the-job training. Employees should be informed of all potential exposure to any major hazards, ensuring that they fully understand the degree of hazard and all necessary precautions. After initial orientation and training has been completed, employees' work habits should be periodically evaluated, and all safety training and orientation should be documented.

DGA—DESIGNATED AREAS OF RESPONSIBILITY

The DGA has deemed that unit production managers shall have overall responsibility for the On Production Injury and Illness Prevention Program (IIPP) from pre-production through completion of production. The delegation by the UPM of authority to others in order to effectuate the purposes of the IIPP does not alter such responsibility. The UPM and first and second assistant directors are asked to meet with the person responsible for the overall studio or production company IIPP. In addition to, or in lieu of such a meeting, some studios or production companies may assign an individual to your specific production to assist in safety coordination.

The UPM, and first and second assistant directors, are each assigned different areas of responsibility in the administration of the IIPP. Together, they must (1) make sure the entire shooting company is thoroughly familiar with the safety program; (2) ensure that the safety program is working; (3) troubleshoot as necessary, addressing all hazardous conditions and concerns; (4) ensure the documentation of safety program activities; (5) deal with emergencies and serious accidents; and (6) deal with OSHA inspectors and other safety investigators. The DGA provides their members with detailed guidelines relating to their individual areas of safety management.

SAFETY BULLETINS

Contact the AMPTP, your studio, or production company safety coordinator for a complete set of safety bulletins issued by the Industry-Wide Labor-Management Safety Committee. Copies of the bulletins should be attached to the daily call sheet when appropriate, and it should be confirmed that cast and crew members whose work and areas of responsibility involve the activities covered in the bulletins are fully aware of the detailed safety guidelines they contain. The safety concerns addressed in the bulletins are as follows:

Bulletin #1	Recommendations for Safety with Firearms
Bulletin #2	Seat Belts and Harnessers
Bulletin #3	Helicopter Safety Procedures
Bulletin #4	Communications Regarding Stunts
Bulletin #5	Safety Awareness
Bulletin #6	Animal Handling Rules for the Motion Picture Industry
Bulletin #7	Scuba Equipment Recommendations for the Motion Picture Industry
Bulletin #8	Guidelines for Insert Camera Cars
Bulletin #9	Safety Guidelines for Multiple Dressing Room Units
Bulletin #10	Guidelines Regarding the Use of Artificially Created Smokes, Fogs, and Lighting Effects
Bulletin #11	Guidelines Regarding the Use of Fixed-Wing Aircraft in Motion Pictures
Bulletin #12	Guidelines for the Use of Exotic Venomous Reptiles
Bulletin #13	Gasoline Operated Equipment
Bulletin #14	Code of Safe Practices—Parachuting and Skydiving
Bulletin #15	Recommendations for Safety with Firearms
Bulletin #16	Recommendations for Safety with Explosives and/or Pyrotechnics
Bulletin #17	Water Hazards
Bulletin #18	Guidelines for the Use of Air Bags
Bulletin #19	Guidelines for Use of Open Flames on Motion Picture Sets
Bulletin #20	Guidelines for Use of Motorcycles
Bulletin #21	Appropriate Clothing and Footwear
Bulletin #22	Guidelines for the Use of Elevating Work Platforms (Scissor Lifts) and Aerial Extensible Boom Platforms

GENERAL SAFETY GUIDELINES FOR PRODUCTION

GENERAL RULES

1. Your working conditions may change from day to day, particularly on location, and a set can be an inherently unsafe place to work. To prevent accidents, you need to be aware of your work environment and the equipment being used. Pay attention to call sheets; they may contain important safety information.
2. There is to be NO SMOKING on any stage. Observe designated smoking areas; extinguish cigarettes in butt cans.
3. Wear appropriate clothing and any necessary protective equipment. Do not wear loose clothing and unnecessary jewelry; long hair should be tied back if working around machinery.
4. If you are taking medication that might interfere with your alertness or ability to work, please let your supervisor know. Do not work under the influence of illegal drugs or alcoholic beverages.
5. Pranks and horseplay should be kept in check.
6. Maintain clear walkways and exit passageways. Keep a four-foot perimeter around the interior of the stage clear. Keep all exit doors unlocked when working.
7. Fire equipment (hydrants, extinguishers, ladders, hoses, fire lanes, etc.) must be accessible at all times and must not be blocked or used for any purpose for which not originally intended.
8. Production days can be long and grueling; make sure you are getting adequate sleep. Exhaustion can cause accidents too.
9. Report all accidents and injuries, no matter how minor, to your supervisor immediately.

LIFTING AND MOVING

1. Follow the correct procedures for lifting. Do not attempt to lift excessive or awkward loads without getting help. If an object is too heavy to move without strain, ask for help!
2. Lift with your legs, not your back. Avoid lifting if possible; use carts, dollies, etc.

COMMON FALL RISKS

1. Temporary stair railings and guard rails are required for any elevated surfaces (over 30 feet) or around pits or holes.
2. Ensure proper lighting at all entrances and exits, stairways, and working areas. Post warning signs if necessary. Use safety harnesses where needed, especially if working above ground level on scaffolding, elevated platforms, etc. or outside areas with guard rails.

HAND TOOLS AND SMALL EQUIPMENT

1. Use the right tool for the job. Do not operate any piece of equipment if you have not been trained to use it; see your supervisor first.
2. Report any defective, damaged, or malfunctioning equipment to your supervisor. Tag "Do Not Use."
3. Operate machinery with all safety guards in place. Wear protective equipment (eye shields, earplugs, respirators), as necessary.
4. Do not use the top two steps of any ladder. Make sure the ladder is adequately supported. Do not leave ladders free-standing against walls—secure them.

FILMING EQUIPMENT AND VEHICLES

1. Use the proper equipment for the job (re: booms, camera and insert cars, process trailers, cranes, etc.). Be aware of load and rider capacities.
2. Never allow more than nine people, including the driver, on an insert car. Only those crew members absolutely essential to the shot should be allowed on the car or trailer.
3. Operators and passengers of all vehicles (including picture vehicles, stunt cars, and

elevated platforms) should always use safety belts or harnessers. Boat passengers should wear life vests.

4. Proceed slowly when driving in congested areas.

5. Be cautious when working around helicopters and other aircraft and on runways. Do not smoke within fifty feet of helicopters, and keep this distance unless you are needed closer. Never approach a helicopter from the rear; make eye contact with the pilot or other individual giving directions.

6. The use of any type of vehicle may require special permits and/or operator certifications. All vehicles and their equipment must undergo thorough safety inspection and testing on a *daily basis* by qualified personnel.

CHEMICALS AND FLAMMABLE MATERIALS

1. Paints, chemicals, and other hazardous materials should not accumulate on stage where they do not belong.

2. Clean up all spills; do not allow spilled oil, wax, water, etc. to remain on the floor.

3. When handling hazardous materials, follow the prescribed safety procedures, especially for their disposal. All containers must be labeled as to their contents.

4. All decorative set materials should be flame retardant or of noncombustible materials.

5. Material Safety Data Sheets (MSDS) should be obtained and kept on file for all chemicals being used and/or stored.

ELECTRICAL SAFETY

1. Ground and properly maintain all electrical equipment and wiring—leave no exposed live parts.

2. Keep electrical panels accessible at all times.

3. Do not place lights too close to props, flags, and other set materials—beware of the danger of fire.

WATER HAZARDS

1. Safetylines, nets, observers, and/or divers should be used when filming in rivers or other bodies of water where hazardous conditions could exist.

2. On watercraft, be aware of load and rider capacity limits. Only persons absolutely needed should be on the craft. If crafts are to be out for extended periods of time, equip all boats with adequate drinking water supplies.

3. Be sure you are comfortable working around water. Know the natural hazards (plant and animal life, etc.); find out if you are unsure.

STUNTS AND SPECIAL EFFECTS

1. Special effects involving pyrotechnics, explosives, and/or fire must be noted in advance on the call sheet.

2. All such effects must be performed by properly licensed individuals. Obtain the proper permits and notify the appropriate regulatory agencies. Explosives must be stored in their proper magazines.

3. All cast and crew members should wear appropriate safety protective equipment. Only persons necessary for the stunt/effect should be in the area.

4. All stunts and special effects require an on-site walk-through with all involved parties before filming.

5. When working indoors, there must be a planned escape route provided. Each person involved should personally check the escape route to ensure its accessibility.

FIREARMS AND LIVE AMMUNITION

1. Treat all firearms as though they are loaded. Do not play around with any weapons—*never* point a weapon at anyone, including yourself.

2. Follow the directions of the prop master regarding all firearms and weapons.

3. Live ammunition will not be used unless absolutely necessary. If used, it must be noted on the call sheet and announced prior to use on the set.

4. The use of firearms and other weapons may require special permits and/or operator certifications. All firearms must undergo thorough safety inspection, testing, and cleaning on a daily basis by qualified, experienced personnel.

5. You should feel comfortable working with firearms and other weapons. Know all the operating features and safety devices. Ask the prop master or weapons expert for help if not.

ANIMALS

1. When working with wild or venomous animals, the set should be closed and notices posted to that effect, including a notice on the call sheet.
2. The animal trainer should address the cast and crew regarding all safety precautions in effect. Defer to the animal trainer at all times.
3. Do not feed, pet, or play with any animal without the permission and direct supervision of its trainer.

Make sure all cast and crew members receive a copy of these safety guidelines. All employees should be required to sign an *Acknowledgement of Safety Guidelines* (sample included in this chapter) attesting to having received, read, and understood these procedures.

Many studios and production companies provide their production units with a supply of Safety Checklists and Work Site Safety Reports to be filled out on a daily basis. Other forms have been devised to note safety concerns while breaking down a script and for documenting safety meetings, training sessions, and various safety compliance measures. If the studio or production company you are working for does not have such forms that you are required you to use, design forms of your own that will specifically address the safety concerns pertaining to your production.

SCREEN ACTORS GUILD— SAFETY REGULATIONS

A. A qualified first-aid person shall be present on all sets where hazardous work is planned. The producer shall properly equip this person, establish the capabilities of nearby medical facilities, and provide transportation and communication with these facilities.

B. Where any of the following conditions are planned as part of a driving sequence and

special expertise is necessary in order to perform such driving sequence in a safe manner, the on-camera driver shall qualify as a stunt performer under Schedule H of the SAG Agreement.

1. When any or all wheels will leave the driving surface.
2. When tire traction will be broken (skids, slides, etc.).
3. When the driver's vision will be substantially impaired by dust, spray (when driving through water, mud, etc.), blinding lights, restrictive covering over the windshield, smoke, or any other conditions that would substantially restrict the driver's normal vision.
4. When the speed of the vehicle will be greater than normally safe for the conditions of the driving surface, or when other conditions—such as obstacles or difficulty of terrain, will exist, or off-road driving—other than normal low-speed driving for which the vehicle was designed, will occur.
5. When any aircraft, fixed-wing or helicopter, is flown in close proximity to the vehicle, creating a hazardous driving condition.
6. Whenever high speed or close proximity of two or more vehicles create conditions dangerous to the drivers, passengers, film crew, or vehicles. Nothing herein shall require the performer to be doubled where the performer has the special expertise to perform the sequence in a safe manner.
7. When for safety reasons a performer is doubled on-camera as the driver of a vehicle, the double shall qualify as a stunt performer under Schedule H of the SAG Agreement. This would also apply to passengers in a vehicle who must be doubled for their safety.

C. When stunts are required, a person qualified in planning, setting up, and/or performing the stunt must be present on the set. Persons involved in the planning and execution of a stunt shall be entitled to inspect any vehicle, mechanical device, and/or equipment to be used in the stunt on the day prior to its use, provided it is available. In any event, such persons shall have reasonable time for such inspections.

No payment shall be due for any inspection. The non–stunt performer shall have the opportunity to consult with this person before being required to perform a stunt.

D. The stunt coordinator shall notify the guild whenever scripted stunts are planned involving non–stunt performers.

E. The producer must always get the performer's consent before asking the performer to engage in a stunt or hazardous activity. They DO NOT have to agree; they may always request a double.

F. All reasonable requests and requirements for safety equipment in connection with the performance of stunts shall be complied with by the producer or the producer's representatives on the set or location.

G. Equipment provided by the producer, for example, autos, cycles, wagons, etc., shall be in suitable repair for the safe and proper performance of the stunt.

SEXUAL HARASSMENT

In promoting practices that provide for a safer and healthier work environment, the matter of sexual harassment must be addressed as well. It is imperative to inform your entire cast and crew that sexual harassment will not be tolerated on your production.

Under federal law, unwelcome sexual advances, requests for sexual favors, and other verbal or physical conduct of a sexual nature constitute sexual harassment when (1) submission to such conduct is made either explicitly or implicitly a term or condition of an individual's employment, (2) submission to or rejection of such conduct by an individual is used as the basis for employment decisions affecting such individual, or (3) such conduct has the purpose or effect of unreasonably interfering with an individual's work performance or creating an intimidating, hostile, or offensive working environment. This can include verbal behavior such as unwanted sexual comments, suggestions, jokes, or pressure for sexual favors; nonverbal behavior, such as suggestive looks or leering; and physical behavior, such as pats or squeezes, or repeatedly brushing against someone's body.

Although many assume that sexual harassment involves a male boss and a female employee, this is not always the case. Sexual harassment often involves co-workers, other employees of the company, or other persons doing business with or for the company. It is against the law for females to sexually harass males or other females, as well as for males to harass other males or females.

Anyone who is being sexually harassed should, if possible, confront the harasser and ask him or her to stop. If this does not stop the behavior, the UPM should be informed of the situation as soon as possible. If, for whatever reason, the UPM cannot be told, the producer should be informed immediately. Sexual harassment or retaliation can be reported in writing or verbally, and may also be reported by someone who is not the subject of the harassment. If the UPM or producer is unable to curb the unwanted behavior, the situation must be reported to the studio or production company, and an investigation will be conducted. Where evidence of sexual harassment or retaliation is found, disciplinary action, up to and including termination, may result. If an employee is found to have engaged in sexual harassment, or if you as a manager know about the conduct and condone it, you may be personally liable for monetary damages.

"ON LOCATION"—PERSONAL SAFETY CONSIDERATIONS AND SUGGESTIONS

This information was prepared by Al Marrewa, President of Powerflex USA, Inc. of Los Angeles, California

VISIT LOCATIONS PRIOR TO FIRST DAY OF SHOOTING

Familiarize yourself with locations—streets, buildings, police and fire departments, hospitals, gas stations, restaurants, and pay telephones. Know the location.

GANG-OCCUPIED LOCATIONS

1. Notify the police department and/or the sheriff's department gang detail unit. Request an increase in security and visibility.
2. Know which gangs can be found in the location area.
3. Suggest to those in power that filming be avoided on Friday and Saturday nights.
4. Remember that gang members can be as young as twelve to thirteen years old.
5. While on location, avoid wearing red/blue/black clothing, such as caps, bandanas, jackets (anything similar to gang attire).
6. While on location, be aware of others wearing red/blue/black clothing, such as caps, bandanas, jackets or team clothing/colors.
7. Be aware of two or more individuals wearing similar clothing of any kind. Many gang members will follow a particular dress code, including having similar haircuts.
8. When gang members are used as extras, notify the police or sheriff's gang detail unit in advance. Request additional security support.
9. Be aware of a vehicle with three or more occupants that is parked or moving slowly down a street or alley.
10. If nearby gunfire breaks out at any time, immediately *drop to the ground, face first.* Stay down until gunfire ceases. Then, get to a safe place.

ADDITIONAL SUGGESTIONS

1. Whenever possible, be with other people from your group or company. There is safety in numbers.
2. Whenever possible, stay in sight of other group or company members.
3. Know how you appear to others at all times. Do you stand out in a particular area because of your race, sex, or dress?
4. Never wear expensive or showy jewelry or clothing (i.e., watch, rings, bracelets, necklace, leather jacket).
5. Carry *small* amounts of cash at any time.
6. Whenever possible, use a buddy system while on location ("I'll keep an eye on you, and you keep an eye on me").

7. Consider carrying a high-powered whistle with you at all times. This can be used to notify others in an emergency.

TAKING ACTION

1. Always walk down the middle of a street, especially at night; walking on sidewalks close to buildings, alleys, bushes, and hidden areas can be dangerous.
2. If you notice a group of men staring at you, glancing at you one at a time, or pointing toward you, run or walk away quickly. (Know where safety is.) If you must walk near them, show no fear. Show confidence in your walk and do not stop. You may choose to look directly at one of them, straight in the eye, acknowledging *confidently* that you see them. Remember, this should be a *nonthreatening* gesture.
3. When dealing with street/neighborhood people—be aware of everything around you (i.e., people, physical environment).

If you get into a precarious situation, ask yourself the following questions:

Am I outnumbered?

Is he/are they outnumbered?

Am I concerned?

Can I get to safety if needed?

Are tempers increasing?

Is he/are they under the influence of alcohol or drugs?

Can I see both of his hands (or are they hidden?)

Can I see a weapon?

How much distance is between this person and myself?

Are *my* actions threatening/challenging him/them?

Do I feel physically threatened?

What/how am I feeling right now?

Am I prepared to fight?

CONFLICT RESOLUTION

1. Treat the other person with respect.
2. Listen until you understand the other person's point of view.

3. Express your own views, needs, feelings.
4. Use body language to communicate with the other person (i.e., face him or her directly/maintain an "open" position/make eye contact).
5. Avoid sarcasm.
6. Negotiate.

SELF-DEFENSE INCLUDES

1. Awareness
2. Assertiveness
3. Communication (verbal and nonverbal)
4. Instinct
5. Intuition
6. Planning
7. Preparation
8. Teamwork

ACKNOWLEDGEMENT OF SAFETY GUIDELINES

This will acknowledge that in accordance with the Injury and Illness Prevention Program
in place at ___XYZ PRODUCTIONS, INC._____ ,
I have received, read and understand the *Production Safety Guidelines* pertaining to the
production of ___HERBY'S SUMMER VACATION_____ .

I am aware that failure to adhere to these procedures could endanger me and my
co-workers, and I will strive to further the company's policy of maintaining a safe work
environment.

___*F. Stopp*_____   ___APRIL 11, 19XX_____
Employee's Signature   Date

___F. STOPP_____   ___DIRECTOR OF PHOTOGRAPHY___
Employee's Name (print or type)   Job Title or Position

(Please return this form to the Production Office when signed.)

CHAPTER TWELVE

Locations

There are many aspects to consider before deciding to shoot at any one location besides how much the owner of the property will charge you for the right to shoot on his or her premises. How much will the permit cost? How much lead time do you need to get a permit? Will you require police and fire safety officers and how many of each? Can you use an off-duty fire officer, or must it be one on active duty? Does this location have restricted hours in which you can shoot? If you are shooting past a certain time at night or before a certain time in the morning, will you need permission from the surrounding neighbors? Will you need neighborhood consent and/or special permits for the use of firearms or special effects at this location? Will you need to close a street? Will you need additional motorcycle police officers for intermittent traffic control? If so, how many? Will you need to *post for parking*? Will you have sufficient parking for your cast and crew at the location or will you have to find a nearby parking lot and *shuttle* everyone to the location site? Will you need to provide evidence of special or additional insurance coverage for use of this location?

The answers will vary from city, to county, to state, to country, with each having its own set of fees and regulations. The sphere of Los Angeles County film permits alone encompasses approximately 35 individual cities in the Los Angeles area plus Los Angeles City and Los Angeles County, each with its own filming guidelines.

Each state has its own film office, and there are approximately 56 metropolitan U.S. cities and 49 international cities (outside of the U.S.) that have their own film office. These offices are set up to enforce their specific film regulations, offer information, promote filmmaking in their city, and assist the filmmakers who choose to shoot in their area.

A good location manager will be able to help determine not only where each location should be, but also to ascertain the specific fees, regulations, and restrictions that come with each site. On bigger shows and shows with several locations to find, it is usually necessary to have an assistant location manager as well.

There are independent location services that will help you find all your locations. Some represent specific properties and others specialize in specific types of locations (only warehouses and office buildings, only mansions, only schools and hospitals, etc.). There are also *film permit services* that provide information, permits (they will pick them up and bring them right to you), police and fire safety officers, and will arrange to post for parking and/or to collect neighborhood signatures when they are necessary.

The number of locations you need to find, the cost of each, and consideration of your budget will determine the combination of location staff and/or services utilized on your show. Clearly, a location manager (or service) working in conjunction with a film permit service is ideal.

FILMMAKER'S CODE OF CONDUCT

If location work is set up properly, with all members of the shooting company knowing up front what is expected of them, residents who reside in the area where you are filming are not unreasonably infringed upon. When filming in a commercial or industrial area, there should be little or no disruption of normal business activities, customer access, and parking, and the rights of the businesses to operate without interference are protected.

Film units that have had little regard for the location where they are shooting or the surrounding neighborhood have not only made it difficult for the next production company that wants to shoot at that location, but their behavior negatively affects the entire industry. Individual property owners and entire communities who have had poor experiences with film companies have ceased to allow any further filming activities on their premises or in their neighborhoods.

In an effort to improve the standards of the film industry and to endorse better community relations and location preservation, leaders within the industry came together to formulate the *Filmmaker's Code of Professional Responsibility* for location filming. These guidelines are being promoted by all the major studios and many unions, guilds, and industry-related organizations. Although rapidly gaining acceptance, code of conduct guidelines are not yet being observed by all production companies. The program needs to be encouraged and implemented throughout the industry, worldwide, extending to the smallest of film units.

Distribute copies of the following to your entire cast and crew, and attach additional copies to daily call sheets when necessary.

Filmmaker's Code of Conduct

1. When filming in a neighborhood or business district, proper notification is to be provided to each merchant or neighbor who is directly affected by the company (this includes parking, base camps and meal areas). The filming notice should include:

a. Name of company

b. Name of production

c. Kind of production (e.g., feature film, movie of the week, TV pilot, etc.)

d. Type of activity and duration (i.e., times, dates, and number of days, including prep and strike)

e. Company contacts (first assistant director, unit production manager, location manager)

The Filmmaker's Code of Professional Responsibility should be attached to the filming notification which is distributed to the neighborhood.

2. Production vehicles arriving on location in or near a residential neighborhood shall not enter the area before the time stipulated in the permit, and park one by one, turning off engines as soon as possible. Cast and crew shall observe designated parking areas.

3. Every member of the crew shall wear a production pass (badge) when issued.

4. Moving or towing of the public's vehicles is prohibited without the express permission of the municipal jurisdiction or the owner of the vehicle.

5. Do not park production vehicles in, or block driveways without the express permission of the municipal jurisdiction or driveway owner.

6. Cast and crew meals shall be confined to the area designated in the location agreement or permit. Individuals shall eat within their designated meal area, during scheduled crew meals. All trash must be disposed of properly upon completion of the meal.

7. Removing, trimming and/or cutting of vegetation or trees is prohibited unless approved by the permit authority or property owner.

8. Remember to use the proper receptacles for disposal of all napkins, plates, and coffee cups that you may use in the course of the working day.

9. All signs erected or removed for filming purposes will be removed or replaced upon completion of the use of that location unless otherwise stipulated by the location agreement or permit. Also remember to

remove all signs posted to direct the company to the location.

10. Every member of the cast and crew shall keep noise levels as low as possible.

11. Do not wear clothing that lacks common sense and good taste. Shoes and shirts must be worn at all times, unless otherwise directed.

12. Crew members shall not display signs, posters or pictures on vehicles that do not reflect common sense or good taste (i.e. pin-up posters).

13. Do not trespass onto other neighbors' or merchants' property. Remain within the boundaries of the property that has been permitted for filming.

14. The cast and crew shall not bring guests or pets to the location, unless expressly authorized in advance by the company.

15. All catering, crafts service, construction, strike and personal trash must be removed from the location.

16. Observe designated smoking areas and *always* extinguish cigarettes in butt cans.

17. Cast and crew will refrain from the use of lewd or improper language within earshot of the general public.

18. The company will comply with the provisions of the parking permit.

In addition to the code of conduct guidelines as listed above, remind your crew to operate with great care when shooting inside of someone's home or office. Be especially aware of potential dents, scratches, and stains that can easily occur while setting up and moving equipment. Protect walls, doors, floors, and carpeting to the best of your ability; cover furniture not being used, and ask that valuables (not needed as props or set dressing) be put away for safe keeping by the owner(s).

LOCATION INFORMATION SHEET

SHOW __HERBY'S SUMMER VACATION__

LOCATION MANAGER __B. SCOUT__

PERMIT SERVICE __PAT'S PERMIT SERVICE__

CONTACT __PAT__

PHONE # __(213) 555-7662__

PRODUCTION # __0100__

(SCRIPTED) LOCATION __HERBY'S DAD'S LAW OFFICE__

DATE(S) __6-15-XX__

☑ INT. ☐ EXT. ☑ DAY ☐ NIGHT

ACTUAL LOCATION
(Address & Phone #)

__1000 ATLANTIC BLVD., SUITE 1200__
__LOS ANGELES, CA 90000__
__(213) 555-6000__

DATE & DAYS

	# of days	dates
Prep:	1	6-14-XX
Shoot:	1	6-15-XX
Strike:	1	6-16-XX

LOCATION OF NEAREST EMERGENCY MEDICAL FACILITY

__BEVERLY HILLS HOSPITAL__
__2000 TINSELTOWN RD.__
__BEVERLY HILLS__

CONTACTS

__OFFICES OF:__
__DEWEY, CHEATEM & HOWE__

Owner(s) Name(s) __CHARLES CHEATEM__

Address __1000 ATLANTIC BLVD. #1200__
__LOS ANGELES, CA 90000__

Phone/FAX # __(310) 555-6000__

Beeper # __(310) 555-1626__

Representative(s)

Company: __LOCATION FINDERS, INC.__

Contact: __BORIS__

Address: __5153 RAILROAD DR.__
__LOS ANGELES CA 90000__

Phone/FAX # __(213) 555-2222__

Beeper # __(213) 555-1246__

LOCATION SITE RENTAL FEE

Full Amount $ __2,000__

Amount for PREP days $ __500__

Amount for SHOOT days $ __1,000__

Amount for STRIKE days $ __500__

Deposit $ __500__ Due on __6/1/XX__

☐ Refundable ☑ Apply to total fee

Balance $ __1,500__ Due on __6/13/XX__

O.T. after __12__ hrs. per day @ $ __100__ per hr.

__ANY__ Additional days @ $ __1,000__ per day

Additional charges:

Phone $ __50/DAY__

Utilities $ __INCL.__

Parking $ __150__

(Other) _____ $ _____

CHECKLIST

- ☑ Location Agreement
- ☑ Certificate of Insurance
- ☑ Permit
- ☑ Fire Safety Officer(s)
- ☐ Police
- ☑ Location Fee
- ☑ Security
- ☐ Intermittent Traffic Control
- ☑ Post for Parking
- ☑ Signed Release from Neighbors
- ☑ Prepared Map to Location

- ☐ Heaters/Fans/Air Conditioners
- ☑ Lay-out Board/Drop Cloths
- ☐ Utilities/Power Supply

Allocated Areas For
- ☑ Extras
- ☑ Dressing Rms.
- ☑ Eating
- ☑ Hair/Makeup
- ☐ School
- ☑ Equipment
- ☑ Special Equipment
- ☐ Animals

Allocated Parking For
- ☑ Equipment
- ☑ Honeywagons
- ☑ Motor Homes
- ☑ Catering Truck
- ☑ Cast Vehicles
- ☑ Crew Vehicles
- ☐ Buses
- ☐ Picture Vehicles
- ☑ Extra Tables & Chairs/Tent
- ☐ Locate Parking Lot if Shuttle is Necessary

© ELH Form #39

LOCATION LIST

SHOW __HERBY'S SUMMER VACATION__   PRODUCTION # __0100__

SET LOCATION	ACTUAL LOCATION (ADDRESS & PHONE)	DATE & DAYS (PREP/SHOOT/STRIKE)	CONTACTS (OWNER & REPRESENTATIVE)		
HERBY'S DAD'S OFFICE	OFFICES OF: DEWEY, CHEATEM & HOWE 1000 ATLANTIC BLVD., SUITE 1200 L.A. 90000 (213) 555-6000	PREP: 6-14-XX SHOOT: 6-15-XX STRIKE: 6-16-XX	CHARLES CHEATEM (213) 555-6000 LOCATION FINDERS, INC. (213) 555-1222 ATTN: BORIS		
HERBY'S HOUSE	WESTER HOME 12436 SOUNDMAN RD. STUDIO VILLAGE, CA 91111	PREP: 6-16-XX SHOOT: 6-17&18 STRIKE: 6-19-XX	K. WESTER H: (818) 555-3221 O: (818) 555-1223		

© ELH Form #40

REQUEST TO FILM DURING EXTENDED HOURS

Dear Resident:

This is to inform you that **XYZ PRODUCTIONS** will be shooting a film entitled **"HERBY'S SUMMER VACATION"** in your neighborhood at the following address: **12353 Rose Street.** Filming activities in residential areas is normally allowed only between the hours of **8:00 a.m.** and **8:00 p.m.** In order to extend the hours before and/or after these times, the City requires that we obtain a signature of approval from the neighbors. The following information pertains to the dates and times of our scheduled shoot and any specific information you may need to know regarding our filming activities.

We have obtained or applied for all necessary City permits and maintain all legally required liability insurance. A copy of our film permit will be on file at the City Film Office and will also be available at our shooting location.

FILMING DAYS/HOURS REQUESTED: on **August 3rd and 4th, 19XX**
      from **10:00 a.m.** to **10:00 p.m.**
      and **August 5th and 6th, 19XX**
      from **12:00 noon** to **12:00 midnight**

THE FOLLOWING ACTIVITIES ARE PLANNED FOR THE EXTENDED HOURS:
A backyard party to include approximately 80 extras, a minimal amount of loud music and a stunt where ten guests fall into the swimming pool.

We appreciate your hospitality and cooperation. We wish to make filming on your street a pleasant experience for both you and us. If you have any questions or concerns before or during the filming, please feel free to call our Production Office and ask for me or the Production Manager.

Sincerely yours,

_____   _____
Location Manager   Production Company

                                      _____
                                        Phone No.

We would very much appreciate it if you would complete and sign where indicated below.
A representative from our company will be by within the next day or two to pick up this form.

— —— —— —— —— —— —— —— —— —— —— —— —— —— —— — —

☐ I DO NOT OBJECT TO THE EXTENDED FILMING HOURS
☐ I DO OBJECT TO THE EXTENDED FILMING HOURS

COMMENTS:

NAME: _____

ADDRESS: _____

             _____

PHONE #: (Optional) _____

Rel #18

CHAPTER THIRTEEN

Distant Location

Distant Location Checklist

- ❑ Contact film commissions representing areas you are considering as location sites
- ❑ Review location photos while weighing the advantages (and disadvantages) of shooting at each site
- ❑ Select a travel agent who is accustomed to working with production companies
- ❑ Scout location sites under consideration
- ❑ Make final location site selections
- ❑ Develop a good working relationship with local film commission representatives in the area(s) where you will be shooting
- ❑ Contact a SAG branch office for jurisdictional guidelines
- ❑ Hire a local location manager, if necessary
- ❑ Hire a local extras casting agency (or extras coordinator), if necessary
- ❑ Consider the purchase of CD ROM cross-referenced telephone directory and map programs
- ❑ Obtain a local phone book to locate needed services and nearby medical facilities
- ❑ Determine the availability of local crew, drivers, office help, etc. and set up interviews
- ❑ Determine whether it would be more economical to rent equipment and supplies on location or to bring them with you

- ❑ Determine whether suitable catering is available locally or if you will have to bring a catering truck and crew to location
- ❑ Secure living accommodations (i.e., hotel, motel, condos) for arriving cast and crew
- ❑ Set up accounts for gasoline, rental cars, motor homes, supplies, etc.
- ❑ Make travel arrangements for cast and crew
- ❑ Prepare a movement list
- ❑ Prepare a list of airline schedules to and from the location(s)
- ❑ Arrange with the airline or travel agency to have someone at the airport to meet cast and crew members and help with arriving equipment
- ❑ Open an account with the airline for the shipment of dailies
- ❑ Obtain a supply of packing slips, air bills, labels, heavy tape, etc. for the shipping of film each night
- ❑ Open a local bank account
- ❑ Have outside phone line(s) installed in the production office if at all possible
- ❑ Rent typewriters, computers and printers (as necessary), and a copier machine for the production office
- ❑ Order a portable screen and projector or a VCR and monitor to screen dailies
- ❑ Prepare a room list
- ❑ Distribute safety and code of conduct guidelines to cast and crew

- [ ] Prepare a local contact list that includes:
  1. Names, addresses, and phone numbers of a doctor, a dentist, paramedics, and a hospital*
  2. Local weather reports for the area
- [ ] Prepare a list of local restaurants, laundry facilities, rental car agencies, etc. for cast/crew members*
- [ ] Prepare a list of local shooting locations*
- [ ] Locate a source for flowers, fruit baskets, etc. for cast and VIP arrivals
- [ ] Locate clothing racks for the wardrobe department (if needed)
- [ ] Arrange to rent a refrigerator, coffee machine, etc. for the production office
- [ ] Find out if refrigerators and microwave ovens are available for cast and crew to rent (if not already in hotel rooms)

Keep maps of how to get to each location in the production office at all times. Tack a call sheet and map to the next day's location on the production office door when you close up for the night.

INTERACTING WITH LOCAL COMMUNITIES

Meeting, working with, and interacting with local people on a shooting location can be a rewarding experience and produce friendships that long outlast your shooting schedule. Most people living outside of big film centers are thrilled to have a film shooting in their town and will extend a great deal of hospitality and support to the visiting production. Keep in mind, however, that the perception any local community has of your shooting company will reflect on the entire film industry. The reaction by the community, good or bad, will directly affect your company's (and future companies') access to location sites, cooperation from local merchants, rates on hotel rooms, site rentals, local services, and everything connected to that location. A negative experience with one film company can motivate an entire city to ban all

---

*Add directions and/or maps whenever possible.

future film production in that area.

Inform local cast and crew members (in addition to reminding those traveling from home base) of Code of Conduct guidelines. This should be done verbally as well as in memo form. In dealing with local merchants, pay your bills in a timely manner and make sure to get what you need without being overly demanding. Be courteous and treat people with respect. Jackets and T-shirts that display vulgarities should not be worn, and noise levels should not get out-of-hand. Do not interfere with the normal activities of the neighborhood unless these activities are authorized as part of your scheduled shoot. Leave location sites cleaned and as you had originally found them (if not better). As time permits, involve the community in your activities as much as possible. A positive rapport with the community will not only help to promote a positive image of the film industry, but it will guarantee that you would be welcomed back with open arms and increasing cooperation on your next shoot at that location.

FILM COMMISSIONS

The purpose of a film commission is to promote and aid film production in a particular city, state, or country. Film commissions are state (or government) based and are found throughout the country and in several countries other than the United States. Some film offices are independent entities, some operate as part of various governors' offices, and others are divisions of tourism boards. They are all members of the Association of Film Commissioners International (AFCI), "an international, non-profit, educational organization of government employees serving as film commissioners. The association's purpose is to act as a liaison between the visual communications industry and local governments or organizations to facilitate on-location production, and to stimulate economic benefit for member governments" (*Locations* magazine).

General information on shooting in various locations can be obtained through *Locations* magazine, the official publication of the AFCI, and also by attending *Location Expo*, a yearly, three-day convention (held in February in Los Angeles) where national and international film commissions exhibit a vast array of locations and location services.

In an effort to persuade you to shoot your picture and spend your production dollars in their state or country, film commission representatives are most helpful in the process of selecting locations and also during production when shooting on a distant location. When you are considering different locations in which to shoot, contact the film office representing each of those locations. They will not only answer questions over the phone, but will also send you photographs of location sites that might meet your needs and provide information on local crew, living accommodations, services, and pertinent tax and/or permit requirements.

If you plan to scout a number of locations before making a final selection, call the film commission representing each area ahead of time. Film commissioners and/or members of their staff will generally meet with you, show you around, and help in any way they can, from cutting through government red tape, to obtaining permits, to helping you get a good rate on hotel rooms.

Once you select a location, working with the local film commission will save you valuable time, energy, and money. You need a person, or persons, who know that area well and are at the same time familiar with the demands of filming and production coordination.

The relationship between production company and film commission should be mutually congenial. More often than not, film commission representatives will become unofficial members of your crew (and should be treated as such). They should be invited to lunch on the set and to cast and crew parties, and most definitely, they should be sent a letter (or gift) of thanks and appreciation before you wrap and head back home. As with the entire community, a positive relationship with the film commission will only enhance the amount of support and cooperation you and other production companies will be afforded in the future. An official AFCI directory of film commissions is listed at the end of this chapter.

SAG BRANCH OFFICES

Even if you have signed an agreement and posted a bond (in one of SAG's main offices) prior to leaving for a distant location, contact the local SAG branch office upon arriving at your location. Local SAG representatives are your best source of information for matters such as what constitutes a local hire within that state, current guidelines on right-to-work state laws (if applicable), casting procedures in that area, the hiring of local extras, drive-to reimbursements, etc. A current list of SAG branch offices can be found at the end of Chapter 7.

WORKING WITH THE HOTEL

Without even being asked, cast and crew members will generally inform you (prior to traveling to location) as to their preferences in hotel rooms. Supply the hotel with a listing of arrivals (names, dates, and times of arrival), what type of room each person is to have and/or requests based on the hotel's availability (a suite, a king-size bed, two beds, a room on the ground floor, etc.), and indicate when each of the rooms is to be vacated. Keep the reservations clerk alerted as to any last-minute additions and/or changes in arrivals and departures.

Reserve additional hotel rooms for a production office, an accounting office, a transportation office, camera and sound equipment, an editing room, and a wardrobe room. Rooms for equipment, editing, and wardrobe should be on the ground floor and should have dead-bolt locks on the doors. Make sure the hotel is aware of the company's parking needs and can supply sufficient parking space for production vehicles and trucks.

Make sure the hotel has rooms ready for check-in when cast and crew members arrive, even if they arrive early in the day (before check-in time). Arrange with the hotel management for cast and crew members to pay for their own incidental charges.

Keep your own list (Hotel Room Log) of when each person checks in and out to compare against hotel bills. It may be helpful to keep two lists—one in alphabetical order for quick reference and one according to the cast and crew lists. Channel all complaints about hotel rooms and facilities through the production office.

If the hotel is busy, think about reserving a couple of extra rooms, just in case the schedule changes and additional cast or crew members have to be brought to location earlier than anticipated (most hotels will not charge you for holding the extra rooms, as long as you release the ones you will not be needing early each afternoon, so they can be rented that night). Find out the status of available rooms should your show run over schedule and the company has to stay longer than anticipated. Check out the availability of rooms at other hotels and motels in the area should they be needed.

Find out if the hotel has a banquet or conference room that could be used to screen dailies each evening or for production meetings if needed. Check the hours of the hotel's coffee shop. If they do not open early enough or stay open late enough, they may be willing to make special arrangements to open early for breakfast (before *call* time) and stay open after wrap.

If the hotel has a beauty shop, check to see if it could be made available to the company early each morning for cast members to have their hair and makeup done before leaving for location.

If the company is shooting nights, make arrangements with Housekeeping for the maids *not* to awaken cast and crew in the morning (and let the coffee shop know your hours have changed). Get permission to post a call sheet in the hotel lobby each night.

SHIPPING DAILIES

You need to open an account with the air cargo division of the airline you choose for the shipment of dailies, and you need to send each night's shipment *over the counter*. Select an airline that flies nonstop to your destination, with the most evening flights. If it is impossible to get a direct flight, choose a route that has as few stops as possible. This will lessen the chances of the film being unloaded at the wrong stop.

If you call the airline, a representative will usually come to your office to open an account

and to give you blank waybills and flight schedules. Keep the flight schedules of more than the one airline in case there is a problem with the airline or their flight schedule does not meet your needs in a *rush* situation and you have to ship dailies via another carrier. You should not have to open accounts with other airlines. On the rare occasion you would be using another carrier, your driver can pay cash and fill out a new waybill at the counter.

Be sure to keep a copy of each waybill in case your shipment is delayed, mislaid, or lost. (They also provide backup to the shipping bills.) It is a good idea to keep a log of every shipment that leaves the production office, indicating: date, waybill #, flight #, arrival and departure times, and the contents of your shipment (the number of reels you are shipping, number of rolls of sound tape and still film, any equipment you may be returning, etc.)

It is best to have a runner from the office or a courier service pick up your daily shipment. This person should go to the airport before you start shipping dailies and introduce himself to the airline personnel who will be handling the film shipment when it comes in each night. (A gratuity or two might also be a good idea in this situation.) Should there be a problem with the flight or the routing of the dailies, it would help to know the airport routine and to be on good terms with the staff.

Once the film starts arriving, your runner or courier will open the box(es) and separate the film for the lab, the 1/4 inch sound tapes, the still film, the envelope(s) for the office (you should *pouch* copies of all your daily paperwork back to the home office via the daily shipment each night), and whatever else you have sent. The runner will drop the film and sound off that night, and deliver the remainder to the office first thing the next morning for distribution.

Labels on the box(es) should be addressed to the production office (always include the office phone number), with the notation: *HOLD FOR PICKUP*. Boxes should also indicate or have labels that read: *UNDEVELOPED FILM—DO NOT X-RAY*.

It is best to ship film on the same flight each evening. The last flight out is the one usually selected to allow a full day's worth of shooting (or most of one) to be sent out. If shooting for the day is not completed by the time the driver has to leave for the airport, the camera crew will have to *break* at a designated time and send what they have.

The driver making the airport run should have the packed boxes, a completed waybill, and a memo indicating the flight information and a description of what is in each of the boxes you are sending. He or she should call the production coordinator from the airport to confirm that the boxes got on board and that the flight was on schedule. If there is a problem, he or she should call to inform production that the boxes had to be sent on another airline or that the flight is going to be delayed. The production coordinator will in turn call the runner or courier on the other end to confirm an estimated arrival time and to give him or her the waybill number. When the driver returns, he or she should give the production coordinator a completed copy of the waybill. Because most labs are closed from Friday night to Sunday night, you should ship Friday and Saturday's footage on Sunday afternoon so that it arrives before midnight on Sunday.

RECEIVING DAILIES VIA FIBEROPTICS

Once the lab receives your daily shipment of footage, the negative is developed and dailies are sent back to you on the following day. The traditional choice is whether to receive dailies on a 35mm work print or videocassette, both of which are sent via *over-the-counter* airline service. There is now another choice, not yet available in all areas nor affordable to all, but certainly an option that will one day soon be both more available and affordable. This new option is to have your dailies sent back to you directly from the lab over fiberoptic lines.

Fiberoptics is growing in popularity and usage as fiberoptic lines are spreading throughout the world. Sports events are being relayed fiberoptically, as are many other live broadcasts. There is virtually no loss of quality, and there is no time delay in the transmission.

The process as it pertains to dailies starts with the transfer of your developed negative and sound track to videocassette. The videocassette is taken to a company that has fiberoptic capability and is sent via a piece of equipment (one manufacturer calls their unit an *Alcatel*) that transmits the picture and sound over a fiberoptic line. It is recovered by a like unit at the other end and is recorded back onto videocassette.

Even if the lab or video facility you are using can transmit fiberoptically, you must be near a hub and have access to a recovery facility in the area where you are shooting. Also, transmission units (such as the Alcatel) are not yet available throughout the entire country. They are installed through local phone companies, and not all phone companies are able to offer the equipment. Check with your lab to see if this process is a possible option for you.

Just as *Kleenex* is synonymous with tissue and *Xerox* is synonymous with photocopying, *Vyvx* has become synonymous with the process of transmitting an image over fiberoptic lines. *Vyvx* is the name of a company that is the leader in the industry of fiberoptics, and "Vyvx it to me" is rapidly becoming a commonly used term.

TRAVEL MOVEMENT

SHOW __HERBY'S SUMMER VACATION__   PROD # __0100__

TRAVEL FROM __LOS ANGELES, CA__ TO __MILWAUKEE, WISCONSIN__

DAY/DATE __MON. SEPT. 20, 19XX__   AIRLINE __WISCONSIN AIR__

TYPE OF AIRCRAFT __747__   MEAL(S) __LUNCH__   MOVIE __YES__

FLIGHT # __230__   DEPARTURE TIME __11:00 A.M.__   ARRIVAL __5:15 P.M.__ FLIGHT STOPS IN _____

CHANGE TO FLIGHT # _____ DEPARTURE _____ ARRIVAL _____

NAME	POSITION	GROUND TRANSPORTATION TO AIRPORT	TO BE PICKED UP @	GROUND TRANSPORTATION FROM AIRPORT
SWIFTY DEALS	PRODUCER	LOU'S LIMO SER.	10:00 A.M.	MILWAUKEE DRIVER TO PICK UP CREW OUTSIDE OF BAGGAGE AREA
SID CELLULOID	DIRECTOR	LOU'S LIMO SER.	9:45 A.M.	
FRED FILMER	UPM	DRIVER TO PICKUP	9:30 A.M.	
F. STOPP	DIR. OF PHOTOG.	DRIVER TO PICKUP	9:45 A.M.	

HOTEL __MILWAUKEE GRAND__

Address __12345 WISCONSIN BLVD.__

__MILWAUKEE, WISCONSIN__

Phone # __(414) 555-2000__

DIRECT # TO PRODUCTION OFFICE __(414) 555-2376__

FAX # __(414) 555-2352__

ADDITIONAL INFO. _____

© ELH Form #41

HOTEL ROOM LOG

SHOW _HERBY'S SUMMER VACATION_

HOTEL _MILWAUKEE GRAND_

LOCATION _MILWAUKEE, WISCONSIN_

PROD # _0100_

CONTACT _JOYCE_

PHONE # _(414) 555-2000_

NAME	POSITION	ROOM #	TYPE OF ROOM	RATE	DATE IN	DATE OUT	TOTAL DAYS
SWIFTY DEALS	PRODUCER	215	SUITE	150	9/20/XX	10/23/XX	33
SID CELLULOID	DIRECTOR	220	SUITE	150	9/20/XX	10/24/XX	34
FRED FILMER	U.P.M.	112	KING	85	9/20/XX	10/30/XX	40
F. STOPP	DIR. OF PHOTOG.	103	KING	85	9/20/XX	10/23/XX	33
A. DEES	1ST ASST. DIR.	330	QUEEN	80	9/20/XX	10/23/XX	33

© ELH Form #42

HOTEL ROOM LIST

SHOW <u>HERBY'S SUMMER VACATION</u> PROD # <u>0100</u>

HOTEL <u>MILWAUKEE, GRAND</u> LOCATION <u>MILWAUKEE, WIS.</u>

ADDRESS <u>12345 WISCONSIN BLVD.</u>

<u>MILWAUKEE, WISCONSIN</u> LOCATION DATES <u>9-20-XX</u>

PHONE # <u>(414) 555-6000</u> FAX # <u>(414) 555-6001</u> Through <u>10-30-XX</u>

NAME	POSITION	ROOM #	DIRECT #
Production Office	----------	103	555-6376
Accounting Office	----------	101	555-6374
Transportation Office	----------	105	555-6372
Editing Room	----------	107	555-6370
SWIFTY DEALS	PRODUCER	215	
SID CELLULOID	DIRECTOR	220	
A. DEES	1ST ASST. DIR.	330	
KATIE KANDU	SCRIPT SUPV'R.	307	
PAULA PROPS	PROPERTY MASTER	217	
MIKE BOOM	SOUND MIXER	302	

© ELH Form #43

MEAL ALLOWANCE

SHOW __HERBY'S SUMMER VACATION__   PROD # __0100__

LOCATION __MILWAUKEE, WISCONSIN__   WEEK OF __SEPT. 20 - 26, 19XX__

MEAL RATES
BREAKFAST $ 8-
LUNCH $ 12-
DINNER $ 20-

NAME	MON 9-20 B	L	D	TUE 9-21 B	L	D	WED 9-22 B	L	D	THUR 9-23 B	L	D	FRI 9-24 B	L	D	SAT 9-25 B	L	D	SUN 9-26 B	L	D	TOTAL	SIGNATURE
A. DEES	-	-	20	-	-	20	-	-	20	-	-	20	-	-	20	-	-	20	8	12	20	200	A. Dees
K. KANDU	-	-	20	-	-	20	-	-	20	-	-	20	-	-	20	-	-	20	8	12	20	200	K. Kandu
M. BOOM	-	-	20	-	-	20	-	-	20	-	-	20	-	-	20	-	-	20	8	12	20	200	M. Boom
P. PROPS	-	-	20	-	-	20	-	-	20	-	-	20	-	-	20	-	-	20	8	12	20	200	P. Props
C. COORDINATES	8	12	20	8	12	20	8	12	20	8	12	20	8	12	20	8	12	20	8	12	20	280	C. Coordinates
A. ACCOUNTANT	8	12	20	8	12	20	8	12	20	8	12	20	8	12	20	8	12	20	8	12	20	280	A. Accountant

TOTAL: $1360-

APPROVED: _Will Filmer_

TRAVEL MEMO TO CAST & CREW

DATE: **June 25, 19XX**

TO: **F. STOPP**

FROM: **FRED FILMER**

RE: TRAVEL & HOTEL ACCOMMODATIONS/LOCATION INFORMATION FOR CAST & CREW
          TRAVELING TO **MILWAUKEE, WISCONSIN**

As per your contract, you will be provided with **one business-**class, round-trip air fare(s) to **Milwaukee.**

At the present time, you are scheduled to travel on **July 5, 19XX** on **Wisconsin Air**, Flight **#45**. The flight departs at **11:00 a.m.** from LAX and arrives at **5:15 p.m.**

Lunch will be served during your flight.

The following ground transportation will be provided for you:

> TO AIRPORT: **AIRPORT SHUTTLE VAN**
> You will be picked up at **9:45 a.m.**
> FROM AIRPORT: **Local Driver will be waiting at airport**

You will be staying at: **MILWAUKEE GRAND HOTEL**
12345 Wisconsin Blvd.
Milwaukee, Wisconsin
(414) 555-2000

The following accommodations have been reserved for you: **Deluxe room with king size bed**

On location, ☒ you will be provided with a vehicle
          ☐ we are not able to provide you with a vehicle
          ☐ you will be sharing the use of a vehicle

Your per diem will be **$100** per day.

Please be aware that upgrading your air fare, bringing guests, reserving a larger room, etc. is to be done at your own expense. You can make additional plane reservations through **Haley** at **Star Studded Travel** at **818/555-4467**, and you will be informed as to the additional costs. All hotel incidental charges (room service, long distance phone calls, etc.) will be charged directly to you by the hotel.

All department heads are requested to supply **Connie** with a list of any equipment/wardrobe/ props, etc. that will need to be shipped to location. We will need to know how many pieces each department will be shipping and if any of the pieces are oversized. Shipping tags and labels can be picked up at the production office.

Also, please let **Connie** know as soon as possible as to any special requests you might have such as renting a car (if one is not provided for you) or a small refrigerator for your room. Every effort will be made to accommodate your requests.

Reports indicate that current weather conditions in **Milwaukee** are **hot (85 degrees) and humid.** We will be shooting **ten** nights and the weather at night for this time of year is anticipated to be **warm and muggy.** Please pack accordingly.

At the present time, your return flight is scheduled for **Friday, August 3, 19XX** on **Wisconsin Air,** Flight **#46**, leaving **Milwaukee** at **9:15 a.m.** and arriving in **Los Angeles** at **11:30 a.m.**

If there are changes in our shooting schedule or unforeseen delays that would extend our location shooting, you will be informed and your return reservations updated.

Your room will be reserved until the completion of ☐ your role ☒ production, and your return flight will be booked accordingly. If you wish to remain at this location or travel elsewhere at the completion of ☒ principal photography ☐ your role, please check with us first as your services may be needed for looping and/or pick-up shots. We may not know immediately if and/or when, but would let you know ASAP. If you choose to remain on location, however, it will be your responsibility to make further arrangements with the hotel and to re-book your own airline tickets. Please just let us know of your plans if you will not be returning with the rest of the company.

If you have any additional questions regarding your travel or location accommodations, please contact **Connie Coordinator** at **555-3331**.

THE OFFICIAL AFCI DIRECTORY OF FILM COMMISSIONS

Organized in Alphabetical Order by Country

AUSTRALIA

NEW SOUTH WALES
New South Wales Film & Television Office
Level 6, 1 Francis Street
Sydney, NSW 2010 Australia
61-2-380-5599   Fax: 61-2-360-1090

QUEENSLAND
Queensland Pacific Film & TV Commission
111 George Street, 16th Floor
Brisbane, Queensland 4000 Australia
61-7-224-4114   Fax: 61-7-224-4077

AUSTRIA

Cineaustria
11601 Wilshire Blvd., Suite 2480
Los Angeles, CA   90025
310-477-3332   Fax: 310-477-5141

BAHAMAS

Bahamas Film And Television Commission
3450 Wilshire Blvd., Suite 208
Los Angeles, CA 90010
213-385-0033   Fax: 213-383-3966

BRITISH VIRGIN ISLANDS

British Virgin Islands Film Commission
Road Town
Chief Minister's Office
Tortola, British V.I.
809-494-4119, ext. 221   Fax: 809-494-6413

CANADA

ALBERTA
Alberta Economic Development & Tourism
10155 102 Street, 12th Floor
Edmonton, AB T5J 4L6 Canada
403-427-2005   Fax: 403-427-5924

CALGARY
Calgary Film Services
P.O. Box 2100, Station M
Calgary, AB T2P 2M5 Canada
403-268-2771   Fax: 403-268-1946

EDMONTON
Edmonton Motion Picture & TV Bureau
9797 Jasper Avenue
Edmonton, AB T5J 1N9 Canada
800-661-6965
403-424-7870   Fax: 403-426-0535

BRITISH COLUMBIA
British Columbia Film Commission
601 West Cordova Street
Vancouver, BC V6B 1G1 Canada
604-660-2732   Fax: 604-660-4790

BURNABY
Burnaby Film Office
4949 Canada Way
Burnaby, BC V5G 1M2 Canada
604-294-7231   Fax: 604-294-7220

OKANAGAN-SIMILKAMEEN
Okanagan-Similkameen Film Commission
27-9015 Westside Road
Kelowna, BC V1Y 8B2 Canada
604-769-1834   Fax: 604-769-1864

THOMPSON-NICOLA
Thompson-Nicola Film Commission
2079 Falcon Road
Kamloops, BC V2C 4J2 Canada
604-372-9336   Fax: 604-372-5048

VICTORIA/VANCOUVER ISLAND
Victoria/Vancouver Island Film Commission
525 Fort Street
Victoria, BC V8W 1E8 Canada
604-386-3976   Fax: 604-385-3552

MANITOBA
CIDO/Location Manitoba
Suite 333-93 Lombard Ave.
Winnipeg, MB R3B 3B1 Canada
204-947-2040   Fax: 204-956-5261

NEW BRUNSWICK
New Brunswick Film/Video Commission
P.O. Box 6000
Fredericton, NB E3B 5H1 Canada
506-453-2553   Fax: 506-453-2416

NEWFOUNDLAND
Service Industries Division, DITT
P.O. Box 8700
St. John's, Newfoundland A1B 4J6 Canada
800-563-2299
709-729-5632   Fax: 709-729-5936

NORTHWEST TERRITORIES
Yellowknife Economic Development Authority
Box 1688
Yellowknife, NT X1A 2P3 Canada
403-873-5772   Fax: 403-920-5649

NOVA SCOTIA
Nova Scotia Film Development Corp./
  Location Services
1724 Granville Street
Halifax, NS B3J 1X5 Canada
902-424-7185   Fax: 902-424-0563

ONTARIO
Ontario Film Development Corporation
175 Bloor Street East, Suite 300
North Tower
Toronto, ONT M4W 3R8 Canada
416-314-6858   Fax: 416-314-6876
(Los Angeles) 213-960-4787 Fax: 213-960-4786

TORONTO
Toronto Film and Television Office
2nd Floor, West City Hall
Toronto, ONT M5H 2N2 Canada
416-392-7570   Fax: 416-392-0675

PRINCE EDWARD ISLAND
Prince Edward Island Film Office
West Royalty Industrial Park
Charlottetown, PEI C1E 1B0 Canada
902-368-6329   Fax: 902-368-6301

QUEBEC
Province of Quebec Film Office
1755, Rene-Levesque Boulevard East, Suite 200
Montreal, QB H2K 4P6 Canada
514-873-7768
514-873-5027   Fax: 514-873-4388

MONTREAL
Montreal Film & Television Commission
5650 D'Iberville, 4th Floor
Montreal, QB H2G 3E4 Canada
514-872-2883   Fax: 514-872-1153

QUEBEC CITY
Quebec City Film Bureau
171 St.-Paul Street, Suite 100
Quebec City, QB G1K 3W2 Canada
418-692-5338   Fax: 418-692-5602

SASKATCHEWAN
Location Saskatchewan (SASKFILM)
2445 13th Avenue, Suite 340
Regina, SASK S4P 0W1 Canada
306-347-3456   Fax: 306-359-7768

REGINA
City of Regina
P.O. Box 1790
Regina, SASK S4P 3C8 Canada
306-777-7486   Fax: 306-777-6803

YUKON
Yukon Film Commission
P.O. Box 2703
Whitehorse, YT Y1A 2C6 Canada
403-667-5400   Fax: 403-667-2634

FRANCE

Rhone-Alpes
Rhone-Alpes Film Commission
7 Place Antonin Poncet
Lyon, Rhone-Alpes 69002 France
33-78-37-4348   Fax: 33-78-37-5041

Var
South of France Film Commission
Rue Emile Miramont
Entrecasteaux, Var 83570 France
33-94-04-4070   Fax: 3-94-04-4998

GERMANY

Munich Film Information Office
Kaiserstrasse 39
D-80801 Muenchen Germany
49-89-38 19 04-0
49-89-38 19 04-32   Fax: 49-89-38 19 04-38

HONG KONG

Hong Kong Film Liaison
10940 Wilshire Blvd, Suite 1220
Los Angeles, CA 90024
310-208-2678   Fax: 310-208-1869

ISRAEL

Israel Film Centre
30 Agron Street
Jerusalem 94190 Israel
972-2-220608   Fax: 972-2-236303
213-658-7924 (Los Angeles)

JAMAICA

Jampro/Jamaica Film & Entertainment Office
35 Trafalgar Road, 3rd Floor
Kingston, 10 Jamaica
809-929-9450
809-926-4613   Fax: 809-924-9650

MEXICO

Instituto Mexicano de Cinematografia
Tepic #40, P.B. Colonia Roma Sur
Mexico City, C.P. 06760 Mexico
525-584-72-83
525-564-41-87   Fax: 525-574-07-12

SRI LANKA

Sri Lanka Film Commission
4269 Via Marina, #9
Marina del Rey, CA 90292-5013
310-301-8173   Fax: 310-823-0862

THAILAND

Thailand Film Promotion Center
599 Bumrung Muang Road
Bangkok, 10100 Thailand
66-2-223-4690,
66-2-223-4474   Fax: 66-2-223-2586

UNITED KINGDOM

British Film Commission
70 Baker Street
London, W1M 1DJ England
44-71-224-5000   Fax: 44-71-224-1013

ENGLAND

BATH
Bath Film Office
The Pump Room, Stall Street
Bath, Avon BA1 1LZ United Kingdom
44-1225-461-111   Fax: 44-1225-481-062

ISLE OF MAN
Isle of Man Film Commission
Sea Terminal Buildings
Douglas, Isle of Man, Great Britain
44-0624-686841   Fax: 44-0624-686800

LIVERPOOL
The City of Liverpool Film Office
William Brown Street, Central Libraries
Liverpool, L3 8EW England
44-51-225-5446   Fax: 44-51-207-1342

NORTH OF ENGLAND
Northern Screen Commission
Stonehills, Shields Road
Gateshead, Tyne/Wear NE10 OHW England
44-91-469-1000   Fax: 44-91-469-7000

YORKSHIRE
Yorkshire Screen Commission
The Workstation, 15 Paternoster Row
Sheffield, Yorkshire S1 2BX United Kingdom
44-7-42-799-115, 44-7-42-796-811
Fax: 44-7-42-798-593   Fax: 44-7-42-796-522

SCOTLAND

Scottish Screen Locations
Filmhouse, 88 Lothian Road
Edinburgh, EH3 9BZ Scotland
44-31-229-1213   Fax: 44-31-229-1070

EDINBURGH
Edinburgh & Lothian Screen Industries
Filmhouse, 88 Lothian Road
Edinburgh, EH3 9BZ Scotland
44-31-228-5960   Fax: 44-31-228-5967

WALES

Gwynedd Film Office/Marketing & Tourism
Gwynedd County Council 2
Bangor, Gwynedd LL57 4BN Wales
44-248-670007   Fax: 44-248-670112

VENEZUELA

Venezuelan Film & Television Office
Centro Profesional Santa Paula, Torre B
Caracas, 1060 Venezuela
58-2-985-2348   Fax: 58-2-985-3734

UNITED STATES

ALABAMA
Alabama Film Office
401 Adams Avenue
Montgomery, AL 36130
800-633-5898   Fax: 205-242-2077

ALASKA
Alaska Film Office
3601 C Street, Suite 700
Anchorage, AK 99503
907-562-4163   Fax: 907-563-3575

ARIZONA
Arizona Film Commission
1800 North Central Avenue, Building D
Phoenix, AZ 85012
800-523-6695
602-280-1380   Fax: 602-280-1384

APACHE JUNCTION
Apache Junction Chamber of Commerce
P.O. Box 1747
Apache Junction, AZ 85217-1747
602-982-3141   Fax: 602-983-3234

COCHISE COUNTY
Cochise County Film Commission
1415 West Melody Lane, Building B
Bisbee, AZ 85603
602-432-9454
602-432-9200   Fax: 602-432-5016

FLAGSTAFF
Greater Flagstaff Economic Council
1300 South Milton, Suite 125
Flagstaff, AZ 86001
602-779-7658   Fax: 602-556-0940

GLOBE MIAMI
Globe Miami Film Commission
P.O. Box 2539
1360 North Broad Street, U.S. 60
Globe, AZ 85502
800-804-5623
602-425-4495   Fax: 602-425-3410

HOLBROOK
Holbrook Film Commission
P.O. Box 70
465 North First Avenue
Holbrook, AZ 86025
602-524-6225   Fax: 602-524-2159

NAVAJO NATION RESERVATION
Navajo Nation Film Office
P.O. Box 2310
Window Rock, AZ 86515
602-871-6656
602-871-6655   Fax: 602-871-7355

PAGE/LAKE POWELL
Page/Lake Powell Film Commission
P.O. Box 727
106 South Lake Powell Blvd.
Page, AZ 86040
602-645-2741   Fax: 602-645-3181

PHOENIX
City of Phoenix Motion Picture Office
200 West Washington, 10th Floor
Phoenix, AZ 85003-1611
602-262-4850   Fax: 602-534-2295

PRESCOTT
City of Prescott
P.O. Box 2059
Prescott, AZ 86302
602-445-3500   Fax: 602-776-6255

SCOTTSDALE
Scottsdale Film Office
3939 Civic Center Blvd.
Scottsdale, AZ 85251
602-994-2636   Fax: 602-994-7780

SEDONA–OAK CREEK
Sedona Film Commission
P.O. Box 2489
Sedona, AZ 86339
602-204-1123

TUCSON
Tucson Film Commission
32 North Stone Avenue, Suite 100
Tucson, AZ 85701
602-791-4000
602-429-1000   Fax: 602-791-4963

WICKENBURG
Wickenburg Film Commission
P.O. Drawer CC
216 North Frontier Street
Wickenburg, AZ 85358
602-684-5479   Fax: 602-684-5470

YUMA
Yuma Film Commission
P.O. Box 230
Yuma, AZ 85366
602-341-1616
602-782-2567   Fax: 602-343-0038

ARKANSAS
Arkansas Motion Picture Development Office
1 State Capital Mall, Room 2C-200
Little Rock, AR 72201
501-682-7676   Fax: 501-682-FILM

EUREKA SPRINGS
Eureka Springs Chamber of Commerce
P.O. Box 551
Eureka Springs, AR 72632
501-253-8737

CALIFORNIA
California Film Commission
6922 Hollywood Blvd., Suite 600
Hollywood, CA 90028-6126
800-858-4PIX
213-736-2465   Fax: 213-736-2522

BIG BEAR LAKE
City of Big Bear Lake Film Office
P.O. Box 10000
39707 Big Bear
Big Bear Lake, CA 92315
909-878-3040   Fax: 909-866-6766

BUTTE COUNTY
Chico Chamber of Commerce
P.O. Box 3038
500 Main Street
Chico, CA 95927
916-891-5556, ext. 326   Fax: 916-891-3613

CATALINA ISLAND
Catalina Island Film Commission
P.O. Box 217
Avalon, CA 90704
310-510-7646   Fax: 310-510-1646

EL DORADO/TAHOE COUNTY
El Dorado/Tahoe Film Commission
542 Main Street
Placerville, CA 95667
800-457-6279
916-626-4400   Fax: 916-642-1624

EUREKA-HUMBOLT
Eureka-Humbolt County Convention
  & Visitors Bureau
1034 Second Street
Eureka, CA 95501-0541
800-346-3482
707-443-5097   Fax: 707-443-5115
(CA only) 800-338-7352

FILLMORE
City of Fillmore Film Commission
P.O. Box 487
524 Sespe Avenue
Fillmore, CA 93016
805-524-3701   Fax: 805-524-5707

KERN COUNTY
Kern County Board of Trade
2101 Oak Street
Bakersfield, CA 93301
800-500-KERN
805-861-2367   Fax: 805-861-2017

LOS ANGELES
Motion Picture and Television Division
6922 Hollywood Blvd., Suite 614
Los Angeles, CA 90028
213-461-8614   Fax: 213-847-5009

MONTEREY COUNTY
Monterey County Film Commission
P.O. Box 111
801 Lighthouse Avenue
Monterey, CA 93942-0111
408-646-0910   Fax: 408-655-9244

ORANGE COUNTY
Orange County Film Office
One City Blvd. West, Suite 401
Orange, CA 92668
714-634-2900   Fax: 714-978-0742

PALM SPRINGS
Palm Springs Desert Resorts
   Convention & Visitors Bureau
69-930 Highway 111, Suite 201
Rancho Mirage, CA 92270
800-96-RESORTS
619-770-9000   Fax: 619-770-9001

PASADENA
City of Pasadena
100 North Garfield Avenue, #103
Pasadena, CA 91109
818-405-4152   Fax: 818-405-4785

PLACER COUNTY
Placer County Film Office
13460 Lincoln Way, #A
Auburn, CA 95603
916-887-2111   Fax: 916-887-2134

REDDING
Redding Convention & Visitors Bureau
777 Auditorium Drive
Redding, CA 96001
800-874-7562
916-225-4100   Fax: 916-225-4354

RIDGECREST
Ridgecrest Film Commission
100 West California Avenue
Ridgecrest, CA 93555
800-847-4830
619-375-8202   Fax: 619-371-1654

RIVERSIDE/SAN BERNARDINO
San Bernardino/Riverside County
   Film Commission
3281 East Guasti Road, Suite 100
Ontario, CA 91761
909-984-3400, ext. 231   Fax: 909-460-7733

SACRAMENTO
Sacramento Area Film Commission
1421 K Street
Sacramento, CA 95814
916-264-7777   Fax: 916-264-7788

SAN DIEGO
San Diego Film Commission
402 West Broadway, Suite 1000
San Diego, CA 92101-3585
619-234-3456   Fax: 619-234-0571

SAN FRANCISCO
San Francisco Film & Video Arts Commission
Mayor's Office
401 Van Ness Avenue, Room 417
San Francisco, CA 94102
415-554-6244   Fax: 415-554-6503

SAN JOSE
San Jose Film & Video Commission
333 West San Carlos, Suite 1000
San Jose, CA 95110
800-726-5673
408-295-9600   Fax: 408-295-3937

SAN LUIS OBISPO
San Luis Obispo County Film Commission
1041 Chorro Street, Suite E
San Luis Obispo, CA 93401
805-541-8000   Fax: 805-543-9498

SANTA BARBARA COUNTY
Santa Barbara County Film Council
P.O. Box 92111
504 State Street
Santa Barbara, CA 93190-2111
805-962-6668   Fax: 805-969-5960

SANTA CLARITA VALLEY
Santa Clarita SCV Film Liaison Office
23920 Valencia Blvd., Suite 125
Santa Clarita, CA 91355-2175
800-4FILMSC
805-259-4787   Fax: 805-259-8628

SANTA CRUZ COUNTY
Santa Cruz County Conference &
  Visitors Council
701 Front Street
Santa Cruz, CA 95060
408-425-1234   Fax: 408-425-1260

SANTA MONICA MOUNTAINS
Santa Monica Mountains NRA
30401 Agoura Road, Suite 100
Aguora Hills, CA 91301
818-597-1036, ext. 212   Fax: 818-597-8537

SONOMA COUNTY
Sonoma County Film Liaison Office
5000 Roberts Lake Road, Suite A
Rohnert Park, CA 94928
707-586-8100
707-586-8110   Fax: 707-586-8111

TEMECULA
Temecula Valley Film Council
43174 Business Park Drive
Temecula, CA 92590
909-699-6267   Fax: 909-694-1999

COLORADO
Colorado Motion Picture & TV Commission
1625 Broadway, Suite 1700
Denver, CO 80202
303-620-4500   Fax: 303-620-4545

BOULDER COUNTY
Boulder County Film Commission
P.O. Box 73
Boulder, CO 80306
800-444-0447
303-442-1044   Fax: 303-938-8837

CANON CITY
Fremont/Custer County Film Commission
P.O. Box 8
Canon City, CO 81212
719-275-5149

COLORADO SPRINGS
Colorado Springs Film Commission
30 South Nevada Avenue, Suite 405
Colorado Springs, CO 80903
719-578-6943   Fax: 719-578-6394

DENVER
Mayor's Office of Art, Culture & Film
280 14th Street
Denver, CO 80202
303-640-2686   Fax: 303-640-2737

FORT MORGAN
Fort Morgan Area Film Commission
P.O. Box 100
710 East Railroad Avenue
Fort Morgan, CO 80701
303-867-3001   Fax: 303-867-3039

GREELEY
Greeley/Weld County Film Commission
1407 8th Avenue
Greeley, CO 80631
303-352-3566   Fax: 303-352-3572

NORTHWEST COLORADO
Yampa Valley Film Board, Inc.
Box 772305
Steamboat Springs, CO 80477
303-879-0882   Fax: 303-879-2543

TRINIDAD
Trinidad Film Commission
136 West Main Street
Trinidad, CO 81082
800-748-1970
719-846-9412   Fax: 719-846-4550

CONNECTICUT
Connecticut Film Office
865 Brook Street
Rocky Hill, CT 06107
203-258-4301   Fax: 203-529-0535

DANBURY
Danbury Film Office
P.O. Box 406
72 West Street
Danbury, CT 06813
800-841-4488
203-743-0546   Fax: 203-794-1439

DELAWARE
Delaware Film Office
P.O. Box 1401
99 Kings Highway
Dover, DE 19903
800-441-8846
302-739-4271   Fax: 302-739-5749

DISTRICT OF COLUMBIA
Washington
Mayor's Office of Motion Picture & TV
717 14th Street, NW, 12th Floor
Washington, D.C. 20005
202-727-6600   Fax: 202-727-3787

FLORIDA
Florida Entertainment Commission
505 17th Street
Miami Beach, FL 33139
305-673-7468   Fax: 305-673-7168

BREVARD COUNTY
Space Coast Film Commission
c/o Brevard County Government Center
2725 St. Johns
Melbourne, FL 32940
800-93-OCEAN
407-633-2110   Fax: 407-633-2112

BROWARD COUNTY
Film & Television Office
200 East Las Olas Blvd., Suite 1850
Fort Lauderdale, FL 33301
305-524-3113   Fax: 305-524-3167

FORT MYERS
Lee County Film Office
P.O. Box 398
2180 West First Street, Suite 306
Fort Myers, FL 33902
800-330-3161
813-335-2481   Fax: 813-338-3227

JACKSONVILLE
Jacksonville Film & TV Office
128 East Forsythe Street, Suite 505
Jacksonville, FL 32202
904-630-2522   Fax: 904-630-1485

KEY WEST
Florida Keys & Key West Film Commission
P.O. Box 984
402 Wall Street
Key West, FL 33040
800-527-8539
305-294-5988   Fax: 305-294-7806

MIAMI/DADE COUNTY
Miami/Dade Office of Film, TV & Print
111 Northwest 1st Street, Suite 2510
Miami, FL 33128
305-375-3288   Fax: 305-375-3266

NORTHWEST FLORIDA/OKALOOSA
Northwest Florida/Okaloosa Film Commission
P.O. Box 4097
1170 Martin Luther King, Jr. Blvd., #717
Fort Walton Beach, FL 32547-4097
904-651-7374   Fax: 904-651-7378

OCALA/MARION COUNTY
Ocala/Marion County Film Commission
110 East Silver Springs Blvd.
Ocala, FL 34470
904-629-2757   Fax: 904-629-1581

ORLANDO
Metro Orlando Film & Television Office
200 East Robinson Street, Suite 600
Orlando, FL 32801
407-422-7159   Fax: 407-843-9514

PALM BEACH COUNTY
Palm Beach County Film Liaison Office
1555 Palm Beach Lakes Blvd., Suite 204
West Palm Beach, FL 33401
407-233-1000   Fax: 407-683-6957

POLK COUNTY
Central Florida Development Council
P.O. Box 1839
600 North Broadway, #300
Bartow, FL 33830
813-534-4371   Fax: 813-533-1247

TAMPA
City of Tampa Motion Picture &
  TV Development
306 East Jackson
Tampa, FL 33602
813-274-8419
813-274-7501   Fax: 813-274-7176

VOLUSIA COUNTY
Volusia County Film Office
P.O. Box 910
123 East Orange Avenue
Daytona Beach, FL 32114
800-544-0415
904-255-0415   Fax: 904-255-5478

GEORGIA
Georgia Film & Videotape Office
285 Peachtree Center Avenue, Suite 1000
Atlanta, GA 30303
404-656-3591   Fax: 404-651-9063

SAVANNAH
Savannah Film Commission
P.O. Box 1027
c/o City Manager's Office
Savannah, GA 31402
912-651-3696   Fax: 912-238-0872

HAWAII
Hawaii Film Office
P.O. Box 2359
Honolulu, HI 96804
808-586-2570   Fax: 808-586-2572

BIG ISLAND OF HAWAII
Big Island Film Office
25 Aupuni Street
Hilo, HI 96720
808-961-8366   Fax: 808-935-1205

KAUAI
Kauai Film Commission
4280-B Rice Street
Lihue, HI 96766
808-241-6390   Fax: 808-241-6399

MAUI
Maui Film Office
200 South High Street
Wailuku, Maui, HI 96793
808-243-7710
808-243-7415   Fax: 808-243-7995

OAHU
Oahu Film Office
530 South King Street, Room 306
Honolulu, HI 96813
808-527-6108   Fax: 808-523-4666

IDAHO
Idaho Film Bureau
Box 83720
700 West State Street, 2nd Floor
Boise, ID 83720-0093
800-942-8338
208-334-2470   Fax: 208-334-2631

ILLINOIS
Illinois Film Office
100 West Randolph, Suite 3-400
Chicago, IL 60601
312-814-3600   Fax: 312-814-6175

CHICAGO
Chicago Film Office
1 North LaSalle, Suite 2165
Chicago, IL 60602
312-744-6415   Fax: 312-744-1378

QUAD CITIES
Quad Cities Development Group/Film Coalition
1830 2nd Avenue, Suite 200
Rock Island, IL 61201
309-326-1005   Fax: 309-788-4964

INDIANA
Indiana Film Commission
1 North Capitol, #700
Indianapolis, IN 46204-2288
317-232-8829   Fax: 317-233-6887

IOWA
Iowa Film Office
200 East Grand Avenue
Des Moines, IA 50309
800-779-3456
515-242-4726   Fax: 515-242-4859

CEDAR RAPIDS
Cedar Rapids Area Film Commission
P.O. Box 5339
119 First Avenue SE
Cedar Rapids, IA 52406-5339
800-735-5557
319-398-5009   Fax: 319-398-5089

DES MOINES
Greater Des Moines Film Commission
601 Locust Street, Suite 222
Des Moines, IA 50309
800-451-2625
515-286-4960   Fax: 515-244-9757

KANSAS
Kansas Film Commission
700 SW Harrison Street, Suite 1300
Topeka, KS 66603
913-296-4927   Fax: 913-296-6988

LAWRENCE, OVERLAND PARK & TOPEKA
Kansas III Film Commission
   Lawrence Convention & Visitors Bureau
734 Vermont
Lawrence, KS 66044
913-865-4411   Fax: 913-865-4400

MANHATTAN
Manhattan Film Commission
555 Poyntz, Suite 290
Manhattan, KS 66502
913-776-8829

WICHITA
Wichita Convention & Visitors Bureau
100 South Main Street, Suite 100
Wichita, KS 67202
316-265-2800   Fax: 316-265-0162

KENTUCKY
Kentucky Film Commission
500 Mero Street, 2200 Capitol Plaza Tower
Frankfort, KY 40601
800-345-6591
502-564-3456   Fax: 502-564-7588

LOUISIANA
Louisiana Film Commission
P.O. Box 44320
Baton Rouge, LA 70804-4320
504-324-8150   Fax: 504-342-7988

JEFF DAVIS PARISH
Jeff Davis Parish Film Commission
P.O. Box 1207
Jennings, LA 70546-1207
318-821-5534   Fax: 318-821-5536

NEW ORLEANS
New Orleans Film & Video Commission
1515 Poydras Street
New Orleans, LA 70112
504-565-8104   Fax: 504-527-0801

SHREVEPORT-BOSSIER
Shreveport-Bossier Film Commission
P.O. Box 1761
Shreveport, LA 71166
800-551-8682
318-222-9391   Fax: 318-222-0056

MAINE
Maine Film Office
State House Station 59
Augusta, ME 04333
207-287-5707   Fax: 207-287-5701

MARYLAND
Maryland Film Commission
601 North Howard Street
Baltimore, MD 21201-4582
800-333-6632
410-333-6633   Fax: 410-333-0044

MASSACHUSETTS
Massachusetts Film Office
10 Park Plaza, Suite 2310
Boston, MA 02116
617-973-8800   Fax: 617-973-8810

BOSTON
Boston Film Bureau
Room 716, Boston City Hall
Boston, MA 02201
617-635-3245   Fax: 617-635-3031

MICHIGAN
Michigan Film Office
P.O. Box 30004
525 West Ottawa
Lansing, MI 48933
800-477-3456
517-373-0638   Fax: 517-373-3872

DETROIT
Mayor's Office For Film & Television
1126 City-County Building
Detroit, MI 48226
313-224-3430   Fax: 313-224-4128

MINNESOTA
Minnesota Film Board
401 North 3rd Street, Suite 460
Minneapolis, MN 55401
612-332-6493   Fax: 612-332-3735

MISSISSIPPI
Mississippi Film Office
Box 849
Jackson, MS 39205
601-359-3297   Fax: 601-359-5757

COLUMBUS
Columbus Film Commission
P.O. Box 789
Columbus, MS 39703
800-327-2686
601-329-1191   Fax: 601-329-8969

MISSISSIPPI GULF COAST
Mississippi Gulf Coast Film Office
P.O. Box 569
Gulfport, MS 39502
601-863-3807   Fax: 601-863-4555

NATCHEZ
Natchez Film Commission
P.O. Box 1485
Natchez, MS 39121
800-647-6724
601-446-6345   Fax: 601-442-0814

OXFORD
Oxford Film Commission
P.O. Box 965
Oxford, MS 38655
601-234-4680   Fax: 601-234-4655

TUPELO
Tupelo Film Commission
P.O. Box 1485
Tupelo, MS 38802-1485
800-533-0611
601-841-6454   Fax: 601-841-6558

VICKSBURG/WARREN COUNTY
Vicksburg Film Commission
P.O. Box 110
Vicksburg, MS 39180
800-221-3536
601-636-9421   Fax: 601-636-9475

MISSOURI
Missouri Film Office
P.O. Box 1157
301 West High, Room 630
Jefferson City, MO 65102
314-751-9050   Fax: 314-751-7258

KANSAS CITY
Kansas City, Missouri Film Office
10 Petticoat Lane, Suite 250
Kansas City, MO 64106
816-221-0636   Fax: 816-221-0189

ST. LOUIS
St. Louis Film Office
100 South 4th Street, Suite 500
St. Louis, MO 63102
314-444-1174   Fax: 314-444-1122

MONTANA
Montana Film Office
1424 9th Avenue
Helena, MT 59620
800-553-4563
406-444-2654   Fax: 406-444-1800

GREAT FALLS
Great Falls Reg. Film Liaison
P.O. Box 2127
815 2nd Street South
Great Falls, MT 59403
800-735-8535   Fax: 406-761-6129

NEBRASKA
Nebraska Film Offices
P.O. Box 94666
Lincoln, NE 68509-4666
800-228-4307
402-471-3797   Fax: 402-471-3026

OMAHA
Omaha Film Commission
6800 Mercy Road, Suite 202
Omaha, NE 68106-2627
402-444-7736
402-444-7737   Fax: 402-444-4511

NEVADA
Motion Picture Division/
  Commission on Economic Development
555 East Washington, Suite 5400
Las Vegas, NV 89161
702-486-2711   Fax: 702-486-2712

RENO/TAHOE
Motion Picture Division/
  Commission on Economic Development
5151 South Carson Street
Carson City, NV 89710
800-336-1600
702-687-4325   Fax: 702-687-4450

NEW_HAMPSHIRE
New Hampshire Film & TV Bureau
P.O. Box 1856
172 Pembroke Road
Concord, NH 03302-1856
603-271-2598   Fax: 603-271-2629

NEW JERSEY
New Jersey Motion Picture/TV Commission
P.O. Box 47023
153 Halsey Street
Newark, NJ 07101
201-648-6279   Fax: 201-648-7350

NEW MEXICO
New Mexico Film Office
1050 Old Pecos Trail
Santa Fe, NM 87503
800-545-9871
505-827-7365   Fax: 505-827-7369

ALBUQUERQUE
Albuquerque TV & Film Commission
P.O. Box 26866
Albuquerque, NM 87125-6866
505-842-9918   Fax: 505-247-9101

LAS CRUCES
Las Cruces Film Commission
311 North Downtown Mall
Las Cruces, NM 88001
800-FIESTAS, 505-524-8521
505-525-2112 (prvt)   Fax: 505-524-8191

NEW YORK
New York State Governor's Office/
  Motion Picture–TV Development
Pier 62 W. 23rd St. at Hudson River, #307
New York, NY 10011
212-929-0240   Fax: 212-929-0506

BUFFALO
Greater Buffalo Convention & Visitors Bureau
107 Delaware Avenue
Buffalo, NY 14202-2801
800-283-3256
716-852-0511, ext. 267   Fax: 716-852-0131

HUDSON VALLEY
Hudson Valley Film & Video Office, Inc.
40 Garden Street, 2nd Floor
Poughkeepsie, NY 12601
914-473-0318   Fax: 914-473-0082

NEW YORK CITY
Mayor's Office - Film, Theater & Broadcasting
1697 Broadway, 6th Floor
New York, NY 10019
212-489-6710   Fax: 212-307-6237

ROCHESTER
Rochester/Finger Lakes Film/Video Office
126 Andrews Street
Rochester, NY 14604-1102
716-546-5490   Fax: 716-232-4822

NORTH CAROLINA
North Carolina Film Office
430 North Salisbury Street
Raleigh, NC 27611
800-232-9227
919-733-9900   Fax: 919-715-0151

ASHEVILLE
Mailing Address:
Western North Carolina Film Commission
P.O. Box 1258
Arden, NC 28704

Street Address:
3 General Aviation Drive
Fletcher, NC 28732
704-687-7234   Fax: 704-687-7552

DURHAM
Durham Convention & Visitors Bureau
101 East Morgan Street
Durham, NC 27701
800-446-8604
919-687-0288   Fax: 919-683-9555

WILMINGTON
Greater Wilmington Film Office
1 Estell Lee Place
Wilmington, NC 28401
910-762-2611   Fax: 910-762-9765

WINSTON-SALEM
Winston-Salem Piedmont Triad
   Film Commission
601 West 4th Street
Winston-Salem, NC 27101
910-777-3787   Fax: 910-761-2209

NORTH DAKOTA
North Dakota Film Commission
604 East Boulevard, 2nd Floor
Bismarck, ND 58505
800-328-2871, 701-328-2874
701-328-2525   Fax: 701-328-4878

OHIO
Ohio Film Commission
P.O. Box 1001
77 South High Street, 29th Floor
Columbus, OH 43266-0413
800-848-1300
614-466-2284   Fax: 614-466-6744

CINCINNATI
Greater Cincinnati Film Commission
435 Elm Street
Cincinnati, OH 45202
513-784-1744   Fax: 513-768-8963

DAYTON
Greater Dayton Film Commission
448 Red Haw Road
Dayton, OH 65405
513-277-8090   Fax: 513-277-8090

OKLAHOMA
Oklahoma Film Office
440 South Houston, Suite 4
Tulsa, OK 74127-8945
800-766-3456
918-581-2660   Fax: 918-581-2244

OREGON
Oregon Film & Video Office
121 SW Salmon Street, Suite 300
Portland, OR 97204
503-229-5832   Fax: 503-229-6869

PENNSYLVANIA
Pennsylvania Film Bureau
Forum Building, Room 449
Harrisburg, PA 17120
717-783-3456   Fax: 717-234-4560

PHILADELPHIA
Greater Philadelphia Film Office
1600 Arch Street, 12th Floor
Philadelphia, PA 19103
215-686-2668   Fax: 215-686-3659

PITTSBURGH
Pittsburgh Film Office
Benedum Trees Building, Suite 1300
Pittsburgh, PA 15222
412-261-2744   Fax: 412-471-7317

PUERTO RICO
Puerto Rico Film Commission
355 F.D. Roosevelt Avenue
Fomento Building #106
San Juan, PR 00918
809-758-4747, ext. 2250-57
809-754-7110   Fax: 809-756-5706

SOUTH CAROLINA
South Carolina Film Office
P.O. Box 7367
Columbia, SC 29202
803-737-0490   Fax: 803-737-3104

UPSTATE SOUTH CAROLINA
Upstate S.C. Film & Video Association
P.O. Box 10048
Greenville, SC 29603
803-239-3712   Fax: 803-282-8549

SOUTH DAKOTA
South Dakota Film Commission
711 East Wells Avenue
Pierre, SD 57501-3369
800-952-3625
605-773-3301   Fax: 605-773-3256

KADOKA
Badlands Film Commission
P.O. Box 58
Kadoka, SD 57543-0058
800-467-9217
605-837-2229   Fax: 605-837-2161

TENNESSEE
Tennessee Film/Entertainment/Music
    Commission
320 6th Avenue North, 7th Floor
Nashville, TN 37243-0790
800-251-8594
615-741-3456   Fax: 615-741-5829

MEMPHIS
Memphis/Shelby County Film Commission
Beale Street Landing/245 Wagner Place, #4
Memphis, TN 38103-3815
901-527-8300   Fax: 901-527-8326

NASHVILLE
Nashville Film Office
161 4th Avenue North
Nashville, TN 37219
615-259-4777   Fax: 615-256-3074

TEXAS
Texas Film Commission
P.O. Box 13246
Austin, TX 78711
512-463-9200   Fax: 512-463-4114

AMARILLO
Amarillo Film Office
1000 South Polk Street
Amarillo, TX 79101
800-692-1338
806-374-1497   Fax: 806-373-3909

AUSTIN
City of Austin
P.O. Box 1088
Austin, TX 78767
512-499-2404   Fax: 512-499-6385

DALLAS/FORT WORTH
Dallas/Fort Worth Regional Film Commission
P.O. Box 610246
DFW Airport, TX 75261
800-234-5699
214-621-0400   Fax: 214-929-0916

EL PASO
El Paso Film Commission
1 Civic Center Plaza
El Paso, TX 79901
800-351-6024
915-534-0698   Fax: 915-532-2963

HOUSTON
Houston Film Commission
801 Congress
Houston, TX 77002
800-365-7575
713-227-3100   Fax: 713-223-3816

IRVING
Irving Texas Film Commission
6309 North O'Connor Road, Suite 222
Irving, TX 75039-3510
800-2-IRVING
214-869-0303   Fax: 214-869-4609

SAN ANTONIO
San Antonio Film Commission
P.O. Box 2277
San Antonio, TX 78230
800-447-3372, ext 730/777
210-270-8700   Fax: 210-270-8782

U.S. VIRGIN ISLANDS
U.S. Virgin Islands Film Promotion Office
P.O. Box 6400
St. Thomas, V.I. 00804 USVI
809-775-1444
809-774-8784   Fax: 809-774-4390

UTAH
Utah Film Commission
324 South State, Suite 500
Salt Lake City, UT 84114-7330
800-453-8824
801-538-8740   Fax: 801-538-8886

CENTRAL UTAH
Central Utah Film Commission
51 South University Ave., Suite 110
Provo, UT 84601
800-222-8824
801-370-8390   Fax: 801-370-8050

KANAB/KANE COUNTY
Kanab/Kane County Film Commission
41 South 100 East
Kanab, UT 84741
800-SEE-KANE
801-644-5033   Fax: 801-644-5923

MOAB
Moab to Monument Valley Film Commission
50 East Center, #1
Moab, UT 84532
801-259-6388
801-587-3235   Fax: 801-259-6399

PARK CITY
Park City Film Commission
P.O. Box 1630
Park City, UT 84060
800-453-1360
801-649-6100   Fax: 801-649-4132

WASHINGTON COUNTY
Washington County Travel/Convention/Film
   Office
425 South 700 East, Dixie Center
St. George, UT 84770
800-869-6635
801-634-5747   Fax: 801-628-1619

VIRGINIA
Virginia Film Office
P.O. Box 798
1021 East Cary Street
Richmond, VA 23206-0798
804-371-8204   Fax: 804-786-1121

RICHMOND
Metro Richmond Convention & Visitors Bureau
   & Film Office
550 East Marshall Street
Richmond, VA 23219
800-365-7272
804-782-2777   Fax: 804-780-2577

WASHINGTON
Washington State Film & Video Office
2001 6th Avenue, Suite 2600
Seattle, WA 98121
206-464-7148   Fax: 206-464-7722

TACOMA-PIERCE COUNTY
Tacoma-Pierce County Film Office
P.O. Box 1754
906 Broadway
Tacoma, WA 98401-1754
206-627-2836   Fax: 206-627-8783

WEST VIRGINIA
West Virginia Film Office
State Capitol, Building 6, Room 525
Charleston, WV 25305-0311
800-982-3386
304-558-2234   Fax: 304-558-1189

WISCONSIN
Wisconsin Film Office
123 West Washington Avenue, 6th Floor
Madison, WI 53702-0001
608-267-3456   Fax: 608-266-3403

MILWAUKEE
City of Milwaukee Film Liaison
809 North Broadway
Milwaukee, WI 53202
414-286-5700   Fax: 414-286-5904

WYOMING
Wyoming Film Commission
I-25 and College Drive
Cheyenne, WY 82002-0240
800-458-6657
307-777-7777   Fax: 307-777-6904

JACKSON HOLE
Jackson Hole Film Commission
P.O. Box E
Jackson, WY 83001
307-733-3316   Fax: 307-733-5585

CHAPTER FOURTEEN

Miscellaneous Production Forms

An actor claims he did not receive the script revisions you know you sent by runner yesterday. A vendor claims not to have received the check you think you mailed with a stack of others last Wednesday. The assistant cameraman wants you to order more raw stock, but you think there should be enough on hand for at least another week.

Working in production means a lot of details to take care of, keep track of, and remember. These forms should help make doing that easier. You may not need all of them, but take advantage of the ones that will help you the most. They are not necessarily considered *standard* and do take time to fill out and keep up, but they will keep you better organized; and being better *organized* will ultimately save you time.

ABBREVIATED PRODUCTION REPORT

SHOW __HERBY'S SUMMER VACATION__   PROD # __0100__

DAY __MONDAY__   DATE __6-7-XX__   DAY # __6__   OUT OF __30__

LOCATION __CITY HALL - DOWNTOWN__

CREW CALL __7A__

FIRST SHOT __9:30A__   MEAL PENALTY __1__

LUNCH __1:30P__ TO __2P__   OVERTIME __½ HR.__

SECOND MEAL _____ TO _____

WRAP __8P__

SCENES __3, 4, 5, 26, 27, 30__

SCENES SCHEDULED BUT NOT SHOT _____

	SCENES	PAGES	MINUTES	SETUPS
PREVIOUS	76	35 2/8	31:37	83
TODAY	6	5 3/8	2:15	23
TOTAL	82	40 5/8	33:52	106

FILM FOOTAGE

GROSS __4590__   GROSS TO DATE __28,830__

PRINT __2720__   PRINT TO DATE __19,630__

N.G. __1510__

WASTE __360__

NOTES
- SCARLET STARLET 30 MIN. LATE REPORTING TO SET
- KATIE KANDU (SCRIPT SUPV'R.) TOOK ILL ON SET & REQUESTED TO BE REPLACED. REPLACEMENT ARRIVED @ NOON.
- COMPUTER USED AS SET DRESSING IN HERBY'S BEDROOM REPORTED MISSING WHEN CREW ARRIVED TO FINISH DRESSING SET.

DAILY COST OVERVIEW

SHOW __HERBY'S SUMMER VACATION__   PROD # __0100__

DATE __6-7-XX__   DAY # __6__

START DATE __5-29-XX__

SCHEDULED FINISH DATE __7-8-XX__

REVISED FINISH DATE __7-9-XX__

	PER CALL SHEET	SHOT	AHEAD/BEHIND
# OF SCENES	6	4	2 BEHIND
# OF PAGES	5 3/8	4 5/8	6/8 BEHIND

	AS BUDGETED AND/OR SCHEDULED	ACTUAL	COST (OVER)/UNDER
CAST OVERTIME	$500	$650	$150
COMPANY SHOOTING HOURS	12	13	$10,000
MEAL PENALTY (5 SAG ACTORS)	$500	$300	($200)
EXTRAS & STAND-INS	$632	$577	($55)
CATERING	$840	$960	$120
RAW STOCK (5,000')	$2,250	$1,687	$563

UNANTICIPATED EXPENSES:

ADDT'L. PROP ASST.	10 HRS. @ $22/HR.		$242
FRINGE			44

TOTAL FOR TODAY __$9,738__

PREVIOUS TOTAL __$4,000__

GRAND TOTAL __$13,738 (OVER)__

PREPARED BY _Aaron Accountant_   APPROVED BY _Ned Filmer_

© ELH Form #19

DISTRIBUTION LIST

SHOW: HERBY'S SUMMER VACATION
PROD. #: 0100

Document	Marvin Mogul	Swifty Deals	Sid Celluloid	Fred Filmer	F. Stopp	A. Dees	Katie Kandu	Connie Coordinates	Aaron Accountant	Total # Copies Needed
Music Cue Sheet	✓	✓								2
Screen Credits	✓	✓	✓	✓			✓			5
Post Prod. Schedule	✓	✓	✓	✓	✓			✓		6
Insur. & WC Claims	✓	✓		✓			✓	✓		5
Cost Reports	✓	✓	✓	✓				✓		5
Abbrev. Prod. Reports	✓	✓	✓	✓		✓	✓	✓		7
Production Reports	✓	✓	✓	✓		✓	✓	✓		7
Call Sheets	✓	✓	✓	✓	✓	✓	✓	✓	✓	9
Travel Info. & Movement	✓	✓	✓	✓		✓	✓	✓		7
Location List	✓	✓	✓	✓	✓	✓	✓	✓	✓	9
Certificates of Insur.				✓			✓			2
Release Forms	✓	✓		✓			✓	✓		5
Location Agreements	✓	✓		✓		✓	✓	✓		6
Cast & Crew Contracts	✓	✓		✓			✓	✓		5
Cast List Without Deals					✓		✓			2
Cast List With Deals	✓	✓	✓	✓		✓	✓	✓		7
Crew & Staff Lists	✓	✓	✓	✓	✓	✓	✓	✓	✓	9
Deal Memos	✓	✓		✓			✓	✓		5
Day-out-of-Days	✓	✓	✓	✓	✓	✓	✓	✓		8
Shooting Schedule	✓	✓	✓	✓	✓	✓	✓	✓	✓	9
Pre-Prod. Schedule	✓	✓	✓	✓	✓	✓	✓	✓		8
Budget	✓	✓	✓					✓	✓	5
Script & Revisions	✓	✓	✓	✓	✓	✓	✓	✓	✓	9

© ELH Form #45

CAST INFORMATION

SHOW *Herby's Summer Vacation* PROD # 0100

EPISODE

(Please fill squares in with dates)

ACTOR	ROLE	START DATE	# OF DAYS WORKING	DEAL MEMO	STATION 12	TRAVEL/HOTEL ACCOMM.	MEDICAL EXAM	SENT SCRIPT	NOTIFIED WARDROBE	SCRIPT REVISIONS (BLUE)	SCRIPT REVISIONS (PINK)	SCRIPT REVISIONS (GREEN)	CONTRACT RECEIVED	CONTRACT TO AGENT/ACTOR	CONTRACT RETURNED	CONT. SIGNED BY PRODUCER	COPIES DISTRIBUTED	NOTES
Clark Grable	Herby	6/18	14	5/27	5/28	✓	5/11	5/3	5/3	6/10	6/16		6/1	6/2	6/9	6/11	6/14	
Rocky Rizzo	Jake	6/18	14	5/27	5/28	✓	5/11	5/5	5/5	6/10	6/16		6/1	6/2	6/9	6/11	6/14	
Scarlet Starlet	Laura	6/21	9	5/29	5/28	✓	5/20	5/11	5/11	6/10	6/16		6/1	6/2	6/9	6/11	6/14	
Nancy Nicely	Mom	6/21	11	6/2	6/4	✓	5/28	5/18	5/18	6/10	6/16		6/8	6/9	6/15	6/16	6/18	
Hollywood Mann	George	6/22	5	6/10	6/10	✓	6/3	5/18	5/18	6/10	6/16		6/4	6/15	6/21	6/22	6/24	
Kenny Smiles	Marc	6/21	8	6/2	6/4	✓	—	5/25	5/25	6/10	6/16		6/17	6/18	6/25	6/29	6/30	
Will Performer	Jed	6/21	8	6/9	6/11	✓	—	5/25	5/25	6/10	6/16		6/17	6/18	6/25	6/29	6/30	
Lloyd Nelson	Police Sgt.	6/24	1	6/15	6/15	✓	—	6/8	6/8	6/10	6/16		6/18	6/19	6/23	6/23	6/24	

© ELH Form #20

BOX/EQUIPMENT RENTAL INVENTORY

PRODUCTION COMPANY ___XYZ PRODUCTIONS, INC.___

SHOW ___HERBY'S SUMMER VACATION___   PROD # ___0100___

EMPLOYEE ___SAM SHUTTER___   POSITION ___STILL PHOTOGRAPHER___

ADDRESS ___8436 LENS AVE.___   SOC.SEC. # ___111-12-1212___

___WONDERLAND, CA 90000___

                                                      PHONE # ___(818) 555-3030___

LOAN OUT COMPANY _____   FED. I.D. # ___95-15693276___

RENTAL RATE $ ___200___   PER   ☐ DAY ☑ WEEK

                                                      ☐ SUBMIT WEEKLY INVOICE

                                                      ☑ RECORD ON WEEKLY TIME CARD

RENTAL COMMENCES ON ___6-18-XX___

INVENTORIED ITEMS:

TWO (2) NIKON CAMERA BODIES - SER# 123456XXX

SER# 654321XXX

THREE (3) LENSES: 70-210 ZOOM (NIKON)

35-105/MACRO (VIVITAR)

28 mm (NIKON)

NIKON MOTOR DRIVE - SER# 4567890XXX

TRI-POD

BLIMP

MISC. FILTERS

Please note: 1. *Box and equipment rentals are subject to 1099 reporting.*

2. *The Production Company is not responsible for any claims of loss or damage to box/equipment rental items that are not listed on the above inventory.*

EMPLOYEE SIGNATURE ___Sam Shutter___   DATE ___6/2/XX___

APPROVED BY ___Fred Filmer___   DATE ___6/2/XX___

© ELH Form #21

INVENTORY LOG

SHOW: HERBY'S SUMMER VACATION   PROD #: 0100   DEPARTMENT: SET DRESSING

ITEM(S)	PURCHASED FROM (Name /Address)	PURCHASE DATE	PURCHASE PRICE	P.O.#	AT COMPLETION OF PRINCIPAL PHOTOGRAPHY			
					IF PORTION USED, HOW MUCH REMAINS	IF SOLD, FOR HOW MUCH	IF RET'D. TO COMPANY, IN WHAT CONDITION	LOCATION OF ITEM
2 OIL PAINTINGS	OTTO'S GALLERY	6/2/XX	$1200 —	1235		$600 —		
FIREPLACE SET	DELL'S DEPT. STORE	6/10/XX	$150 —	1576			GOOD	COMPANY'S STORAGE
HALL MIRROR	COUNTRY ANTIQUES	6/11/XX	$300 —	1592			SCRATCHED	"

© ELH Form #22

PURCHASE ORDER LOG

SHOW __HERBY'S SUMMER VACATION__   PROD # __0100__

| P.O. # | DATE | TO | FOR | PRICE | CHECK ONE | | | RENTAL RET'D | TO INVENTORY | P.O. ASSIGNED TO |
					PURCHASE	RENTAL	SERVICE			
1001	6/21/XX	LARRY'S LUMBER	MISC. CONST.	$2500 -	✓					CONST. COORDINATOR
1002	6/21/XX	PAUL'S PROP HOUSE	HAND PROPS	$250 -		✓		7/3/XX		PROPERTY MASTER
1003	6/22/XX	JONES' SANITATION	TRASH REMOVAL	$500 -			✓			CONST. COORDINATOR

CREW START-UP AND DATA SHEET

NAME	POSITION	SOC. SEC. #	NAME OF CORP. FED. I.D. #	DEAL MEMO	START SLIP	W-4 I-9	START DATE	WRAP DATE	PAYCHECK TO EMPLOYEE	PAYCHECK TO MAIL
ALICE DEES	1ST ASST. DIR.	555·21·1234		7/3/XX	✓	✓	7/5	9/10	✓	
KATIE KANDU	SCRIPT SUPV'R.	543·62·3762		7/10/XX	✓	✓	7/26	9/14	✓	
MIKE BOOM	SOUND MIXER	331·42·9776	BOOM AUDIO RENTALS #15-1234567	7/15/XX	✓	✓	7/15	9/13	✓	
F. STOPP	DIR. OF PHOTOG.	137·62·8371		7/2/XX	✓	✓	7/19	9/10		✓

© ELH Form #24

TIME CARDS/INVOICES
WEEKLY CHECK-OFF LIST

NAME	POSITION	SOC. SEC. # / FED. I.D. #	TIME CARDS AND/OR INVOICES TURNED IN EACH WEEK							
			W/E 7.31	W/E 8.7	W/E 8.14	W/E 8.21	W/E 8.28	W/E 9.4	W/E 9.11	W/E 9.18
A. Dees	1st Asst. Dir.	555-21-1234	✓	✓	✓	✓	✓	✓	✓	
Katie Kandu	Script Supv'r.	543-37-6732		✓	✓	✓	✓	✓	✓	
Mike Boom	Sound Mixer	#95-1234567		✓	✓	✓	✓	✓		
Paula Propps	Property Master	321-77-4476	✓	✓	✓	✓	✓	✓	✓	✓
E. Stopp	Dir. of Photog.	132-64-3217	✓	✓	✓	✓	✓	✓	✓	✓

© ELH Form #25

Miscellaneous Production Forms **201**

INDIVIDUAL PETTY CASH ACCOUNT

NAME __PAULA PROPPS__   DEPARTMENT __PROPERTY__

SHOW __HERBY'S SUMMER VACATION__   PROD # __0100__

                               FLOAT $ __500—__

DATE	CHECK#/CASH RECV'D FROM	AMOUNT RECV'D	ACCOUNTED FOR	BALANCE
7/2/xx	CHECK #1243	$500—		$500—
7/10			$432—	$ 68—
7/11	CHECK #1536	$432—		$500—
7/15	CASH FROM F. FILMER	$250—		$750—
7/23			$830—	$ (80)
7/28	CHECK #1732	$580—		$ 500—

© ELH Form #26

INVOICE

TO: XYZ PRODUCTIONS
1234 FLICK DR.
HOLLYWOOD, CA 90038

FROM: ASHLEY WILKES   DATE 3/17/XX
(Address) 123 TWELVE OAKS AVE.
ATLANTA, GEORGIA
(Phone #) 555-3824

PAYEE SS# OR FED. ID# 521-76-3535   1099 ✓

FOR SERVICES RENDERED ON _____ OR WEEK/ENDING 3/15/XX

DESCRIPTION OF SERVICE/RENTAL/CAR ALLOWANCE

DIALOGUE COACH TO HELP CAST WITH SOUTHERN ACCENT	
22.5 HRS @ $100 PER HOUR	

TOTAL AMOUNT DUE $ 2,250

EMPLOYEE SIGNATURE _Ashley Wilkes_

APPROVED BY _Fred Gilmer_

PD. BY CHECK # 2376   DATE 3/20/XX

© ELH Form #27

CASH OR SALES RECEIPT   DATE 8/24/XX   No. 93

RECIPIENT/
SOLD TO: IRMA'S SWAP MEET

ADDRESS: 4226 ORANGE BOWL AVE.

PASADENA, CA

PHONE # (818) 555-4344

FOR PURCHASE OF: OLD BOOKS & RECORDS
(SET DRESSING)

WRITTEN
AMOUNT FIFTY-TWO DOLLARS ————— $52

☑ CASH   ☐ 1099   Soc. Sec. # 123-32-1323

☐ CHECK   Fed. I.D. #

ACCOUNT CODING 823-51

APPROVED BY _Fred Filmer_   RECV'D BY _Irma Price_

© ELH Form #28

THE CHECK'S IN THE MAIL

CHECK MADE OUT TO	CHECK NUMBER	CHECK DATED	ADDRESS SENT TO	DATE MAILED	PAY-ROLL	INV.
CAL'S COMPUTERS	1032	2/14/XX	9876 FLORES ST. STUDIO VILLAGE, CA	2/15		✓
XXX AUDIO SERVICES	1053	2/15	123 MAIN ST. HOLLYWOOD, CA	2/16		✓
A. PAINE, M.D.	1059	2/15	3327 INJECTION BLVD. LOS ANGELES, CA	2/16		✓
ASHLEY WILKES	1075	2/20	123 TWELVE OAKS AVE. ATLANTA, GEORGIA	2/22		✓
F. STOPP (D.P.)	1082	2/20	2486 MADONNA LN. BEVERLY HILLS, CA	2/22	✓	

© ELH Form #29

MILEAGE LOG

NAME: **GARY GOFER**   WEEK ENDING **3/25/XX**

SHOW: **HERBY'S SUMMER VACATION**   PROD # **0100**

| DATE | LOCATION | | PURPOSE | MILEAGE |
	FROM	TO		
3/20	OFFICE	SCREEN ACTORS GUILD	PICKUP RATE BOOK	10
	SAG OFFICE	ORIN'S OFFICE SUPPLY	OFFICE SUPPLIES	5
	ORIN'S	OFFICE		15
3/21	OFFICE	SCARLET STARLET HOME	DELIVER SCRIPT	8
	SCARLET STARLET'S	KENNY SMILE'S HOME	DELIVER SCRIPT	5
	KENNY SMILE'S	NANCY NICELY'S APARTMENT	DELIVER SCRIPT	3
	NANCY NICELY'S	OFFICE		7

TOTAL MILES: **53**

53 MILES @ **31** ¢ Per Mile = $ **16.43**

Approved By: *Fred Filmer*   Date: **3/30/XX**

Pd. By Check # **2976**   Date **3/31/XX**

RAW STOCK INVENTORY

SHOW _HERBY'S SUMMER VACATION_   PROD # _0100_

WEEK ENDING _____

EPISODE/WEEKLY TOTALS	52 _47_	52 _93_	52 _96_	52 _____
Print	7865	6,050	7,086	_____
No Good	2,390	1,769	1,807	_____
Waste	980	823	1,230	_____
Total **	11,235	8,642	10,123	_____

PURCHASED

Previously Purchased	50,000	50,000	50,000	_____
Purchased This Episode/Week	+ 15,000	15,000	20,000	_____
Total Stock Purchased	65,000	65,000	70,000	_____

USED

Stock Used To Date	33,705	25,926	30,369	_____
Used This Episode/Week**	+ 11,235	8,642	10,123	_____
Total Stock Used	44,940	34,568	40,492	_____

Total Purchased	65,000	65,000	70,000	_____
Total Used	- 44,940	34,568	40,492	_____
Estimated Remaining Stock	20,060	30,432	29,508	_____
(Remaining Stock As Per Assistant Cameraman)	20,060	28,400	29,600	_____

RAW STOCK PURCHASES MADE DURING
THIS EPISODE/WEEK:

P.O. # _2076_	15,000	15,000	—	_____
P.O. # _2093_	—	—	20,000	_____
P.O. # _____	_____	_____	_____	_____
P.O. # _____	_____	_____	_____	_____
TOTAL	_____	_____	_____	_____

NOTES:

© ELH Form #31

DAILY RAW STOCK LOG

SHOW __HERBY'S SUMMER VACATION__   PROD # __0100__

DATE __OCT. 21, 19XX__   DAY # __32__

CAMERA	ROLL #	GOOD	N.G.	WASTE	TOTAL
A	1	550	350	100	1,000
B	1	210	140	60	410
C	1	100	100	200	400
A	2	330	210	20	560
B	2	190	130	140	460
B	3	310	80	70	460
B	4	160	140	20	320

	DRAWN	GOOD	N.G.	WASTE	TOTAL
PREVIOUS	15,463	6,186	3,788	2,010	27,447
TODAY	4,730	1,850	1,150	610	3,610
TOTAL	20,193	8,036	5,038	2,620	31,057

UNEXPOSED ON HAND	18,820'	TOTAL EXPOSED	31,057'

© ELH Form #32

REQUEST FOR PICK UP

DATE __7·5·XX__

SHOW __HERBY'S SUMMER VACATION__   PROD # __0100__

PICK UP REQUESTED BY __FRED FILMER__

ITEMS TO BE PICKED UP __SAG THEATRICAL CONTRACT BOOKS__

_____

_____

_____

_____

PICK UP FROM __FRONT RECEPTION DESK__

(COMPANY) __SCREEN ACTORS GUILD__   PHONE # __(213)   600__

ADDRESS __5757 WILSHIRE BLVD.__

__LOS ANGELES__

DIRECTIONS (if needed) _____

_____

_____

_____

_____

☐ MUST BE PICKED UP BY _____ (A.M.)(P.M.)

☑ PICK UP AS SOON AS POSSIBLE

☐ PICK UP TODAY, NO SPECIFIC TIME

☐ NO RUSH — WHENEVER YOU CAN

COMMENTS/SPECIAL INSTRUCTIONS __BOOKS ARE "ON HOLD" AT__
__RECEPTION DESK. ASK FOR PICKUP FOR__
__XYZ PRODUCTIONS.__

_____

DATE & TIME OF PICK UP __11:30 A.M.   7/5/XX__

ITEM(S) DELIVERED TO __FRED FILMER__

(ALL PICK UP SLIPS ARE TO BE KEPT ON FILE IN THE PRODUCTION OFFICE)

© ELH Form #33

REQUEST FOR DELIVERY

DATE __7/23/XX__

SHOW __HERBY'S SUMMER VACATION__   PROD # __0100__

DELIVERY REQUESTED BY __CASTING DEPT.__

ITEMS TO BE DELIVERED _____

__SCRIPT__

_____

_____

_____

DELIVER TO __ROBERT BLUFORD__

(COMPANY) _____   PHONE # __555-7321__

ADDRESS __7364 SUNDANCE DR.__

__HOLLYWOOD HILLS, CA__

DIRECTIONS (if needed) _____

_____

_____

☑ MUST BE DELIVERED BY __10__ (A.M.)(P.M.)

☐ DELIVER AS SOON AS POSSIBLE

☐ DELIVER TODAY, NO SPECIFIC TIME

☐ NO RUSH — WHENEVER YOU CAN

COMMENTS/SPECIAL INSTRUCTIONS __IF NO ONE IS HOME TO ACCEPT__
__SCRIPT, LEAVE ON FRONT PORCH.__

_____

DATE & TIME OF DELIVERY __9:55 a.m.__

RECEIVED BY __R. Bluford__

(ALL DELIVERY SLIPS ARE TO BE KEPT ON FILE IN THE PRODUCTION OFFICE)

© ELH Form #34

DRIVE-TO

SHOW __HERBY'S SUMMER VACATION__   DATE __8·10·XX__

EPISODE __"BOY'S NIGHT OUT"__   PROD # __0100__

LOCATION __TARA LAKE__

MILEAGE: __18__   MILES @ __30__   ¢ PER MILE = $ __5.40__

	NAME	SOC. SEC. #	POSITION	SIGNATURE
1.	F. STOPP	111·76·3251	DIR. OF PHOTOG.	_F. Stopp_
2.	A. DEES	723·13·2763	1ST ASST. DIR.	_A. Dees_
3.	K. KANDU	447·63·3331	SCRIPT SUPV'R.	_K. Kandu_
4.	A. WILKES	123·45·6789	DIALOGUE COACH	_A. Wilk_
5.				
6.				
7.				
8.				
9.				
10				
11.				
12.				
13.				
14.				
15.				
16.				
17.				
18.				
19.				
20.				
21.				
22.				
23.				
24.				
25.				
26.				
27.				
28.				
29.				

TOTAL ALLOCATION: __75__   People x $ __5.40__   = $ __405__

APPROVED _F. Filmer_   DATE __8/10/XX__

© ELH Form #35

WALKIE-TALKIE SIGN-OUT SHEET

SHOW __HERBY'S SUMMER VACATION__   PROD # __0100__

SERIAL #	PRINT NAME	DATE OUT	DATE IN	SIGNATURE
AB 376 227	ALICE DEES	7/5/XX	7/5	*(signature)*
AB 376228	FRED FILMER	7/5/XX	7/5	*(signature)*
AB 376229	JOHN SMITH	7/6/XX	7/6	*(signature)*
AB 376230	PHIL WYLLY	7/6/XX	7/6	*(signature)*

WALKIE-TALKIES RENTED FROM: __XXX AUDIO SERVICES__

ADDRESS __123 MAIN ST.__   PHONE # __555-5311__

__HOLLYWOOD, CA__   FAX # __555-5312__

CONTACT __GEORGE__   HOURS __8A-6P__

© ELH Form #36

BEEPER SIGN-OUT SHEET

SHOW ___HERBY'S SUMMER VACATION___ PROD # ___0100___

SERIAL #	PRINT NAME	DATE OUT	DATE IN	SIGNATURE
XXX 1234	FRED FILMER	4/13/XX	5/20	Fred Filmer
XXX 2345	CONNIE COORDINATES	4/15	5/18	Connie Coordinates
XXX 3456	ALICE DEES	3/25	6/30	A. Dees

BEEPERS RENTED FROM: ___ABC CELLULAR, INC.___

ADDRESS ___1717 HIGHLIGHT DR.___ PHONE # ___555-4321___

___LOS ANGELES, CA___ FAX # ___555-4322___

CONTACT ___JOE___ HOURS ___9A-7P___

© ELH Form #37

VEHICLE RENTAL SHEET

PRODUCTION COMPANY __XYZ PRODUCTIONS, INC.__   DATE __9.5.XX__

ADDRESS __1234 FLICK DR.__

__HOLLYWOOD, CA 90038__

PHONE # __555-3331__

The vehicle as described below is to be rented for use on the film tentatively entitled: __HERBY'S SUMMER VACATION__

YEAR, MAKE, MODEL __1992 MERCEDES BENZ - SL__

LICENSE NUMBER __1PAL222__

VEH. ID # __X944312967LMP3760__

VALUE __$45,000-__

SPECIAL EQUIPMENT/ATTACHMENTS _____

RENTAL PRICE $ __250-__   Per (Day) Week/Month

OWNER'S NAME __ROMEO JONES__

ADDRESS __4321 BEVERLY HILLS LANE__

__BEVERLY HILLS, CA__

PHONE # __555.6643__

DRIVER OF VEHICLE (if not owner) _____

START DATE __2.19.XX__   COMPLETION DATE __2.19.XX__

INSURANCE TO BE SUPPLIED BY __XYZ PRODUCTIONS__

INSURANCE COMPANY __ABC INSURANCE CO.__

POLICY # __5362732LT__

INSURANCE AGENCY REP. __DARRYL DEDUCTIBLE__

PHONE # __555-7373__

REQUIRED MAINTENANCE _____

FUEL _____

VEHICLE TO BE USED FOR __PICTURE VEHICLE FOR SC.#25 / PROPS__ (DEPARTMENT)

CERTIFICATE OF INSURANCE ☑TO OWNER   ☑IN VEHICLE   ☑ON FILE

AGREED TO:

BY: _Romeo Jones_   BY: _Alex Autos_

OWNER   TRANSPORTATION COORDINATOR

© ELH Form #38

CHAPTER FIFTEEN

Wrap

Wrap schedules vary based on budgetary considerations, the type of show you are doing, and where the show was shot. The wrap times of department heads and crew members vary depending on their areas of responsibility and applicable union and guild policies, and generally range from a day or two to a few weeks. The amount of time it will take to tie up loose ends will depend on factors such as sets to be struck, practical locations to be repaired and restored, paperwork to be turned in, rentals to be returned, company inventory to be itemized and stored (or sold), props and wardrobe to be pulled for reshoots or inserts, insurance claims to be prepared and submitted, and offices to be closed up.

Production managers, production coordinators, and production accountants will generally take longer to wrap than other crew members. Again, budgetary considerations and the type of show you are doing will determine how many weeks will be needed to complete the work. Wrap time for production personnel is often shorter for those working for a studio or an established production company than for those working for smaller independent companies that do not have in-house production staffs.

Taking all variables into consideration, prepare a wrap schedule prior to the end of principal photography and confirm with each crew member when his or her last day will be. This information is crucial in determining final shooting costs.

Although post production personnel start at the beginning of principal photography, the most important and busiest parts of their jobs begin after the shooting has been completed. Those working in conjunction with the post production crew to facilitate the completion of the picture include: the producer, the post production accountant (who takes over when the production accountant leaves the show), and, depending on the production company, possibly a few in-house staff members. Shows that are not wrapped properly can create major difficulties for these members of the post contingent. Clearing up unresolved matters pertaining to the shoot can be quite difficult and time consuming, especially for those who were not involved in the production process. Unresolved issues created by a *sloppy* wrap can cost valuable time, money, and energy needed to complete the picture.

The following is a checklist to assist you during the wrap process:

WRAP CHECKLIST

Legal
❑ All signed contracts and releases are countersigned, returned, copies distributed and filed

Paperwork
❑ Final cast list
❑ Final crew and staff list
❑ Final script with all change pages
❑ Final shooting schedule
❑ Final day-out-of-days
❑ Final location list
❑ Final contact list
❑ Completed and organized production files
❑ Final production book

Closing Production Office
❑ Submit move-out notice
❑ Submit change-of-address to post office (if necessary)
❑ Submit forwarding phone number to phone company (if necessary)
❑ Return office furniture
❑ Return office machines
❑ Disconnect phones and utilities
❑ Turn in office keys
❑ Cancel bottled water/coffee service
❑ Return refrigerator
❑ Pack up remaining forms and supplies
❑ Pack up production files

Guild Related
❑ All SAG contracts countersigned, returned, distributed, and filed
❑ All SAG Production Time Reports submitted
❑ Final Casting Data Reports submitted
❑ Final SAG Cast List submitted
❑ All DGA Weekly Work Sheets submitted
❑ DGA Employment Data Report filed
❑ DGA and WGA final screen credit approval

Note: SAG requires submission of final screen credits and music cue sheets at the completion of post production

Return
❑ Equipment
❑ Vehicles
❑ Walkie-talkies
❑ Beepers/cellular phones
❑ Props
❑ Set dressing
❑ Wardrobe
❑ Greens
❑ Flats/cycs/backdrops

Insurance
❑ Submit all insurance claims not previously submitted
❑ Prepare breakdown of pending and unsettled claims

Locations
❑ All signed location agreements are returned, copies distributed and filed
❑ All practical locations are thoroughly wrapped, cleaned, and restored to original (or better) condition

Company-Owned Inventory
❑ Collect all inventory logs, indicating condition and location of all inventory
❑ Balance raw stock inventory, match totals to assistant cameraman's records; account for differences, if any

Sell or Store Remaining:
❑ Short ends
❑ Wardrobe
❑ Props
❑ Set dressing
❑ Computer software
❑ Fans/heaters
❑ Tools/lumber/building supplies
❑ Expendables
❑ Office supplies/forms

❑ Arrange storage of inventoried items not sold, if company does not already have storage facilities

Accounting Related

❑ Collect all refundable deposits
❑ Collect outstanding accounts receivable
❑ Collect outstanding petty cash
❑ Prepare 1099 list
❑ Prepare final vendor list (in alphabetical order)
❑ Prepare final budget
❑ Prepare final cost report

Turn Over to Post Production

❑ Script supervisor's final notes
❑ Script supervisor's final script
❑ Continuity Polaroids
❑ Final cast list
❑ Final camera reports and sound reports
❑ First draft of screen credits—main titles and end credits (including all credits based on contractual obligations and union and guild regulations)

Fun Stuff

❑ Plan and have wrap party
❑ Order and distribute show gifts (i.e., T-shirts and jackets)
❑ Send out special thank you notes to those whose contributions meant the most to you during production

Once the show (including post production) has been completed and before the files are packed and stored, prepare a *Final Production Book* containing all the pertinent information you may need to refer to at a later date. Keep this information in one or two large three-ring binders and use dividers to separate the following:

❑ Corporate (signatory papers) information
❑ Bank information (bank, contact, account number, copy of signature cards, etc.)
❑ Bank reconciliation
❑ Trial balance
❑ Final budget
❑ Final cost report
❑ Cast list and final SAG cast list
❑ Chart-of-account and vendor list
❑ Contact list (local and location)
❑ Final staff and crew list
❑ Crew deal memos
❑ Location list (including dates and deals)
❑ Call sheets
❑ Production reports
❑ Final shooting schedule
❑ Final day-out-of-days
❑ Key correspondence
❑ Copies of major deals
❑ Copies of signed union and guild contract agreements
❑ Information on insurance claims
❑ Final script
❑ Dates of delivery and delivery requirements
❑ Inventory logs and location of inventory

CHAPTER SIXTEEN

Immigration, Customs, and Visa Information

Our business continues to become increasingly *international* as more U.S.-based films are being shot in other countries and cast and crew members from other countries are being recruited to work on U.S. films. There is a definite controversy over this continuing trend, but whether you agree or not, you should have a basic knowledge of what it entails. The following is a brief description of immigration, customs, and visa information. Because this is an area that requires a considerable amount of legal expertise—in addition to the precise preparation of petitions and applications, consultations with labor and management organizations, documentation of work searches, etc.—it is an area primarily handled by attorneys who specialize in immigration-related matters. Consult with your attorney before any definitive plans are made to shoot out of the country or to bring foreign performers or crew members into the United States.

FILMING IN A FOREIGN COUNTRY

Producers, name directors, and top-name performers are generally welcome in most foreign countries, but justification for bringing in lesser known talent is considerably more difficult in an effort to protect local workforces. As each country has its own set of regulations, the first step is to call the embassy or consulate of the country where you wish to film to find out their specific immigration policies and requirements. Be aware that in addition to requirements to enter certain foreign countries, several also impose a *departure tax*, a fee to leave their country. Some will require that this tax be paid in its exact amount in their country's currency. Others will accept the fee in U.S. dollars. Your travel agent or the embassy you are dealing with will inform you if the country you wish to travel to has a departure tax, how much it is, and how it is to be paid.

Some countries have their own film office and/or film industry representatives to handle inquiries and to work with you. Less developed countries tend to have less stringent policies; but regardless of which country it is, assume you will have to apply for a permit, and allow plenty of time to do so.

Arrangements for cast and crew members to work in a foreign country are made through *immigration*. Arrangements for the shipment of equipment, wardrobe, props, etc. to that same foreign country are made through *customs*. It is important to select and retain a local *customs broker* specializing in the entertainment industry who will assist with all your import needs and interact with an affiliate broker at your point of entry if necessary.

Depending on your destination, one of three different procedures will be required in the importation of any necessary items: (1) carnets, (2) duplicate lists, and (3) duplicate lists with bond or cash deposit requirements.

A *carnet*, which is not accepted in all countries, is a document that lists all the equipment by serial number and description.

The goods are inspected by customs prior to departure and at each point of entry and departure to ensure that all goods stay with the carriers. A *bond* based on 40% of the value of the goods is required to protect against claims on the carnet (although in a couple of countries the figure is slightly higher). The bond will cost 1% of the 40% figure, or a financial statement of the company applying may be sufficient to underwrite the bond. Information on carnets, carnet applications, and bond forms can be obtained from one of the eight *United States Council for International Business* offices throughout the country, located in

NEW YORK CITY—HEADQUARTERS
1212 Avenue of the Americas, 21st Floor
New York, NY 10036
(212) 354-4480   Fax: (212) 944-0012

NEW YORK CITY—DOWNTOWN OFFICE
39 Broadway, Suite 1915
New York, NY 10006
(212) 747-1800   Fax: (212) 747-1948

MASSACHUSETTS
21 Custom House Street, Suite 240
Boston, MA 02110
(617) 951-1411   Fax: (617) 951-1468

MARYLAND
Executive Plaza I, Suite 105
11350 McCormick Road
Hunt Valley, MD 21031
(410) 771-6102   Fax: (410) 771-6104

FLORIDA
8725 N.W. 18th Terrace, Suite 402
Miami, FL 33172
(305) 592-6929   Fax: (305) 592-9537

ILLINOIS
1930 Thoreau Drive, Suite 101
Schaumburg, IL 60173
(708) 490-9696   Fax: (708) 885-8710

TEXAS
2 Northpoint Drive, Suite 720
Houston, TX 77060-3237   Fax: (713) 847-0700
(713) 847-5693   or Fax: (713) 847-4440

CALIFORNIA
5000 East Spring Street, Suite 400
Long Beach, CA 90815
(310) 420-2777   Fax: (310) 420-3838

425 California Street, Suite 700
San Francisco, CA 94104
(415) 765-6639   Fax: (415) 391-2716

Some countries require less complicated *duplicate lists*. At importation, the equipment is checked against a list, again with serial numbers required, and then rechecked at exportation to ensure that nothing has remained in the country. On the list, a *CIF* value (Cost Including Freight) will be required, which is the value of the goods at the point of entry, plus the insurance and freight paid to get the shipment there added to the total cost of the goods. Some countries require *cash deposits*, others will accept banker's guarantees, or you may be able to obtain a *TIB* (*Temporary Importation Bond*) from the customs broker in that country.

Again, each country has different regulations. Canada, for example, has what they call an *Equivalency Requirement*: If equivalent equipment is available in Canada, you may have difficulty bringing similar U.S. goods across the border. So allow yourself enough lead time to ascertain requirements and restrictions, apply for permits, fill out applications, gather serial numbers and the value of your equipment, and post bonds and/or deposits. Customs and immigration are government entities, and no matter how urgent our needs may be, they will work within their own time frame and will not make exceptions for anyone, even filmmakers.

TEMPORARY EMPLOYMENT OF TALENT AND TECHNICAL PERSONNEL FROM OTHER COUNTRIES

The following summarizes the requirements for bringing cast and crew members from other countries into the United States. *The Immigration Act of 1990* introduced the newly created *O and P visa classifications* for the entry of importation of artists, entertainers, athletes, performers, and related support per sonnel. Prior to the 1990 act, these individuals would have entered under the H-1B classification of distinguished merit and ability. With the introduction of the O and P visas, the *H-1B classification* is now limited to individuals in *specialty occupations*. The *H-2B classification*, although more complicated to qualify for, remains an option for those who do not qualify in the *O Non-immigrant visa* and *P Non-immigrant visa* categories.

O VISAS

O-1 Visa: This visa is granted to those who possess *extraordinary ability* in the arts, sciences, education, business, or athletics, or have a demonstrated record of extraordinary achievement in the motion picture and television industry.

O-2 Visa: Granted to those entering the United States temporarily and solely for the purpose of accompanying and assisting an O-1 alien of extraordinary ability. These individuals must be highly skilled, possess all appropriate qualifications and significant prior experience, and perform support services that cannot be readily performed by U.S. workers. Documentation is not only required to establish the qualifications of the O-2 petitioner, but also the past working relationship with the O-1 alien.

O-3 Visa: Granted to accompanying family members of O-1 or O-2 aliens.

Before a petition may be approved for the O category, a *consultation requirement* must be met. In the field of motion pictures and television, consultation with both a labor union or guild and a management organization in the area of the alien's ability is required. The mandatory consultation requirement allows unions to have input on all O-1 and O-2 petitions requiring services in the motion picture and television industry, which affects the adjudication of these petitions. However, it is important to note that consultation with a management organization is also required, which may not be consistent with the union. Further, these consultations are advisory in nature only and are not binding on the ultimate decision of the Immigration Service.

The O-1 and O-2 visa petition may only be approved for the time required to complete a specific event or performance, and may not exceed three years. Extensions are granted one year at a time to continue or complete the same event or activity.

P VISAS

The standard of eligibility is less restrictive than that of the O visas, because the P visas encompass a smaller scope of services.

P-1 Visa: This classification pertains to athletes who perform at an internationally recognized level of performance and seek to enter the United States temporarily for the purpose of competing at a specific competition or tournament, or for a limited athletic season. It also pertains to those who are members of internationally recognized entertainment groups. (The Attorney General may waive the international recognition requirement under special circumstances for a group that is nationally recognized.)

A *P-1 entertainment group* must have been established for at least one year, and 75% of the performers and entertainers in the group must have been performing in the group for at least one year. This classification additionally covers aliens who function as support personnel to individual athletes, an athletic team, or an entertainment group. Again, the P-1 visa is granted only for the period of time necessary to complete the performance or event.

P-2 Visa: This category is reserved for an alien who performs as an artist or entertainer, either individually or as part of a group, and is to perform under a *Reciprocal Exchange Program* that is between an organization(s) in the United States and an organization in one or more foreign states. The P-2 entertainer petition must be accompanied by evidence that the group has been established and performing regularly for a period of at least one year, and must contain a statement from the petitioner listing each member of the group and the exact dates during which that member has been employed on a regular basis by the group. Evidence must also be submitted to substantiate the international recognition of the group. These petitions must also include: (1) a copy of the formal reciprocal exchange agreement; (2) a statement from the sponsoring organization describing the reciprocal exchange as it relates to the specific petition for which P-2 classification is sought; (3) evidence that the appropriate labor organization in the United States was involved in negotiation, or has concurred with the reciprocal exchange; and (4) evidence that the aliens and U.S. artists or entertainers subject to the reciprocal exchange possess comparable skills and experience. Unlike the P-3 visa, it is important to note that the P-2 visa does not require a finding of cultural or ethnic uniqueness.

P-3 Visa: An alien who performs as an artist or entertainer, individually or as part of a group, and seeks to enter the United States to perform, teach, or coach as such an artist or entertainer, or with such a group, under a commercial or noncommercial program that is culturally unique may qualify for this classification. A P-3 petition must be accompanied by substantiation from recognized experts attesting to the authenticity and excellence of the alien's or group's skills in performing or presenting the unique or traditional art form. Evidence must also be submitted indicating that most of the performances or presentations will be culturally unique events sponsored by educational, cultural, or governmental agencies.

P-4 Visa: The family of a P-1, P-2, or P-3 alien who is accompanying or following to join such alien may enter on this visa.

As with the O non-immigrant category, a *consultation requirement* is also required with the P non-immigrant category. Written evidence of consultation with an appropriate labor organization regarding the nature of the work to be done and the alien's qualifications is mandatory. The permitted length of stay for all P classifications is generally the time necessary to complete the event or events for which non-immigrant status is sought with a maximum period of one year. Extensions of stay may be granted for periods of one year to complete the event.

Performers' agents, who routinely negotiate employment for their clients, are allowed to file O and P classification petitions on their behalf. Such petitions must provide a complete itinerary of the event(s) as well as the contract(s) between the third-party employer(s) and the alien. The contract between the agent and the alien specifying the wage offered and the conditions of employment must also be submitted.

Once the Immigration Service approves a petition on Form I-797, the applicant must apply for a visa at a U.S. Consulate abroad by presenting the original Approval Notice and completing a visa application form. When the visa is issued, the applicant may enter the United States and work on the project authorized by the approved petition.

H-2B VISAS

Entertainment personnel who do not qualify as aliens of extraordinary or exceptional ability to be classified in the O and P categories, or as support personnel of an O-1 or P alien, will have to consider using the H-2B classification. For a lesser known entertainer or technician, or support personnel involved with a project begun abroad that needs to be completed in the United States, when the principal entertainer is a U.S. citizen, this category is the best option available.

Requirements for the H-2B classification are as follows: (1) the position to be filled by the alien is one for which the employer has a temporary need, and (2) certification is sought from the U.S. Department of Labor that unemployed persons capable of performing the labor are not available in the United States and the employment of the alien will not adversely affect the wages and working conditions of workers similarly employed in the United States.

The *Department Of Labor* (DOL) has published detailed guidelines for the criteria and procedures to be followed for all H-2 requests in the entertainment industry. Applications for temporary *Labor Certification* should be filed at least forty-five days prior to the proposed commencement of services to ensure completion and processing by the DOL. In addition to submitting *Form ETA-750*,

Part A, the application must include an itinerary of locations where the alien will work, together with the duration of work in each location, as well as documentation of any recruitment efforts taken by the employer. Proof is required to establish that there are not sufficient U.S. workers able, willing, qualified, and available for the employment. Two principal sources of recruitment are always required: an advertisement placed in a national (trade) publication six weeks prior to filing the paperwork, advertising for this particular position/role, and a request to the appropriate labor union regarding membership availability.

With regard to *talent*, casting session information and a letter from the casting director stating the particulars of the casting search in the United States and reasons for the use of an actor from another country should be included. It must be stressed in the letter that this particular actor is the only one who can properly portray the part as it is written.

The Department of Labor grants labor certifications for periods not exceeding twelve months. If the intended duration of employment is more than one year, a new application must be submitted for any additional year or part thereof; but *temporary employment* must not exceed three years.

All applications, itineraries, labor certifications, letters, and documentations are to be submitted to the *Employment Development Department—Alien Certification Office*. After reviewing these materials, they will then forward everything to the *United States Department of Labor*. The Department of Labor will then certify or turn down all requests for U.S. work permits.

With regard to talent, a copy of all applications and documentations should also be sent to the *Screen Actors Guild*, where they are reviewed and a recommendation of acceptance or denial is then issued and forwarded to the *Immigration and Naturalization Service* (INS). Check with your local SAG office to find out who your contact is pertaining to the employment of aliens.

After certification approval has been obtained from the Department of Labor, the *temporary labor certification*, together with completed *I-129H forms*, are sent to the Regional Service Center of the *Immigration and Naturalization Service* having jurisdiction over the intended place of employment. This form is three pages long and requires information on the petitioner, the beneficiary, and the signature of the petitioner.

As the DOL determination is only advisory, INS can still approve H-2B classification even in the absence of the certification. Petitions submitted to the INS should include a statement from the employer explaining the reasons it is unfeasible to hire U.S. workers to fill the position offered and the factors that make the position offered temporary in nature.

Once the I-129H form is processed and labor certification is cleared, the applicant can go to the *American Consulate* in their country and apply for their visa. They cannot apply until it has been approved and cleared in this country. The Immigration Service will notify the petitioning employer, as well as the appropriate consulate, that said individual has been approved for a visa. With respect to talent, when the Immigration Service has finalized everything, the actors must be cleared with SAG, either checked through *Station 12* or *Taft-Hartleyed*, before they can work.

For further information, first contact your attorney and then the *Employment Development Department—Alien Certification Office*, *United States Department Of Labor*, and *Immigration and Naturalization Service* office closest to your base of operations.

Note: The information on visas was provided by Peter Loewy, Esq., Managing Partner of the law firm, Fragomen, Del Rey, and Bernsen, P.C., a national law firm practicing solely in the area of immigration and nationality law. Mr. Loewy is based in the West Los Angeles, California office.

CHAPTER SEVENTEEN

Visual Effects

Visual effects are created when outside elements, such as animation, matte shots, and computer-generated characters and effects, are integrated with original photography. The term *visual effect* also refers to the more familiar—reverses, dupes, flops, freeze frames, etc. The creation of certain effects may also include the fabrication and development of miniatures, prosthetics, and mechanically operated puppets, robots, and creatures.

As current production trends and competition for box office revenues create the desire for bigger, better, and more innovative effects, this entire aspect of filmmaking is expanding and becoming increasingly complex. Studios and production companies are now routinely employing visual effects units, headed by a visual effects supervisor, to oversee the entire process. The number of people needed to facilitate the effects on any one show will depend on the number of effects to be created, how complicated the work will be, how many effects houses will be utilized, and, most importantly—what all film work boils down to—budgetary and scheduling considerations.

If the effects house(s) you will be using is planning to assign their own supervisor to the job, or if your budget is tight and you think you can coordinate the effects work yourself, think again. Do not make the mistake of trying to save money by not hiring your own effects supervisor. Depending on the effects, you will need at least one person, and possibly more, with a good working knowledge of visual effects (and related methodology) to coordinate

and evaluate the work being created from multiple sources, schedule production work that must be done in conjunction with certain effects, monitor costs, make sure delivery dates are met, and watch out, at all times, for the interest of the production.

The most common misconception regarding visual effects is that it is strictly a facet of post production. It isn't! The visual effects process must begin at the very earliest stages of pre-production, and it generally continues right up through the end of post production. Avoid committing to any effects work before confirming that you have a sufficient budget in which to do them correctly and sufficient time to complete them on schedule. Waiting too long to start the process will, at the very least, create added expenses and scheduling delays.

The steps one takes when contemplating visual effects are as follows:

1. Breakdown your script by highlighting every single shot that cannot be achieved by conventional production photography.
2. Have someone who specializes in conceptual design work storyboard all effects shots with clearly defined drawings.
3. List each visual effects shot. Discuss and assess the methods to be used to accomplish each.
4. Send the breakdowns and storyboards out to four or five visual effects houses for bids. Select houses that specialize in the type of effects work you are trying to create. The bids should include estimated

time frames needed to accomplish the work, as well as estimates on the cost of doing the work.

Once bids have come in, you may want to

1. Make script changes to eliminate or modify effects that are too costly and/or too time consuming to create as currently written.
2. Go back to studio executives or funding source to request a budget increase if your current effects budget is not sufficient.
3. Extend your delivery date to accommodate the time necessary to create certain desired effects.

Once bids have been accepted, your visual effects supervisor will work with the various effects houses in creating an overall schedule. Upon budget and schedule approval, the work must start immediately. Absolutely no time should be wasted in building models, creating animation, constructing puppets and creatures, etc. Some effects may take six months to a year to develop and perfect; and creating computer-generated effects is also a very lengthy process. Certain effects will take longer to create than anticipated, and concept or design changes are often made along the way. Starting the process as early as possible will enable you to better accommodate these delays and changes.

Your effects supervisor will work with the UPM and first assistant director to schedule portions of effects shots, such as background plates, that must be done during production. A special crew and/or unit may be required for the shoot. The effects supervisor will also let the UPM know in advance if any special equipment will be needed, such as a blue screen, green screen, a *motion control* camera system, etc. A motion control system has the capacity to memorize its exact movements and can create the identical moves and focus, shooting separate elements at a later time.

All effects-related production needs—shooting, crew, and equipment—must be worked into the budget and schedule during pre-production. If the proper time and budgetary requirements are not considered up front, it could become a much more costly and time-consuming process to squeeze them into the schedule at a later date or after the completion of principal photography. Also, not having the necessary production footage in a timely manner may likely hold up the work being done at the effects house.

Certain effects elements, such as smoke and rain, can be added during post production; but, remember, visual effects is not just a function of post production—it requires planning and work that must begin during the very earliest stages of pre-production. Not being able to anticipate and integrate the elements essential to achieving the effects you desire may prove to be disastrous to your budget, to your schedule, and, perhaps, to your picture.

CHAPTER EIGHTEEN

Interactive

Interactive is becoming a popular and increasingly used word, as it is also becoming a rapidly growing industry. Interactive may refer to a video, computer, or arcade game; a show for television or cable; or a feature film. Interactive formats can be found on the Internet; and department store catalogs are also now being sent out on interactive CDs. In all of these formats, it is a program that allows participants to influence the action, characters, and eventual outcome of the scenario being played out by use of a computer keyboard, a mouse, a remote control, a joy stick, or a set of buttons on a pistol grip device attached to a theater armrest. The ability to control an interactive program by voice-activated means is just around the corner. *Virtual reality* is also interactive, with a computer generating a 3-D environment that allows viewers to interact with it.

All interactive media are computer based. Now that the software has advanced to the point that live action and video can be incorporated into both computer programs and CD ROMs, producers of interactive programs have the ability to replace computer-generated characters with live performers. By combining computer-generated graphics and effects with live action, you now have a multimedia program requiring a specific mixture of elements that must be facilitated by a multimedia trained staff. All conventional rules have changed with this nontraditional form of production.

Once an interactive program is designed and its elements are determined, producers and their crews must have the expertise to budget, schedule, coordinate, and supervise animators, artists, technicians, live film or video production, editors, and a generally intensive post production process. It is the responsibility of the creative director to make sure all graphic and live action elements are interfaced properly and work well together. Knowledge in the fields of post production technology, software programming, computer platforms (IBM, Mac, SEGA, Nintendo, etc.), electronics, and basic film and video is extremely beneficial. As the field expands, so does the number of people qualified to oversee the medium.

Interactive production companies do exist, as do interactive *divisions* of traditional production companies, studios, post production houses, and effects houses. Working in conjunction with programmers, these facilities must have the technology to blend and manipulate all the completed elements into a finished product.

Actors find working on interactive programs quite different from conventional productions. Schedules generally move much faster; and instead of sets, they are often filmed in front of blue or green screens. Each scene must be performed in various versions, ultimately allowing viewers to choose the scenario they wish. (Keeping continuity of multiple takes and versions of each scene is a formidable task for the script supervisor.)

As live production for interactive/multimedia programs has increased, so has the involvement of the industry's unions and guilds. The Directors Guild of America and the Writers Guild of America both offer interactive agreements. The DGA has crew stipulations, and both guilds require payment of all appropriate pension, health, and welfare benefits. Beyond that, their interactive contracts are negotiated on a project-by-project basis. The most detailed guild contract is the one offered by the Screen Actors Guild.

In June of 1993, SAG created the first *Interactive Agreement* in the entertainment industry. It covers all forms of media production, including but not limited to film, videotape, and other forms of electronic publishing. SAG's Interactive/Multimedia Agreement is the official contract under which all guild members must be hired and to which producers wishing to use SAG talent must become signatory.

To learn more about this field, a large selection of books and magazines are available on the subject. Information can also be obtained at Show-Biz Expo and other annual conventions featuring electronic multimedia systems. Classes and seminars are available as well.

CHAPTER NINETEEN

A Little Post Production

Many production people find that their knowledge of post production and its ever changing technology is somewhat limited. Hired at the beginning of pre-production, they work through the end of production and take a few weeks to wrap before moving on to the next picture. It is assumed that the *post production supervisor* will handle all necessary tasks associated with completing the film. But even with a good post production supervisor on board, production personnel often find themselves involved with certain facets of post production prior to the end of principal photography.

Post production is a vast and complicated subject, worthy of an entire book in itself. Just as budgets, schedules, and the selection of equipment were once based on whether a film was for television or theatrical release, the field grows increasingly more complex as current and developing technologies offer more choices, visual effects become more complicated and more widely used, films are being made strictly for video, and interactive is the latest craze. Moviolas are becoming extinct as editors must now be proficient computer operators and adept at a variety of different editing programs, and post production personnel must keep up with technology that is evolving in leaps and bounds.

But unless you are working in the field, having a good *overview* of the various stages and technological processes should suffice as far as effectively performing your job in a production capacity. It is also important to be aware of just how significant post production is to your finished picture.

A fundamental understanding of post production (and post production–related costs) is needed to prepare more accurate budgets. Other basics that are beneficial to know are the differences between film and electronic editing, how to plan a *post production schedule* (including the time needed to complete and incorporate complicated visual effects), guidelines for preparing *screen credits*, and some essential terminology.

It is also beneficial to be aware of standard *delivery requirements*, those elements (i.e., film, sound track, script, contracts, cast list, stills) that must be turned over to the distributor of your film when post production has been completed. Much of the necessary paperwork can be accumulated ahead of time (during principal photography) to save on time during post production.

Post production is the time used to assemble and complete your picture. It begins during pre-production with the preparation of a post production budget and schedule, the lining up of crew and facilities, and the planning of arrangements that must be made for any necessary special processes (such as visual effects). It is imperative to know what is involved, up front, and to anticipate how long the post production process will take before committing to a delivery date. Changes and delays along the way are not uncommon, but the more thorough the planning, the better chances are that the picture will remain on budget and on schedule.

Once your film has been edited, the remaining components needed to complete the picture are as follows: inserts and pickup shots, sound effects and foley, music, ADR, titles (main titles and end credits), opticals, and visual effects. Simplified, these are the elements that are *mixed* together to create a finished product ready for release. Although there were at one time standard methods utilized to produce this finished product, there are now many more options and considerations. One of the most critical decisions to be made for each show is whether the post production will be done entirely on film, done entirely by electronic methods, or accomplished with a combination of both.

FILM VERSUS ELECTRONIC EDITING

The traditional method of editing has been to cut on film. The *work print* (selected takes printed from the developed negative) is literally *cut*, either on a moviola or a flatbed. The cuts are manually spliced together, and sequences are stored on reels or cores. Changes requiring deletions, additions, or alterations require the time-consuming process of going back through *trims* (pieces of work print not used from cut sequences) and *outs* (scenes that were printed but not cut or used). When the picture is locked-in, the negative is cut to match the edited work print. Release prints are then struck from the conformed negative. This is a much slower process than editing electronically, but the cost of renting moviolas and flatbeds is a fraction of the cost of electronic equipment. An entire second editing crew can, and often is, hired for what it would cost to cut a picture on one of the digital systems. There are also editors who are not comfortable using computers and enjoy physically handling the film during the editing process.

Videotape editing was popular for quite some time and is still used by some. Of the videotape editing systems available, some are *linear* and some are *nonlinear*. Digital editing, which is a nonlinear system, is currently very much the system of choice. A nonlinear system allows the editor to insert, remove, or alter scenes without affecting any of the scenes preceding or following the change. Linear systems do not easily allow for this option. Cutting digitally equates to cutting on a computer, and the two most popular such systems are *Lightworks* and *AVID*.

Digital editing is fast and allows you the time and ease of cutting different versions of each scene, jumping back and forth until one variation is deemed better than the others. There is some amount of instant gratification in being able to restructure scenes and *play* with different options, as well as being able to create (temporary) visual and special effects right in the editing room. Using these systems can shave weeks off your schedule, especially in television, where schedules are tight. The faster pace of editing will often eliminate the need for additional editors. You will also realize savings on your sound package, as you will no longer have to order reprints of production takes for sound effects and dialogue editing. Sound tracks can be duplicated digitally directly from your system. In addition, because digital editing systems produce high quality sound and the ability to incorporate music and effects into the *cut*, *temp dubs* may no longer be necessary.

The down side to digital editing is the expense of the equipment, which is considerably higher than that of traditional editing equipment. If the time you save and the additional staff you may not have to hire compensates for the higher costs, then you are well advised to go with one of the digital systems. Even if you are not on a tight schedule, if you can afford the extra cost of the electronic equipment and want the versatility it can offer, then it is also a wise choice. Be aware, however, that using this method does not *necessarily* equate to saving time and therefore money. As the equipment is so expensive, editing rooms often run twenty-four hours a day, with assistant editors working in shifts— one at night to load footage from the previous day's shoot and another to work days with the editor.

Having the ability to experiment with and create special and visual effects digitally during the editing process can be a tremendous help; but, while instantly gratifying, the process can easily get out of hand, and become expensive. It is easy to forget that all effects must eventually be recreated at an optical or effects house, and transferred to negative.

DGA directors exercising their right to a lengthy number of specified *director's cut* days, retakes, and/or visual effects that need to be incorporated into the picture later than anticipated, and producers who schedule several previews and continually experiment with new ways to cut the picture, are all elements that may contribute to a schedule that turns out to be just as lengthy as it would have been cutting the picture by more conventional means.

Dailies and screenings created from electronically edited footage are viewed on the system's computer monitor or downloaded onto videotape for viewing elsewhere. Another factor to consider with the use of digital equipment is that if your dailies or screenings are to be viewed on a big screen or you plan to *preview* the picture, you will have to have the work print cut to conform to your electronic edit. Once you start adding film elements and the cost of another editor or assistant to conform the work print, any anticipation of savings you might have had become negligible.

New and ever-evolving technology has produced new and varied choices to make concerning every phase of post production. Your post production supervisor and/or producer must be aware of what each alternative offers, including both the benefits and possible problems associated with each. There is much to be considered before budgets and schedules are finalized, systems are selected, a lab is chosen, equipment is ordered, sound and visual effects houses are retained, and post production personnel are hired.

POST PRODUCTION SOUND

Sound editing, ADR, foley, and dubbing are the components of post production sound. Most of this work is done by sound effects houses, and more than 50% of the work done at sound effects houses is done digitally. Sound editing equipment and software have been developed to be compatible with (and to read the files of) digital editing systems such as Lightworks and AVID. Presently, it takes separate software programs to read the files of each system, but new software is being developed that will be able to read the files of any editing system.

Files from a digitally edited show are loaded onto the sound editing system's computer with the help of an edit decision list (EDL). Without an EDL, each take [either on 1/4 inch mag or digital audiotape (DAT)] must be manually loaded into the system, taking three times as long.

The cost of using digital equipment for sound editing is more expensive than the conventional analog-based equipment, but the quality it produces is better. Digital equipment also allows sound editors and sound *designers* (individuals who specialize in creating sound effects for big action sequences or sequences that require unique and distinctive sounds) the ability to listen to several tracks simultaneously while in the process of building their sound effects units.

Sound effects houses are now frequently getting involved with pictures during preproduction by working in conjunction with sound mixers in relation to production sound and how it will be recorded. Most houses also now offer what is called the *ADE System*. The ADE produces a database and time code during the normal transfer of dailies, creating an EDL that allows for the automatic loading and assembly of the production sound for sound editorial.

Various release print sound track systems have been developed by different studios and companies (Dolby being one of the better known) and are available in both digital and analog formats. (Optical tracks are still used as well.) The producing entity of your picture, where it is being dubbed, the cost of a licensing fee (if applicable) for the use of a specific system, overall budgetary and scheduling considerations, and personal preferences will help you and your post production supervisor determine which system should be used for your film.

SAMPLE POST PRODUCTION SCHEDULES

Post production schedules can vary. Half-hour television shows are being completed in two weeks; one-hour shows in four to six weeks; and two-hour movies for television in twelve weeks. Theatrical features have been completed in twelve weeks from the completion of principal photography, and some take eight to ten months. Schedules vary greatly depending on the form in which your picture is to be released (i.e., television, theatrical, video), how it is structured to meet delivery date and budgetary obligations, and whether the post production is to be done on film, electronically, or using a combination of both.

The following are three different versions of a *reasonable* post production schedule based on a modestly budgeted film—not overly extravagant, yet allowing enough time to make sure everything is done properly. All are subject to interruption and change, and are to be used as guidelines only.

None of these sample schedules include *previewing*, which is when a picture that is not *locked-in* (or final) is screened for a full movie audience. The audience's comments and reactions are assessed and changes are made accordingly. Predubbing is necessary prior to each preview, and a certain amount of restructuring is required following each preview to facilitate appropriate changes. Most lower (and some moderately) budgeted films cannot afford the additional time and expense to preview, whereas larger budgeted films often have several previews before a final cut is locked in. Each preview adds at least one week to your post schedule time.

The first schedule utilizes the traditional method of doing everything on film. The second, which is quite commonly used, illustrates a combined use of film and electronic methods. The third reflects an all-electronic scenario, with delivery on videotape.

The process of editing begins during principal photography. The film shot on the set each day is taken to the lab each evening to be developed. It is either printed (creating a work print) or transferred to videotape (in *Telecine*), and then loaded onto the digital editing system. The 1/4 inch sound tapes (*production sound*) are taken in to be transferred to 35mm mag stock or directly onto videotape. Even if you are cutting digitally, syncing the sound track to a work print will allow you to screen dailies on a large screen the following day. (You may also view dailies from the videotape.) If the

entire editing process is to be done electronically, *dailies* are synced-up in Telecine, which is a more costly process.

The editor can begin cutting as soon as filming has been completed on an entire sequence. The following reflects the weeks *following* the completion of principal photography.

POST PRODUCTION PROCESS DONE ENTIRELY ON FILM

Week 1

The editor receives the last batch of dailies and the script supervisor's final notes. She continues her *assembly*.

Week 2

The producer starts assembling a list of tentative screen credits. By the end of this week, the editor should have a completed *assembly* of the picture (sometimes referred to as the *editor's cut).*

Weeks 3–6

Once the editor's cut is completed, the director then takes the next several weeks to add his changes. It is reasonable to assume he will complete a *first cut* by the end of Week 4 and a final *director's cut* by the end of Week 6.

DGA regulations specify that the director of a *feature film* budgeted over $1,500,000 is to receive up to ten weeks or one day of editing time for each two days of originally scheduled photography, whichever is greater (following the editor's assembly of the picture) to complete the director's cut. The director has up to 20 days to complete his cut on a *television motion picture* running 120 minutes or less; and on a television motion picture running more than 2 hours, he has 20 days, plus 5 days for each additional hour in excess of 2 hours.

Although the director is entitled to the above-specified number of days in which to have his cut, those who work well with their editor(s) and are also cognizant of delivery date requirements and the financial concerns of the company will not generally take the full allotted time and will complete their cut within a *reasonable* time frame.

Week 7

Producer screens the director's cut and starts adding his own changes to the picture.

Spot the picture with the composer, sound effects, and dialogue editors. Although not final, a cassette of the picture (without time code) should be given to each so they can begin their work.

Week 8

Inserts, retakes, and visual effects (other than *dissolves* and *fades*) should all be completed and cut in no later than this week.

Producer should complete his changes by the end of this week, constituting the *final cut* and *locking in* the picture.

Transfer the final cut to video (with time code) for sound effects, dialogue, and music editors and the composer.

Week 9

Main titles and screen credits should be finalized.

Assistant editor starts ordering opticals (dissolves, fades, wipes, etc.).

If the picture is for theatrical release, the editor starts cutting the television version.

Negative cutter begins cutting the negative.

Week 11

Begin looping (ADR) actors.

Begin color correcting.

Begin answer printing.

Weeks 10–13

During these weeks (while the sound effects and foley editors, dialogue editor, and the composer are preparing their work), the opticals are finalized, the opticals and credits are cut into the picture, and the negative cutter continues cutting the negative.

Weeks 14–16

Assuming the sound track of this picture will be recorded in stereo, it will take approximately five weeks to *dub* the show. It would be cost effective to spend the first three weeks predubbing. If predubbing is done during these three weeks, this is also the time when the picture is scored (prior to the final dub).

Weeks 17 and 18

Final dub (or mix)

View *first trial print* minus any missing elements, such as end credits not yet approved or opticals not completed.

Week 19

Add any sound *fixes* to (or *sweeten*) the picture. If there are any major sound fixes, they should be made to the master tracks. Minor fixes can be done at the same time as print mastering.

Make a print master.

Make a mono master.

Make M & E (music & effects) *tracks* for foreign distribution.

If required, make a television/stereo version of the picture.

Time the picture for color.

Strike a first answer print.

Week 20

Strike a final *answer print*.

Prepare *delivery requirements*.

POST PRODUCTION SCHEDULE BASED ON EDITING DIGITALLY AND COMPLETING THE PROCESS ON FILM

You can reduce your editing time and subsequent post production schedule by two or three weeks by cutting on digital equipment rather than using a moviola or flatbed and cutting on film. If, however, this reduction infringes upon the DGA's allocated time frame given for the director's cut, you must receive permission from your director to waive his full time allotment.

Assuming this schedule is approved by both the producer and director, Weeks 1 and 2 remain the same. Weeks 3–6 now become Weeks 3 and 4, and everything else is moved up by two weeks, creating an eighteen week schedule. If you can cut three weeks off your editing time instead of two, everything is moved up an additional week, producing a seventeen week schedule.

Again, if dailies are to be viewed on a large screen (even if it is for the first few days for the purpose of checking camera work and film quality), the work print must be cut to conform to the electronic edit from the beginning. If the work print is to be cut for the purpose of a preview, it might be done following a second cut toward the end of Week 4. If you do not preview but still wish to screen a final cut for the producer and director, then the work print should be conformed during Week 5.

Unless you are delivering your picture on a one-inch videotape master only, the negative will need to be cut to conform to the electronic edit (whether you have previously cut the work picture or not). This would be done during the same time frame as would an all film post schedule. Both the work print and negative are conformed using an *edit decision list* prepared by the assistant editor.

In addition to picture editing, the popularity of editing sound effects and music digitally is also on the rise. Most pictures are being done with a combination of both. The type of equipment being used for each phase of the post process will help determine both schedule and budget, because speed and versatility are constantly being weighed against costs. A well-informed post production supervisor and editor, along with the producer, should be able to make the best choices for each picture. When using qualified post production facilities and personnel, whether the equipment is film based or electronic, the end result will remain the same.

ENTIRE POST PRODUCTION SCHEDULE DONE ELECTRONICALLY

Week 1

The editor receives the last batch of dailies and the script supervisor's final notes. She continues the *assembly*.

The producer starts assembling a list of tentative screen credits.

Week 2

By the end of this week, the editor should have a completed assembly of the picture (*editor's cut*).

Weeks 3 and 4

The director uses this time for his cut. Again, if this reduced schedule infringes upon his DGA allocated time, he must waive the remainder of the time he is entitled to.

Inserts, retakes, etc. should be completed and incorporated into the picture.

Spot the picture with the composer, sound effects, and dialogue editors.

Week 5

This week should be used for the producer's changes and to lock in the picture. It is also the time to finalize the main titles and screen credits.

Week 6

Order opticals.

Cut television version.

If you are required to deliver *release prints*, the negative cutter should receive a cut list, so she can start cutting the negative to conform to the final edit. If the picture is for video or television release, and you are only required to deliver a one-inch master, this step is not necessary.

By the end of this week, start ADR.

Weeks 7–10

Begin on-line process in which picture is transferred to a one-inch master and all color corrections are made.

If the negative has been cut and the negative cutting has been completed, a first trial print can be struck.

These are the weeks in which the sound effects, foley, and dialogue editors, in addition to the composer, are finalizing their work.

Weeks 11–13

Predub

Weeks 14 and 15

Final dub (or mix)

Week 16

Fixes

Make M & E tracks for foreign distribution.

Prepare delivery requirements.

BASIC POST PRODUCTION TERMINOLOGY

FILM-RELATED TERMS

These terms are listed in order of progression through the post production process.

Work Print (or Dailies)

A (positive) print made from the director's selected takes. This is what the editor works with in assembling the picture.

Negative Cutter

Your negative cutter is responsible for accepting the exposed negative from the lab. She breaks the negative down into individual scenes and maintains a log of each scene by key numbers (numbers on the edge of the film used to match the work print to the negative). The negative cutter pulls sections of negative for reprints and opticals, and, most importantly, cuts the negative to match the final cut work print. This person is hired prior to the start of principal photography.

Syncing Dailies

The matching or synchronization of the sound track to the picture. This is accomplished by matching the sound of the clapping slate from the sound track with the exact spot in the picture where the slate comes together.

Coding Dailies

Printing matching numbers on the edge of the work print and the sound track for the purpose of maintaining synchronization while cutting the picture.

Inserts

Inserts are brief shots that are used to accentuate a story point. They are usually close-ups or extreme close-ups and can include anything from the time on a wristwatch to a hand writing a note. If time restrictions did not allow for inserts to be shot during production or if it is decided after the completion of principal photography that an insert is needed, they can easily be shot on a small insert stage anywhere and at any time. Depending on the shot, the actual actors are generally not needed. It is important, however, that the props and the wardrobe match exactly.

Opticals

Visual effects such as dissolves, fades, enlargements, etc. This may also include titles when they appear over action.

Spotting

Running the picture with the composer to determine where music will begin and end for each scene. Separately running the picture for the sound effects editors to determine where and what sound effects are to be added and/or enhanced, and for the dialogue editor to determine where dialogue needs to be replaced and/or added.

Sound Effects

The adding, replacing, or enhancing of sounds of any kind that are not recorded during production or were recorded but deemed unusable. Sound effects can include anything from the sound of a kiss to that of a major explosion.

Foley

A method of recording sound effects that involve physical movement, such as footsteps, that can be duplicated on a sound stage. These effects are recorded by a foley artist, who reproduces the exact movement on the stage while watching the action being projected on a screen.

Looping (or ADR—Automatic Dialogue Replacement)

Re-recording production dialogue that has been deemed unusable for any number of reasons (airplane flying overhead during the take, unintelligible dialogue, etc.). The actors repeat the dialogue while watching themselves projected on a screen and listening to the sound track on earphones as it was originally recorded on the set. The new dialogue that is being recorded must match the lip movement of the actor on the screen.

Looping also encompasses the adding of off-stage dialogue that had not been previously recorded or miscellaneous crowd or background voices (walla). These are also done while the actors view the projected scene.

Scoring

The recording of the music that is to be used in the film.

Predubbing

When there are so many sound tracks being used that it makes it difficult to maintain control, it is advantageous to mix several sound tracks together prior to the final mix. This is usually done with dialogue when mixing in stereo. However, if you have a large number of sound effects tracks, you may also want to premix some of them. Once the dialogue tracks are mixed, the effects and the music are balanced accordingly.

Dubbing

As a film term, this can also be referred to as *mixing*. It is the blending of dialogue, music, and sound effects.

Fixes or Sweetening

This involves going back after the dubbing has been completed to make adjustments to the sound track.

Print Master

Combining all mastered stereo tracks into a single piece of magnetic sound track.

Optical Sound Track

The transferring of the print master from magnetic tape stock to optical stock, which is then combined with the negative to make a release print.

Timing

This is a process in which the color and density of the picture are balanced from one scene to another throughout the picture. It is done at the lab with the lab's color timer, the editor, and, occasionally, the director of photography.

First Trial Print

This is a first complete print of the film with sound track, opticals, and titles struck from the cut negative. This print will indicate where additional minor color and density adjustments have to be made. Several trial prints may be necessary before an answer print is struck.

Answer Print (Release Print)

The first acceptable release print struck from the negative.

ELECTRONIC TERMS

The following list represents the tip of the iceberg. There are many, many more terms associated with electronic post production, which can be found in books, magazines, and operational manuals, or can be learned in classes and seminars dedicated to the field. For the purposes of this book, however, a limited and select number of basic terms are sufficient. These terms are listed in alphabetical order.

Analog

The common form of any magnetic recording (i.e., audiotape or videotape) in which the recorded waveform signal maintains the shape of the original waveform signal. (Digital recording converts an analog audio or video signal to a digital signal.)

Cut List

A list of edits (containing picture key numbers) given to a negative cutter to conform the negative to match an electronically cut picture.

D1 (Component)

A digital method of recording a signal in which the elements of luminance (brightness and darkness) and the three primary colors of red, green, and blue are recorded separately rather than combined, allowing each to be enhanced individually. It provides the highest quality video signal available.

D2 (Composite)

A digital method of recording in which the elements have been combined. D2 (composite video) is easier to transmit, although the quality is not as high as D1 (component video). D1s and D2s are generally used to record completed one-inch master videotapes during the final stages of the post process, most commonly to fulfill delivery requirements.

DAT

Digital audiotape.

Digital

Converting an analog (waveform) signal to a numerical signal.

Digital Cut

Outputting digitized material (footage, sound, and music) onto videotape.

Digitizing

The loading of material—footage (on videotape), sound, and music—into a digital editing system.

Dubbing

The process of duplicating a videotape.

Edit Decision List (EDL)

List of edits used to conform the one-inch master to the (off-line) edited version during the on-line process.

Layback

Transferring the finished audio track back to the master videotape.

NTSC (National Television Standards Committee)

This defines the 525-line, 30 frame-per-second television standard currently being used in the United States, Canada, Mexico, Japan, and a few other countries.

Off-Line

The process of electronic editing.

On-Line

This process is to an electronic edit what a negative cutter is to a picture completed on film. On-line operators conform videotapes containing daily production footage to the completed (off-line) edited version. It is also possible to mix audio tracks and to add titles and opticals during the on-line process. The end result is a one-inch master videotape.

PAL (Phase Alternate Line)

The 625-line, 25 frame-per-second television standard used in Western Europe, India, China, Australia, New Zealand, Argentina, and parts of Africa.

SECAM (Systeme Electronique pour Couleur Avec Memoire)

The 625-line, 25 frame-per-second television system developed in France and used in France, Eastern Europe, Russia, and parts of Africa.

Note: When ordering videotapes for distribution requirements, always be aware of which system—NTSC, PAL, or SECAM—the videotapes must be transferred to.

(SMPTE) Time Code

An electronic indexing method used for editing and timing video programs. The time code denotes hours, minutes, seconds, and frames elapsed on a videotape. SMPTE refers to the Society of Motion Picture and Television Engineers, the organization that set up this time code system.

Sweetening

The process of mixing sound effects, music, and announcer audio tracks with the audio tracks of the edited master tape.

Telecine

The process of, or place where, film is transferred to videotape.

SCREEN CREDITS

One of the things a production manager or coordinator is often asked to do before wrapping a show is to supply the company or producer with a list of tentative screen credits. Screen credits vary greatly from picture to picture, but there are basic guidelines that apply to all productions.

Union and guild requirements govern the placement of certain screen credits. Some credits are given based on an unwritten industry-accepted pecking order, some are negotiated before the beginning of principal photography, and others are given at the sole discretion of the producer after the completion of principal photography.

The following are basic union/guild regulations pertaining to screen credits and examples of what a *reasonable* set of credits might look like, both for a motion picture and a movie for television. Note that you are not bound by any of the union/guild requirements if you are not a signatory to that particular union or guild; however, many of the union rules pertaining to screen credit placements are also routinely utilized on non-union shows. Again, be aware that much of the positioning is negotiated and is determined by the producer.

DIRECTORS GUILD OF AMERICA (DGA)

Director—Theatrical Motion Pictures

The director of the film shall be accorded credit on a separate card on all positive prints and all videodiscs/videocassettes of the film in size of type not less than 50% of the size in which the title of the motion picture is displayed or of the largest size in which credit is accorded to any other person, whichever is greater. Such credit shall be on the last title card appearing prior to principal photography or the first card following the last scene of the picture.

Director—Television

The director shall be given credit in the form *Directed by* on a separate card, which shall be the last title card before the first scene of the picture or the first title card following the last scene of the picture. However, in the case of split credits, where credit is given to any person before the first scene of the picture, the director shall be given the last solo credit card before the first scene of the picture. The director's name on the screen shall be no less than 40% of the episode or series title, whichever is larger.

Unit Production Manager/First Assistant Director/Second Assistant Director—Theatrical Motion Pictures and Television

Employer shall accord credit in a *prominent place* (no less than a separate card, or its equivalent in a crawl, shared by no more than three names) on all positive prints of each feature or television motion picture. The only *technical* credits that may receive a more prominent place shall be those of the director of photography, the art director, and the film editor. The order of names on the card shall be the unit production manager, first assistant director, and second assistant director; and each of such names on the card or crawl shall be of the same size and style of type. If you wish to give your unit production manager the screen credit of *production manager*, it must be with the prior approval of the DGA.

Note: The DGA requires that you submit your tentative screen credits to them for approval of "compliance with credit provisions." The above is a brief synopsis of their credit provisions. Check the DGA basic agreement for a complete list of their credit guidelines.

SCREEN ACTORS GUILD (SAG)

Performers— Theatrical Motion Pictures

Producer agrees that a cast of characters on at least one card will be placed at the end of each theatrical feature motion picture, naming the performer and the role portrayed. All credits on this card shall be in the same size and style of type, with the arrangement, number, and selection of performers listed to be at the sole discretion of the producer. In all feature motion pictures with a cast of fifty or less, all performers shall receive credit. In all other feature motion pictures, not less than fifty shall be listed in the cast of characters required at the end of each feature motion picture in connection with theatrical exhibition, excluding performers identified elsewhere in the picture. Stunt performers need not be identified by role.

Performers—
Television Motion Pictures

As for theatrical motion pictures, there should be at least one card at the end of each television motion picture naming the performer and role portrayed. Any performer identified by name and role elsewhere in the picture, or any performer playing a major continuing role and identified by name elsewhere in the picture, need not be listed in the cast of characters at the end of the picture.

WRITERS GUILD OF AMERICA (WGA)

Writers—
Theatrical Motion Pictures

Credit for the screenplay authorship of a feature-length photoplay shall be on a single card and read, *Screenplay by*. When the screenplay is based on a story and no other source material, the screen credit shall read, *Story by*. When the screenplay is based on source material, the credit shall read, *From a Story by* or *Based on a Story by*. Screen credit on photoplays in which one or more writers has written both the story and the screenplay shall be worded, *Written by*; and screen credit for a screenplay will not be shared by more than two writers. Writing credits as finally determined shall appear on a card immediately preceding the card for the director. No other credit, except source material credit, may appear on the writer's card. Credit for screenplay writer shall be in the same style and size of type as that used for the individual producer or director, whichever is larger.

Writers—Television

Credit shall be given on the screen for the authorship of stories and teleplays, and shall be worded, *Teleplay by*, or *Story by* (based on a story with no source material), or *Written by* (for story and teleplay). Screen credit for teleplay will not be shared by more than two writers. Writing credit, including source mate-rial credit, may appear on a separate card or cards immediately following the title card of a particular episode, or immediately prior to or following immediately after the director's credit.

Note: Check your Writers Guild Basic Agreement for requirements relating to the submission of Tentative Screen Credits.

MISCELLANEOUS LOCAL CRAFT UNIONS

Director of Photography

Credit shall be given on a separate card adjacent to the group of cards for the writer, producer, and director in whichever order such cards appear in such grouping.

Film Editor

Credit shall read: *Edited by* or *Editor*, and such credit shall be on a separate card in a prominent place (it is generally placed adjacent to the art director credit). This credit is given only to the editor who edits the material for content, continuity, and narration concept.

Art Director

Credit shall be on a separate card adjacent to the director of photography credit and read *Art Director* or *Art Directors*. If the latter is used and joint credit is given, the names shall be joined by the word *and*. If you wish to give *production designer* or *production design(ed) by* credit, prior permission must be obtained from the local union.

Costume Designer

While credit is not mandatory, it may only be given to a member of the Costume Designers Guild. If given, it should read, *Costumes Designed by*, *Costumes by*, or *Costume Designer*.

Set Decorator

There is no regulation calling for the specific placement of this credit other than in a *prominent place*. It usually appears directly after or shortly after the DGA (UPM, first assistant director, and second assistant director) card in the end credits.

Makeup Artist/Hair Stylist

The requirement of this local is just that both the makeup artist and the hair stylist receive screen credit. Placement is at the discretion of the producer.

MAIN TITLES AND END TITLES

Main titles refer to the screen credits that appear before the picture begins and *end credits* appear following the picture. If your film is for television, check the network's delivery requirements as to their *format*, which will indicate the amount of time you have to run screen credits. The number of screen credits a producer is able to give (other than those that are contractual or required by the unions and guilds) is greatly influenced by the limited amount of time allowed to run them. Producers of theatrical features, on the other hand, do not share the same time restrictions and have the freedom to give credit to whomever they wish. Before your screen credits are finalized, have them checked over and approved by your legal and/or business affairs office and/or your production executive.

SAMPLE MAIN TITLES
Movie For Television

Card #1   (Show Title)
Card #2   Starring

      _____   (lead cast)
Card #3   _____   (cast)
Card #4   _____   (cast)
Card #5   _____   (cast)
Card #6   And

      _____   (last cast member as listed and the "And/as"
       as _____   makes this a "special" credit)

Card #7   Editor (or "Edited by")   _____
Card #8   Art Director
         (or "Production Designer")   _____
Card #9   Director of Photography   _____
Card #10   Executive Producer   _____
Card #11   Produced by   _____
Card #12   Written by   _____
Card #13   Directed by   _____

SAMPLE MAIN TITLES
Theatrical Motion Picture

Card #1   _____ Presents   (name of producing entity)
Card #2   A _____ Production   (name of producer or
                                                  producer's company)

Card #3   A _____ Film (name of director)
Card #4   _____ (lead cast)
Card #5   _____ (2nd lead)
Card #6   (Picture Title)
Card #7   Starring

       _____ (cast)
Card #8   _____ (cast)
Card #9   _____ (all cast members
       _____ may not receive
       _____ single card credit)

Card #10   And   (the last cast credit is
       _____   almost as special as the
                                              first and is accentuated
                                              by the "And...")

Card #11   Casting by   _____
Card #12   Music by   _____
Card #13   Costume Designer   _____   (this credit is sometimes
                                                  listed in the end credits)

Card #14   Associate Producer   _____
Card #15   Edited by   _____
Card #16   Production Designed by   _____
Card #17   Director of Photography   _____
Card #18   Executive Producer   _____
Card #19   Produced by   _____
Card #20   Screenplay by   _____
Card #21   Directed by   _____

SAMPLE END CREDITS
Theatrical Motion Picture

Note: Depending upon your contractual obligations, the amount of time you have to run the end credits, and the producer's "discretion" as to the exact placement of names, your credits will look different. This is merely a simplified example of what your end credits might look like.

Card #1   Associate Producer   _____ __

Card #2   Co-Starring

           _____ as _____
           _____ as _____
           _____ as _____
           _____ as _____

Card #3   Featuring

           _____ as _____
           _____ as _____
           _____ as _____
           _____ as _____
           _____ as _____
           _____ as _____

Card #4   Casting by   _____   (If #4 & #5 are not in the main titles, this is a good place for them)

Card #5   Music Composed by   _____

Card #6   _____   Unit Production Manager
           _____   First Assistant Director
           _____   Second Assistant Director

Card #7   _____   Set Decorator
           _____   Gaffer
           _____   Property Master
           _____   Script Supervisor
           _____   Sound Mixer

Card #8   _____   Camera Operator
           _____   Costume Supervisor
           _____   Key Grip
           _____   Location Manager
           _____   Production Coordinator

Card #9   _____   Post Production Supervisor
           _____   Assistant Film Editor
           _____   Music Editor
           _____   Sound Editor
           _____   Negative Cutter
           _____   Rerecording Mixer

Card #10   _____   Make-up Artist
           _____   Hair Stylist
           _____   Production Accountant
           _____   Transportation Coordinator
           Extra Casting

Card #11   Catering by   _____
           Color by   _____
           Titles & Opticals by   _____
           Lenses & Camera Equipment by   _____
           Rerecorded at   _____

Card #12   Copyright © 19XX by   _____
           All Rights Reserved
           Music Copyright © 19XX by   _____
           All Rights Reserved   I.A.T.S.E. bug (if applicable)

Card #13   Executive In Charge of Production   _____

Card #14   (Production Company Logo)

SAMPLE END CREDITS
Movie for Television

Note: These credits will probably run on a "crawl"; and again, remember, this is just an example.

CAST OF CHARACTERS

—————————— as ——————————
—————————— as ——————————
—————————— as ——————————
—————————— as ——————————

—————————— Unit Production Manager
—————————— First Assistant Director
—————————— Second Assistant Director

—————————— Second Unit Director

—————————— Choreographer

—————————— Art Director
—————————— Set Decorator

—————————— Costume Supervisor
—————————— Men's Costumer
—————————— Women's Costumer

—————————— Camera Operator
—————————— Steadicam Operator
—————————— First Assistant Cameraman
—————————— Second Assistant Cameraman
—————————— Script Supervisor

—————————— Sound Mixer
—————————— Boom Operator
—————————— Utility Sound Technician

—————————— Additional Film Editor
—————————— Assistant Film Editor
—————————— Apprentice Editor

—————————— Supervising Sound Editor
—————————— ADR Editor
—————————— Sound Editor
—————————— Music Editor

—————————— Chief Lighting Technician (or Gaffer)
—————————— Asst Chief Lighting Tech (Best Boy)
—————————— Electricians
—————————— Key Grip
—————————— Second Company Grip (Best Boy/Grip)
—————————— Dolly Grip
—————————— Grips

—————————— Set Designer
—————————— Property Master
—————————— Assistant Property Master
—————————— Lead Man
—————————— Swing Gang

SAMPLE END CREDITS—cont'd
Movie for Television

_____	Supervising Make-up Artist
_____	Make-up Artist
_____	Supervising Hair Stylist
_____	Hair Stylist
_____	Construction Coordinator
_____	Stand-by Painter
_____	Production Illustrator
_____	Art Department Coordinator
_____	Special Effects Coordinator
_____	Stunt Coordinator
_____	Location Manager
_____	Production Coordinator
_____	Production Secretary
_____	Production Accountant
_____	Assistant Production Accountant
_____	Unit Publicist
_____	Still Photographer
_____	First Aid
_____	Extras Casting
_____	Craft Service
_____	Transportation Coordinator
_____	Transportation Captain
_____	Drivers
_____	Head Wrangler
_____	Wranglers
_____	Assistant to (Producer)
_____	Assistant to (Director)
_____	Production Assistants
_____	Musical Supervision
_____	Music Coordinator
_____	Rerecording Mixers
_____	Music Engineer
_____	Music Scoring Mixer
_____	Orchestrations
_____	Orchestra Conductor
_____	Negative Cutter
_____	Color Timer
_____	Titles & Opticals

(SECOND UNIT CREW)

_____	First Assistant Director
_____	Second Assistant Director
_____	Camera Operator
_____	Script Supervisor

SAMPLE END CREDITS—cont'd
Movie for Television

(STUNTS BY)

_____   _____
_____   _____
_____   _____
_____   _____
_____   _____

(MUSIC CREDITS)

"Song Title"   _____
Written by   _____
Performed by   _____
Courtesy of   _____ Records

THIS FILM WAS SHOT ON LOCATION IN _____
_____

THE PRODUCERS WISH TO THANK

_____
_____
_____
_____
_____
_____

Color by   _____
Lenses & Cameras by _____
Rerecorded at   _____

Dolby Stereo (R) (logo)

MPAA (logo)   I.A.T.S.E. (bug)

Copyright © 19XX by   _____
All Rights Reserved

The events, characters, and firms depicted in this photoplay are fictitious, any similarity to actual events or firms, is purely coincidental.

Ownership of this motion picture is protected by copyright and other
applicable laws, and any unauthorized duplication, distribution or
exhibition of this motion picture could result in criminal prosecution
as well as civil liability.

A (Name of Producing Entity) Production

Distributed by_____
            (Company Logo)

STANDARD DELIVERY REQUIREMENTS

Delivery requirements are those elements that must be turned over to the distributor of your picture at the completion of post production. The sooner you get a list of delivery requirements from your distributor, the sooner you can start assembling the necessary elements.

The following is a list of some standard delivery requirements. You may not be asked for everything on this list or may be asked for something that is not here, but the specifications will be similar, as these are fairly standard requirements. Your distributor will let you know the quantity needed of each element requested.

Composite Answer Print or 35mm Release Print

A complete first class composite 35mm positive print of the picture, fully color corrected with complete main and end titles and composite sound track.

Negative

The complete 35mm picture negative and the optical sound negative in perfect synchronization with the picture negative cut and assembled to conform in all respects to the work print.

Interpositive (IP)

A *fine grain* positive print of the picture made from the cut negative and used to make a duplicate (dupe) negative.

Duplicate Negative

A second-generation negative made from the *interpositive* for the purpose of striking additional release prints.

Low-Contrast (Low-Con) Print

A positive print of the picture made from the dupe negative on special low-contrast film stock for the purpose of transferring the picture to videotape.

One-Inch Videotape

A D1 NTSC one-inch videotape format of the picture transferred from the low-con print. The one-inch videotape is used to make (dub) additional (3/4 inch and 1/2 inch) videotapes of the picture. One-inch videotapes are often supplied to television and cable networks.

Original Sound Recording

Complete original 1/4 inch master magnetic recording of the sound track of the picture (original *production* sound).

Magnetic Master Composite Mix

A magnetic 1/4 inch or 35mm master composite recording or original digital audio master (if available) of the complete sound track of the picture conforming in all respects to the answer print.

Magnetic Music Master

A magnetic 1/4 inch track of the original music score for the picture.

Textless Background

A clear background interpositive and dupe negative of all scenes, including main and end titles, which would normally have lettering superimposed over them (used to make foreign-language prints).

Work Print

The edited work picture and all corresponding dialogue, music, and sound effects work tracks.

Three-Stripe Magnetic Master

A complete dubbed and re-recorded 35mm magnetic master of the sound track of the picture composed of separate dialogue, music, and sound effects tracks (three-stripe).

English Language Sound Track

A 35mm magnetic printmaster of the complete English-language sound track in synchronization with the original cut picture negative, suitable for the manufacture of optical sound track negatives and digital stereomaster, if applicable.

Music and Effects (M & E) Track

A 35mm sound track of the dubbed music and sound effects (each on separate channels) for purposes of looping dialogue into foreign language versions of the picture.

Sound System License

A copy of the Producer's Licensing Agreement (if applicable) for a specific sound system used in the dubbing (final mix) of the picture (i.e., Dolby, Sony, etc.).

Television Version

The negative and positive print(s), or a D2 video master, and sound tracks for all alternate scenes and/or takes, cover shots, looped dialogue lines, and other material that can be used in place of all scenes containing nudity, violence, and objectionable language in the picture for the purpose of conforming to *rating* or television requirements.

Foreign Version

The negative, positive print(s), and sound tracks for any alternate scenes and/or takes, cover shots, etc. that may contain nudity, violence, or language that were shot for the purpose of foreign distribution.

Information Pertaining to Foreign Dubbing

Copies of dubbing and subtitling restrictions relating to the replacement of actors' voices, including the dubbing of dialogue in a language other than that in which the picture was originally recorded.

Cuts and Trims

The negative and positive prints of all outtakes, trims, second takes, tests, sound effects tracks, dialogue tracks, and music tracks made in connection with the picture, which may be used to manufacture trailers and for purposes of exhibiting and exploiting the picture.

Access Letters

Letters sent by the producer to the lab(s) and/or any storage facility where elements of the picture (not already delivered to the distributor) are being stored that give the distributor access to these elements. The distributor will require copies of all access letters in addition to the name(s) and location(s) of the facilities where all undelivered elements are being stored and a detailed inventory of the elements being kept at each location.

Stills

Original black-and-white and color negatives, black-and-white contact proof sheets, still photographs, and color transparencies taken in connection with the picture.

Publicity Material

All publicity and advertising material that may have been prepared in connection with the picture, including press books, posters, biographies of featured players, and production notes pertaining to the making of the picture.

Continuity Script

A script containing the exact dialogue and action continuity of the completed picture.

Screenplay

The final screenplay or shooting script, the script supervisor's lined script and notes, and the film editor's notes and code books.

Synopsis

A brief synopsis of the story of the picture.

Music Cue Sheets

Copies of the music cue sheets of the picture and any other materials that contain music. The music cue sheets are to include (1) the title of the musical compositions and sound recordings if applicable; (2) names of the composers and their performing rights society affiliation; (3) names of the recording artists; (4) the nature, extent, and exact timing of the uses made of each musical composition in the picture; (5) the name and address of the owner of the copyright of each musical composition and sound recording; and (6) the name and address of the publisher and company that controls the sound recording.

Song Lyrics

Copies of all song lyrics (if applicable) for closed captioning.

Composer's Score

The entire musical score used by the composer and/or conductor, together with all original music, manuscripts, instrumental and vocal parts, and other music prepared in connection with the picture.

Proof of Copyright Ownership

Copies of the producer's registration, claim to copyright in the picture, and the screenplay upon which the picture is based; and, when available, copies of the Certificate of Registration.

Contracts

Copies of all licenses, contracts, releases, clearances, assignments, and/or other written permissions from the proper parties for the use of any musical, literary, dramatic, and other materials of whatever nature (including logos, trademarks, art work, brand names, etc.) used in the production of the picture (including but not limited to all employment contracts with actors, directors, producers, writers, and composers).

M.P.A.A. Rating

A paid rating certificate from the Code and Rating Administration of America, Inc. and a production code number.

Screen Credits

A complete list of screen credits and the names of all persons to whom the producer is contractually obligated to accord credit in any paid advertising, publicity, or exploitation of the picture.

Final Cast and Crew Lists

Final Cost Report

Proof of Errors and Omissions Insurance

A certificate of insurance evidencing Producer's Errors and Omissions policy covering the picture and adding the distributor as an additional named insured.

Television Residuals

A statement containing the following information for purposes of determining television residual payments: (1) Date principal photography commenced; (2) name and address (and loan-out information if applicable) of each writer, director, actor, unit production manager, first and key second assistant directors, and any other personnel entitled to residuals, together with the following information concerning each: (1) Social Security number, (2) W-4 classification (marital status and number of dependents claimed), (3) length of employment of SAG personnel, (4) a copy of Notice of Tentative Writing Credits, and (5) a list of all DGA personnel employed on the picture.

Ownership

A certified statement containing the name and address of each participant in net profits to whom the distributor must account and make payment.

CHAPTER TWENTY

Creating Your Own Niche

Breaking into the film industry is not an easy feat, and, once in, it is often just as difficult to remain gainfully employed. Building a successful and steady career is quite an accomplishment in light of aggressive competition, a limited number of jobs, technologies and trends that change rapidly, and studio executives who are there one week and gone the next.

Unless you are fortunate enough to land in the exact right place at the right time, find the perfect mentor, have a relative in the business, can afford to start your own production company, possess needed skills that few others can provide, or are just lucky, finding jobs and staying employed in this business takes a great deal of continuous effort. Contacts must be cultivated and maintained as networking becomes your middle name and perseverance your credo.

We need all the help we can get—rookies and veterans alike. Hopefully, this chapter will provide some useful tips and insights into both entering and surviving in the film business.

GETTING WORK

Unlike many other businesses, relatively few people are hired by one studio or production company and remain there until it's time to retire. Studio positions are typically limited in duration as top management teams come and go (their staffs along with them), and salaries are generally too high for many independents to retain full-time production personnel unless

they're in production. Staff jobs within the industry do exist, but the majority of film-related work is freelance. And *freelance* means that every time the job or show you are working on is over, you are back out looking for a new job or show. Unfortunately, no matter what positions we hold when we are working, our secondary occupation is that of perpetually having to look for work.

When searching for work, keep in mind that there will be a number of people competing for the same jobs you're going after. Be aware of your own personal qualities, recognize what makes you special and what it is that will make you stand out above the others. Whether it's a specific personality trait, a sense of confidence, or a specialized talent, find a way to emphasize your personal strength(s) when communicating with prospective employers.

An essential key to job hunting is the ability to remain persistent, pleasant, and patient. You will undoubtedly be faced with a certain amount of rejection and will run into your share of rude people. Do not take it personally; stay upbeat and do not get discouraged. I once worked as an assistant to the head of production for an independent production company. Someone called one day looking for work. I explained that we didn't have any openings and suggested he send us a resume to keep on file for future reference. He was extremely pleasant and asked if he could call me every week or two just to check in. He knew my boss wouldn't take the time to call him back but just made me promise that I would write his name down on the boss's daily phone log. This person called every week. He was consistently friendly, and I was consistently writing his name down on the phone log. This went on for months and months, until one day there was an opening. It wasn't a big job, it wasn't going to pay much nor would it last long, but my boss and I both immediately thought of this person who had been calling for the past several months. We brought him in for a meeting, he took the job, and today he is running his own company.

If you aren't having much luck landing a job, another option you might want to consider is working for nothing. It may not sound terribly appealing, but if you can afford to do so, it is one of the very best ways to get your foot in a door. Find a person or company you want to work for or a specific show you want to work on, and volunteer your services. Make yourself useful, work hard, learn as much as you can while you are there, and show everyone how terrific you are. You may be able to exchange your time for free lunches, mileage money, and a screen credit on the film. Chances are good that you will be officially hired as soon as there is an opening or will be hired on the company's next show. If nothing else, you have made some new contacts, gained some needed experience, and have a show to add to your resume.

Here are some additional job-hunting tips:

1. NETWORK! NETWORK! NETWORK!!!

2. Make sure you have a professional-looking resume printed on good stationery, and that it is always sent out with an equally professional-looking cover letter.

3. Include references (with phone numbers) on your resume.

4. If you have a varied background, prepare more than one version of your resume, so that each accentuates a different area of your experience. Submit the resume that best matches the qualifications a prospective employer is looking for.

5. If you have gone to film school or have taken related classes or seminars, include your professors and teachers in your network. Use them as references, solicit their advice, and ask for introductions to their contacts.

6. In addition to teachers, ask friends and acquaintances to introduce you to, or help you to get, meetings with their contacts—people you cannot get in to see on your own.

7. Regularly check the trade papers and magazines for information regarding shows in development or in prep that you can submit resumes to.

8. Consider placing a cleverly worded ad in the trade papers under "Situations Wanted."

9. Join any organization or group you are eligible to join (e.g., Women in Film) that would enable you to network with other people who do what you do and/or with people who might be in a position to hire you.

10. Send notes and/or make calls to contacts and acquaintances, letting them know you are available and asking them to let you know if they hear of anything you might be right for.

11. When calling the offices of prospective employers, remain *persistently charming* and *charmingly persistent*. The person on the other end of the phone may try to brush you off or may be rude, but do not respond in kind. Remain polite and upbeat.

12. If upon calling, you are told there are no openings, ask if you could possibly come in for a brief meeting, just for future reference. Some people drop off resumes in person, hoping to introduce themselves while there. This only works if the person you want to meet is in at the time and is available to see you.

13. Follow up all meetings and interviews with a note thanking the person you met for his or her time. Consider writing your note on a unique-looking notecard. If it's special enough, it might not get thrown away. And if left out, it will be a constant and subtle reminder of who you are.

14. It is also fitting to send a thank you note to an assistant or secretary who has been particularly nice or helpful to you on the phone. Think of these people as *gate-keepers*, because they are often the ones who will get you in to meet the potential

employers you have been trying to connect with.

15. Keep up with changing technologies and be aware of new production-related computer software.

16. There are some job referral services for certain categories of jobs. Check your industry reference books for information on these services.

17. Also listed in the reference books are employment agencies that specialize in the placement of production assistants, receptionists, secretaries, and sundry "assistants to."

18. Find out if you are eligible to apply for the Assistant Directors' Training Program. If you can pass their exam and are selected for the program, it is an excellent way to get a start in the business.

19. Keep up your contacts by staying in touch, even when you are not looking for work. Send notes, make lunch dates, and just call to say hello every so often.

20. Remain friendly and helpful to others. You never know who may be in a position to help or recommend you at a later time.

21. As difficult as it may be at times, keep a positive attitude and never appear desperate.

PAYING YOUR DUES

Several years ago, while working at my second job in the industry, I found myself exasperated and complaining to a co-worker. I was spending a great deal of time every day running errands for my boss—getting her coffee, getting her lunch, going to the bank for her, etc. I was bright, had some previous experience, and felt that these tasks were a tremendous waste of my time and abilities. My friend just looked at me and asked, "Are you ready to make the big decisions and negotiate the deals?" I had to admit I wasn't, to which he replied, "There are only two of you working in that office. If one of you has to make the deals and one of you has to get the coffee, and you're not ready to make the deals yet—where does that leave you?" What a revelation! Until I was ready, I would have to be the one to get the coffee.

It is perfectly natural to complete film

school and/or get your feet wet on a couple of films and feel you are ready for a very important position. This does happen occasionally, but more often than not, it doesn't. Be prepared to pay your dues. Give yourself time to learn, to learn how to learn more, to network, and to gain experience.

With your first job comes the good news that you have a job in your chosen field. The bad news is that you are starting at the bottom of the proverbial ladder and will typically be given the most menial tasks for the lowest salary. If you are working as an *intern*, you will probably be receiving no salary at all. Starting off as a production assistant, runner, apprentice, or secretary, you can generally expect to work long, hard hours and have a lot of people giving you orders.

The trick is to be the very best production assistant, runner, apprentice, or secretary that ever existed. Short of being totally abused and terribly exploited, don't groan when asked to do something you don't want to do. No one is asking you to do anything just to make your life miserable. If it has to be done and falls within your sphere of responsibility, you don't have much choice. Do not complain. Everyone is busy, and no one wants to hear it. Be a pleasure to have around; be a team player; and if you have any extra time, volunteer to help others with their work. Everyone will agree that you are wonderful, and they will all want you to work on their next picture and the next one after that. And so the ascent begins.

Use your time at the bottom to start absorbing information, read whatever you can get your hands on, ask questions when it's appropriate to do so, and make an effort to learn a little about everyone else's job. Get a good sense of how a set is run, who does what, what goes on in the production office, and how the entire picturemaking process works. The exposure will not only allow you to find the one area of filmmaking that really excites you, but it will give you a good foundation for becoming a production coordinator, production manager, or producer later on. Once in a supervisory position, you won't have to be proficient at each job yourself; but a good, basic understanding of any one job is essential if you're going to know when someone working in that capacity is effective.

ONCE YOU'VE GOT YOUR FOOT IN THE DOOR, HOW DO YOU LEARN WHAT YOU DON'T ALREADY KNOW?

Some knowledge only comes with experience; and the person you are working for may have good intentions, but may be too busy to teach you much. If you want to learn more, be better at your job, and move up faster—take an active role in your own continuing education.

1. Again, do not hesitate to ask questions and seek advice.

2. Take notes on things happening around you that you want to remember for future reference.

3. Find a bookstore that specializes in industry-related books or one that has a good film section. Start collecting books that will assist you in your work. Purchase industry reference books (e.g., *LA 411* and *New York Production Guide*).

4. Subscribe to industry-related publications (e.g., *On Production*).

5. Obtain union and guild contracts or books that summarize the contracts, and familiarize yourself with basic union and guild rates and regulations. Get to know union and guild representatives.

6. Collect production manuals from previous employers, or make copies of manuals your friends may have from other studios and production companies. Each one has useful information that the other ones do not.

7. Talk to representatives from the equipment houses your company has accounts with. Ask questions, and if possible, make arrangements to stop by when it's convenient. Someone should be available to show you the different types of equipment and to explain how the equipment is used. Keep copies of updated equipment catalogs for reference.

8. Ask for a tour of the lab your company uses.

9. Sign up for production-related classes and seminars.

10. Go to annually held production-related conventions, such as *Show-Biz Expo* and *Location Expo*. Pick up and keep information on equipment, production services, location services, current technology, etc.

11. Have a good working knowledge of computer software programs that will help you with your work.

12. Stay in touch and network with others who work in the same general field as you. It could be through a union, guild, industry-related organization, or just a group of friends and acquaintances. Exchange information, share tips on solving common problems, discuss changing industry trends, and help each make new contacts and find new jobs.

13. Start your own production files and keep them in an easily transportable file box. File headings should include:

    Production Services (equipment, caterers, expendables, etc.)

    Union and Guild Information

    Location Information

    Local Stages

    Cast Lists (collected from previous shows)

    Crew Lists (collected from previous shows)

    Contact Lists (collected from previous shows)

    Sample Budgets (collected from previous shows)

    Resumes (of people you enjoyed working with and would like to recommend or work with again)

    Blank Forms and Releases

    Post Production Information

    Safety Regulations and Code of Conduct

    Always keep a file with an ongoing list of your personal industry contacts.

14. When someone asks you to do something you don't think can be done, don't automatically say "no." Take a few minutes and think about it carefully. It may be difficult, but within reasonable means; try to find a way to do it. Learn to draw on your resources, use your contacts, stretch your capabilities, and be creative.

Tear-Out Blank Forms

INSURANCE CLAIM WORKSHEET

(THEFT)

STOLEN ☐ EQUIPMENT
☐ WARDROBE
☐ PROPS
☐ SET DRESSING
☐ VEHICLE

PRODUCTION _____

DATE ITEM(S) WERE DISCOVERED MISSING _____

DESCRIPTION OF ITEM(S) STOLEN (Include I.D.#'s If Available) _____
_____
_____
_____
_____
_____
_____

DEPARTMENT USED BY _____
PERSON USED BY _____

WHERE WERE ITEM(S) LAST SEEN _____

WHO DISCOVERED ITEM(S) MISSING _____

ITEM(S) ☐ PURCHASED FOR SHOW—PURCHASE PRICE $ _____
☐ RENTED FOR SHOW
RENTED FROM _____
ADDRESS _____
_____
PHONE# _____
CONTACT _____

VALUE $ _____
RENTAL PRICE $ _____ PER ☐ DAY
☐ WEEK
☐ MONTH

☐ POLICE REPORT ATTACHED
☐ OTHER ATTACHMENTS _____
_____

SUBMITTED TO INSURANCE AGENCY ON _____
ATTENTION _____
CLAIM # _____
INSURANCE COMPANY CLAIMS REP. _____

INSUR. CLAIM WORKSHEET COMPLETED BY _____
DATE _____ TITLE _____

AMOUNT CREDITED TO AGGREGATE DEDUCTIBLE $ _____ DATE _____
REIMBURSEMENT CHECK PAID TO _____
AMOUNT $ _____ DATE _____

INSURANCE CLAIM WORKSHEET

DAMAGE TO ☐ EQUIPMENT
☐ WARDROBE
☐ PROPS
☐ SET DRESSING
☐ LOCATION/PROPERTY

PRODUCTION _____

DATE OF OCCURRENCE _____ TIME _____

WHAT WAS DAMAGED _____
_____
_____

LOCATION OF OCCURRENCE _____
_____

HOW DID DAMAGE OCCUR _____
_____
_____
_____
_____

WITNESS _____ POSITION _____
PHONE# _____

DAMAGED ITEM(S) ☐ PURCHASED FOR SHOW—PURCHASE PRICE $_____
☐ RENTED FROM/OWNER _____
ADDRESS _____
_____
PHONE # _____
CONTACT _____

RENTAL PRICE $_____ PER ☐ DAY
☐ WEEK
☐ MONTH

VALUE OF DAMAGED ITEM(S) $_____
ESTIMATE TO REPAIR $_____
☐ ATTACHMENTS _____
_____

SUBMITTED TO INSURANCE AGENCY ON _____
ATTENTION _____
CLAIM # _____
INSURANCE COMPANY CLAIMS REP. _____

INSURANCE CLAIM WORKSHEET COMPLETED BY _____
DATE _____ TITLE _____

AMOUNT CREDITED TO AGGREGATE DEDUCTIBLE $_____ DATE _____
REIMBURSEMENT CHECK PAID TO _____
AMOUNT $_____ DATE _____

© ELH Form #02

INSURANCE CLAIM WORKSHEET

☐ CAST
☐ EXTRA EXPENSE
☐ FAULTY STOCK

PRODUCTION _____

DATE OF OCCURRENCE _____ TIME _____

DESCRIPTION OF INCIDENT _____
_____
_____
_____
_____
_____
_____

IF CAST CLAIM, WHICH ARTIST _____

WAS A DOCTOR CALLED IN ☐ YES ☐ NO

NAME OF DOCTOR _____
ADDRESS _____
_____
PHONE # _____

COULD COMPANY SHOOT AROUND INCIDENT ☐ YES ☐ NO
IF YES, FOR HOW LONG _____

HOW MUCH DOWN TIME WAS INCURRED DUE TO THIS INCIDENT _____
_____
_____

AVERAGE DAILY COST $_____

BACKUP TO CLAIM TO INCLUDE _____
_____
_____
_____
_____
_____

SUBMITTED TO INSURANCE AGENCY ON _____
ATTENTION _____
CLAIM # _____
INSURANCE COMPANY CLAIMS REP. _____
INSURANCE AUDITOR _____

INSURANCE CLAIM WORKSHEET COMPLETED BY _____
DATE _____ TITLE _____

AMOUNT CREDITED TO DEDUCTIBLE $_____ DATE _____
REIMBURSEMENT CHECK PAID TO _____
AMOUNT $_____ DATE _____

INSURANCE CLAIM WORKSHEET

AUTOMOBILE ACCIDENT

PRODUCTION _____

DATE OF OCCURRENCE _____ TIME _____

LOCATION OF OCCURRENCE _____
_____
_____

HOW DID ACCIDENT OCCUR _____
_____
_____
_____
_____
_____
_____

<u>INSURED VEHICLE</u> (Year, Make, Model) _____
VEHICLE I.D. # _____ LIC. PLATE # _____
OWNER OF VEHICLE _____
ADDRESS _____
PHONE # _____ CONTACT _____

DRIVER _____
POSITION _____
DRIVER'S LIC. # _____ USED W/PERMISSION ☐ YES ☐ NO
ADDRESS _____
_____
PHONE # _____

WHERE CAN CAR BE SEEN _____
WHEN _____

DAMAGE TO CAR _____
_____
_____

ESTIMATE(S) TO REPAIR $_____ $_____

<u>DAMAGE TO OTHER VEHICLE</u> (Year, Make, Model) _____
_____ LIC. PLATE # _____
DRIVER OF OTHER VEHICLE _____
ADDRESS _____
_____
PHONE(S) # _____ # _____

WHERE CAN CAR BE SEEN _____
WHEN _____

DAMAGE TO CAR _____
_____
_____

ESTIMATE(S) TO REPAIR $_____ $_____

© ELH Form #04 (Pg. 1)

INSURANCE CLAIM WORKSHEET—AUTOMOBILE ACCIDENT
PAGE #2

INJURED _____   _____
ADDRESS _____   _____
PHONE # _____   _____
EXTENT OF INJURY _____   _____
                  _____   _____
                  _____   _____
                  _____   _____

WITNESS(ES) _____   _____
    ADDRESS _____   _____
            _____   _____
    PHONE # _____   _____

☐ POLICE REPORT ATTACHED
☐ OTHER ATTACHMENTS _____
                      _____
                      _____

SUBMITTED TO INSURANCE AGENCY ON _____
                      ATTENTION _____
                        CLAIM # _____
   INSURANCE COMPANY CLAIMS REP. _____

INSURANCE CLAIM WORKSHEET COMPLETED BY _____
DATE _____   TITLE _____

INSURANCE ADJUSTER TO SEE INSURED VEHICLE ON _____
              TO SEE OTHER VEHICLE ON _____

AMOUNT CREDITED TO DEDUCTIBLE $_____ DATE _____
REIMBURSEMENT CHECK PAID TO _____
                   AMOUNT $_____ DATE _____
                       TO _____
                   AMOUNT $_____ DATE _____

NOTES: _____
_____
_____
_____
_____
_____
_____
_____
_____
_____
_____

CAST DEAL MEMO

PRODUCTION COMPANY _____   DATE _____
ADDRESS _____   PHONE # _____
_____   FAX # _____
SHOW _____   EPISODE _____
CASTING DIRECTOR _____   PROD # _____

ARTIST _____   SOC.SEC. # _____
ADDRESS _____   PHONE # _____
_____   MESSAGES _____
ROLE _____   START DATE _____

☐ ACTOR   ☐ THEATRICAL   ☐ DAY PLAYER
☐ SINGER   ☐ TELEVISION   ☐ 3-DAY PLAYER
☐ STUNT   ☐ OTHER _____   ☐ WEEKLY
☐ OTHER _____

COMPENSATION $_____ PER   ☐ DAY ☐ WEEK   ☐ SHOW

	# DAY/WEEKS	DATES
TRAVEL	_____	_____
REHEARSAL/FITTINGS	_____	_____
PRINCIPAL PHOTOGRAPHY	_____	_____
ADDITIONAL SHOOT DAYS	_____	_____
POST PRODUCTION DAYS	_____	_____

PER DIEM/EXPENSES _____
_____

TRANSPORTATION/TRAVEL _____
_____

ACCOMMODATIONS _____
_____

OTHER _____
_____

BILLING _____
_____

☐ PAID ADVERTISING

AGENT _____   HOME # _____
AGENCY _____   OFFICE # _____
ADDRESS _____   FAX # _____
_____

☐ LOAN OUT
CORPORATION NAME _____
Address _____
_____

Federal I.D. # _____
CONTRACT PREPARED BY _____   DATE SENT OUT _____

SENT: ☐ To Agent   ☐ To Artist   ☐ To Set

☐ SENT SCRIPT   ☐ NOTIFIED WARDROBE   ☐ STATION 12   ☐ INSURANCE PHYSICAL

APPROVED BY _____   TITLE _____

© ELH Form #13

CREW DEAL MEMO

PRODUCTION CO. _____ DATE _____

SHOW _____ PROD # _____

NAME _____ SOC.SEC. # _____

ADDRESS _____ PHONE (Home) _____

_____ (Beeper) _____

START DATE _____ (Fax) _____

JOB TITLE _____ ACCOUNT # _____

UNION/GUILD _____ ☐ Exempt ☐ Non-Exempt *(to be paid on hourly basis only)*

RATE (In Town) _____ Per [Hour][Day][Week] for a [5][6]___ -day week

(Distant Loc.) _____ Per [Hour][Day][Week] for a [5][6]___ -day week

ADDITIONAL DAY(S) PRO-RATED @ _____ (th) Of a week

OVERTIME _____ After _____ hours _____ After _____ hours

BOX RENTAL _____ Per Day/Week

EQUIPMENT/VEHICLE RENTAL _____ Per Day/Week

MILEAGE ALLOWANCE _____ Per Day/Week

> NOTE: Box & Equipment rental & mileage allowance are subject to 1099 reporting.—Any equipment rented by the Production Co. from the employee must be listed or inventoried before rental can be paid.

TRAVEL/ACCOMMODATIONS _____

_____

_____

EXPENSES/PER DIEM _____

_____

_____

OTHER _____

_____

_____

☐ LOAN OUT

CORP. NAME _____ FED. ID# _____

ADDRESS (If Different From Above) _____

AGENT _____ AGENCY _____

ADDRESS _____ PHONE # _____

_____ FAX # _____

EMPLOYER OF RECORD _____

ADDRESS _____ PHONE # _____

_____ FAX # _____

IF AWARDED SCREEN CREDIT, HOW WOULD YOU LIKE YOUR NAME TO READ _____

_____

APPROVED BY _____ TITLE _____

ACCEPTED _____ DATE _____

© ELH Form #14

WRITER'S DEAL MEMO

PRODUCTION COMPANY _____ DATE _____

ADDRESS _____ PHONE # _____

_____ FAX # _____

SHOW _____ PROD # _____

EPISODE _____

WRITER _____ PHONE # _____

SOC. SEC. # _____ MESSAGES _____

ADDRESS _____ FAX # _____

_____

DATES OF EMPLOYMENT _____

_____

_____

COMPENSATION _____

_____

ADDITIONAL TERMS OF EMPLOYMENT _____

_____

_____

_____

BILLING _____

_____

_____

☐ PAID ADVERTISING

WRITER'S AGENT _____ DIRECT # _____

AGENCY _____ PHONE # _____

ADDRESS _____ FAX # _____

_____

☐ LOAN OUT

CORPORATION NAME _____

ADDRESS _____

_____

FED. I.D. # _____

CONTRACT PREPARED BY _____

DATE SENT OUT _____

APPROVED BY _____

TITLE _____ DATE _____

WRITING TEAM DEAL MEMO

PRODUCTION COMPANY _____   DATE _____

ADDRESS _____   PHONE # _____

_____   FAX # _____

SHOW _____   PROD # _____

EPISODE _____

WRITERS _____   _____

SOC.SEC. # _____   _____

ADDRESS _____   _____

_____   _____

PHONE # _____   _____

FAX # _____   _____

DATES OF EMPLOYMENT _____

_____

COMPENSATION _____

_____

ADDITIONAL TERMS OF EMPLOYMENT _____

_____

_____

BILLING _____

_____

☐ PAID ADVERTISING

WRITER'S AGENTS _____   _____

AGENCY _____   _____

ADDRESS _____   _____

_____   _____

PHONE # _____   _____

☐ LOAN OUT   ☐ LOAN OUT

CORP. NAME _____   _____

ADDRESS _____   _____

_____   _____

FED. I.D. # _____   _____

CONTRACT PREPARED BY _____

DATE SENT OUT _____

APPROVED BY _____

TITLE _____   DATE _____

© ELH Form #16

DIRECTOR DEAL MEMORANDUM

This confirms our agreement to employ you to direct the project described as follows:

Name: _____ S.S. # _____

Loanout (if applicable): _____ Tel. # _____

Address: _____

Salary: $_____ ☐ per week   ☐ per day   ☐ per show

Additional Time: $_____ ☐ per week   ☐ per day

Start date: _____ Guaranteed Period: _____ ☐ pro rata

Project Information:

    Picture or Series Title: _____

    Episode/Segment Title: _____ Epsd.#_____

    Length of Program: _____ Is this a Pilot? ☐ Yes   ☐ No

Produced Primarily/Mainly for:

    ☐ Theatrical   ☐ Network   ☐ Syndication

    ☐ Basic Cable   ☐ Disc/Cassette   ☐ Pay-TV: _____
                                                                       (service)

Theatrical Film Budget (check one)   Free Television/Pay Television

    ☐   A. Under $500,000   ☐ Network Prime Time (type)

    ☐   B. Between $500,000 and $1,500,000   ☐ Other than Network Prime Time (type)

    ☐   C. Over $1,500,000

Check one (if applicable):   ☐ Segment   ☐ Second Unit

The INDIVIDUAL having final cutting authority over the film is: _____

Other conditions (including credit above minimum): _____

_____

This employment is subject to the provisions of the Directors Guild of America Basic Agreement of 1993.

Accepted and Agreed: Signatory Co: _____

Employee: _____   By: _____

Date: _____   Date: _____

RC300/070193

ADDENDUM TO THE DIRECTOR'S DEAL MEMORANDUM
POST PRODUCTION SCHEDULE
(FOR A THEATRICAL MOTION PICTURE OR TELEVISION MOTION PICTURE 90 MINUTES OR LONGER)

DIRECTOR'S NAME: _____ DATE FOR SPECIAL PHOTOGRAPHY
                                              & PROCESSES (IF ANY): _____

SOCIAL SECURITY #: _____ DATE FOR DELIVERY OF ANSWER PRINT: _____

PROJECT TITLE: _____ DATE OF RELEASE (THEATRICAL FILM): _____

COMPANY NAME: _____

DIRECTOR'S CUT:START DATE: _____ DATE OF NETWORK BROADCAST
                                               (IF APPLICABLE): _____

           FINISH DATE: _____

UNIT PRODUCTION MANAGER AND
ASSISTANT DIRECTOR FILM DEAL MEMORANDUM

This confirms our agreement to employ you on the project described below as follows:

Name: _____   S.S. #:_____

Loanout: _____   Tel. #:_____

Address: _____

_____   ☐ Unit Production Manager
☐ First Assistant Director
☐ Key Second Assistant Director
☐ Principal Photography   ☐ 2nd Second Assistant Director
☐ Second Unit   ☐ Additional Second Assistant Director
☐ Both   ☐ Technical Coordinator

Salary: $_____ $_____   ☐ per week   ☐ per day
                  (studio)   (location)

Production Fee: $_____ $_____
                    (studio)   (location)

Start Date: _____   Guaranteed Period: _____

Film or Series Title: _____

Episode Title: _____   Length of Show: _____

Intended Primary Market:
      ☐ Theaters   ☐ Network   ☐ Syndication
      ☐ Basic Cable   ☐ Discs/Cassettes ☐ Pay TV: _____
                                                           (service)

Other Terms (e.g., credit, suspension, per diem, etc.): _____

_____

_____

      ☐ Studio   ☐ Distant Location   ☐ Both
      ☐ Check if New York Area Amendment Applies

This Employment is subject to the Provisions of the Directors Guild of America, Inc. Basic Agreement of 1993.

Accepted and Agreed: Signatory Co.: _____

Employee: _____   By: _____

Date: _____   Date: _____

RC301/070193

EXTRA TALENT VOUCHER

DATE WORKED _____

PRODUCTION _____ PROD # _____

EXTRA CASTING AGENCY _____

CONTACT _____ PHONE # _____

EMPLOYER OF RECORD _____

    ADDRESS _____

    PHONE # _____

NAME (Please Print) _____

    ADDRESS _____

    PHONE # _____
SOC. SEC. # _____

☐ Married   ☐ Single   ____ Exemptions   ☐ Completed I-9

	BASE RATE	
REPORTING TIME _____	____ HRS. of S.T. @ _____ per. hr. _____	
MEAL _____	____ HRS. of 1 1/2X @ _____ per. hr. _____	
2ND MEAL _____	____ HRS. of 2X @ _____ per. hr. _____	
DISMISSAL TIME _____	ADJUSTMENT(S)	
	_____ _____	
	_____ _____	
TOTAL HRS. WORKED: _____	GROSS TOTAL: _____	

MILEAGE REIMBURSEMENT _____

WARDROBE REIMBURSEMENT _____

OTHER REIMBURSEMENT _____

I acknowledge receipt of the compensation stated herein as payment in full for all services rendered by me on the days indicated. I hereby grant to my employer permission to photograph me and to record my voice, performances, poses, acts, plays and appearances, and use my picture, photograph, silhouette and other reproductions of my physical likeness and sound in the above-named production and in the unlimited distribution, advertising, promotion, exhibition and exploitation of the production by any method or device now known or hereafter devised in which the same may be used. I agree that I will not assert or maintain against you, your successors, assigns and licensees, any claim, action, suit or demand of any kind or nature whatsoever in connection with your authorized use of my physical likeness and sound in the production as herein provided.

SIGNATURE _____
                 (If minor, parent or guardian must sign)

APPROVED BY _____

    TITLE _____

LOANOUT AGREEMENT

This agreement, dated as of _____ , is between

_____ , ("Producer") and

_____ , ("Employer")

for the services of _____ , ("Employee")

in connection with the _____

tentatively entitled _____ .

You, the Employer, warrant and represent that you have the exclusive right to lend Employee's services to Producer under all terms and conditions hereof, and that Employee is free to render such services. Employer maintains that if applicable, Employee is a member in good standing of such union or guild as may have jurisdiction, to the extent required by law and applicable collective bargaining agreements. You further warrant and represent to us that you are a duly organized and existing corporation and are currently in good standing under the laws of the state or country of your incorporation.

In consideration of the mutual covenants and agreements herein contained, Producer and Employer agree as follows:

Producer shall pay directly to you all of the compensation that would have been payable to Employee had Employee rendered services directly for us, and we shall not be obligated to make any such payments of any nature whatsoever directly to Employee. In no event shall your failure to pay any amount to Employee be deemed a breach of this agreement.

Producer will not withhold, report or pay payroll taxes from the compensation payable to Employer. Should Producer be subjected to any expenses or other liability by reason of such failure to withhold, report or pay such taxes (including but not limited to penalties, interest and reasonable attorneys' fees), Employer agrees that Employer and Employee will indemnify and hold Producer harmless therefrom.

Employer has, and will maintain at all times while Employee is rendering services hereunder, Workers' Compensation insurance as required by law.

Kindly sign this agreement in the space provided below to confirm your understanding of our agreement.

Very truly yours,

AGREED TO AND ACCEPTED

By _____   By _____

_____   _____
                Title   Name of Production Company
Name of Corporation _____   Address _____

                                                                              _____

Federal ID# _____   Phone Number _____

THE PERFORMER MAY NOT WAIVE ANY PROVISION OF THIS CONTRACT WITHOUT THE WRITTEN CONSENT OF SCREEN ACTORS GUILD, INC.

SCREEN ACTORS GUILD

**DAILY CONTRACT
(DAY PERFORMER)
FOR TELEVISION MOTION PICTURES OR VIDEOTAPES**

Company _____

Date _____

Production Title _____

Performer Name _____

Production Number _____

Address _____

Date Employment Starts _____

Telephone No.: (____) _____

Role _____

Social Security No. _____

Daily Rate $_____

Date of Performer's next engagement _____

Weekly Conversion Rate $_____

Wardrobe supplied by performer   Yes ☐   No ☐

If so, number of outfits _____ @ $_____

(formal) _____ @ $_____

COMPLETE FOR "DROP-AND-PICK-UP" DEALS ONLY:
Firm recall date on _____
or on or after * _____
("On or after" recall only applies to pick-up as Weekly Performer)
As   ☐ Day Performer   ☐ Weekly Performer
*Means date specified or within 24 hours thereafter.

THIS AGREEMENT covers the employment of the above-named Performer by _____ in the production and at the rate of compensation set forth above and is subject to and shall include, for the benefit of the Performer and the Producer, all of the applicable provisions and conditions contained or provided for in the applicable Screen Actors Guild Television Agreement (herein called the "Television Agreement"). Performer's employment shall include performance in non-commercial openings, bridges, etc., and no added compensation shall be payable to Performer so long as such are used in the role and episode covered hereunder in which Performer appears; for other use, Performer shall be paid the added minimum compensation, if any, required under the provisions of the Screen Actors Guild agreements with Producer.

Producer shall have all the rights in and to the results and proceeds of the Performer's services rendered hereunder, as are provided with respect to "photoplays" in Schedule A of the applicable Screen Actors Guild Codified Basic Agreement and the right to supplemental market use as defined in the Television Agreement.

Producer shall have the unlimited right throughout the world to telecast the film and exhibit the film theatrically and in supplemental markets in accordance with the terms and conditions of the Television Agreement.

If the motion picture is rerun on television in the United States or Canada and contains any of the results and proceeds of the Performer's services, the Performer will be paid for each day of employment hereunder the additional compensation prescribed therefor by the Television Agreement, unless there is an agreement to pay an amount in excess thereof as follows:

_____

_____

If there is foreign telecasting of the motion picture as defined in the Television Agreement, and such motion picture contains any of the results and proceeds of the Performer's services, the Performer will be paid the amount in the blank space below for each day of employment hereunder, or if such blank space is not filled in, then the Performer will be paid the minimum additional compensation prescribed therefor by the Television Agreement. $_____

If the motion picture is exhibited theatrically anywhere in the world and contains any of the results and proceeds of the Performer's services, the Performer will be paid $_____ , or if this blank is not filled in, then the Performer will be paid the minimum additional compensation prescribed therefor by the Television Agreement.

If the motion picture is exhibited in supplemental markets anywhere in the world and contains any of the results and proceeds of the Performer's services, then Performer will be paid the supplemental market fees prescribed by the applicable provisions of the Television Agreement.

If the Performer places his or her initials in the box below, he or she thereby authorizes Producer to use portions of said television motion picture as a trailer to promote another episode or the series as a whole, upon payment to the Performer of the additional compensation prescribed by the applicable provisions of the Television Agreement.

Initial

By _____
Producer

_____
Performer

Production time reports are available on the set at the end of each day, which reports shall be signed or initialed by the Performer.

NOTICE TO PERFORMER: IT IS IMPORTANT THAT YOU RETAIN A COPY OF THIS CONTRACT FOR YOUR PERMANENT RECORDS.

THE PERFORMER MAY NOT WAIVE ANY PROVISION OF THIS CONTRACT WITHOUT THE WRITTEN CONSENT OF SCREEN ACTORS GUILD, INC.

MINIMUM THREE-DAY CONTRACT
FOR TELEVISION MOTION PICTURES OR VIDEOTAPES
THREE-DAY MINIMUM EMPLOYMENT

THIS AGREEMENT is made this _____ day of _____ , 19____ , between

_____ , a corporation, hereinafter called "Producer," and

_____ , hereinafter called "Performer."

WITNESSETH:

1. **Photoplay: Role and Guarantee.** Producer hereby engages Performer to render service as such in the role of _____ , in a photoplay produced primarily for exhibition over free television, the working title of which is now _____ . Performer accepts such engagement upon the terms herein specified. Producer guarantees that it will furnish Performer not less than _____ days' employment. (If this blank is not filled in, the guarantee shall be three (3) days.)

2. **Salary.** The Producer will pay to the Performer, and the Performer agrees to accept for three (3) days (and pro rata for each additional day beyond three (3) days) the following salary rate: $_____ .

3. Producer shall have the unlimited right throughout the world to telecast the film and exhibit the film theatrically and in Supplemental Markets in accordance with the terms and conditions of the applicable Screen Actors Guild Television Agreement (herein referred to as the "Television Agreement").

4. If the motion picture is rerun on television in the United States or Canada and contains any of the results and proceeds of the Performer's services, the Performer will be paid the additional compensation prescribed therefor by the Television Agreement, unless there is an agreement to pay an amount in excess thereof as follows:

_____

_____

5. If there is foreign telecasting of the motion picture as defined in the Television Agreement, and such motion picture contains any of the results and proceeds of the Performer's services, the Performer will be paid the amount in the blank space below plus an amount equal to one-third (1/3) thereof for each day of employment in excess of three (3) days, or, if such blank space is not filled in, then the Performer will be paid the minimum additional compensation prescribed therefor by the Television Agreement. $_____ .

6. If the motion picture is exhibited theatrically anywhere in the world and contains any of the results and proceeds of the Performer's services, the Performer will be paid $_____ , plus an amount equal to one-third (1/3) thereof for each day of employment in excess of three (3) days. If this blank is not filled in, the Performer will be paid the applicable minimum additional compensation prescribed therefor by the Television Agreement.

7. If the motion picture is exhibited in Supplemental Markets anywhere in the world and contains any of the results and proceeds of the Performer's services, the Performer will be paid the supplemental market fees prescribed by the applicable provisions of the Television Agreement.

8. **Term.** The term of employment hereunder shall begin on _____ , on or about* _____ and shall continue thereafter until the completion of the photography and recordation of said role.

* The "on or about clause" may only be used when the contract is delivered to the Performer at least three (3) days before the starting date.

9. **Incorporation of Television Agreement.** The applicable provisions of the Television Agreement are incorporated herein by reference. Performer's employment shall include performance in non-commercial openings, closings, bridges, etc., and no added compensation shall be payable to Performer so long as such are used in the role and episode covered hereunder and in which Performer appears; for other use, Performer shall be paid the added minimum compensation, if any, required under the provisions of the Screen Actors Guild agreements with Producer. Performer's employment shall be upon the terms, conditions and exceptions of the provisions applicable to the rate of salary and guarantee specified in Paragraphs 1. and 2. hereof.

10. **Arbitration of Disputes.** Should any dispute or controversy arise between the parties hereto with reference to this contract, or the employment herein provided for, such dispute or controversy shall be settled and determined by conciliation and arbitration in accordance with and to the extent provided in the conciliation and arbitration provisions of the Television Agreement, and such provisions are hereby referred to and by such reference incorporated herein and made a part of this agreement with the same effect as though the same were set forth herein in detail.

11. **Performer's Address.** All notices which the Producer is required or may desire to give to the Performer may be given either by mailing the same addressed to the Performer at _____, or such notice may be given to the Performer personally, either orally or in writing.

12. **Performer's Telephone.** The Performer must keep the Producer's casting office or the assistant director of said photoplay advised as to where the Performer may be reached by telephone without unreasonable delay. The current telephone number of the Performer is (_____)_____ .

13. If Performer places his initials in the box, he thereby authorizes Producer to use portions of said television motion picture as a trailer to promote another episode or the series as a whole, upon payment to the Performer of the additional compensation prescribed by the Television Agreement.

14. **Furnishing of Wardrobe.** The Performer agrees to furnish all modern wardrobe and wearing apparel reasonably necessary for the portrayal of said role; it being agreed, however, that should so-called "character" or "period" costumes be required, the Producer shall supply the same. When Performer supplies any wardrobe, Performer shall receive the cleaning allowance and reimbursement specified in the Television Agreement.

15. **Next Starting Date.** The starting date of Performer's next engagement is _____.

IN WITNESS WHEREOF, the parties have executed this agreement on the day and year first above written.

By _____
Producer

_____
Performer

_____
Social Security No.

Production time reports are available on the set at the end of each day. Such reports shall be signed or initialed by the performer.

Attached hereto for your use is a Declaration Regarding Income Tax Withholding ("Part Year Employment Method of Withholding"). You may utilize such form by delivering same to Producer.

NOTICE TO PERFORMER: IT IS IMPORTANT THAT YOU RETAIN A COPY OF THIS CONTRACT FOR YOUR PERMANENT RECORDS.

**THE PERFORMER MAY NOT WAIVE ANY PROVISION OF THIS CONTRACT
WITHOUT THE WRITTEN CONSENT OF SCREEN ACTORS GUILD, INC.**

SCREEN ACTORS GUILD
MINIMUM FREE LANCE WEEKLY CONTRACT
FOR TELEVISION MOTION PICTURES OR VIDEOTAPES
**Continuous Employment – Weekly Basis – Weekly Salary
One Week Minimum Employment**

THIS AGREEMENT is made this _____ day of _____ , 19____ , between
_____ , a corporation, hereinafter called "Producer," and
_____ , hereinafter called "Performer."

WITNESSETH:

1. **Photoplay: Role and Guarantee.** Producer hereby engages Performer to render services as such, in the role of _____ , in a photoplay produced primarily for exhibition over free television, the working title of which is now _____ . Performer accepts such engagement upon the terms herein specified. Producer guarantees that it will furnish Performer not less than _____ weeks employment. (If this blank is not filled in, the guarantee shall be one week.)

2. **Salary.** The Producer will pay to the Performer, and the Performer agrees to accept weekly (and pro rata for each additional day beyond guarantee) the following salary rate: $_____ per "studio week." (Schedule B Performers must receive an additional overtime payment of four (4) hours at straight time rate for each overnight location sixth day).

3. Producer shall have the unlimited right throughout the world to telecast the film and exhibit the film theatrically and in Supplemental Markets, in accordance with the terms and conditions of the applicable Screen Actors Guild Television Agreement (herein referred to as the "Television Agreement").

4. If the motion picture is rerun on television in the United States or Canada and contains any of the results and proceeds of the Performer's services, the Performer will be paid the additional compensation prescribed therefor by the Television Agreement, unless there is an agreement to pay an amount in excess thereof as follows:

_____

_____

5. If there is foreign telecasting of the motion picture, as defined in the Television Agreement, and such motion picture contains any of the results and proceeds of the Performer's services, the Performer will be paid $_____ plus pro rata thereof for each additional day of employment in excess of one week, or, if this blank is not filled in, the Performer will be paid the minimum additional compensation prescribed therefor by the Television Agreement.

6. If the motion picture is exhibited theatrically anywhere in the world and contains any of the results and proceeds of the Performer's services, the Performer will be paid $_____ plus pro rata thereof for each additional day of employment in excess of one week, or, if this blank is not filled in, the Performer will be paid the minimum additional compensation prescribed therefor by the Television Agreement.

7. If the motion picture is exhibited in Supplemental Markets anywhere in the world and contains any of the results and proceeds of the Performer's services, the Performer will be paid the supplemental market fees prescribed by the applicable provisions of the Television Agreement.

8. **Term.** The term of employment hereunder shall begin on _____ , on or about*_____ and shall continue thereafter until the completion of the photography and recordation of said role.

*The "on or about clause" may only be used when the contract is delivered to the Performer at least three (3) days before the starting date.

The Complete Film Production Handbook   **271**

9. **Incorporation of Television Agreement.** The applicable provisions of the Television Agreement are incorporated herein by reference. Performer's employment shall include performance in non-commercial openings, closings, bridges, etc., and no added compensation shall be payable to Performer so long as such are used in the role and episode covered hereunder and in which Performer appears; for other use, Performer shall be paid the added minimum compensation, if any, required under the provisions of the Screen Actors Guild agreements with Producer. Performer's employment shall be upon the terms, conditions and exceptions of said provisions applicable to the rate of salary and guarantee specified in Paragraphs 1. and 2. hereof.

10. **Arbitration of Disputes.** Should any dispute or controversy arise between the parties hereto with reference to this contract, or the employment herein provided for, such dispute or controversy shall be settled and determined by conciliation and arbitration in accordance with and to the extent provided in the conciliation and arbitration provisions of the Television Agreement, and such provisions are hereby referred to and by such reference incorporated herein and made a part of this agreement with the same effect as though the same were set forth herein in detail.

11. **Performer's Address.** All notices which the Producer is required or may desire to give to the Performer may be given either by mailing the same addressed to the Performer at _____ , or such notice may be given to the Performer personally, either orally or in writing.

12. **Performer's Telephone.** The Performer must keep the Producer's casting office or the assistant director of said photoplay advised as to where the Performer may be reached by telephone without unreasonable delay. The current telephone number of the Performer is (_____)_____ .

13. If Performer places his initials in the box, he thereby authorizes Producer to use portions of said television motion picture as a trailer to promote another episode or the series as a whole, upon payment to the Performer of the additional compensation prescribed by the Television Agreement.

14. **Furnishing of Wardrobe.** The Performer agrees to furnish all modern wardrobe and wearing apparel reasonably necessary for the portrayal of said role; it being agreed, however, that should so-called "character" or "period" costumes be required, the Producer shall supply the same. When Performer supplies any wardrobe, Performer shall receive the cleaning allowance and reimbursement specified in the Television Agreement.

15. **Next Starting Date.** The starting date of Performer's next engagement is _____ .

IN WITNESS WHEREOF, the parties have executed this agreement on the day and year first above written.

By _____
_____ Producer

_____ Performer

_____ Social Security No.

Production time reports are available on the set at the end of each day. Such reports shall be signed or initialed by the performer.

NOTICE TO PERFORMER: IT IS IMPORTANT THAT YOU RETAIN A COPY OF THIS CONTRACT FOR YOUR PERMANENT RECORDS.

THE PERFORMER MAY NOT WAIVE ANY PROVISION OF THIS CONTRACT WITHOUT THE WRITTEN CONSENT OF SCREEN ACTORS GUILD, INC.

DAILY STUNT PERFORMER CONTRACT
FOR TELEVISION MOTION PICTURES OR VIDEOTAPES

Company _____

Date Employment Starts _____

Role _____

    Stunt Double for* _____

    Other (description) _____

Production Title _____

Date _____

Stunt Performer Name _____

Address _____

Telephone No.: (____)_____

Social Security No. _____

Daily Rate $_____

Weekly Conversion Rate $_____

Stunt Adjustment(s):

$_____ for _____ No. of takes _____

$_____ for _____ No. of takes _____

Wardrobe supplied by performer Yes ☐ No ☐

If so, number of outfits _____ @ $_____

        (formal) _____ @ $_____

Date of Stunt Performer's next engagement: _____

COMPLETE FOR "DROP-AND-PICK-UP" DEALS ONLY:

Firm recall date on _____

or on or after * _____

("On or after" recall only applies to pick-up as Weekly Performer)

As   ☐ Day Performer   ☐ Weekly Performer

*Means date specified or within 24 hours thereafter.

WITNESSETH:

1. THIS AGREEMENT covers the employment of the above-named Performer by _____ in the production and at the rate of compensation set forth above and is subject to and shall include, for the benefit of the Performer and the Producer, all of the applicable provisions and conditions contained or provided for in the Screen Actors Guild Television Agreement (herein called the "Television Agreement"). Performer's employment shall include performance in non-commercial openings, bridges, etc., and no added compensation shall be payable to Performer so long as such are used in the role and episode covered hereunder in which Performer appears.

2. Producer shall have the unlimited right throughout the world to telecast the film and exhibit the film theatrically and in supplemental markets in accordance with the terms and conditions of the Television Agreement.

3. If the motion picture is rerun on television in the United States or Canada and contains any of the results and proceeds of the Performer's services, the Performer will be paid for each day of employment hereunder the additional compensation prescribed therefor by the Television Agreement, unless there is an agreement to pay an amount in excess thereof as follows: _____

_____

_____

* NOTE: STUNT DAY PERFORMERS MUST RECEIVE A SEPARATE DAY'S PAY AND CONTRACT FOR EACH PERSON DOUBLED

4. If there is foreign telecasting of the motion picture as defined in the Television Agreement, and such motion picture contains any of the results and proceeds of the Performer's services, the Performer will be paid in the amount in the blank space below for each day of employment hereunder, or if such blank space is not filled in, then the Performer will be paid the minimum additional compensation prescribed therefor by the Television Agreement. $_____

5. If the motion picture is exhibited theatrically anywhere in the world and contains any of the results and proceeds of the Performer's services, the Performer will be paid $_____ , or if this blank is not filled in, then the Performer will be paid the minimum additional compensation prescribed therefor by the Television Agreement.

6. If the motion picture is exhibited in supplemental markets anywhere in the world and contains any of the results and proceeds of the Performer's services, then Performer will be paid the supplemental market fees prescribed by the applicable provisions of the Television Agreement.

By _____

Producer

_____

Stunt Performer

Production time reports are available on the set at the end of each day, which reports shall be signed or initialed by the Performer.

Attached hereto for your use are the following: (1) Declaration Regarding Income Tax Withholding ("Part Year Employment Method of Withholding") and (2) Declaration Regarding Income Tax Withholding. You may utilize the applicable form by delivering same to Producer. Only one of such forms may be used.

NOTICE TO PERFORMER: IT IS IMPORTANT THAT YOU RETAIN A COPY OF THIS CONTRACT FOR YOUR PERMANENT RECORDS.

SCREEN ACTORS GUILD

STUNT PERFORMER'S
MINIMUM FREELANCE THREE-DAY CONTRACT
FOR TELEVISION MOTION PICTURES

STUNT PERFORMER _____ DATE OF AGREEMENT _____

ADDRESS _____

_____

TELEPHONE ( ) – _____ SOCIAL SECURITY NO. ___ – ___ – _____

COMPANY/PRODUCER_____

PRODUCTION TITLE _____ PRODUCTION NO. _____

AGENT/AGENCY _____

ADDRESS _____

_____

1. **DESCRIPTION OF SERVICES:** Producer hereby engages Stunt Performer to render services as _____ _____. Stunt Performer accepts such engagement upon the terms herein specified.

2. **COMPENSATION/TERM/GUARANTEE:** Producer will pay Stunt Performer and Stunt Performer agrees to accept the following three-day compensation (excluding location premiums) of $_____ (and pro rata services). The total guaranteed compensation shall be $_____ for the total guaranteed period of _____. If this space is not filled in, the guarantee shall be three (3) days. Stunt Performer shall receive sixth day location premium where applicable.

3. **START DATE:** The term of engagement shall begin on _____. or "on or about" *_____.

4. **NEXT START DATE:** The start date of Stunt Performer's next engagement is _____.

5. **STUNT ADJUSTMENTS:** It is understood that the rate of compensation specified may be adjusted depending upon the nature of the stunt activities Producer may require. If so, a stunt adjustment will be agreed upon between the parties through good faith bargaining and said adjustment shall be noted on Stunt Performer's daily time report or time card.

   The parties shall agree upon the compensation to be paid before the stunt is performed if they may readily do so; however, it is expressly agreed that production shall not be delayed for the purpose of first determining the compensation for a stunt. Such adjustment shall increase Stunt Performer's compensation for the three-days in the manner prescribed in Schedule H-II or H-III of the Screen Actors Guild Codified Basic Agreement.

6. **INCORPORATION OF PRODUCER-SCREEN ACTORS GUILD COLLECTIVE BARGAINING AGREEMENT:** All provisions of the Screen Actors Guild Codified Basic Agreement as the same may be supplemented and/or amended to date shall be deemed incorporated herein. Stunt Performer's engagement shall include performance in non-commercial openings, closings, bridges, etc., and no added compensation shall be payable to Stunt Performer so long as such are used in the Motion Picture covered hereunder and in which Stunt Performer appears or with respect to which Stunt Performer is paid compensation hereunder. Stunt Performer's engagement shall be upon the terms, conditions and exceptions of said provisions applicable to the rate of compensation specified.

*The "on or about" clause may only be used when this Agreement is delivered to Stunt Performer at least three (3) days before the Start Date.

7. **RIGHTS:** Producer shall have the unlimited right throughout the universe and in perpetuity to exhibit the Motion Picture in all media, now or hereafter known, and Producer, as employer-for-hire of Stunt Performer, shall own all rights in the results and proceeds of Stunt Performer's services hereunder.

8. **ADDITIONAL COMPENSATION:** If the Motion Picture covered hereby is exhibited, containing any of the results and proceeds of Stunt Performer's services hereunder, in any of the following media:

   (i) "Free" television reruns in the United States or Canada, or both;
   (ii) Television exhibition anywhere in the universe outside the United States and Canada;
   (iii) Theatrical exhibition anywhere in the universe;
   (iv) Supplemental Market exhibition anywhere in the universe;
   (v) Basic Cable exhibition anywhere in the universe,

   as to each such medium in which the motion picture is so exhibited, Producer will pay, and Stunt Performer will accept as payment in full, the minimum additional compensation provided therefor in the Screen Actors Guild Codified Basic Agreement or Television Agreement, as the case may be, except as compensation in excess of such minimum, if any, has been provided in this Agreement.

9. **CONTINUOUS EMPLOYMENT AND RIGHT TO ROLE (when applicable):** If Stunt Performer portrays a role or has dialogue, Stunt Performer shall be entitled to "continuous employment" and "Right to Role," if any, only to the extent prescribed by the Screen Actors Guild Codified Basic Agreement. Stunt Performer shall receive a separate contract for such services.

10. **MOTION PICTURE AND TELEVISION FUND:** Stunt Performer [does] [does not] hereby authorize Producer to deduct from the compensation hereinabove specified an amount equal to _____ percent of each installment of compensation due Stunt Performer hereunder, and to pay the amount so deducted to the Motion Picture and Television Fund of America, Inc.

11. **WAIVER:** Stunt Performer may not waive any provision of the Screen Actors Guild Codified Basic Agreement or Television Agreement, whichever is applicable, without the written consent of the Screen Actors Guild, Inc.

12. **SIGNATORY:** Producer makes the material representation that either it is presently a signatory to the Screen Actors Guild collective bargaining agreement covering the engagement contracted for herein, or that the Motion Picture is covered by such collective bargaining agreement under the "Independent Production" provisions (Section 24) of the General Provisions of the Screen Actors Guild Codified Basic Agreement.

Signing of this Agreement in the spaces below signifies acceptance by Producer and Stunt Performer of all of the above terms and conditions and those on the reverse hereof and attached hereto, if any, as of the date specified above.

PRODUCER _____ STUNT PERFORMER_____

BY_____

Production time reports and/or time cards are available on the set at the beginning and end of each day, which reports and/or time cards shall be signed or initialed by Stunt Performer and must indicate any agreed stunt adjustments.

NOTICE TO STUNT PERFORMER: IT IS IMPORTANT THAT YOU RETAIN A COPY OF THIS AGREEMENT FOR YOUR PERMANENT RECORDS.

 **SCREEN ACTORS GUILD**

**STUNT PERFORMER
MINIMUM FREE LANCE WEEKLY CONTRACT
FOR TELEVISION MOTION PICTURES OR VIDEOTAPES**

Weekly Basis—Weekly Salary
One Week Minimum Employment

THIS AGREEMENT, made this _____ day of _____ , 19___ , between

_____ , a corporation, hereinafter called "Producer."

and _____ , hereinafter called "Performer."

WITNESSETH:

1. PHOTOPLAY, ROLE AND GUARANTEE. Producer hereby engages Performer to render services as such,

    Check One:

    ☐ in the Role of _____ , or

    ☐ as Stunt Double for _____ , or

    ☐ as Utility Stunt Performer, or

    ☐ other (describe work) _____

    in a photoplay produced primarily for exhibition over free television, the working title of which is now
    _____ . Performer accepts such engagement upon the terms
    herein specified. Producer guarantees that it will furnish Performer not less than _____ weeks employment.
    (If this blank is not filled in, the guarantee shall be one week.)

2. SALARY. The Producer will pay to the Performer, and the Performer agrees to accept weekly (and pro rata for
    each additional day beyond guarantee) the following salary rate: $_____ per "studio week." (Schedule H-II
    Performers must receive an additional overtime payment for four (4) hours at straight time rate for each overnight
    location Saturday.)

3. STUNT ADJUSTMENTS. It is understood between the parties that the salary rate specifed above may require
    adjustment depending upon the nature of the stunt activities Producer requires. If so, a Stunt Adjustment will be
    agreed upon between the parties through good faith bargaining and said adjustment shall be noted on the
    Performer's daily time sheet or time card. Such adjustment shall increase the Performer's compensation for the
    week in the manner prescribed in Schedule H of the Screen Actors Guild Codified Basic Agreement.

4. Producer shall have the unlimited right throughout the world to telecast the film and exhibit the film theatrically
    and in supplemental markets, in accordance with the terms and conditions of the Screen Actors Guild Tele-
    vision Agreement (herein referred to as the "Television Agreement").

5. If the motion picture is rerun on television in the United States or Canada and contains any of the results and
    proceeds of the Performer's services, the Performer wili be paid the additional compensation prescribed therefor
    by the Television Agreement unless there is an agreement to pay an amount in excess thereof as follows:

    _____

6. If there is foreign telecasting of the motion picture as defined in the Television Agreement, and such motion pic-
    ture contains any of the results and proceeds of the Performer's services, the Performer will be paid $_____
    plus pro rata thereof for each day of employment in excess of one week, or, if this blank is not filled in, then the
    Performer will be paid the minimum additional compensation prescribed therefor by the Television Agreement.

7. If the motion picture is exhibited theatrically anywhere in the world and contains any of the results and proceeds of the Performer's services, the Performer will be paid $_____ plus pro rata thereof for each day of employment in excess of one week, or, if this blank is not filled in, the Performer will be paid the minimum additional compensation prescribed therefor by the Television Agreement.

8. If the motion picture is exhibited in supplemental markets anywhere in the world and contains any of the results and proceeds of the Performer's services, then Performer will be paid the supplemental market fees prescribed by the applicable provisions of the Television Agreement.

9. TERM. The term of employment hereunder shall begin

   on _____ , OR on or about*_____

10. CONTINUOUS EMPLOYMENT AND RIGHT TO ROLE. If the Stunt Performer portrays a role or has dialogue, such Performer shall be entitled to continuous employment and "right to role" and shall receive payment for the entire period from the Performer's first call to work on the picture until completion of the photography and recordation of said role.

11. INCORPORATION OF TELEVISION AGREEMENT. The applicable provisions of the Television Agreement are incorporated herein by reference. Performer's employment shall include performance in non-commercial openings, closings, bridges, etc., and no added compensation shall be payable to Performer so long as such are used in the role(s) and episode(s) covered hereunder and in which Performer appears. Performer's employment shall be upon the terms, conditions and exceptions of said provisions applicable to the rate of salary and guarantee specified in Paragraphs 1 and 2 hereof.

12. PERFORMER'S ADDRESS. All notices which the Producer is required or may desire to give to the Performer may be given either by mailing the same addressed to the Performer at _____ or such notice may be given to the Performer personally, either orally or in writing.

13. PERFORMER'S TELEPHONE. The Performer must keep the Producer's casting office or the assistant director of said photoplay advised as to where the Performer may be reached by telephone without unreasonable delay. The current telephone number of the Performer is _____ .

14. NEXT STARTING DATE. The starting date of the Performer's next engagement is _____ .

IN WITNESS WHEREOF, the parties have executed this agreement on the day and year first above written.

PRODUCER _____ STUNT PERFORMER _____

BY_____ SOCIAL SECURITY # _____

*The "on or about" clause may only be used when the contract is delivered to the Performer at least three (3) days before the starting date.

The Production time reports are available on the set at the end of each day, which reports shall be signed or initialed by the Performer and must indicate any agreed stunt adjustments.

Attached hereto for your use is a Declaration Regarding Income Tax Withholding.

NOTICE TO STUNT PERFORMER: IT IS IMPORTANT THAT YOU RETAIN A COPY OF THIS CONTRACT FOR YOUR PERMANENT RECORDS.

THE PERFORMER MAY NOT WAIVE ANY PROVISION OF THIS CONTRACT WITHOUT THE WRITTEN CONSENT OF SCREEN ACTORS GUILD, INC.

SCREEN ACTORS GUILD

**DAILY CONTRACT
(DAY PERFORMER)
FOR THEATRICAL MOTION PICTURES**

Company _____   Date _____

Date Employment Starts _____   Performer Name _____

Production Title _____   Address _____

Production Number _____   Telephone No.: ( ) _____

Role _____   Social Security No. _____

Daily Rate $ _____   Legal Resident of (State) _____

Weekly Conversion Rate $ _____   Citizen of U.S. ☐ Yes ☐ No

Wardrobe supplied by Performer Yes ☐   No ☐

COMPLETE FOR "DROP-AND-PICK-UP" DEALS ONLY:

Firm recall date on _____

or on or after * _____

("On or after" recall only applies to pick-up as Weekly Performer)

As ☐ Day Performer   ☐ Weekly Performer

*Means date specified or within 24 hours thereafter.

If so, number of outfits _____ @ $_____

(formal) _____ @ $_____

Date of Stunt Performer's next engagement: _____

The employment is subject to all of the provisions and conditions applicable to the employment of DAY PERFORMER contained or provided for in the Producer-Screen Actors Guild Codified Basic Agreement as the same may be supplemented and/or amended.

The performer [does][does not] hereby authorize the Producer to deduct from the compensation hereinabove specified an amount equal to _____ per cent of each installment of compensation due the Performer hereunder, and to pay the amount so deducted to the Motion Picture and Television Relief Fund of America, Inc.

Special Provisions: _____

PRODUCER _____   PERFORMER _____

BY _____

Production time reports are available on the set at the end of each day. Such reports shall be signed or initialed by the Performer.

Attached hereto for your use is Declaration Regarding Income Tax Withholding.

NOTICE TO PERFORMER: IT IS IMPORTANT THAT YOU RETAIN A COPY OF THIS CONTRACT FOR YOUR PERMANENT RECORDS.

**THE PERFORMER MAY NOT WAIVE ANY PROVISION OF THIS CONTRACT
WITHOUT THE WRITTEN CONSENT OF SCREEN ACTORS GUILD, INC.**

SCREEN ACTORS GUILD

**SCREEN ACTORS GUILD
MINIMUM FREE LANCE CONTRACT
FOR THEATRICAL MOTION PICTURES**

Continuous Employment—Weekly Basis—Weekly Salary
One Week Minimum Employment

THIS AGREEMENT, made this _____ day of _____ , 19_____ , between _____
_____ , hereafter called "Producer," and
_____ , hereafter called "Performer."

1. PHOTOPLAY, ROLE, SALARY AND GUARANTEE. Producer hereby engages Performer to render services as such in the role of _____ , in a photoplay, the working title of which is now _____ , at the salary of $_____ per "studio week" (Schedule B Performers must receive an additional overtime payment of four (4) hours at straight time rate for each overnight location Saturday). Performer accepts such engagement upon the terms herein specified. Producer guarantees that it will furnish Performer not less than _____ week's employment (if this blank is not filled in, the guarantee shall be one week). Performer shall be paid pro rata for each additional day beyond guarantee until dismissal.

2. TERM: The term of employment hereunder shall begin on

on _____

on or about* _____

and shall continue thereafter until the completion of the photography and recordation of said role.

3. BASIC CONTRACT. All provisions of the collective bargaining agreement between Screen Actors Guild, Inc. and Producer, relating to theatrical motion pictures, which are applicable to the employment of the Performer hereunder, shall be deemed incorporated herein.

4. PERFORMER'S ADDRESS. All notices which the Producer is required or may desire to give to the Performer may be given either by mailing the same addressed to the Performer at _____ or such notice may be given to the Performer personally, either orally or in writing.

5. PERFORMER'S TELEPHONE. The Performer must keep the Producer's casting office or the assistant director of said photoplay advised as to where the Performer may be reached by telephone without unreasonable delay. The current telephone number of the Performer is_____.

6. MOTION PICTURE AND TELEVISION RELIEF FUND. The Performer [does] [does not] hereby authorize the Producer to deduct from the compensation hereinabove specified an amount equal to _____ per cent of each installment of compensation due the Performer hereunder, and to pay the amount so deducted to the Motion Picture and Television Relief Fund of America, Inc.

7. FURNISHING OF WARDROBE. The (Producer) (Performer) agrees to furnish all modern wardrobe and wearing apparel reasonably necessary for the portrayal of said role; it being agreed, however, that should so-called "character" or "period" costumes be required, the Producer shall supply the same. When Performer furnishes any wardrobe, Performer shall receive the cleaning allowance and reimbursement, if any, specified in the basic contract.

Number of outfits furnished by Performer _____ @ $_____
(formal) _____ @ $_____

*The "on or about" clause may only be used when the contract is delivered to the Performer at least seven days before the starting date. See Codified Basic Agreement, Schedule B, Schedule C, otherwise a specific starting date must be stated.

8. ARBITRATION OF DISPUTES. Should any dispute or controversy arise between the parties hereto with reference to this contract, or the employment herein provided for, such dispute or controversy shall be settled and determined by conciliation and arbitration in accordance with the conciliation and arbitration provisions of the collective bargaining agreement between the Producer and Screen Actors Guild relating to theatrical motion pictures, and such provisions are hereby referred to and by such reference incorporated herein and made a part of this Agreement with the same effect as though the same were set forth herein in detail.

9. NEXT STARTING DATE. The starting date of Performer's next engagement is _____.

10. The Performer may not waive any provision of this contract without the written consent of Screen Actors Guild, Inc.

11. Producer makes the material representation that either it is presently a signatory to the Screen Actors Guild collective bargaining agreement covering the employment contracted for herein, or that the above-referred-to photoplay is covered by such collective bargaining agreement under the Independent Production provisions of the General Provisions of the Screen Actors Guild Codified Basic Agreement as the same may be supplemented and/or amended.

IN WITNESS WHEREOF, the parties have executed this agreement on the day and year first above written.

PRODUCER _____ PERFORMER _____

BY _____ Social Security No. _____

Production time reports are available on the set at the end of each day, which reports shall be signed or initialed by the Performer.

Attached hereto for your use are the following: (1) Declaration Regarding Income Tax Withholding ("Part Year Employment Method of Withholding") and (2) Declaration Regarding Income Tax Withholding. You may utilize the applicable form by delivering same to Producer. Only one of such forms may be used.

NOTICE TO PERFORMER: IT IS IMPORTANT THAT YOU RETAIN A COPY OF THIS CONTRACT FOR YOUR PERMANENT RECORDS.

SCREEN ACTORS GUILD

STUNT PERFORMER'S
DAILY CONTRACT
FOR THEATRICAL MOTION PICTURES

STUNT PERFORMER _____ DATE OF AGREEMENT _____

ADDRESS _____

_____

TELEPHONE (___) - _____ SOCIAL SECURITY NO. ____ – ____ – _____

COMPANY/PRODUCER _____

PRODUCTION TITLE _____ PRODUCTION NO. _____

AGENT/AGENCY _____

ADDRESS _____

_____

DAILY RATE _____ SERIES _____

WEEKLY CONV. RATE $ _____ START DATE _____

1. **DESCRIPTION OF SERVICES:** Producer hereby engages Stunt Performer to render services as _____
_____. Stunt Performer accepts such engagement upon the terms herein specified.

2. **TERM/GUARANTEE:** Producer guarantees to furnish Stunt Performer not less than _____ days engagement.
If this space is not filled in, the guarantee shall be one (1) day.

3. **STUNT ADJUSTMENTS:** It is understood that the rate of compensation specified may be adjusted depending
upon the nature of the stunt activities Producer may require. If so, a stunt adjustment will be agreed upon
between the parties through good faith bargaining and said adjustment shall be noted on Stunt Performer's
daily time report or time card. The parties shall agree upon the compensation to be paid before the stunt is
performed if they may readily do so; however, it is expressly agreed that production shall not be delayed for the
purpose of first determining the compensation for a stunt. Such adjustment shall increase Stunt Performer's
compensation for the day in the manner prescribed in Schedule H of the Screen Actors Guild Codified Basic
Agreement.

4. **INCORPORATION OF PRODUCER-SCREEN ACTORS GUILD COLLECTIVE BARGAINING AGREEMENT:** All
provisions of the Screen Actors Guild Codified Basic Agreement and Television Agreement as the same may be
supplemented and/or amended to date shall be deemed incorporated herein. Stunt Performer's engagement
shall be upon the terms, conditions and exceptions of said provisions applicable to the rate of compensation
and guarantee specified.

5. **RIGHTS:** Producer shall have the unlimited right throughout the universe and in perpetuity to exhibit the Motion
Picture in all media, now or hereafter known, and Producer, as employer-for-hire of Stunt Performer, shall own
all rights in the results and proceeds of Stunt Performer's services hereunder.

6. **ADDITIONAL COMPENSATION:** If the Motion Picture covered hereby is exhibited, containing any of the
results and proceeds of Stunt Performer's services hereunder, in any of the following media:
(i) "Free" television exhibition anywhere in the universe;
(ii) Supplemental market exhibition anywhere in the universe;
(iii) Basic Cable exhibition anywhere in the universe,

as to each such medium in which the motion picture is so exhibited, Producer will pay, and Stunt Performer will accept as payment in full, the minimum additional compensation provided therefor in the Screen Actors Guild Codified Basic Agreement or Television Agreement, as the case may be, except as compensation in excess of such minimum, if any, has been provided in this Agreement.

7. **CONTINUOUS EMPLOYMENT AND RIGHT TO ROLE (when applicable):** If Stunt Performer portrays a role or has dialogue, Stunt Performer shall be entitled to "continuous employment" and "Right to Role," if any, only to the extent prescribed by the Screen Actors Guild Codified Basic Agreement. Stunt Performer shall receive a separate contract for such services.

8. **MOTION PICTURE AND TELEVISION FUND:** Stunt Performer [does] [does not] hereby authorize Producer to deduct from the compensation hereinabove specified an amount equal to _____ percent of each install- ment of compensation due Stunt Performer hereunder, and to pay the amount so deducted to the Motion Picture and Television Fund of America, Inc.

9. **WAIVER:** Stunt Performer may not waive any provision of the Screen Actors Guild Codified Basic Agreement without the written consent of the Screen Actors Guild, Inc.

10. **SIGNATORY:** Producer makes the material representation that either it is presently a signatory to the Screen Actors Guild collective bargaining agreement covering the engagement contracted for herein, or that the Motion Picture is covered by such collective bargaining agreement under the "Independent Production" provisions (Section 24) of the General Provisions of the Screen Actors Guild Codified Basic Agreement.

Signing of this Agreement in the spaces below signifies acceptance by Producer and Stunt Performer of all of the above terms and conditions and those on the reverse hereof and attached hereto, if any, as of the date specified above.

PRODUCER _____ STUNT PERFORMER _____

BY _____

Production time reports and/or time cards are available on the set at the beginning and end of each day, which reports and/or time cards shall be signed or initialed by Stunt Performer and must indicate any agreed stunt adjustments.

NOTICE TO STUNT PERFORMER: IT IS IMPORTANT THAT YOU RETAIN A COPY OF THIS AGREEMENT FOR YOUR PERMANENT RECORDS.

S-3 (7-92)

SCREEN ACTORS GUILD

STUNT PERFORMER'S
MINIMUM FREELANCE WEEKLY CONTRACT
FOR THEATRICAL MOTION PICTURES

STUNT PERFORMER _____ DATE OF AGREEMENT _____

ADDRESS _____

_____

TELEPHONE ( ) - _____ SOCIAL SECURITY NO. ___ – ___ – _____

COMPANY/PRODUCER _____

PRODUCTION TITLE _____ PRODUCTION NO. _____

AGENT/AGENCY _____

ADDRESS _____

_____

---

1. **DESCRIPTION OF SERVICES:** Producer hereby engages Stunt Performer to render services as _____ _____. Stunt Performer accepts such engagement upon the terms herein specified.

2. **COMPENSATION/TERM/GUARANTEE:** Producer will pay Stunt Performer and Stunt Performer agrees to accept the following weekly compensation (excluding location premiums) of $_____ (and pro rata for each additional day beyond the guarantee until completion of services). The total guaranteed compensation shall be $_____ for the total guaranteed period of _____ . If this space is not filled in, the guarantee shall be one (1) week. Stunt Performer shall receive sixth day location premium where applicable.

3. **START DATE:** The term of engagement shall begin on _____ . or "on or about" * _____ .

4. **NEXT START DATE:** The start date of Stunt Performer's next engagement is _____ .

5. **STUNT ADJUSTMENTS:** It is understood that the rate of compensation specified may be adjusted depending upon the nature of the stunt activities Producer may require. If so, a stunt adjustment will be agreed upon between the parties through good faith bargaining and said adjustment shall be noted on Stunt Performer's daily time report or time card.

   The parties shall agree upon the compensation to be paid before the stunt is performed if they may readily do so; however, it is expressly agreed that production shall not be delayed for the purpose of first determining the compensation for a stunt. Such adjustment shall increase Stunt Performer's compensation for the week in the manner prescribed in Schedule H-II or H-III of the Screen Actors Guild Codified Basic Agreement.

6. **INCORPORATION OF PRODUCER-SCREEN ACTORS GUILD COLLECTIVE BARGAINING AGREEMENT:** All provisions of the Screen Actors Guild Codified Basic Agreement as the same may be supplemented and/or amended to date shall be deemed incorporated herein. Stunt Performer's engagement shall be upon the terms, conditions and exceptions of said provisions applicable to the rate of compensation and guarantee specified.

7. **RIGHTS:** Producer shall have the unlimited right throughout the universe and in perpetuity to exhibit the Motion Picture in all media, now or hereafter known, and Producer, as employer-for-hire of Stunt Performer, shall own all rights in the results and proceeds of Stunt Performer's services hereunder.

The "on or about" clause may only be used when this Agreement is delivered to Stunt Performer at least three (3) days before the Start Date.

8. **ADDITIONAL COMPENSATION:** If the Motion Picture covered hereby is exhibited, containing any of the results and proceeds of Stunt Performer's services hereunder, in any of the following media:

(i) "Free" television reruns in the United States or Canada, or both;
(ii) Television exhibition anywhere in the universe outside the United States and Canada;
(iii) Theatrical exhibition anywhere in the universe;
(iv) Supplemental Market exhibition anywhere in the universe;
(v) Basic Cable exhibition anywhere in the universe,

as to each such medium in which the motion picture is so exhibited, Producer will pay, and Stunt Performer will accept as payment in full, the minimum additional compensation provided therefor in the Screen Actors Guild Codified Basic Agreement or Television Agreement, as the case may be, except as compensation in excess of such minimum, if any, has been provided in this Agreement.

9. **CONTINUOUS EMPLOYMENT AND RIGHT TO ROLE (when applicable):** If Stunt Performer portrays a role or has dialogue, Stunt Performer shall be entitled to "continuous employment" and "Right to Role," if any, only to the extent prescribed by the Screen Actors Guild Codified Basic Agreement. Stunt Performer shall receive a separate contract for such services.

10. **MOTION PICTURE AND TELEVISION FUND:** Stunt Performer [does] [does not] hereby authorize Producer to deduct from the compensation hereinabove specified an amount equal to _____ percent of each installment of compensation due Stunt Performer hereunder, and to pay the amount so deducted to the Motion Picture and Television Fund of America, Inc.

11. **WAIVER:** Stunt Performer may not waive any provision of the Screen Actors Guild Codified Basic Agreement or Television Agreement, whichever is applicable, without the written consent of the Screen Actors Guild, Inc.

12. **SIGNATORY:** Producer makes the material representation that either it is presently a signatory to the Screen Actors Guild collective bargaining agreement covering the engagement contracted for herein, or that the Motion Picture is covered by such collective bargaining agreement under the "Independent Production" provisions (Section 24) of the General Provisions of the Screen Actors Guild Codified Basic Agreement.

Signing of this Agreement in the spaces below signifies acceptance by Producer and Stunt Performer of all of the above terms and conditions and those on the reverse hereof and attached hereto, if any, as of the date specified above.

PRODUCER _____ STUNT PERFORMER _____

BY _____

Production time reports and/or time cards are available on the set at the beginning and end of each day, which reports and/or time cards shall be signed or initialed by Stunt Performer and must indicate any agreed stunt adjustments.

NOTICE TO STUNT PERFORMER: IT IS IMPORTANT THAT YOU RETAIN A COPY OF THIS AGREEMENT FOR YOUR PERMANENT RECORDS.

S-2 (7-92)

SCREEN ACTORS GUILD

PERFORMER CONTRACT FOR INTERACTIVE PROGRAMMING

Company _____   Date _____

Production Title _____   Performer Name _____

Production Number _____   Address _____

Date Employment Starts _____   Telephone No.: (____) _____

Role _____   Social Security No.: _____

Daily Rate $_____   Date of Performer's next engagement _____

3 Day Rate $_____

Weekly Rate $_____

Special Provisions $_____

_____

Wardrobe supplied by Performer ☐ Yes ☐ No

If so, number of outfits _____ @ $_____

(formal) _____ @ $_____

> **Complete for "Drop-And-Pick-Up" Deals ONLY:**
>
> Firm recall date on _____
>
> or on or after* _____
>
> ("On or after" recall only applies to pick-up as Weekly Performer)
>
> As ☐ Day Performer ☐ Weekly Performer
>
> *Means date specified or within 24 hours thereafter.

THIS AGREEMENT covers the employment of the above-named Performer by _____ in the production and at the rate of compensation set forth above and is subject to and shall include, for the benefit of the Performer and the Producer, all of the applicable provisions and conditions contained or provided for in the applicable Screen Actors Guild Interactive Agreement, and/or the Screen Actors Guild Television Agreement. Performer's employment shall include performance in non-commercial openings, bridges, etc., and no added compensation shall be payable to Performer so long as such are used in the role and project(s) covered hereunder in which Performer appears; for other use, Performer shall be paid the added minimum compensation, if any, required under the provisions of the Screen Actors Guild agreements with Producer.

Producer shall have all the rights in and to the results and proceeds of the Performer's services rendered hereunder, as are provided with respect to "photoplays" in Schedule A of the applicable Screen Actors Guild Codified Basic Agreement and the right to supplemental market use as defined in the Television Agreement.

Producer shall have the unlimited right throughout the world to telecast the film and exhibit the film theatrically and in supplemental markets in accordance with the terms and conditions of the Television Agreement.

By _____   _____
                               Producer   Performer

                                          _____
                                          Performer's Social Security No.

Production time reports are available on the set at the end of each day, which reports shall be signed or initialed by the Performer.

NOTICE TO PERFORMER: IT IS IMPORTANT THAT YOU RETAIN A COPY OF THIS CONTRACT FOR YOUR
#37A   PERMANENT RECORDS.

SCREEN ACTORS GUILD
TAFT/HARTLEY REPORT

ATTENTION: _____ ATTACHED?: ☐ RESUME* ☐ PHOTO

EMPLOYEE INFORMATION

NAME _____ SS# _____

ADDRESS _____ AGE (IF MINOR) _____

CITY/STATE _____ ZIP _____ PHONE ( ) _____

EMPLOYER INFORMATION

NAME _____ Check one: ☐ AD AGENCY
                                            ☐ STUDIO
ADDRESS _____   ☐ PRODUCTION COMPANY

CITY/STATE _____ ZIP _____ PHONE ( ) _____

EMPLOYMENT INFORMATION

Check one: CONTRACT: ☐ DAILY   CATEGORY: ☐ ACTOR
                        ☐ 3-DAY   ☐ SINGER   ☐ OTHER
                        ☐ WEEKLY   ☐ STUNT

WORK DATE(S) _____ SALARY _____

PRODUCTION TITLE _____ PROD'N/COM'L # _____

SHOOTING LOCATION (City & State) _____

REASON FOR HIRE (be specific) _____

_____

_____

_____

_____

Employer is aware of General Provision, Section 14 of the Basic Asreement that applies to Theatrical and Television production, and Schedule B of the Commercials Contract, wherein Preference of Employment shall be given to qualified professional actors (except as otherwise stated). Employer will pay to the Guild as liquidated damages, the sums indicated for each breach by the Employer of any provision of those sections.

SIGNATURE _____ DATE _____
          Producer or Casting Director – Indicate which

PRINT NAME _____ PHONE ( ) _____

*PLEASE BE CERTAIN RESUME LISTS ALL TRAINING AND/OR EXPERIENCE IN THE ENTERTAINMENT INDUSTRY.

SAG EXTRA

TAFT/HARTLEY REPORT

ATTENTION: _____ ATTACHED?: ☐ RESUME   ☐ PHOTO

EMPLOYEE INFORMATION

NAME _____ SS#_____

ADDRESS _____ AGE (IF MINOR) _____

CITY/STATE _____ ZIP _____ PHONE (____)_____

EMPLOYER INFORMATION

NAME _____ Check one: ☐ CASTING OFFICE
                                                    ☐ STUDIO
ADDRESS _____   ☐ PRODUCTION COMPANY

CITY/STATE _____ ZIP _____ PHONE (____)_____

EMPLOYMENT INFORMATION

CHECK ONE: General Extra ☐   Special Ability Extra ☐   Dancer ☐

WORK DATE(S) _____ SALARY_____

PRODUCTION TITLE _____

SHOOTING LOCATION (City & State) _____

REASON FOR HIRE (be specific) _____

_____

_____

_____

_____

Employer is aware of General Provision, Section 14.G of the Screen Actors Guild Codified Basic Agreement of 1989 for Independent Producers as amended that applies to Theatrical and Television production, wherein Preference of Employment shall be given to qualified professional extras (except as otherwise stated). Employer will pay to the Guild as liquidated damages, a sum which shall be determined by binding arbitration for each breach by the Employer of any provision of those sections.

SIGNATURE_____ DATE _____
           Producer or Casting Director (indicate which)

PRINT NAME _____ PHONE (____)_____

SAG EXTRA VOUCHER

PRODUCER:

| DATE | NAME (PRINT) | PRODUCTION NO. OR TITLE | | DISMISSAL TIME |

TYPE OF CALL

STARTING TIME

SAG NO.

SOCIAL SECURITY NO. MUST BE PROVIDED TO MAKE PAYMENT

☐ SINGLE ☐ MARRIED ☐ MARRIED but withheld at higher single rate

Total number of allowances you are claiming: ___

Additional amount, if any, you want deducted $ ___

If claiming exemption from withholding, write exempt and year in box ___ 19__

BASIC WAGE RATE

TRAVEL TIME
ARRIVE LOCATION: ___
LEAVE LOCATION: ___

PENALTIES

INTERVIEW ☐

HOURS WORKED

MEAL PERIODS
OUT / IN
OUT / IN

ASST. DIR.-APPROVED FOR PAYMENT

FITTING ☐

MEALS
B ☐
L ☐
D ☐

WARDROBE | PROPS | VEHICLE | MILEAGE

EMPLOYEE: PLEASE PRINT INFORMATION LISTED ABOVE AND SIGN WHERE INDICATED

"I, the undersigned, certify that the number of income tax withholding exemptions claimed on this certificate does not exceed the number of which I am entitled.

"I agree to accept the sum properly computed based upon the times and the basic wage rate shown as payment in full for all services heretofore rendered by me for said employer.

"I further agree that the said sum, less all deduction required by law, may be paid to me by negotiable check issued by said company, said check to be addressed to me at my last reported address and deposited in the United States mail within the time periods provided by law.

"I hereby give and grant to the company named all rights of every kind and character whatsoever in and to all work heretofore done, and all poses, acts, plays and appearances heretofore made by me for you and in to all of the results and proceeds of my services heretofore rendered for you, as well as in and to the right to use my name, likeness and photographs, either still or moving for commercial and advertising purposes. I further give and grant to the said company the right to reproduce in any manner whatsoever any recordations heretofore made by said company of my voice and all instrumental, musical, or other sound effects produced by me. I further agree that in the event of a retake of all or any of the scenes in which I participate, or if additional scenes are required (whether originally contemplated or not) I will return to work and render my services in such scenes at the same basic rate of compensations as that paid me for the original taking.

"By signing this form, I hereby agree that said employer may take deductions from my earnings to adjust previous overpayments if and when said overpayments may occur."

Signature _____ Date _____

Address _____ Apt # ___

City _____ State ___ Zip ___

Phone Number _____

BACK OF WHITE COPY MUST BE COMPLETED

YOUR EMPLOYER OF RECORD IS _____
IF OTHER THAN A PAYROLL COMPANY, EMPLOYER'S FEDERAL I.D. NUMBER IS _____

DO NOT WRITE IN THIS SPACE

TYPE OF WORK	PAY CODE	HOURS		AMOUNT	
		WORK	PAY		BASIC RATE
DAY		.	.	.	
NIGHT		.	.	.	ADJUSTMENTS
O/T		.	.	.	OVERTIME
WET		.	.	.	
SMOKE		.	.	.	ALLOWANCES
OTHER		.	.	.	
OTHER		.	.	.	GROSS
OTHER					

white—PAYROLL COPY
yellow—PRODUCTION COPY
pink—SAG COPY
golden rod—EXTRAS COPY

Screen Actors Guild
Kenmar Printing 357
Form No. 451

SCREEN ACTORS GUILD THEATRICAL & TELEVISION SIGN-IN SHEET

PRODUCER: _____

PROD'N CO: _____

PROD'N OFFICE _____

PHONE # _____

CASTING REP: _____

CASTING REP. PHONE: _____

PRODUCTION TITLE: _____

EPISODE: _____

AUDITION DATE: _____

CASTING REP:

Please fill in time seen for each actor

Casting Director's Signature _____

(1) NAME	(2) SOCIAL SECURITY	(3) ROLE	(4) AGENT	(5) PROVIDED?		(6) ARRIVAL TIME	(7) APPT. TIME	(8) TIME SEEN (Cast. rep.)	(9) TIME OUT	(10) TAPED?	(11) ACT. INI.
				PARK	SCRIPT						

SCREEN ACTORS GUILD
ACTORS PRODUCTION TIME REPORT

PICTURE TITLE: _____ PROD. # _____ DATE _____

IS TODAY A DESIGNATED DAY OFF?* YES ☐ NO ☐

CAST - WEEKLY & DAY PLAYERS Worked - W / Started - S / Travel - TR, Rehearsal - R / Hold - H, Finished - F / Test - T		W H S F R T TR	MAKEUP WDBE.	WORKTIME		B K F S T	MEALS		TRAVEL TIME				STUNT ADJUST.	WARDROBE NO. OF OUTFITS PROVIDED	ACTORS SIGNATURE
CAST	CHARACTER			REPORT ON SET	DISMISS ON SET		1ST MEAL	2ND MEAL	LEAVE FOR LOCA-TION	ARRIVE ON LOCA-TION	LEAVE LOCA-TION	ARRIVE AT STUDIO			

* This refers to the 2 days (1 day on overnight location) which producer can designate as day(s) off for the production.

SCREEN ACTORS GUILD

CASTING DATA REPORT

See Reverse For Instructions

THIS FORM MUST BE COMPLETED FOR EACH MOTION PICTURE AND EACH EPISODE OF EACH SERIES PRODUCED FOR THE QUARTER IN WHICH PRINCIPAL PHOTOGRAPHY WAS COMPLETED.

1) PRODUCTION COMPANY _____

2) QUARTER and YEAR _____

3) PROJECT (Title, Prod. No., etc.) _____

4) DESCRIPTION (Feature, M.O.W., TV Series, etc.) _____

5) TOTAL NO. OF DAYS OF PRODUCTION (Principal Photography Only) _____

6) DATA SUBMITTED BY _____
   NAME

   TELEPHONE NUMBER _____

7) CHECK IF APPROPRIATE ☐ NO STUNTS

PART I

CATEGORY		FORM OF HIRING			CAST TOTALS	NO. OF DAYS WORKED	AGE:		
		DAILY	WEEKLY	SERIES	9)	10)	UNDER 40	40 and OVER	UNKNOWN
		8)					11)		
MALE	LEAD								
	SUPPORT								
FEMALE	LEAD								
	SUPPORT								

PART II

CATEGORY		FORM OF HIRING								NO. OF DAYS WORKED		AGE					
		DAILY		WEEKLY		SERIES						UNDER 40		40 and OVER		UNKNOWN	
		M	F	M	F	M	F	M	F	M	F	M	F	M	F	M	F
		12)								13)		14)					
ASIAN/PACIFIC	LEAD																
	SUPPORT																
BLACK	LEAD																
	SUPPORT																
CAUCASIAN	LEAD																
	SUPPORT																
LATINO / HISPANIC	LEAD																
	SUPPORT																
N. AMERICAN INDIAN	LEAD																
	SUPPORT																
UNKNOWN / OTHER	LEAD																
	SUPPORT																

INSTRUCTIONS

(After reading the following, if you have any further questions, please call 213/549-6644.) (For your convenience, our fax number is 213/549-6647.)

1. Indicate the name of the signatory Production Company (e.g., "THE ABC COMPANY").

2. Indicate the quarter/year when ***principal photography*** was completed (e.g., "1st quarter 1981"). Make one report only for full project even though it might span more than one quarter.

   The quarters consist of:

January	-	March	(1st)
April	-	June	(2nd)
July	-	September	(3rd)
October	-	December	(4th)

3. Indicate the <u>name</u> of the film for which you are reporting.

4. Indicate the <u>type</u> of project (feature, television movie, television pilot, television series, animation.

5. Use a number to respond to this question.

6. Indicate the name of person completing this form and the telephone number for same.

7. Two separate reports are required, one for <u>Performers</u> only and one for <u>Stunt Performers</u> only. If there were no Stunt Performers employed on the film, check the "No Stunt" box. If Stunt Performers were employed, complete the casting data report form for Stunt Performers.

8. **Part I.** Indicate the total number of lead and supporting Performers in each of the applicable categories. Series performers column is provided for episodic TV shows only. Daily column is for daily contract & 3-day contract performers only. Weekly column is for weekly contract and run-of-the-picture performers. A day contract performer upgraded to a weekly contract performer in a drop/pick-up situation should be listed in the weekly column (**do <u>not</u> count** the performer twice).

9. Use numbers only to indicate the total number of Performers in the category.

10. Use numbers only to indicate the total number of days worked by <u>ALL</u> Performers in the category. (Include all days paid for including hold, rehearsal days, etc.)

11. Use numbers only to indicate how many Performers were in each age group.

12. **Part II.** Indicate the total number of males and females in each category.

13. Use number only to indicate the total number of days worked by <u>ALL</u> the Performers in male and female category.

14. Use numbers only to indicate how many Performers were in each age group.

NOTE: PLEASE MAKE EVERY EFFORT TO INSURE THAT YOUR NUMBERS CORRESPOND ACROSS AND AMONG <u>PART I AND PART II</u>.

Screen Actors Guild

CASTING DATA REPORT FOR STUNT PERFORMERS ONLY

THIS FORM MUST BE COMPLETED FOR EACH MOTION PICTURE AND EACH EPISODE OF EACH SERIES PRODUCED FOR THE QUARTER IN WHICH PRINCIPAL PHOTOGRAPHY WAS COMPLETED.

See Reverse For Instructions

1) PRODUCTION COMPANY _____

2) QUARTER and YEAR _____

3) PROJECT (Title, Prod. No., etc.) _____

4) DESCRIPTION (Feature, M.O.W., TV Series, etc.) _____

5) TOTAL NO. OF DAYS OF PRODUCTION (Principal Photography Only) _____

6) DATA SUBMITTED BY _____
   NAME

   TELEPHONE NUMBER _____

7) NAME OF STUNT COORDINATOR _____

PART I

8) CATEGORY	9) FORM OF HIRING						10) NUMBER DAYS WORKED	11) AGE			12) STUNT SUMMARY	
	DAILY		WEEKLY		SERIES		PERFORMER TOTALS	UNDER 40	40 AND OVER	UNKNOWN	DESCRIPT	NON-DESCRIPT
MALE												
FEMALE												

PART II

13) CATEGORY	14) FORM OF HIRING												15) NUMBER DAYS WORKED						16) AGE								STUNT SUMMARY			
	DAILY		WEEKLY		SERIES				UNDER 40		40 AND OVER		UNKNOWN		DESCRIPT		NON-DESCRIPT	
	M	F	M	F	M	F			M	F	M	F	M	F	M	F	M	F
ASIAN/PACIFIC																		
BLACK																		
CAUCASIAN																		
LATINO / HISPANIC																		
N. AMERICAN INDIAN																		
OTHER / UNKNOWN																		

STUNT INSTRUCTIONS

**There are two separate report forms required.
Complete one report for Performers and one report for Stunt Performers.

(After reading the following, if you have any further questions, please call 213/549-6644.) (For your convenience, our fax number is 213/549-6647.)

1. Indicate the Production Company (e.g., "THE ABC COMPANY").

2. Indicate the quarter/year (e.g., "1st quarter 1981").

   The quarters consist of:

January	- March	(1st)
April	- June	(2nd)
July	- September	(3rd)
October	- December	(4th)

3. Indicate the <u>name</u> of the film for which you are reporting.

4. Indicate the <u>type</u> of project (feature, television movie, television pilot, television series, animation.

5. Use a number to respond to this question.

6. Indicate the name of person completing this form and the telephone number for same.

7. Provide the name of the stunt coordinator for the film.

Part I

8. Indicate the total number of males and females in each category.

9. Use numbers only to indicate the total number of stunt performers in the category.

10. Use numbers only to indicate the total amount of days worked by all stunt performers in the category.

11. Use numbers only to indicate how many stunt performers are in a certain age group.

12. Use numbers only to indicate the stunts as **descript*** or **non-descript***.

   *Descript   =   A stunt performer who doubles for an actor.

   *Non-descript =   A stunt performer doing a utility or faceless stunt.

Part II

13. Indicate the total number of males and females in each category.

14. Use numbers only to indicate the total number of days worked by <u>all</u> the Performers in each category.

15. Use numbers only to indicate how many performers were in each age group.

16. Indicate the stunts as descript or non-descript.

NOTE: **Please make every effort to insure that your numbers correspond across categories and among <u>Part I and Part II</u>.**

SCREEN ACTORS GUILD

LOW-BUDGET
AFFIRMATIVE ACTION
CASTING DATA REPORT

See Reverse
For Instructions

THIS FORM MUST BE COMPLETED FOR EACH MOTION PICTURE AND EACH EPISODE OF EACH SERIES PRODUCED FOR THE QUARTER IN WHICH PRINCIPAL PHOTOGRAPHY WAS COMPLETED.

1) PRODUCTION COMPANY _____

2) QUARTER and YEAR _____

3) PROJECT (Title, Prod. No., etc.) _____

4) DESCRIPTION (Feature, M.O.W., TV Series, etc.) _____

5) TOTAL NO. OF DAYS OF PRODUCTION (Principal Photography Only) _____

6) DATA SUBMITTED BY _____ NAME

TELEPHONE NUMBER _____

7) CHECK IF APPROPRIATE   ☐ NO STUNTS

PART I

8) CATEGORY		FORM OF HIRING				9) CAST TOTALS	10) NO. OF DAYS WORKED	11) AGE:		
		DAILY	WEEKLY		SERIES			UNDER 40	40 TO 60	60 & OVER
MALE	LEAD									
	SUPPORT									
FEMALE	LEAD									
	SUPPORT									

PART II

12) CATEGORY		FORM OF HIRING								13) NO. OF DAYS WORKED		14) AGE					
		DAILY		WEEKLY		SERIES						UNDER 40		40 TO 60		60 & OVER	
		M	F	M	F	M	F			M	F	M	F	M	F	M	F
ASIAN/PACIFIC	LEAD																
	SUPPORT																
BLACK	LEAD																
	SUPPORT																
CAUCASIAN	LEAD																
	SUPPORT																
LATINO / HISPANIC	LEAD																
	SUPPORT																
N. AMERICAN INDIAN	LEAD																
	SUPPORT																
UNKNOWN / OTHER	LEAD																
	SUPPORT																

INSTRUCTIONS

1. Indicate the Production Company (e.g., "THE ABC COMPANY").

2. Indicate the quarter/year (e.g., "1st quarter 1981").

   The quarters consist of:

January	–	March	(1st)
April	–	June	(2nd)
July	–	September	(3rd)
October	–	December	(4th)

3. Indicate the <u>name</u> of the film for which you are reporting.

4. Indicate the <u>type</u> of project (feature, television movie, television pilot, television series, animation).

5. Use a number to respond to this question.

6. Indicate the name of person completing this form and the telephone number for same.

7. Two separate reports are required, one for <u>Performers</u> only and one for <u>Stunt Performers</u> only. If there were no Stunt Performers employed on the film, check the "No Stunt" box. If Stunt Performers were employed, complete the casting data report form for Stunt Performers.

8. <u>Part I</u>. Indicate the total number of lead and supporting Performers in each of the applicable categories.

9. Use numbers only to indicate the total number of Performers in the category.

10. Use numbers only to indicate the total number of days worked by <u>ALL</u> Performers in the category.

11. Use numbers only to indicate how many Performers were in each age group.

12. <u>Part II</u>. Indicate the total number of males and females in each category.

13. Use number only to indicate the total number of days worked by <u>ALL</u> the Performers in male and female category.

14. Use numbers only to indicate how many performers were in each age group.

NOTE: PLEASE MAKE EVERY EFFORT TO INSURE THAT YOUR NUMBERS CORRESPOND ACROSS AND AMONG <u>PART I AND PART II.</u>

SCREEN ACTORS GUILD

FINAL CAST LIST INFORMATION SHEET

DATE
FILED: _____

PICTURE TITLE _____   SHOOTING LOCATION _____

PRODUCTION COMPANY _____   START DATE _____   COMPLETION DATE _____

ADDRESS _____   FEDERAL I.D. # _____   STATE I.D. # _____

PHONE (___) _____ CONTACT _____   PICTURE # _____

DISTRIBUTOR _____

Check
One: MP ☐   MOW ☐   OTHER TV ☐   INDUSTRIAL ☐   OTHER ☐

To establish Residual payments, see Section 5.2 of the 1980 Basic Agreement.

PLAYER NAME & SOCIAL SECURITY NUMBER	PLAYER ADDRESS INCLUDING ZIP	(1) PERIOD WORKED # DYS	(1) PERIOD WORKED # WKS	(1) START DATE	(1) FINISH DATE	(2) CONTRACT TYPE	(3) PLAYER TYPE	(4) TOTAL GROSS SALARY	(5) BASE SALARY	TIME UNITS	SALARY UNITS	TOTAL UNITS	FOR SAG USE ONLY

(1) Include days not worked, but considered worked under continuous employment provisions. Report contractually guaranteed work period or actual time worked, whichever is longer.

(2) Insert D for Daily or W for Weekly type of contract.

(3) Insert: A = Actor; ST = Stunt; P = Pilot; SG = Singer; ADR = Automated Dialogue Replacement.

(4) Include all salary, Overtime, Premium, and Stunt Adjustments. Do not include any Penalties paid (e.g., Meal Penalties, Forced Calls, etc.).

(5) List base contractual salary (e.g., $1,500.00/week or $500.00/day).

To establish Residual payments, see Section 5.2 of the 1980 Basic Agreement.

PLAYER NAME & SOCIAL SECURITY NUMBER	PLAYER ADDRESS INCLUDING ZIP	(1) PERIOD WORKED # WKS	(1) PERIOD WORKED # DYS	(1) START DATE	(1) FINISH DATE	(2) CONTRACT TYPE	(3) PLAYER TYPE	(4) TOTAL GROSS SALARY	(5) BASE SALARY	TIME UNITS	SALARY UNITS	TOTAL UNITS	FOR SAG USE ONLY

(1) Include days not worked, but considered worked under continuous employment provisions. Report contractually guaranteed work period or actual time worked, whichever is longer.

(2) Insert D for Daily or W for Weekly type of contract.

(3) Insert: A = Actor; ST = Stunt; P = Pilot; SG = Singer; ADR = Automated Dialogue Replacement.

(4) Include all salary, Overtime, Premium, and Stunt Adjustments. Do not include any Penalties paid (e.g., Meal Penalties, Forced Calls, etc.).

(5) List base contractual salary (e.g., $1,500.00/week or $500.00/day).

SCREEN ACTORS GUILD
MEMBER REPORT
ADR THEATRICAL/TELEVISION

It is the responsibility of the reporting member to file a copy of this report with the Screen Actors Guild within forty-eight (48) hours of each session and to deliver a copy to the employer or the employer's representative at the conclusion of each session. If there is a contractor, he shall assume these responsibilities with respect to each session.

Work Date _____ Title _____

Episode Title _____ Prod. No. _____

Production Co./
Employer _____

Studio
Facility _____

Sound Supervisor
Editor _____

Address_____

Address_____

Sound Engineer/
Mixer _____

_____

_____

ADR Supervisor _____

_____

_____

Employer Rep. _____

Phone # (___) _____

Phone # (___) _____

Type of Film: Theatrical ☐   TV Series ☐   TV MOW ☐   TV Pilot ☐   Other _____

Performer's Name	Performer's Social Security #	Character of 6+ Lines (sync)	Additional sets of up to 3 characters under 5 sync lines each	Hours Employed Studio Time Report/Dismiss	Meal Period From/To	Performer's Initials

Reel #s Recorded: _____

NOTES: _____

_____

This engagement shall be governed by and be subject to the applicable terms of the Screen Actors Guild Codified Basic or Television Agreement.

Production Co./EMPLOYER _____

Signature of Employer or
Employer Representative _____

SAG Reporter _____ (Print name) _____

SAG Reporter's Phone # (___) _____ Date _____

SCHEDULE A – EXHIBIT I

DIRECTORS GUILD OF AMERICA
WEEKLY WORK LIST

From: _____
(signatory company)

_____
(address)

_____

Return to:
Directors Guild of America, Inc.

Week Ending: _____

Name	Soc. Sec. #	Cat.	Project

Prepared by _____

Phone # _____

RC314/031489

DGA EMPLOYMENT DATA REPORT

DATE: _____ PREPARED BY: _____ PHONE #: _____

SIGNATORY COMPANY: _____

QUARTER COVERED: _____

PROJECT: _____

DIRECTOR

	C	B	H	A	AI	UNKNOWN
MALE						
FEMALE						

UNIT PRODUCTION MANAGER

	C	B	H	A	AI	UNKNOWN
MALE						
FEMALE						

FIRST ASSISTANT DIRECTOR

	C	B	H	A	AI	UNKNOWN
MALE						
FEMALE						

SECOND ASSISTANT DIRECTOR

	C	B	H	A	AI	UNKNOWN
MALE						
FEMALE						

FIRST TIME DIRECTOR

	C	B	H	A	AI	UNKNOWN
MALE						
FEMALE						

INSTRUCTIONS

The minority codes utilized in this report represent the following:

C	-	CAUCASIAN
B	-	BLACK
H	-	HISPANIC
A	-	ASIAN
AI	-	AMERICAN INDIAN

When completing this report the employment statistics must be reported in order that two (2) types of statistics can be obtained; the first statistic will indicate the number of persons employed in the respective category (referenced above) during that quarter. The second statistic will indicate the number of days worked or guaranteed in the respective categories for that quarter. Therefore in each category, there will be two (2) separate sets of statistics, one on top of the other, separated by a horizontal slash (example below). The top statistic will represent the number of employees working, the bottom statistic will be the number of days worked or guaranteed during the same quarter.

Example:

DIRECTOR

	C	B	H	A	AI	UNKNOWN
MALE	1/56					
FEMALE		1/25				

In the above example there was one (1) male Caucasian Director working during the quarter for a total of fifty-six (56) days worked or guaranteed. There was one (1) female Black Director working for a total of twenty-five days worked or guaranteed.

This report is to be submitted on a per-production basis not on a per episode basis. In instances where the same DGA employee is employed for multiple episodes in a continuing series, such employee will only be counted once in the number of employee statistics but such employee's cumulative days worked shall be included in that statistic.

NOTICE OF TENTATIVE WRITING CREDITS—THEATRICAL

Date _____

TO: Writers Guild of America

  <u>AND</u>

  All Participating Writers (or to the current agent if that participant so elects)

<u>NAMES OF PARTICIPATING WRITERS</u>   <u>ADDRESS</u>

_____   _____

_____   _____

_____   _____

_____   _____

Title of Photoplay _____

Executive Producer _____

Producer _____

Director _____

Other Production Executives, including their titles, if
  Participating Writers _____

According to the provisions of Schedule A of the Writers Guild of America Theatrical and Television Basic Agreement of 1985 credits are now being determined on the above entitled production.

ON SCREEN, the tentative writing credits are as follows:

SOURCE MATERIAL upon which the photoplay is based, if any:

ON SCREEN, <u>FORM</u> of Source Material credit, if any:

PRESENTATION or PRODUCTION credits, if any, which are intended for use in advertising and/or on-screen:

The above tentative writing credits will become final unless a protest is communicated to the undersigned not later than 6:00 P.M. on _____

_____
(Signatory Company)

BY _____

NAME _____

ADDRESS _____

PHONE _____

Revised

Feb. 1985

NOTICE OF TENTATIVE WRITING CREDITS—TELEVISION

Date _____

TO: Writers Guild of America

         <u>AND</u>

         Participating Writers

<u>NAMES OF PARTICIPATING WRITERS</u>   ADDRESS

_____   _____

_____   _____

_____   _____

_____   _____

Title of Episode _____ Prod. No. _____
           (If Pilot or MOW or other special or unit program, indicate Network and length.)

Series Title _____

Producing Company _____

Executive Producer _____

Producer _____ Assoc. Producer _____

Director _____ Story Editor _____
                            (or Consultant)

Other Production Executives, if
    Participating Writers _____

Writing credits on this episode are tentatively determined as follows:

ON SCREEN:

Source Material credit ON THIS EPISODE (on separate card, unless otherwise indicated), if any:

Continuing source material or Created By credit APPEARING ON ALL EPISODES OF SERIES (on separate card):

Revised final script was sent to participating writers on _____.

The above tentative writing credits will become final unless a protest is communicated to the undersigned not later than 6:00 P.M. on _____ .

                         _____
                                      (Company)

           BY _____

BREAKDOWN SHEET

BREAKDOWN PAGE # _____

SHOW _____   PRODUCTION # _____

EPISODE _____   DATE _____

LOCATION _____

SCENE #'S	DESCRIPTION		NO. OF PAGES
	(INT)(EXT)	(DAY)(NIGHT)	
		TOTAL	

NO.	CAST	BITS/DOUBLES	ATMOSPHERE
		WARDROBE	PROPS/SET DRESSING
		SPEC. EFFECTS	TRANS/PIC VEHICLES
	STUNTS	MUSIC/SOUND/CAMERA	WRANGLERS/LIVESTOCK
	HAIR/MAKE-UP	SPECIAL REQUIREMENTS	

DAY-OUT-OF-DAYS

PRODUCTION COMPANY _____

PRODUCTION TITLE _____

EPISODE TITLE _____

PRODUCTION # _____

SCRIPT DATED _____

DATE _____

PRODUCER _____

DIRECTOR _____

UNIT PRODUCTION MGR. _____

FIRST ASST. DIRECTOR _____

MONTH →

DAY OF WEEK →

SHOOTING DAYS →

NAME	CHARACTER								TRAVEL	START	FINISH	WORK	IDLE	TOTAL
1														
2														
3														
4														
5														
6														
7														
8														
9														
10														
11														
12														
13														
14														
15														
16														
17														
18														
19														
20														
21														
22														
23														
24														
25														
26														
27														
28														
29														
30														
31														

© ELH Form #06

CALL SHEET

PRODUCTION COMPANY _____

SHOW _____

SERIES EPISODE _____

PROD# _____ DAY # _____ OUT OF _____

IS TODAY A DESIGNATED DAY OFF? ☐ YES ☐ NO

CREW CALL _____

LEAVING CALL _____

SHOOTING CALL _____

DATE _____

DIRECTOR _____

PRODUCER _____

LOCATION _____

SUNRISE _____ SUNSET _____

ANTICIPATED WEATHER _____

☐ Weather Permitting   ☐ See Attached Map

☐ Report to Location   ☐ Bus to Location

Set Description	Scene Nos.	Cast	D/N	Pages	Location

Cast	Part Of	Leave	Makeup	Set Call	Remarks

Atmosphere & Stand-ins	

NOTE: No forced calls without previous approval of unit production manager or assistant director.   All calls subject to change.

Advance Schedule Or Changes

Assistant Director _____   Production Manager _____

© ELH Form #07

PRODUCTION REQUIREMENT

SHOW: _____ PROD #: _____ DATE: _____

NO.	STAFF & CREW	TIME	NO.	STAFF & CREW	TIME	NO.	EQUIPMENT
	Production Mgr.			Gaffer			Cameras
	1st Asst. Dir.			Best Boy			
	2nd Asst. Dir.			Lamp Oper.			Dolly
	2nd 2nd Asst. Dir.			Lamp Oper.			Crane
	DGA Trainee			Lamp Oper.			Condor
	Script Supervisor			Local 40 Man			
	Dialogue Coach						Sound Channel
	Prod. Coordinator			Prod. Designer			
	Prod. Sect'y			Art Director			Video
	Prod. Accountant			Asst. Art Dir.			
	Asst. Accountant			Set Designer			Radio Mikes
	Location Manager			Sketch Artist			Walkie/talkies
	Asst. Location Mgr.						
	Teacher/Welfare Worker			Const. Coord.			Dressing Rooms
	Production Assts.			Const. Foreman			Schoolrooms
				Paint Foreman			Rm. for Parents
	Dir. of Photography			Labor Foremen			
	Camera Operator			Const. First Aid			Projector
	Camera Operator						Moviola
	SteadyCam Operator			Set Decorator			
	Asst. Cameraman			Lead Person			Air Conditioners
	Asst. Cameraman			Swing Crew			Heaters
	Asst. Cameraman			Swing Crew			Wind Machines
	Still Photographer			Swing Crew			
	Cameraman-Process			Drapery			
	Projectionist						
				Technical Advisor			

NO.	STAFF & CREW	TIME	NO.	STAFF & CREW	TIME	NO.	SUPPORT PERSONNEL	TIME
	Mixer			Publicist				
	Boomman			**MEALS**			Policemen	
	Cableman			Caterer			Motorcycles	
	Playback			Breakfasts			Fireman	
	Video Oper.			Wlkg. Breakfasts rdy @			Guard	
				Gals. Coffee			Night Watchman	
	Key Grip			Lunches rdy @ Crew @				
	2nd Grip			Box Lunches				
	Dolly Grip			Second Meal				
	Grip							
	Grip							

NO.	STAFF & CREW	TIME	NO.	DRIVERS	TIME	NO.	VEHICLES	
	Grip			Trans. Coord.			Prod. Van	
				Trans. Capt.			Camera	
	Greensman			Driver			Grip	
				Driver			Electric	
	S/By Painter			Driver			Effects	
	Craftservice			Driver			Props	
	First Aid			Driver			Wardrobe	
				Driver			Makeup	
	Spec. Efx			Driver			Set Dressing	
	Spec. Efx			Driver			Crew Bus	
				Driver			Honeywagon	
	Propmaster			Driver			Motorhomes	
	Asst. Props			Driver			Station Wagons	
	Asst. Props			Driver			Mini-buses	
				Driver			Standby Cars	
	Costume Designer			Driver			Crew Cabs	
	Costume Supervisor			Driver			Insert Cars	
	Costumer			Driver			Generators	
	Costumer			Driver			Water Wagon	
				Driver			Picture Cars	
	Makeup Artist			Driver				
	Makeup Artist			Driver				
	Body Makeup							
	Hairstylist			Stunt Coord.				
	Hairstylist			Wranglers				
				Animal Handlers			Livestock	
	Editor						Animals	
	Asst. Editor							
	Apprentice Editor							

DEPARTMENT	SPECIAL INSTRUCTIONS

© ELH Form #07A

DAILY PRODUCTION REPORT

	1st Unit	2nd Unit	Reh.	Test	Travel	Holidays	Change Over	Retakes & Add. Scs.	Total	Schedule	
No. Days Sched										Ahead	
No. Days Actual										Behind	

Title _____ Prod. # _____ Date _____

Producer _____ Director _____

Date Started _____ Scheduled Finish Date _____ Est. Finish Date _____

Sets _____

Location _____

Crew Call _____ Shooting Call _____ First Shot _____ Lunch _____ Til _____

1st Shot After Lunch _____ 2nd Meal _____ Til _____ Camera Wrap _____ Last Man Out _____

Company dismissed at ☐ Studio ☐ Location ☐ Headquarters   Round Trip Mileage _____   Is Today A Designated Day Off? ☐ YES ☐ NO

								RETAKES	
SCRIPT SCENES AND PAGES			MINUTES		SETUPS		ADDED SCENES	PAGES	SCENES
	SCENES	PAGES	Prev.		Prev.		Prev.	Prev.	
			Today		Today		Today	Today	
Script			Total		Total		Total	Total	
Taken Prev.			Scene No.						
Taken Today									
Total to Date			Added Scenes						
To be Taken			Retakes				Sound Tracks		

FILM STOCK	FILM USE	GROSS	PRINT	NO GOOD	WASTE	1/4" ROLLS	FILM INVENTORY	
	Prev.						Starting Inv.	
	Today						Additional Rec'd.	
	To Date						Today	
							Total	
FILM STOCK	FILM USE	GROSS	PRINT	NO GOOD	WASTE		FILM INVENTORY	
	Prev.						Starting Inv.	
	Today						Additional Rec'd.	
	To Date						Today	
							Total	
FILM STOCK	FILM USE	GROSS	PRINT	NO GOOD	WASTE		FILM INVENTORY	
	Prev.						Starting Inv.	
	Today						Additional Rec'd.	
	To Date						Today	
							Total	

CAST - WEEKLY & DAY PLAYERS				WORKTIME			MEALS		TRAVEL TIME				
Worked - W Rehearsal - R Finished - F Started - S Hold - H Test - T Travel - TR		W H S F R T TR	MAKEUP WDBE.	REPORT ON SET	DISMISS ON SET	OUT	IN	LEAVE FOR LOC.	ARRIVE ON LOC.	LEAVE LOCATION	ARRIVE AT HDQ.	STUNT ADJ.
CAST	CHARACTER											

XX = N.D. BREAKFAST   * = DISMISS TIME INCLUDES 15 MIN. MAKEUP / WARD. REMOVAL

X = NOT PHOTOGRAPHED   S = SCHOOL ONLY

EXTRA TALENT													
No.	Rate	1st Call	Set Dismiss	Final Dismiss	Adj.	MPV	No.	Rate	1st Call	Set Dismiss	Final Dismiss	Adj.	MPV

Assistant Director _____   Production Manager _____

© ELH Form #08

| SHOW: | | | PROD #: | | | DATE: | |

NO.	STAFF & CREW	TIME	NO.	STAFF & CREW	TIME	NO.	EQUIPMENT
	Production Mgr.			Gaffer			Cameras
	1st Asst. Dir.			Best Boy			
	2nd Asst. Dir.			Lamp Oper.			Dolly
	2nd 2nd Asst. Dir.			Lamp Oper.			Crane
	DGA Trainee			Lamp Oper.			Condor
	Script Supervisor			Local 40 Man			
	Dialogue Coach						Sound Channel
	Prod. Coordinator			Prod. Designer			
	Prod. Sect'y			Art Director			Video
	Prod. Accountant			Asst. Art Dir.			
	Asst. Accountant			Set Designer			Radio Mikes
	Location Manager			Sketch Artist			Walkie/talkies
	Asst. Location Mgr.						
	Teacher/Welfare Worker			Const. Coord.			Dressing Rooms
	Production Assts.			Const. Foreman			Schoolrooms
				Paint Foreman			Rm. for Parents
	Dir. of Photography			Labor Foremen			
	Camera Operator			Const. First Aid			Projector
	Camera Operator						Moviola
	SteadyCam Operator			Set Decorator			
	Asst. Cameraman			Lead Person			Air Conditioners
	Asst. Cameraman			Swing Crew			Heaters
	Asst. Cameraman			Swing Crew			Wind Machines
	Still Photographer			Swing Crew			
	Cameraman-Process			Drapery			
	Projectionist						
				Technical Advisor		**SUPPORT**	
	Mixer			Publicist		**PERSONNEL**	**TIME**
	Boomman			**MEALS**			Policemen
	Cableman			Caterer			Motorcycles
	Playback			Breakfasts			Fireman
	Video Oper.			Wlkg. Breakfasts rdy @			Guard
				Gals. Coffee			Night Watchman
	Key Grip			Lunches rdy @ Crew @			
	2nd Grip			Box Lunches			
	Dolly Grip			Second Meal			
	Grip						
	Grip						
	Grip			**DRIVERS**			**VEHICLES**
				Trans. Coord.			Prod. Van
	Greensman			Trans. Capt.			Camera
				Driver			Grip
	S/By Painter			Driver			Electric
	Craftservice			Driver			Effects
	First Aid			Driver			Props
				Driver			Wardrobe
	Spec. Efx			Driver			Makeup
	Spec. Efx			Driver			Set Dressing
				Driver			Crew Bus
	Propmaster			Driver			Honeywagon
	Asst. Props			Driver			Motorhomes
	Asst. Props			Driver			Station Wagons
				Driver			Mini-buses
	Costume Designer			Driver			Standby Cars
	Costume Supervisor			Driver			Crew Cabs
	Costumer			Driver			Insert Cars
	Costumer			Driver			Generators
				Driver			Water Wagon
	Makeup Artist			Driver			Picture Cars
	Makeup Artist			Driver			
	Body Makeup						
	Hairstylist			Stunt Coord.			
	Hairstylist			Wranglers			
				Animal Handlers			Livestock
	Editor						Animals
	Asst. Editor						
	Apprentice Editor						

COMMENTS-DELAYS (EXPLANATIONS)-CAST, STAFF & CREW ABSENCE

CHECK REQUEST

SHOW _____   PROD # _____

COMPANY _____

ADDRESS _____   PHONE # _____

_____   FAX # _____

DATE _____   AMOUNT $ _____

CHECK PAYEE _____

ADDRESS _____

_____

PHONE # _____   FAX # _____

ATTN: _____

PAYEE SS # OR FED. I.D. # _____

DESCRIPTION	CODING	AMOUNT

TAX: _____

TOTAL: $ _____

☐ PURCHASE
☐ RENTAL   CHECK NEEDED: ☐ IMMEDIATELY
☐ DEPOSIT   ☐ WITHIN NEXT DAY OR TWO
☐ ADVANCE   ☐ WITHIN NORMAL PROCESSING TIME
☐ 1099
☐ INVENTORY

WHEN READY: ☐ PLEASE MAIL CHECK
               ☐ PLEASE GIVE CHECK TO _____

CHECK REQUESTED BY _____   DEPT. _____

APPROVED BY _____   DATE _____

(INVOICE SUBSTANTIATION MUST FOLLOW THIS REQUEST)

PAID BY CHECK # _____   DATE _____

© ELH Form #09

PURCHASE ORDER

DATE _____   P.O. # _____

SHOW _____   PROD # _____

COMPANY _____

ADDRESS _____   PHONE # _____

_____   FAX # _____

VENDOR _____   PHONE # _____

ADDRESS _____   FAX # _____

_____

CONTACT _____

VENDOR SS # OR FED. I.D. # _____

☐ PURCHASE   ☐ RENTAL   ☐ SERVICE

DESCRIPTION	CODING	AMOUNT

INCL. TAX IF APPLICABLE: _____

SET #(s) _____   TOTAL COST: $ _____

Per Show ☐
Day ☐
Week ☐
Month ☐

IF TOTAL COST CANNOT BE DETERMINED
AT THIS DATE, ESTIMATE OF COSTS WILL
NOT EXCEED $ _____

IF P.O. IS FOR A <u>RENTAL</u>, PLEASE ESTIMATE DATE OF RETURN _____

ORDER PLACED BY _____   DEPT. _____

APPROVED BY _____   DATE _____

cc: Vendor (Orig)   Accounting Dept.
       Production Manager   Department Head

© ELH Form #10

PETTY CASH ACCOUNTING

NAME _____

SHOW _____   AMOUNT RECEIVED $ _____   ENVELOPE # _____

DEPARTMENT _____   FROM _____ 19 _____   TO _____ 19 _____ *   DATE _____

CHECK # _____

DATE	NO.	PAID TO	FOR	ACCOUNT	AMOUNT
				TOTAL: **	

FOR ACCOUNTING USE ONLY

ACCOUNT	AMOUNT

AMOUNT ADVANCED* _____
TOTAL ACCOUNTED FOR** _____
CASH ON HAND _____
-OR-
AMT. TO BE REIMBURSED _____

NOTE: EACH RECEIPT SHOULD BE CLEARLY LABELED WITH A DATE AND DESCRIPTION AS TO WHAT THEY ARE FOR AND ATTACHED IN THE SAME ORDER IN WHICH THEY APPEAR ON THE ENVELOPE.

APPROVED _____

AUDITED _____   ENTERED _____

SIGNATURE _____

PETTYCASH ADVANCE/REIMBURSEMENT

RECEIVED IN CASH $ _____   ON _____ , 19 _____

© ELH Form #11

The Complete Film Production Handbook   **315**

AMOUNT $ _____   NO. _____

RECEIVED OF PETTY CASH

DATE _____

NAME _____

DEPARTMENT _____

DESCRIPTION _____

_____

_____

_____

☐ *PETTY CASH TO BE ACCOUNTED FOR*

APPROVED BY   RECEIVED BY

_____   _____

© ELH Form #12

LOCATION AGREEMENT

Dear

You have advised the undersigned that you are producing a _____ tentatively entitled
_____ (the "Picture"). In consideration of your payment to the
undersigned for the sum of $_____,_____ you and the undersigned hereby agree as follows:

1. The undersigned hereby irrevocably grants you and your agents, employees, licensees, successors and assigns:

    (a) The right to enter and remain upon the property, which shall include not only real property but any fixtures, equipment or other personal property thereat or thereon, located at: _____
    _____ (the "Property"), with personnel and equipment (including without limitations, props, temporary sets, lighting, camera and special effects equipment) for the purpose of photographing scenes and making recordings of said Property in connection with the production of the Picture on the following date(s): Prep: _____ ; Shoot: _____ ; Strike: _____. If the weather or other conditions are not favorable for such purpose on such date(s), the date(s) shall be postponed to _____ .

    (b) The right to take motion pictures, videotapes, still photographs and/or sound recordings on and of any and all portions of the Property and all names associated there with or which appear in, on or about the Property.

    (c) All rights of every nature whatsoever in and to all films and photographs taken and recordings made hereunder, including without limitation of all copyrights therein and renewals and extensions thereof, and the exclusive right to reproduce, exhibit, distribute, and otherwise exploit in perpetuity throughout the universe (in whole or in part) such films, photographs and recordings in any and all media, whether now known or hereafter devised, including without limitation in and in connection with the Picture and the advertising and other exploitation thereof.

2. You agree to indemnify and to hold the undersigned harmless from and against all liability or loss which the undersigned may suffer or incur by reason of any injury to or death of any person, or damage to any property (ordinary wear and tear excepted), directly caused by any of your agents or employees when present on the Property or by reason of the use by any of your agents or employees or any equipment brought by them on to the property.

3. The undersigned warrants and represents (as a condition to the payment of the compensation referred to above), that the undersigned has the full right and authority to enter into this agreement and grant the rights herein granted, and that the consent or permission of no other person, firm, or entity is necessary in order to enable you to exercise or enjoy the rights herein granted.

4. The undersigned hereby releases you from, and covenants not to sue you for, any claim or cause of action, whether known or unknown, for defamation, invasion of his privacy, right of publicity or any similar matter, or any other claim or cause of action, based upon or relating to the exercise of any of the rights referred to in Paragraph 1 hereof; provided, however, that the foregoing shall not affect your obligations to indemnify the undersigned pursuant to Paragraph 2 hereof.

5. The undersigned further warrants neither he/she or anyone acting for him/her, gave or agreed to give anything of value, except for use of the Property, to anyone at _____
    or anyone associated with the production for using the Property as a shooting location.

6. This agreement shall inure to benefit of and shall be binding upon your and our respective successors, licensees, assigns, heirs and personal representatives. You shall not be obligated actually to exercise any of the rights granted to you hereunder; it being understood that your obligations shall be fully satisfied hereunder by payment of the compensation referred to above. The agreement constitutes the entire agreement between the parties with respect to the subject matter hereof and cannot be amended except by a written instrument signed by the parties.

Very truly yours,

ACCEPTED & AGREED TO:

_____
(Signature)

By _____

_____
(Please print name)

_____
(Title)

_____
(Address)

_____

_____
(Phone Number)

_____
(Business Phone)

_____
(Fed. ID # or Soc. Sec. #)

Rel #01

PERSONAL RELEASE

Gentlemen:

I, the undersigned, hereby grant permission to _____
to photograph me and to record my voice, performances, poses, acts, plays and appearances, and use my picture, photograph, silhouette and other reproductions of my physical likeness and sound as part of the _____ tentatively entitled _____ (the "Picture") and the unlimited distribution, advertising, promotion, exhibition and exploitation of the Picture by any method or device now known or hereafter devised in which the same may be used, and/or incorporated and/or exhibited and/or exploited.

I agree that I will not assert or maintain against you, your successors, assigns and licensees, any claim, action, suit or demand of any kind or nature whatsoever, including but not limited to, those grounded upon invasion of privacy, rights of publicity or other civil rights, or for any other reason in connection with your authorized use of my physical likeness and sound in the Picture as herein provided. I hereby release you, your successors, assigns and licensees, and each of them, from and against any and all claims, liabilities, demands, actions, causes of action(s), costs and expenses whatsoever, at law or in equity, known or unknown, anticipated or unanticipated, which I ever had, now have, or may, shall or hereafter have by reason, matter, cause or thing arising out of your use as herein provided.

I affirm that neither I, nor anyone acting for me, gave or agreed to give anything of value to any of your employees or any representative of any television station, network or production entity for arranging my appearance on the Picture.

I have read the foregoing and fully understand the meaning and effect thereof and, intending to be legally bound, I have signed this release.

Very truly yours,

_____
(Signature)

_____
(Please print name)

_____
(Address)

_____
(Phone number)

Rel #02

PERSONAL RELEASE - PAYMENT

Gentlemen:

In consideration of payment to me of the sum of $ _____ , receipt of which is hereby acknowledged, I, the undersigned, hereby grant permission to _____ to photograph me and to record my voice, performances, poses, acts, plays and appearances, and use my picture, photograph, silhouette and other reproductions of my physical likeness and sound as part of the _____ tentatively entitled _____ (the "Picture") and the unlimited distribution, advertising, promotion, exhibition and exploitation of the Picture by any method or device now known or hereafter devised in which the same may be used, and/or incorporated and/or exhibited and/or exploited.

I agree that I will not assert or maintain against you, your successors, assigns and licensees, any claim, action, suit or demand of any kind or nature whatsoever, including but not limited to, those grounded upon invasion of privacy, rights of publicity or other civil rights, or for any other reason in connection with your authorized use of my physical likeness and sound in the Picture as herein provided. I hereby release you, your successors, assigns and licensees, and each of them, from and against any and all claims, liabilities, demands, actions, causes of action(s), costs and expenses whatsoever, at law or in equity, known or unknown, anticipated or unanticipated, which I ever had, now have, or may, shall or hereafter have by reason, matter, cause or thing arising out of your use as herein provided.

I affirm that neither I, nor anyone acting for me, gave or agreed to give anything of value to any of your employees or any representative of any television station, network or production entity for arranging my appearance on the Picture.

I have read the foregoing and fully understand the meaning and effect thereof and, intending to be legally bound, I have signed this release.

Very truly yours,

_____
(Signature)

_____
(Please print name)

_____

_____
(Address)

_____
(Phone number)

_____
(Fed. ID # or Soc. Sec. #)

Rel #03

GROUP RELEASE

Gentlemen:

I, the undersigned, hereby grant permission to _____ to photograph me and to record my voice, performances, poses, acts, plays and appearances, and use my picture, photograph, silhouette and other reproductions of my physical likeness and sound as part of the _____ tentatively entitled _____ (the "Picture") and the unlimited distribution, advertising, promotion, exhibition and exploitation of the Picture by any method or device now known or hereafter devised in which the same may be used, and/or incorporated and/or exhibited and/or exploited.

I agree that I will not assert or maintain against you, your successors, assigns and licensees, any claim, action, suit or demand of any kind or nature whatsoever, including but not limited to, those grounded upon invasion of privacy, rights of publicity or other civil rights, or for any other reason in connection with your authorized use of my physical likeness and sound in the Picture as herein provided. I hereby release you, your successors, assigns and licensees, and each of them, from and against any and all claims, liabilities, demands, actions, causes of action(s), costs and expenses whatsoever, at law or in equity, known or unknown, anticipated or unanticipated, which I ever had, now have, or may, shall or hereafter have by reason, matter, cause or thing arising out of your use as herein provided.

I affirm that neither I, nor anyone acting for me, gave or agreed to give anything of value to any of your employees or any representative of any television station, network or production entity for arranging my appearance on the Picture.

I have read the foregoing and fully understand the meaning and effect thereof and, intending to be legally bound, I have signed this release.

NAME	ADDRESS	SOC. SEC. #
_____	_____	_____
_____	_____	_____
_____	_____	_____
_____	_____	_____
_____	_____	_____
_____	_____	_____
_____	_____	_____
_____	_____	_____
_____	_____	_____
_____	_____	_____

Rel #04

USE OF NAME

Gentlemen:

For good and valuable consideration, receipt of which I hereby acknowledge, I hereby grant to you and to your successors, assigns, distributees and licensees forever, throughout the universe, the sole, exclusive and unconditional right and license to use, simulate and portray my name to such extent and in such manner as you in your sole discretion may elect, in or in connection with your _____ _____ tentatively entitled _____ (including reissues, remakes of and sequels to any such production) prepared by you or any successor to your interest therein, together with the right to publish synopses thereof, and to advertise, exploit, present, release, distribute, exhibit and/or otherwise utilize said productions and publications throughout the world.

I agree that I will not bring, institute or assert or consent that others bring, institute or assert any claim or action against you or your successors, licensees, distributees, or assigns, on the ground that anything performed in any such production or contained in the advertising or publicity issued in connection therewith is libelous, reflects adversely upon me, violates my right of privacy, or violates any other rights, and I hereby release, discharge, and acquit you and them of and from any and all such claims, actions, causes of action, suits and demands whatsoever that I may now or hereafter have against you or them.

In granting of the foregoing rights and licenses, I acknowledge that I have not been induced so to do by any representation or assurance by you or on your behalf relative to the manner in which any of the rights or licenses granted hereunder may be exercised; and I agree that you are under no obligation to exercise any of the rights or licenses granted hereunder.

Very truly yours,

_____
(Signature)

ACCEPTED & AGREED TO:

_____
(Please print name)

By _____

_____
(Address)

_____
(Phone Number)

USE OF TRADEMARK OR LOGO

Gentlemen:

For good and valuable consideration, receipt of which is hereby acknowledged, the undersigned hereby grants to you, your successors, licensees and assigns, the non-exclusive right, but not the obligation to use and include all or part of our trademark(s), logo(s), and/or animated or identifiable characters (the Mark(s)) listed below in the _____ tentatively entitled _____ _____ (the "Picture"), and to utilize and reproduce the Mark(s) in connection with the Picture, without limitation as to time or number of runs, for reproduction, exhibition and exploitation, throughout the world, in any and all manner, methods and media, whether now known or hereafter known or devised, and in the advertising, publicizing, promotion, trailers and exploitation thereof.

The undersigned acknowledges, as does the company which he represents, that, under the Federal Communications Act, it is a federal offense to give or agree to give anything of value to promote any product, service or venture in connection with the Picture on the air, and warrants and represents that neither he nor they have done or will do so.

The undersigned and the company he represents, hereby warrant, represent and affirm that he and the company have the right to grant the rights granted herein, free of claims by any person or entity.

Mark(s): _____

Very truly yours,

_____
(Signature)

_____
(Please print name)

ACCEPTED & AGREED TO:

_____
(Title)

By _____

_____

_____
(Address)

_____
(Phone Number)

Rel #06

USE OF LITERARY MATERIAL

Gentlemen:

I am informed that you are producing a _____ tentatively entitled
_____ (the "Picture") and that you have requested that I
grant you the right to use the title and/or portions of the following literary material owned and published by the
undersigned for inclusion in the Picture:

_____

For good and valuable consideration, receipt of which is hereby acknowledged, I (the undersigned) do
hereby confirm the consent hereby given you with respect to your use of the above title and/or literary
material (the "Materials") in connection with the Picture, and I do hereby grant to you, your successors,
assigns and licensees, the perpetual right to use the Materials in connection with the Picture. I agree that
you may record the Materials on tape, film or otherwise and use the Materials and recordings in and in
connection with the exhibition, advertising, promotion, exploitation, and any other use of the Picture as
you may desire.

I hereby release you, your agents, successors, licensees and assigns, and each of them, from and
against any and all claims, liabilities, demands, actions, causes of action, costs and expenses, whatsoever, at law or in equity, known or unknown, anticipated or unanticipated, suspected or unsuspected,
which I ever had, now have, or may, shall or hereafter have by any reason, matter, cause or thing
whatsoever, arising out of your use of the Materials as provided herein in connection with the Picture.
I realize that in using the Materials, you are relying upon the rights granted to you hereunder.

Very truly yours,

ACCEPTED & AGREED TO:

_____
(Signature)

By _____

_____
(Please print name)

_____

_____
(Address)

_____
(Phone Number)

Rel #07

USE OF STILL PHOTOGRAPH(S)
(Person in Photo/Free)

Gentlemen:

For good and valuable consideration, receipt of which is hereby acknowledged, I, the undersigned, hereby grant to you, your successors, licensees and assigns, the non-exclusive right, but not the obligation to use and include my physical likeness in the form of still photograph(s) (the Still(s)) as described below in the _____ tentatively entitled _____ _____ (the "Picture"), and to utilize and reproduce the Still(s) in connection with the Picture, without limitation as to time or number of runs, for reproduction, exhibition and exploitation, throughout the world, in any and all manner, methods and media, whether now known or hereafter known or devised, and in the advertising, publicizing, promotion, trailers and exploitation thereof.

I agree that I will not assert or maintain against you, your successors, assigns and licensees, a claim, action, suit or demand of any kind or nature whatsoever, including but not limited to, those grounded upon invasion of privacy, rights of publicity or other civil rights, or for any other reason in connection with your authorized use of the Still(s) in the Picture as herein provided. I hereby release you, your successors, assigns and licensees from any and all such claims, actions, causes of action, suits and demands whatsoever that I may now or hereafter have against you or them.

In the granting of the foregoing rights and licenses, I acknowledge that I have not been induced to do so by any representative or assurance by you or on your behalf relative to the manner in which any of the rights or licenses granted hereunder may be exercised; and I agree that you are under no obligation to exercise any of the rights or licenses granted hereunder.

Description of the Still(s): _____

_____

_____

Very truly yours,

ACCEPTED & AGREED TO:

_____
(Signature)

By _____

_____
(Please print name)

_____
(Title)

_____

_____
(Address)

_____
(Phone Number)

Rel #08

USE OF STILL PHOTOGRAPH(S)
(Person in Photo/Payment)

Gentlemen:

In consideration of the payment of the sum of $ _____ and other good and valuable consideration, receipt of which is hereby acknowledged, I, the undersigned hereby grant to you, your successors, licensees and assigns, the non-exclusive right, but not the obligation to use and include my physical likeness in the form of the still photograph(s) (the Still(s)) as described below in the _____ tentatively entitled _____ (the "Picture"), and to utilize and reproduce the Still(s) in connection with the Picture, without limitation as to the number of runs, for reproduction, exhibition and exploitation, throughout the world, in any and all manner, methods and media, whether now known or hereafter known or devised, and in the advertising, publicizing, promotion, trailers and exploitation thereof.

I agree that I will not assert or maintain against you, your successors, assigns and licensees, a claim, action, suit or demand of any kind or nature whatsoever, including but not limited to, those grounded upon invasion of privacy, rights of publicity or other civil rights, or for any other reason in connection with your authorized use of the Still(s) in the Picture as herein provided. I hereby release you, your successors, assigns and licensees from any and all such claims, actions, causes of action, suits and demands whatsoever that I may now or hereafter have against you or them.

In the granting of the foregoing rights and licenses, I acknowledge that I have not been induced to do so by any representative or assurance by you or on your behalf relative to the manner in which any of the rights or licenses granted hereunder may be exercised; and I agree that you are under no obligation to exercise any of the rights or licenses granted hereunder.

Description of the Still(s): _____

_____

_____

Very truly yours,

_____
(Signature)

ACCEPTED & AGREED TO:

_____
(Please print name)

By _____

_____
(Address)

_____
(Phone Number)

_____
(Fed. ID # or Soc. Sec. #)

Rel #09

USE OF STILL PHOTOGRAPH(S)
(Copyrighted Owner
Not Person in Photo/Free)

Gentlemen:

For good and valuable consideration, receipt of which is hereby acknowledged, the undersigned Licensor hereby grants to you, the Licensee, your successors, licensees and assigns, the non-exclusive right, but not the obligation to use and include the still photograph(s) (the Still(s)) as described below in the _____ tentatively entitled _____ _____ (the "Picture"), and to utilize and reproduce the Still(s) in connection with the Picture, without limitation as to time or number of runs, for reproduction, exhibition and exploitation, throughout the world, in any and all manner, methods and media, whether now known or hereafter known or devised, and in the advertising, publicizing, promotion, trailers and exploitation thereof.

You agree to indemnify and hold harmless the undersigned Licensor and its respective agents, representatives, associates, affiliates, predecessors, successors and assigns, parent and subsidiary corporations, and their officers, directors, and employees and each and all of them, of and from any and all claims, losses, costs, damage, liability and expenses, including reasonable attorneys' fees and costs, arising out of any claim which may arise as the result of the broadcast or release of the Picture.

The undersigned Licensor acknowledges, as does the company which he represents, that, under the Federal Communications Act, it is a federal offense to give or agree to give anything of value to promote any product, service or venture in connection with the Picture on the air, and warrants and represents that neither he nor they have done or will do so.

The undersigned and the company he represents, hereby warrant, represent and affirm that he and the company have the right to grant the rights granted herein, free of claims by any person or entity.

Description of the Still(s): _____
_____
_____

Very truly yours,

ACCEPTED & AGREED TO:

_____
(Signature)

By _____

_____
(Please print name)

_____
(Title)

_____

_____
(Address)

_____
(Phone Number)

USE OF STILL PHOTOGRAPH(S)
(Copyrighted Owner
Not Person in Photo/Payment)

Gentlemen:

In consideration of the payment of the sum of $_____ and other good and valuable consideration, receipt of which is hereby acknowledged, the undersigned Licensor hereby grants to you, the Licensee, your successors, licensees and assigns, the non-exclusive right, but not the obligation to use and include the still photograph(s) (the Still(s)) as described below in the _____ tentatively entitled _____ (the "Picture"), and to utilize and reproduce the Still(s) in connection with the Picture, without limitation as to time or number of runs, for reproduction, exhibition and exploitation, throughout the world, in any and all manner, methods and media, whether now known or hereafter known or devised, and in the advertising, publicizing, promotion, trailers and exploitation thereof.

You agree to indemnify and hold harmless the undersigned Licensor and its respective agents, representatives, associates, affiliates, predecessors, successors and assigns, parent and subsidiary corporations, and their officers, directors, and employees and each and all of them, of and from any and all claims, losses, costs, damage, liability and expenses, including reasonable attorneys' fees and costs, arising out of any claim which may arise as the result of the broadcast or release of the Picture.

The undersigned Licensor acknowledges, as does the company which he represents, that, under the Federal Communications Act, it is a federal offense to give or agree to give anything of value to promote any product, service or venture in connection with the Picture on the air, and warrants and represents that neither he nor they have done or will do so.

The undersigned and the company he represents, hereby warrant, represent and affirm that he and the company have the right to grant the rights granted herein, free of claims by any person or entity.

Description of the Still(s): _____
_____
_____

ACCEPTED & AGREED TO:

By _____

Very truly yours,

_____
(Signature)

_____
(Please print name)

_____
(Title)

_____
(Address)

_____
(Phone Number)

_____
(Fed. ID # or Soc. Sec. #)

Rel #11

WORDING FOR MULTIPLE SIGNS

(To be placed in several clearly visible locations)

IN A STUDIO WHEN TAPING OR FILMING BEFORE A LIVE AUDIENCE:

PLEASE BE ADVISED THAT YOUR PRESENCE AS A MEMBER OF THE STUDIO AUDIENCE DURING THE _____ OF THE PROGRAM ENTITLED _____ CONSTITUTES YOUR PERMISSION TO _____ TO USE YOUR LIKENESS ON THE AIR IN ANY FORM AND AS OFTEN AS THEY DEEM APPROPRIATE AND DESIRABLE FOR PROMOTIONAL OR BROADCAST PURPOSES.

IF FOR ANY REASON YOU OBJECT TO YOUR LIKENESS BEING SO USED, YOU SHOULD LEAVE THE STUDIO AT THIS TIME. IF YOU REMAIN, YOUR PRESENCE AT THIS TAPING/FILMING WILL CONSTITUTE YOUR APPROVAL OF THE FOREGOING.

Rel #12A

WORDING FOR MULTIPLE SIGNS

(To be placed in several clearly visible locations)

IN AN "AREA" DURING THE TAPING OR FILMING OF A SHOW:

PLEASE BE ADVISED THAT _____ IS TAKING PLACE IN CONNEC-
TION WITH THE PRODUCTION OF A _____ TENTATIVELY
ENTITLED _____ PEOPLE ENTERING THIS
AREA MAY APPEAR IN THE PICTURE. BY ENTERING THIS AREA, YOU
GRANT TO _____ THE RIGHT TO FILM AND PHOTO-
GRAPH YOU AND RECORD YOUR VOICE AND TO USE YOUR VOICE AND
LIKENESS IN CONNECTION WITH THE PICTURE AND THE DISTRIBUTION
AND EXPLOITATION THEREOF, AND YOU RELEASE _____
AND ITS LICENSEES FROM ALL LIABILITY IN CONNECTION THEREIN.
YOU AGREE AND UNDERSTAND THAT _____ WILL
PROCEED IN RELIANCE UPON SUCH GRANT AND RELEASE.

_____ DOES NOT ASSUME RESPONSIBILITY FOR
ANY INJURY TO YOUR PERSON OR DAMAGE OR LOSS TO YOUR
PROPERTY.

**THE USE OF CAMERAS AND RECORDING EQUIPMENT IS PROHIBITED DUE TO
UNION AND COPYRIGHT REGULATIONS.**

SMOKING IS PROHIBITED IN THIS AREA . . . THANK YOU!

Rel #12B

SUPPLYING A FILM/TAPE CLIP OF YOUR SHOW
FOR PROMOTIONAL PURPOSES

Gentlemen:

The undersigned hereby authorizes you to use a FILM/TAPE CLIP from the _____ _____ tentatively entitled _____ for promotional purposes only in the program entitled _____ currently scheduled for broadcast on _____ .

The undersigned hereby affirms that neither he nor anyone acting on his behalf or any company which he may represent, gave or agreed to give anything of value (except for the FILM/TAPE CLIP) which was furnished for promotional purposes solely on or in connection with _____ to any member of the production staff, anyone associated in any manner with the program or any representative of _____ for mentioning or displaying the name of any company which he may represent or any of its products, trademarks, trade-names or the like.

The undersigned understands that any broadcast identification of the FILM/TAPE CLIP (or the name of any company, product, etc. which he may represent) which _____ may furnish, shall, in no event, be beyond that which is reasonable related to the program content.

The undersigned is aware, as is the company which he may represent, that it is a federal offense unless disclosed to _____ prior to broadcast if the undersigned gives or agrees to give anything of value to promote any product, service or venture on the air.

The undersigned represents that he is fully empowered to execute this letter on behalf of any company which he may represent.

The undersigned warrants that he or the company which he may represent has the right to grant the license herein granted, and agrees to indemnify you for all loss, damage and liability, excluding the payment of any guild related talent fees or performing rights fees in the music included in said clip, if any (which you agree to pay or cause to be paid), arising out of the use of the above material.

Very truly yours,

ACCEPTED & AGREED:

By _____

_____
(Signature)

_____
(Please print name)

_____
(Title)

PRODUCT PLACEMENT RELEASE

Gentlemen:

The undersigned ("Company") agrees to provide the following product(s) and/or service(s) to
_____ for use in the motion picture now entitled _____
_____ (the "Picture"):

_____
_____
_____
_____
_____
_____

The Company grants to you, your successors, licensees and assigns, the non-exclusive right, but not the obligation to use and include all or part of the trademark(s), logo(s) and/or identifiable characters (the "Mark(s)") associated with the above listed product(s) and/or service(s) in the Picture, without limitation as to time or number of runs, for reproduction, exhibition and exploitation, throughout the world, in any and all manner, methods and media, whether now known or hereafter known or devised, and in the advertising, publicizing, promotion, trailers and exploitation thereof.

The Company warrants and represents that it is the owner of the product(s) or direct provider of the service(s) as listed above or a representative of such and has the right to enter this agreement and grant the rights granted to _____ hereunder.

In full consideration of the Company providing the product(s) and/or service(s) to _____,
_____ agrees to accord the Company screen credit in the end titles of the positive prints of the Picture in the following form: "_____ furnished by
_____ ."

The Company understands that any broadcast identification of its products, trademarks, trade names or the like which _____ may furnish, shall in no event, be beyond that which is reasonably related to the program content.

As it applies to any and all television broadcasts of the Picture, the Company is aware that it is a federal offense to give or agree to give anything of value to promote any product, service or venture on the air. The Company affirms that it did not give or agree to give anything of value, except for the product(s) and/or service(s) to any member of the production staff, anyone associated in any manner with the Picture or any representative of _____ for mentioning or displaying the name of the Company or any of its products, trademarks, trade names, or the like.

I represent that I am an officer of the Company and am empowered to execute this form on behalf of the Company.

I further represent that neither I nor the Company which I represent will directly or indirectly publicize or otherwise exploit the use, exhibition or demonstration of the above product(s) and/or service(s) in the Picture for advertising, merchandising or promotional purposes without the express written consent of
_____ .

Sincerely yours,

_____
(Authorized Signatory)

ACCEPTED & AGREED TO:

By _____

_____
(Please print name)

_____
(Title)

_____
(Name of Company)

_____

_____
(Address)

_____
(Phone Number)

Rel #14

FILM/TAPE FOOTAGE RELEASE

LICENSOR: _____

LICENSEE: _____

DESCRIPTION OF THE FILM/TAPE FOOTAGE: _____

_____

LENGTH OF FOOTAGE: _____

PRODUCTION: _____ (The "Picture")

LICENSE FEE, if any _____

Licensor hereby grants to Licensee, Licensor's permission to edit and include all or portion of the above-mentioned Footage in the Picture as follows:

1. Licensor grants to Licensee a non-exclusive license to edit and incorporate the Footage in the Picture. Licensee may broadcast and otherwise exploit the Footage in the Picture, and in customary advertising and publicity thereof, throughout the world in perpetuity in any media now known or hereafter devised.

2. Licensee shall not make any reproductions whatsoever of or from the Footage except as described hereunder.

3. Licensee agrees to obtain, at Licensee's expense, all required consents of any person whose appearances are contained in the Footage pursuant to this agreement, and to make any payments to such persons, guilds or unions having jurisdiction thereof and music publishers, when necessary. Licensor agrees to supply the identity of such persons, if known.

4. Licensor represents and warrants that: (1) Licensor has the right and power to grant the rights herein granted, and (2) neither Licensee's use of the Footage pursuant to this license nor anything contained therein infringes upon the rights of any third parties.

5. Licensor and Licensee each agree to indemnify and hold the other harmless from and against any and all claims, losses liabilities, damages and expenses, including reasonable attorneys' fees, which may result from any breach of their respective representations and warranties hereunder.

6. As between Licensor and Licensee, the Picture shall be Licensee's sole and exclusive property. Licensee shall not be obligated to use the Footage or the rights herein granted or to produce or broadcast the Picture.

7. Licensor acknowledges that, under the Federal Communications Act, it is a Federal offense to give or agree to give anything of value to promote any product, service or venture in the Picture, and Licensor warrants and represents that Licensor has not and will not do so.

8. This agreement constitutes the entire understanding between the parties, supersedes any prior understanding relating thereto and shall not be modified except by a writing signed by the parties. This agreement shall be irrevocable and shall be binding upon and inure to the benefit of Licensor's and Licensee's respective successors, assigns and licensees.

Kindly sign below to indicate your acceptance of the foregoing.

Licensor:

_____
(Signature)

CONFIRMED:

_____
(Please print name)

By _____

_____
(Title)

_____
(Company)

_____

_____
(Address)

_____
(Phone Number)

_____
(Fed. ID # or Soc. Sec. #)

Rel #15

TALENT
USE OF NAME & LIKENESS
IN A FILM OR TV CLIP

Dear

I am writing to you with regard to a _____ being produced by
_____ and tentatively entitled _____
(the "Picture"). The Picture is scheduled for _____ on _____ .

A brief description of the Picture is as follows:

_____
_____
_____

In conjunction with this Picture, we are requesting permission to use the appearance of _____
_____ in a clip from _____
_____ .

In consideration for _____ 's permission and in conjunction with the current SAG
Agreement, _____ hereby offers to pay _____
a fee of $ _____ . This sum represents the total payment for _____ 's
use of _____ 's name and likeness in the above described clip in and in
connection with the Picture and in promotion for the Picture. Compensation to _____
for any further use of the Picture in any media shall be governed by the then applicable collective bargaining
agreements pertaining to such use.

I would appreciate it if you would have _____ complete the information requested below
and acknowledge _____ assent to the Agreement by signing below. Once executed, please return a copy of
this letter to us for our records.

Please do not hesitate to call should you have any questions.

Sincerely yours,

ACCEPTED & AGREED TO:

By: _____   Date _____

_____   SS# _____

_____   Fed. Tax ID# _____

_____
Loan-Out Corporation Name and Address

Rel #16

REQUEST FOR VIDEOCASSETTE

Dear

You accept delivery of the _____ videocassette ("Recording") of _____ (the "Picture"), and in consideration of our delivery of it, agree as follows:

1. You warrant, represent and agree that the Recording shall be used solely for your private, personal library purpose or for screenings in connection with an in-house demo reel; and the Recording will never be publicly exhibited in any manner or medium whatsoever. You will not charge or authorize the charge of a fee for exhibiting the Recording. You will not duplicate or permit the duplication of the Recording. You will retain possession of the Recording at all times.

2. All other rights in and to the Picture, under copyright or otherwise, including but not limited to title to, are retained by _____.

3. The permission which we have granted to you for the use of the Recording itself will be non-assignable and non-transferable.

4. You agree to indemnify us against and hold us harmless from claims, liabilities and actions arising out of your breach of this agreement.

5. You agree to reimburse us for the cost of making the Recording available to you.

This will become a contract between you and us upon your acceptance of delivery of the Recording.

Sincerely yours,

ACCEPTED & AGREED:

By _____

_____
(Signature)

_____
(Please print name)

_____

_____
(Address)

_____
(Phone Number)

Rel #17

ACKNOWLEDGEMENT OF SAFETY GUIDELINES

This will acknowledge that in accordance with the Injury and Illness Prevention Program in place at _____ ,
I have received, read and understand the *Production Safety Guidelines* pertaining to the production of _____ .

I am aware that failure to adhere to these procedures could endanger me and my co-workers, and I will strive to further the company's policy of maintaining a safe work environment.

_____   _____
Employee's Signature   Date

_____   _____
Employee's Name (print or type)   Job Title or Position

(Please return this form to the Production Office when signed.)

LOCATION INFORMATION SHEET

SHOW _____   PRODUCTION # _____
LOCATION MANAGER _____   (SCRIPTED) LOCATION _____
PERMIT SERVICE _____
    CONTACT _____   DATE(S) _____
    PHONE # _____   ☐ INT.   ☐ EXT.   ☐ DAY   ☐ NIGHT

ACTUAL LOCATION
(Address & Phone #)

CONTACTS

Owner(s)   Name(s) _____
    Address _____

DATE & DAYS

	# of days	dates
Prep:		
Shoot:		
Strike:		

Phone/FAX # _____
Beeper # _____

Representative(s)

Company: _____
Contact: _____
Address: _____

LOCATION OF NEAREST EMERGENCY
MEDICAL FACILITY

Phone/FAX # _____
Beeper # _____

LOCATION SITE RENTAL FEE

Full Amount $ _____   O.T. after _____ hrs. per day @ $ _____ per hr.

Amount for PREP days $ _____   _____ Additional days @ $ _____ per day

Amount for SHOOT days $ _____   Additional charges: Phone $ _____

Amount for STRIKE days $ _____   Utilities $ _____

Deposit $ _____ Due on _____   Parking $ _____

☐ Refundable   ☐ Apply to total fee   (Other) _____ $ _____

Balance $ _____ Due on _____

CHECKLIST

☐ Location Agreement	☐ Heaters/Fans/Air Conditioners	Allocated Parking For
☐ Certificate of Insurance	☐ Lay-out Board/Drop Cloths	☐ Equipment
☐ Permit	☐ Utilities/Power Supply	☐ Honeywagons
☐ Fire Safety Officer(s)	Allocated Areas For	☐ Motor Homes
☐ Police	☐ Extras	☐ Catering Truck
☐ Location Fee	☐ Dressing Rms.	☐ Cast Vehicles
☐ Security	☐ Eating	☐ Crew Vehicles
☐ Intermittent Traffic Control	☐ Hair/Makeup	☐ Buses
☐ Post for Parking	☐ School	☐ Picture Vehicles
☐ Signed Release from Neighbors	☐ Equipment	☐ Extra Tables & Chairs/Tent
☐ Prepared Map to Location	☐ Special Equipment	☐ Locate Parking Lot if
	☐ Animals	Shuttle is Necessary

© ELH Form #39

LOCATION LIST

SHOW _____ PRODUCTION # _____

SET LOCATION	ACTUAL LOCATION (ADDRESS & PHONE)	DATE & DAYS (PREP/SHOOT/STRIKE)	CONTACTS (OWNER & REPRESENTATIVE)

© ELH Form #40

REQUEST TO FILM DURING EXTENDED HOURS

Dear Resident:

This is to inform you that _____ will be shooting a film entitled
_____ in your neighborhood at the following address:
_____.
Filming activities in residential areas is normally allowed only between the hours of _____ and _____.
In order to extend the hours before and/or after these times, the City requires that we obtain a signature of approval from the neighbors. The following information pertains to the dates and times of our scheduled shoot and any specific information you may need to know regarding our filming activities.

We have obtained or applied for all necessary City permits and maintain all legally required liability insurance. A copy of our film permit will be on file at the City Film Office and will also be available at our shooting location.

FILMING DAYS/HOURS REQUESTED: on _____ (date(s))
     from _____ to _____
     and on _____ (date(s))
     from _____ to _____

THE FOLLOWING ACTIVITIES ARE PLANNED FOR THE EXTENDED HOURS:
_____
_____
_____
_____

We appreciate your hospitality and cooperation. We wish to make filming on your street a pleasant experience for both you and us. If you have any questions or concerns before or during the filming, please feel free to call our Production Office and ask for me or the Production Manager.

Sincerely yours,

_____   _____
Location Manager   Production Company

                                         _____
                                         Phone No.

We would very much appreciate it if you would complete and sign where indicated below. A representative from our company will be by within the next day or two to pick up this form.

☐ I DO NOT OBJECT TO THE EXTENDED FILMING HOURS
☐ I DO OBJECT TO THE EXTENDED FILMING HOURS

COMMENTS:

NAME: _____

ADDRESS: _____
              _____

PHONE #: (Optional) _____

Rel #18

TRAVEL MOVEMENT

SHOW _____ PROD # _____

TRAVEL FROM _____ TO _____

DAY/DATE _____ AIRLINE _____

TYPE OF AIRCRAFT _____ MEAL(S) _____ MOVIE _____

FLIGHT # _____ DEPARTURE TIME _____ ARRIVAL _____ FLIGHT STOPS IN _____

CHANGE TO FLIGHT # _____ DEPARTURE _____ ARRIVAL _____

NAME	POSITION	GROUND TRANSPORTATION TO AIRPORT	TO BE PICKED UP @	GROUND TRANSPORTATION FROM AIRPORT

DIRECT # TO PRODUCTION OFFICE _____

FAX # _____

ADDITIONAL INFO. _____

HOTEL _____

Address _____

Phone # _____

HOTEL ROOM LOG

SHOW _____
HOTEL _____
LOCATION _____

PROD # _____
CONTACT _____
PHONE # _____

NAME	POSITION	ROOM #	TYPE OF ROOM	RATE	DATE IN	DATE OUT	TOTAL DAYS

© ELH Form #42

HOTEL ROOM LIST

SHOW _____   PROD # _____

HOTEL _____   LOCATION _____

ADDRESS _____

_____   LOCATION DATES _____

PHONE # _____   FAX # _____   Through

_____

NAME	POSITION	ROOM #	DIRECT #
Production Office	----------		
Accounting Office	----------		
Transportation Office	----------		
Editing Room	----------		

© ELH Form #43

The Complete Film Production Handbook   **345**

MEAL ALLOWANCE

SHOW _____

LOCATION _____

PROD # _____

WEEK OF _____

MEAL RATES

BREAKFAST $ ___

LUNCH $ ___

DINNER $ ___

NAME	MON			TUE			WED			THUR			FRI			SAT			SUN			TOTAL	SIGNATURE
DAY / DATE	B	L	D	B	L	D	B	L	D	B	L	D	B	L	D	B	L	D	B	L	D		

APPROVED _____

TOTAL: _____

TRAVEL MEMO TO CAST & CREW

DATE: _____

TO: _____

FROM: _____

RE: TRAVEL & HOTEL ACCOMMODATIONS/LOCATION INFORMATION FOR CAST & CREW TRAVELING TO

_____

As per your contract, you will be provided with ____   _____ class, round-trip air fare(s) to _____ .

At the present time, you are scheduled to travel on _____ on _____
Airlines, Flight _____ . The flight departs at _____ (a.m.) (p.m.) from _____
and arrives at _____ (a.m.) (p.m.).

_____ will be served during your flight.

The following ground transportation will be provided for you:
        TO AIRPORT: _____
        You will be picked up at _____ (a.m.) (p.m.)
        FROM AIRPORT: _____

You will be staying at: _____ (hotel)
                           _____ (address)
                           _____
                           _____ (phone #)

The following accommodations have been reserved for you: _____ .

On location,   ☐   you will be provided with a vehicle
               ☐   we are not able to provide you with a vehicle
               ☐   you will be sharing the use of a vehicle

Your per diem will be $_____ per day.

Please be aware that upgrading your air fare, bringing guests, reserving a larger room, etc. is to be done at your own expense. You can make additional plane reservations through _____ at _____ , and you will be informed as to the additional costs. All hotel incidental charges (room service, long distance phone calls, etc.) will be charged directly to you by the hotel.

All department heads are requested to supply _____ with a list of any equipment/wardrobe/ props, etc. that will need to be shipped to location. We will need to know how many pieces each department will be shipping and if any of the pieces are oversized. Shipping tags and labels can be picked-up at the production office.

Also, please let _____ know as soon as possible as to any special requests you might have such as renting a car (if one is not provided for you) or a small refrigerator for your room. Every effort will be made to accommodate your requests.

Reports indicate that current weather conditions in _____ are _____ .
We will be shooting _____ nights and the weather at night for this time of year is anticipated to be _____ .
Please pack accordingly.

At the present time, your return flight is scheduled for _____ on _____
Airlines, Flight _____ leaving _____ at _____ and arriving in _____
at _____ (a.m.) (p.m.).

If there are changes in our shooting schedule or unforeseen delays that would extend our location shooting, you will be informed and your return reservations updated.

Your room will be reserved until the completion of ☐ your role ☐ production, and your return flight will be booked accordingly. If you wish to remain at this location or travel elsewhere at the completion of ☐ principal photography ☐ your role, please check with us first as your services may be needed for looping and/or pick-up shots. We may not know immediately if and/or when, but would let you know ASAP. If you choose to remain on location, however, it will be your responsibility to make further arrangements with the hotel and to re-book your own airline tickets. Please just let us know of your plans if you will not be returning with the rest of the company.

If you have any additional questions regarding your travel or location accommodations, please contact _____
_____ at _____.

ABBREVIATED PRODUCTION REPORT

SHOW _____   PROD # _____

DAY _____   DATE _____   DAY # _____ OUT OF _____

LOCATION _____

CREW CALL _____

FIRST SHOT _____   MEAL PENALTY _____

LUNCH _____   TO _____   OVERTIME _____

SECOND MEAL _____   TO _____

WRAP _____

SCENES _____

_____

SCENES SCHEDULED BUT NOT SHOT _____

_____

	SCENES	PAGES	MINUTES	SETUPS
PREVIOUS				
TODAY				
TOTAL				

FILM FOOTAGE

GROSS _____   GROSS TO DATE _____

PRINT _____   PRINT TO DATE _____

N.G. _____

WASTE _____

NOTES _____

_____

_____

_____

_____

_____

_____

_____

_____

_____

_____

_____

DAILY COST OVERVIEW

SHOW _____   PROD # _____

DATE _____   DAY # _____

START DATE _____

SCHEDULED FINISH DATE _____

REVISED FINISH DATE _____

	PER CALL SHEET	SHOT	AHEAD/BEHIND
# OF SCENES			
# OF PAGES			

	AS BUDGETED AND/OR SCHEDULED	ACTUAL	COST (OVER)/UNDER
CAST OVERTIME	_____	_____	_____
COMPANY SHOOTING HOURS	_____	_____	_____
MEAL PENALTY	_____	_____	_____
EXTRAS & STAND-INS	_____	_____	_____
CATERING	_____	_____	_____
RAW STOCK	_____	_____	_____

UNANTICIPATED EXPENSES:

_____   _____   _____

_____   _____   _____

_____   _____   _____

_____   _____   _____

TOTAL FOR TODAY _____

PREVIOUS TOTAL _____

GRAND TOTAL _____

PREPARED BY _____   APPROVED BY _____

© ELH Form #19

DISTRIBUTION LIST

SHOW _____

PROD. # _____

	Script & Revisions	Budget	Pre-Prod. Schedule	Shooting Schedule	Day-out-of-Days	Deal Memos	Crew & Staff Lists	Cast List With Deals	Cast List Without Deals	Cast & Crew Contracts	Location Agreements	Release Forms	Certificates of Insur.	Location List	Travel Info. & Movement	Call Sheets	Production Reports	Abbrev. Prod. Reports	Cost Reports	Insur. & WC Claims	Post Prod. Schedule	Screen Credits	Music Cue Sheet

TOTAL # COPIES NEEDED:

© ELH Form #45

CAST INFORMATION

SHOW

EPISODE

PROD #

ACTOR

ROLE

(Please fill squares in with dates)

	START DATE	# OF DAYS WORKING	DEAL MEMO	STATION 12	TRAVEL/HOTEL ACCOMM.	MEDICAL EXAM	SENT SCRIPT	NOTIFIED WARDROBE	SCRIPT REVISIONS (BLUE)	SCRIPT REVISIONS (PINK)	SCRIPT REVISIONS (GREEN)	CONTRACT RECEIVED	CONTRACT TO AGENT/ACTOR	CONTRACT RETURNED	CONT. SIGNED BY PRODUCER	COPIES DISTRIBUTED	NOTES

BOX/EQUIPMENT RENTAL INVENTORY

PRODUCTION COMPANY _____

SHOW _____ PROD # _____

EMPLOYEE _____ POSITION _____

ADDRESS _____ SOC.SEC. # _____

_____

LOAN OUT COMPANY _____ PHONE # _____

RENTAL RATE $ _____ FED. I.D. # _____

PER ☐ DAY ☐ WEEK

☐ SUBMIT WEEKLY INVOICE

☐ RECORD ON WEEKLY TIME CARD

RENTAL COMMENCES ON _____

INVENTORIED ITEMS:

_____
_____
_____
_____
_____
_____
_____
_____
_____
_____
_____
_____
_____
_____
_____
_____
_____
_____
_____
_____
_____
_____
_____

Please note: 1. *Box and equipment rentals are subject to 1099 reporting.*

2. *The Production Company is not responsible for any claims of loss or damage to box/equipment rental items that are not listed on the above inventory.*

EMPLOYEE SIGNATURE _____ DATE _____

APPROVED BY _____ DATE _____

INVENTORY LOG

SHOW _____

PROD # _____

DEPARTMENT _____

ITEM(S)	PURCHASED FROM (Name /Address)	PURCHASE DATE	PURCHASE PRICE	P.O.#	AT COMPLETION OF PRINCIPAL PHOTOGRAPHY			LOCATION OF ITEM
					IF PORTION USED, HOW MUCH REMAINS	IF SOLD, FOR HOW MUCH	IF RET'D. TO COMPANY, IN WHAT CONDITION	

PURCHASE ORDER LOG

SHOW _____   PROD # _____

| P.O. # | DATE | TO | FOR | PRICE | CHECK ONE | | | RENTAL RET'D | TO INVENTORY | P.O. ASSIGNED TO |
					PURCHASE	RENTAL	SERVICE			

© ELH Form #23

CREW START-UP AND DATA SHEET

NAME	POSITION	SOC. SEC. #	NAME OF CORP. FED. I.D. #	DEAL MEMO	START SLIP	W-4 I-9	START DATE	WRAP DATE	PAYCHECK TO	
									EMPLOYEE	MAIL

TIME CARDS/INVOICES
WEEKLY CHECK-OFF LIST

NAME	POSITION	SOC. SEC. # FED. I.D. #	TIME CARDS AND/OR INVOICES TURNED IN EACH WEEK							
			W/E	W/E	W/E	W/E	W/E	W/E	W/E	W/E

© ELH Form #25

INDIVIDUAL PETTY CASH ACCOUNT

NAME _____   DEPARTMENT _____

SHOW _____   PROD # _____

FLOAT $ _____

DATE	CHECK#/CASH RECV'D FROM	AMOUNT RECV'D	ACCOUNTED FOR	BALANCE

© ELH Form #26

INVOICE

TO: _____

_____

_____

_____

FROM: _____   DATE _____

(Address) _____

_____

(Phone #) _____

PAYEE SS# OR FED. ID# _____ 1099 ___

FOR SERVICES RENDERED ON _____ OR WEEK/ENDING _____

DESCRIPTION OF SERVICE/RENTAL/CAR ALLOWANCE

TOTAL AMOUNT DUE $ _____

EMPLOYEE SIGNATURE _____

APPROVED BY _____

PD. BY CHECK # _____ DATE _____

CASH OR SALES RECEIPT

DATE _____ No. _____

RECIPIENT/
SOLD TO: _____

ADDRESS: _____

_____

PHONE # _____

FOR PURCHASE OF: _____

_____

WRITTEN
AMOUNT _____ $ _____

☐ CASH   ☐ 1099   Soc. Sec. # _____

☐ CHECK   Fed. I.D. # _____

ACCOUNT CODING _____

APPROVED BY _____   RECV'D BY _____

© ELH Form #28

THE CHECK'S IN THE MAIL

CHECK MADE OUT TO	CHECK NUMBER	CHECK DATED	ADDRESS SENT TO	DATE MAILED	PAY-ROLL	INV.

MILEAGE LOG

NAME: _____   WEEK ENDING _____

SHOW: _____   PROD # _____

DATE	LOCATION		PURPOSE	MILEAGE
	FROM	TO		

TOTAL MILES: _____

_____ MILES @ _____ ¢ Per Mile = $ _____

Approved By: _____   Date: _____

Pd. By Check # _____   Date _____

© ELH Form #30

362   The Complete Film Production Handbook

RAW STOCK INVENTORY

SHOW _____ PROD # _____

WEEK ENDING _____

	52_____	52_____	52_____	52_____
EPISODE/WEEKLY TOTALS				
Print	_____	_____	_____	_____
No Good	_____	_____	_____	_____
Waste	_____	_____	_____	_____
Total **	======	======	======	======
PURCHASED				
Previously Purchased	_____	_____	_____	_____
Purchased This Episode/Week	+ _____	_____	_____	_____
Total Stock Purchased	======	======	======	======
USED				
Stock Used To Date	_____	_____	_____	_____
Used This Episode/Week**	+ _____	_____	_____	_____
Total Stock Used	======	======	======	======
Total Purchased	_____	_____	_____	_____
Total Used	− _____	_____	_____	_____
Estimated Remaining Stock	======	======	======	======
(Remaining Stock As Per Assistant Cameraman)	_____	_____	_____	_____

RAW STOCK PURCHASES MADE DURING
THIS EPISODE/WEEK:

P.O. # _____	_____	_____	_____	_____
P.O. # _____	_____	_____	_____	_____
P.O. # _____	_____	_____	_____	_____
P.O. # _____	_____	_____	_____	_____
TOTAL	_____	_____	_____	_____

NOTES:

© ELH Form #31

DAILY RAW STOCK LOG

SHOW _____ PROD # _____

DATE _____ DAY # _____

CAMERA	ROLL #	GOOD	N.G.	WASTE	TOTAL

	DRAWN	GOOD	N.G.	WASTE	TOTAL
PREVIOUS					
TODAY					
TOTAL					

UNEXPOSED ON HAND	TOTAL EXPOSED

© ELH Form #32

REQUEST FOR PICK UP

DATE _____

SHOW _____   PROD # _____

PICK UP REQUESTED BY _____

ITEMS TO BE PICKED UP _____

_____

_____

_____

_____

PICK UP FROM _____

(COMPANY) _____   PHONE # _____

ADDRESS _____

_____

DIRECTIONS (if needed) _____

_____

_____

_____

☐ MUST BE PICKED UP BY _____ (A.M.)(P.M.)

☐ PICK UP AS SOON AS POSSIBLE

☐ PICK UP TODAY, NO SPECIFIC TIME

☐ NO RUSH — WHENEVER YOU CAN

COMMENTS/SPECIAL INSTRUCTIONS _____

_____

_____

_____

DATE & TIME OF PICK UP _____

ITEM(S) DELIVERED TO _____

(ALL PICK UP SLIPS ARE TO BE KEPT ON FILE IN THE PRODUCTION OFFICE)

REQUEST FOR DELIVERY

DATE _____

SHOW _____ PROD # _____

DELIVERY REQUESTED BY _____

ITEMS TO BE DELIVERED _____

_____

_____

_____

_____

DELIVER TO _____

(COMPANY) _____ PHONE # _____

ADDRESS _____

_____

DIRECTIONS (if needed) _____

_____

_____

_____

☐ MUST BE DELIVERED BY _____ (A.M.)(P.M.)

☐ DELIVER AS SOON AS POSSIBLE

☐ DELIVER TODAY, NO SPECIFIC TIME

☐ NO RUSH — WHENEVER YOU CAN

COMMENTS/SPECIAL INSTRUCTIONS _____

_____

_____

_____

DATE & TIME OF DELIVERY _____

RECEIVED BY _____

(ALL DELIVERY SLIPS ARE TO BE KEPT ON FILE IN THE PRODUCTION OFFICE)

DRIVE-TO

SHOW _____   DATE _____

EPISODE _____   PROD # _____

LOCATION _____

MILEAGE: _____ MILES @ _____ ¢ PER MILE = $ _____

	NAME	SOC. SEC. #	POSITION	SIGNATURE
1.				
2.				
3.				
4.				
5.				
6.				
7.				
8.				
9.				
10				
11.				
12.				
13.				
14.				
15.				
16.				
17.				
18.				
19.				
20.				
21.				
22.				
23.				
24.				
25.				
26.				
27.				
28.				
29.				

TOTAL ALLOCATION: _____ People x $ _____ = $ _____

APPROVED _____   DATE _____

© ELH Form #35

WALKIE-TALKIE SIGN-OUT SHEET

SHOW _____ PROD # _____

SERIAL #	PRINT NAME	DATE OUT	DATE IN	SIGNATURE

WALKIE-TALKIES RENTED FROM: _____

ADDRESS _____ PHONE # _____

_____ FAX # _____

CONTACT _____ HOURS _____

© ELH Form #36

BEEPER SIGN-OUT SHEET

SHOW _____   PROD # _____

SERIAL #	PRINT NAME	DATE OUT	DATE IN	SIGNATURE

BEEPERS RENTED FROM: _____

ADDRESS _____   PHONE # _____

_____   FAX # _____

CONTACT _____   HOURS _____

© ELH Form #37

VEHICLE RENTAL SHEET

PRODUCTION COMPANY _____   DATE _____

ADDRESS _____

_____

PHONE # _____

The vehicle as described below is to be rented for use on the film tentatively entitled: _____

YEAR, MAKE, MODEL _____

LICENSE NUMBER _____

VEH. ID # _____

VALUE _____

SPECIAL EQUIPMENT/ATTACHMENTS _____

_____

RENTAL PRICE $ _____   Per Day/Week/Month

OWNER'S NAME _____

ADDRESS _____

_____

PHONE # _____

DRIVER OF VEHICLE (if not owner) _____

START DATE _____   COMPLETION DATE _____

INSURANCE TO BE SUPPLIED BY _____

INSURANCE COMPANY _____

POLICY # _____

INSURANCE AGENCY REP. _____

PHONE # _____

REQUIRED MAINTENANCE _____

FUEL _____

VEHICLE TO BE USED FOR _____ (DEPARTMENT)

CERTIFICATE OF INSURANCE   ☐ TO OWNER   ☐ IN VEHICLE   ☐ ON FILE

AGREED TO:

BY: _____   BY: _____
    OWNER   TRANSPORTATION COORDINATOR

© ELH Form #38

Index

A

Accident coverage, guild/union, 16
Acknowledgment of Safety Guidelines, 155
Actors Production Time Report, 87
Adaptation rights, 145
ADE System, 229
AFTRA (American Federation of Television and Radio Artists), 41
Aircraft liability, non-owned, 19
All States' Endorsement, 16
American Humane Association, 93
AMPTP (Alliance of Motion Picture and Television Producers), 41–42
Animals
  mortality insurance, 19
  working with, 92–93
ASCAP (American Society of Composers, Authors, and Publishers), 145, 149
Auto liability, hired, loaned, donated, or non-owned, 14–15
Auto physical damage, hired, loaned, donated, or non-owned, 15

B

Bereavement coverage, 17
BMI (Broadcast Music, Inc.), 145, 149
Booking slip, 85

C

Cable, movies for, 28–29
Carnet defined, 218–19
Cash, petty, 10–11
Cast

insurance, 16–17
lists, 85
Certificates of Insurance forms, 14
Characters, fictional, 116
Check requests, 10
Child labor laws, 90
CIF (Cost Including Freight), 219
Claims; *See also* Insurance
  reporting procedures, 21
  submitting, 21–22
Clearances
  defined, 143
  and release forms, 115–42
  talent, 118–20
    feature films, 119
    news footage, 118–19
    television programs, 120
Clearances, music, 115
  and commercials, 147
  and copyright owners, 145
  cue sheets defined, 145–46
  and fair use, 146
  guide to, 143–50
  and hiring composers, 149
  and home video distribution, 148
  obtaining rights, 145
  obtaining rights for one's own projects, 150
  ownership, 144
  personnel, 148
  proper, 144–45
  and the Rear Window decision, 144
  and release forms, 116
  responsibilities, 144
  rights
    for distributing programs, 148–49
    licensing for feature films, 148
    and public broadcasting stations, 148–49
  songs, 149

Index of Forms

Note: **Bold face** entries indicate blank form. *Italicized entries* indicate a grouping of forms.

The companion CD-ROM contains the many necessary forms including standard production forms, deal memos, and release forms that are found in this book. The on-line versions of the forms are delivered as Microsoft® Word 6.0 templates. These templates consist of text fields and check boxes that can be filled in on-line and then printed. Additionally these forms can be printed and then filled in on paper. Installation instructions can be found in the readme.doc file.

Microsoft Word is a registered trademark of Microsoft Corporation.

3 ½" DISKS ARE AVAILABLE IN BOTH PC AND MACINTOSH FORMATS (2 DISKS EACH). TO ORDER A SET, PLEASE RETURN THE ENCLOSED CD-ROM TO THE FOLLOWING ADDRESS, AND THE 3 ½" DISKS WILL BE MAILED TO YOU FREE OF CHARGE.

MAIL REQUESTS TO:

BUTTERWORTH-HEINEMANN
225 WILDWOOD AVENUE
WOBURN, MA 01801

Please specify PC (Item Number DI 02365 PC) or Macintosh (Item Number DI 02365 Mac).

If you have any questions, please contact a customer service representative at 1-800-366-BOOK or 1-617-928-2500.